Eisenhower
and
Israel

Isaac Alteras

☆ Eisenhower

and

✡ Israel

U.S.-Israeli

Relations,

1953–1960

University Press of Florida
Gainesville
Tallahassee
Tampa
Boca Raton
Pensacola
Orlando
Miami
Jacksonville

Copyright 1993 by the Board of
Regents of the State of Florida
Printed in the United States of
America on acid-free paper
All rights reserved

Alteras, Isaac.
Eisenhower and Israel: United
States-Israeli relations, 1953–1960
/ Isaac Alteras.
p.   cm.
Includes bibliographical references
and index.
ISBN 0-8130-1205-8 (hard: alk.
paper)—ISBN 0-8130-1206-6
(pbk.: alk. paper)
    1. United States—Foreign
relations—Israel. 2. Israel—
Foreign relations—United States.
3. United States—Foreign
relations—1953–1961. 4.
Eisenhower, Dwight D. (Dwight
David), 1890–1969. I. Title.
E183.8.I7A44 1993
327.7305694′09′045—
dc20   92-44703

Cover and frontispiece: President
Dwight D. Eisenhower and Prime
Minister David Ben-Gurion of
Israel meeting in the president's
White House office, March 10,
1960. Photo by the National Park
Service; from the Dwight D.
Eisenhower Library collection.

The University Press of Florida is
the scholarly publishing agency for
the State University System of
Florida, comprised of Florida
A & M University, Florida Atlantic
University, Florida International
University, Florida State
University, University of Central
Florida, University of Florida,
University of North Florida,
University of South Florida, and
University of West Florida.

University Press of Florida
15 Northwest 15th Street
Gainesville, FL 32611

To
my
daughters
Sabina
and
Tanya

Contents

Preface

This book, a detailed diplomatic history of the relations between the United States and Israel during the 1950s, is an analysis of U.S. policy toward Israel in the context of U.S. (Western) military, economic, and political interests in the Middle East as seen by Dwight D. Eisenhower and John Foster Dulles. It is also an examination of the actions and reactions of Israeli leaders to U.S. policy formulations and implementations from the vantage point of Israeli security and national interests. This divergence of interests between the two countries before, during, and in the aftermath of the Sinai campaign of 1956 caused strains in the relations between them. Relations would improve toward the end of the decade, due in large part to Nasser's subversion of Western interests and expansion of Soviet influence in the region.

The general topic of U.S.-Israeli relations has, of course, been discussed in other studies.[1] This one, however, is focused on a specific period and includes declassified Israeli and U.S. primary and archival materials that have not been previously explored. It has also been possible for me to expand on the subject by introducing information from private papers, oral histories, and a discussion with Abba Eban, Israel's ambassador to Washington during most of the decade. This information provides a better understanding and perspective of the decision-making process in both countries and helps explain the circumstances, motivations, and interests of the personalities who shaped relations between the United States and Israel during the difficult 1950s.

Many individuals and institutions deserve my thanks and gratitude for making this book possible. The research for this book was supported by grants from the City University of New York PSC-CUNY Research Award Program, for which I am very grateful. Archivists at several institutions in the United States provided me with valuable advice throughout the research phase of this project: David Haight at the Eisenhower Library in Abilene, Kansas; Jean Holliday and Nancy A. Young at the Seeley G. Mudd Manuscript Library of Princeton University; and William B. Mahoney and Sally M. Marks at the National Archives in Washington, D.C. I was also fortunate to be assisted by dedicated archivists in Israel: Tuvia Friling at the Ben-Gurion Research Center, S'deh Boker; Dr. Yehoshua Freundlich and Gilad Livne at the Israel State Archives; and Dr. Michael Hayman at the Central Zionist Archives in Jerusalem. A portion of this manuscript has been reprinted by permission of Greenwood Press from my article "Dwight D. Eisenhower and the State of Israel: Supporter or Distant Sympathizer?" published in *Dwight D. Eisenhower: Soldier, President, Statesman,* edited by Joann P. Krieg.

I would like to thank my professional colleagues, especially Frank Merli, Edmund Leites, and Gad Nahshon, for their advice, insights, and support of this project. Any factual errors, omissions, or misinterpretations that remain are, of course, my responsibility. I also wish to express my gratitude to Mrs. Grayce Romeo, who graciously typed and corrected parts of the manuscript. Special thanks to Bobbe Hughey for her meticulous copyediting of my work and to Michael Senecal for overseeing production of the manuscript.

Finally, I owe a special debt of gratitude to my mentor, Keith Eubank, professor emeritus of history at Queens College. A scholar, dedicated teacher, and incisive critic, he has guided me throughout my academic career, providing me with invaluable insights and wise counsel. He was kind enough to read the manuscript in an early draft and made suggestions for improving both the content and the writing. I will always be deeply grateful for his generous support.

Isaac Alteras
Queens College, CUNY

Introduction

In August 1990 Iraq invaded and conquered its small, oil-rich neighbor, Kuwait. That act of unprovoked aggression set off a military and diplomatic crisis in the region and the world. The leader of Iraq, Saddam Hussein, vowed that he would never relinquish his conquest, declared Kuwait to be Iraq's nineteenth province, and all but dared the West to interfere with his "correction" of his nation's historic boundaries. President George W. Bush condemned Iraq's action and told the world that its aggression would not stand. He called upon Hussein for an immediate withdrawal from Kuwait, but he did not stop with words and warnings. Because he had little confidence in Hussein, whom he likened to Hitler, Bush set in motion a carefully calibrated campaign of diplomatic and military initiatives to achieve the liberation of Kuwait.

When Hussein threatened to widen his conquest by an attack on Saudi Arabia, the president dispatched hundreds of thousands of U.S. troops with their armor and equipment to defend the desert Arab kingdom. He also sent powerful naval and air units to support them. Simultaneously, he and his Secretary of State, James A. Baker III, in a brilliant and effective diplomatic campaign, succeeded in forming a coalition of twenty-eight countries. Coalition members contributed troops and financial assistance to the effort of dislodging Iraq from Kuwait. In addition to Britain and France, the most important partners were Arab countries—Saudi Arabia,

Egypt, Syria, and Morocco—all of which sent troops to fight alongside the Europeans and Americans against Iraq's Hussein. Arab participation in the coalition was crucial. The Arabs "invited" U.S. troops to Saudi soil and helped dispel the notion among the Arab masses that the conflict was between Iraq and despised colonialists bent on the conquest of the oil-rich region. Arab participation in the campaign also made it more difficult for Hussein to portray the conflict as one between an Arab country and the West. After Iraq refused to withdraw its troops by the date set in UN Security Council resolutions, the United States and its allies, on January 16, 1991, began bombing Iraqi military installations as part of the first phase of the liberation of Kuwait. For the first time in its history the United States became involved in a major war in the Middle East.

Although wholeheartedly supporting the allied effort against Iraq, Israel deliberately stayed out of the fighting. Months before the outbreak of hostilities, the United States had in fact asked Israel to maintain a low profile of total noninvolvement to avoid giving Hussein any pretext for characterizing the conflict as a U.S.-Israeli campaign against Iraq. Such a linkage of U.S.-Israeli interests might rupture the fragile coalition of Arab states.

Despite U.S. and Israeli wishes, within twenty-four hours after the coalition planes began bombing Iraq, Israel became a front-line state. Iraq began launching Scud-B missiles on densely populated areas in Tel Aviv and northern Israel. These attacks damaged buildings and took human lives. During the six-week Persian Gulf war, Israelis counted eighteen missile attacks on Israel, in which a total of thirty-nine Scuds were fired. One person was killed as a direct result of a missile, twelve persons suffered missile-related deaths such as heart attacks or suffocation while wearing gas masks, and nearly two hundred Israelis were injured. In the Greater Tel Aviv area, 4,095 buildings were damaged, some 200 of them leveled.

Hussein had launched the Scud attacks on Israel in an effort to incite Israeli retaliation and to turn the war into an Arab-Israeli conflict, thus destroying the coalition against him. Initially, the Israeli government wished to retaliate. After all, retaliation for acts of violence against the Jewish state had been traditional Israeli policy. But President Bush and Secretary of State Baker immediately telephoned the Israeli Prime Minister, Yitzhak Shamir, to plead with him to forgo retaliation, despite the magnitude of the provocation. They pointed out that the Iraqi attacks were political, aimed at involving Israel in the conflict and thereby gaining support for Hussein in the Arab world. If the Iraqi leader succeeded in his ploy of bringing Israel into the war, he might force nations such as Egypt and Syria out of the U.S.-led alliance and threaten their leaders with popular unrest in their own countries. Israel's entry into the war, they argued, would transform it from a conflict of Iraq versus the world to one of Iraq versus Israel. By changing the nature of the war, Hussein hoped to immobilize the Arab forces fighting alongside the United States.

In the president's view, Israeli retaliation would widen the conflict. Israeli planes flying to Iraq would have to violate Jordanian airspace. If Jordan were to shoot at Israeli planes with Hawk surface-to-air missiles or if the Israelis were to destroy Jordanian batteries, Jordan would be drawn into the war. That would add a new, dangerous dimension to the conflict. Most of all, the president sought to make clear that the United States and its allies were already heavily engaged in bombing the missile sites in western Iraq from which the Scuds were being launched against Israel.

In deference to U.S. requests, Israeli leaders decided to forgo retaliation despite continued Scud attacks. The policy of restraint, so out of character for the Israelis, won them effusive praise from the president of the United States and other world leaders.

Matching words with deeds, the president ordered the immediate dispatch to Israel of two batteries of Patriot antimissile systems, complete with U.S. crews, to intercept incoming Iraqi Scud missiles. For the first time in Israel's history, U.S. troops had been deployed there in defense of the country. In addition, the president ordered the dispatch of the aircraft carrier *Forrestal* to the eastern Mediterranean off the Israeli coast to aid in Israel's defense against Iraqi airplanes. Simultaneously, the U.S. Deputy Secretary of State, Lawrence S. Eagleburger, arrived in Israel to coordinate military and diplomatic action with Israeli leaders. Upon his arrival he declared: "We have a common cause with Israel now." Secretary of State Baker told his Israeli counterpart that when the crisis was over, he intended to coordinate every diplomatic move with Israel. All in all, the Gulf war further strengthened U.S.-Israeli relations and brought into focus a new shared strategic interest. This was an unexpected development, unique in the relations between the two countries. President Dwight David Eisenhower and his Secretary of State, John Foster Dulles, would not have taken such a step.

Indeed, the relations between the two nations have come a long way since the days of the Eisenhower presidency. Then, U.S. policy makers viewed Israel as a burden and a hindrance to U.S. interests in the Middle East. Those interests stemmed from the strategic location of the region and Western dependence on the area's petroleum resources and military facilities. As a result, the United States sought to bring the region into its global system of containment and deterrence, free from Soviet influence. The attainment of such an objective required courting the Arab states and drawing them into the Western camp. But U.S. pursuit of Arab goodwill as a means of blocking Soviet penetration meant, publicly at least, a lessening of U.S. support of Israeli policies.

Moreover, U.S. policy toward Israel was formulated in the context of a broad and relentless effort by Eisenhower and Dulles to establish and maintain stability in the region, for only peace and stability would ensure that pro-Western leaders would remain in power, that oil would flow uninterruptedly to the West, and that Soviet influence would be contained. Hence, the Eisenhower administration made major attempts to solve the Arab-Israeli conflict—a conflict that threatened regional stability and offered the Soviet Union opportunities of gaining a foothold in the area.

In pursuing those goals, President Harry S Truman's policy of a "special relationship" with Israel gave way to an evenhanded policy of "friendly impartiality" in the Arab-Israeli conflict. While Abba Eban diplomatically characterized the policy as "benevolent condescending, not especially invigorating," in reality, the policy of "friendly impartiality" had been very troubling to Israel, given the Jewish state's dependence on U.S. political, economic, and military support.

Since U.S. recognition of Israel in May 1948, throughout the 1950s and beyond, the attitude of the United States dominated the whole range of Israel's foreign policy. In the calculations of Israeli decision makers, the U.S. factor assumed paramount importance. During the Eisenhower presidency, Israeli leaders made a relentless effort to become an ally of the United States. They stressed the values the nations shared, such as a Western form of democracy and a pioneering spirit. But Eisenhower and Dulles listened politely to Israel's entreaties, whether a request for U.S.

arms or a security pact with the United States, and rebuffed them. The U.S. policy of "friendly impartiality" in essence required a certain distance in Israeli relations. The United States did not wish to be seen by Arabs as Israel's ally and protector.

Israel, however, considered an evenhanded U.S. policy between a small beleaguered state and hostile Arab neighbors supported by the Soviet Union unfair and even immoral. Thus frictions, misunderstandings, and mistrust between the two countries were inevitable.

The strain in U.S.-Israeli relations had been especially acute from September 1955 on, when, in the aftermath of the massive Egyptian-Soviet arms deal, the United States refused to supply Israel with arms as a counterbalance. While Israel viewed U.S. weapons supply as imperative to its survival, the United States urged Israel to seek weapons elsewhere and turn to the United Nations for security. Eisenhower and Dulles were aware that other sources of supply were available to Israel in Europe, especially in France. They suspected with good reason that Israel's insistence on U.S. weapons was designed to open the door for U.S. security guarantees or a defense treaty, something the United States refused to grant lest it alienate the Arab states. Israel's surprise attack in collusion with France and Britain on Egypt in late October 1956 further aggravated the relationship between the two countries. It became necessary for the United States to threaten sanctions if Israel refused to withdraw from the Sinai, the Gaza Strip, and Sharm es-Sheikh.

The turning point in relations came in mid-1957, when it became apparent to the United States that, despite its condemnation of the British-French-Israeli attack on Egypt and its successful effort to save Egypt from a military debacle, Gamal Abdel Nasser, Egypt's president, would show no gratitude for U.S. favors. On the contrary, he rejected the Eisenhower Doctrine and undermined U.S. interests in the Arab world. Washington now viewed Nasser as the Soviets' principal agent. Nasser, and not Israel, stood in the way of stemming the spread of Soviet influence in the region. Moreover, in the course of frequent crises in the Middle East due to Nasserite subversions of pro-Western governments, the United States began to appreciate Israel as the only stable pro-Western country in the Middle East. Israel's presence and military strength helped confine anti-U.S. elements in the area and facilitated U.S. successes in stabilizing the situation in Lebanon and Jordan during July-August 1958.

The improvement in the relationship between the two countries became apparent by the inclusion of Israel in the Eisenhower Doctrine and by increases in U.S. economic aid to that country for development purposes. The new spirit culminated with a meeting at the White House between the Israeli Prime Minister, David Ben-Gurion, and Eisenhower in March 1960. The stage had been set for further improvements in relations. In subsequent decades new initiatives made possible the strategic cooperation and coordination evidenced before and during the Persian Gulf war. In a sense, the period of the Eisenhower presidency, at least in its first term, constituted a stage of transition from strained relations to eventual cooperation.

One of my major aims in this book is to show that despite all the difficulties in the relations between the two countries stemming from U.S. perceptions of its strategic regional and global interests, the United States never wavered in its commitment to the legitimacy and the survival of the state of Israel. Moral and humanitarian principles, sympathy for a small beleaguered democratic state—recognized first by the United States—all figured prominently in the policy formulations of Eisenhower and Dulles.

Within this larger theme, I focus on some basic questions. What was the chain of command in the decision-making processes of both countries? Were the president and his secretary of state in full agreement on policy toward Israel? What role did the officials in the Division of Near Eastern Affairs and other agencies play in policy formulation and implementation? How effective was the Israeli ambassador to Washington in presenting Israel's case, and what input if any did he have in formulating his country's response to U.S. policies? Did Congress exercise any influence? Did domestic political considerations impact Eisenhower's decisions? What role did U.S. Jewish leaders play in their attempts to steer U.S. policy in a pro-Israel direction? Most important, how effective were they in rallying the U.S. Jewish community and the public at large to prevent the imposition of economic sanctions in the aftermath of the Sinai campaign? It is my hope that the answers to such questions will shed new light on this crucial and difficult period in the relations between the United States and Israel.

Abbreviations

AIPAC	American Israel Public Affairs Committee
AZC	American Zionist Council
CIA	U.S. Central Intelligence Agency
DMZ	Demilitarized Zone
DPs	Displaced Persons
MAC	Mixed Armistice Commission
MEDO	Middle East Defense Organization
MSA	Mutual Security Act
NATO	North Atlantic Treaty Organization
NE	Division of Near Eastern Affairs, NEA
NEA	Office of Near Eastern, South Asian, and African Affairs, U.S. Department of State
NSC	National Security Council
OCB	Operations Coordinating Board
PCC	Palestine Conciliation Commission
RCC	Revolutionary Command Council
TVA	Tennessee Valley Authority
UNEF	United Nations Emergency Force
UNTSO	United Nations Troop Supervision Organization
USIA	United States Information Agency
ZOA	Zionist Organization of America

Eisenhower
and
Israel

The Truman Legacy

When David Ben-Gurion, Israel's first prime minister, came to New York in March 1967 on behalf of the United Jewish Appeal, he received a telephone call from former president Harry S. Truman. After small talk about the years during which they had led their respective countries and inquiries about each other's health, Ben-Gurion told Truman: "I can't leave America without saying what my people in Israel and many Jews throughout the world feel for what you have done for the establishment of Israel. Our hearts are with you. You have become immortal in our country."[1]

Ben-Gurion, who had first met with President Truman in 1951, recalled in an interview one conversation with the president that obviously moved him deeply.

At our last meeting, after a very interesting talk, just before he left me—it was in a New York hotel suite—I told him that as a foreigner I could not judge what would be his place in American history; but his helpfulness to us, his constant sympathy with our aims in Israel, his courageous decision to recognize our new State so quickly and his steadfast support since then had given him an immortal place in Jewish history. As I said that, tears suddenly sprang to his eyes. And his eyes were still wct when he bade me goodbye. I had rarely seen anyone so moved. I tried to hold him for a few minutes until he had become more composed, for I recalled that the hotel corridors were full of waiting journalists and photographers. He left. A little later, I too had to go out, and a correspondent came up to me to ask, "Why was President Truman in tears when he left you?"[2]

The state of Israel came into being at 4:00 P.M. Israel time, Friday, May 14, 1948, at a meeting of the National Council held at the Tel Aviv Museum on Rothschild Boulevard. The first country to recognize the new state was the United States. On the same day, at 6:11 P.M. Washington, D.C., time (12:11 A.M. May 15 in Israel), President Truman issued a statement: "This government has been informed that a Jewish state has been proclaimed in Palestine, and recognition has been requested by the provisional government thereof. The United States recognizes the provisional government as the *de facto* authority of the new State of Israel."[3]

With this historic act, Truman became the first head of state to recognize a sovereign Jewish state after two thousand years of nonexistence. He laid the foundations for the future relationship between the United States and Israel, a relationship that would prove in years to come to be of utmost importance to Israel's survival.

While Truman's action evoked Jewish gratitude, it had the opposite effect in the Arab world, whose armies were at that moment invading the newly born state with the aim of crushing it in its infancy.

The United Nations' reaction to Truman's statement was one of "anger, incredulity and shock mixed with relief."[4] The U.S. delegates sat in their seats as surprised as any of the other delegates; "they knew nothing, no official word had come to them."[5]

In his *Memoirs*, Truman recounted the events of that historic day: "I was well aware that some of the State Department experts would want to block recognition of the Jewish State. . . . I was told that to some of the career men of the State Department it came as a surprise. It should not have been if these men had faithfully supported my policy."[6]

Truman's action illustrated the divergence over Palestine policy since the end of World War II between the White House on the one hand and the State Department, the Defense Department, and the intelligence community on the other. In foreign policy in general, the president allowed his secretary of state great latitude. But he reacted strongly and decisively when he felt that diplomacy impinged on domestic politics or ran counter to his wishes. No area of foreign policy illustrated that fact more than his attitude in the Palestine question. Overriding State Department recommendations that sided with British policies in Palestine favoring the Arabs, in 1946 Truman demanded the admission into Palestine of 100,000 displaced Jewish survivors of the Holocaust. Failing to move the British to accept his proposals and always subject to conflicting pressures both within and outside his administration, the president forced a reluctant State Department in 1947 to go along with a UN partition resolution dividing Palestine into a Jewish and Arab state and including the Negev Desert in southern Palestine in the Jewish part. When he wanted to grant quick recognition to the new state of Israel, he did so against the advice of his Secretary of State, George C. Marshall, the Under Secretary of State, Robert Lovett, and the Near Eastern, South Asian, and African Affairs Office of the State Department.

By early May 1948, the president, advised by three of his closest White House aides, Clark M. Clifford, David Niles, and Max Lowenthal, became convinced that recognizing the Jewish state was both morally and pragmatically the right course of action. On the other hand, most of those concerned with Middle Eastern affairs in the State and Defense departments feared that a pro-Jewish policy in Palestine would alienate the Arabs and possibly the entire Moslem world, cause Anglo-U.S. friction, destroy Western influence in that strategically important area with its vast oil resources, and provide new opportunities for Soviet exploitation. General Dwight D. Eisenhower, in his capacity as chief of staff of the army and later as commander of the North Atlantic Treaty Organization, held a similar view. But ultimately, humanitarian and moral imperatives (the Holocaust), domestic political considerations (the Jewish vote and funds for the upcoming presidential elections), and the national interest (preempting Soviet recognition of the Jewish state and the need to strengthen the United Nations) combined to prevail over the oil-centered realpolitik views of State and Defense Department strategists.[7] Moreover, recent Jewish military gains on the ground in Palestine helped seal the decision in favor of recognition.

But the tug of war within the Truman administration over the Palestine question did not end with the act of recognition of the Jewish state. In spite of State Department objections, on June 22, 1948, Truman appointed James G. MacDonald as the special representative of the United States in Israel. MacDonald, who had been connected with Jewish and Palestine affairs since 1933, was known for his sympathy with Zionist aspirations and his belief in strong U.S. support for Israel. All that recommended him to President Truman, but not to Under Secretary Lovett, who preferred a career diplomat, one who shared the viewpoint of State Department experts.[8] The president, however, "stressed his desire to share his own independent means of communication and of information to and from the State of Israel."[9]

The president's policy in regard to the Bernadotte proposals of September 1948 further illustrated the policy difference between the White House and State Department, and the intrusion of domestic politics in the foreign policy decision-making process. On May 15, 1948, the armies of the neighboring Arab states invaded Israel, aiming at the destruction of the Jewish community. In the words of Azzam Pasha, the secretary general of the Arab League, "This would be a war of extermination and a momentous massacre which will be spoken of like the Mongolian massacres and the Crusades."[10] The U.S. representative in the Security Council, Warren Austin, told the council that the Arab armies had marched "to blot out an existing independent government . . . it was therefore a matter of international concern and a violation of the Charter." The Security Council decided to call for a month's truce, which came into effect on June 11, 1948. The real purpose of the truce was to reopen the territorial question in Palestine. Count Folke Bernadotte of Sweden, an experienced diplomat who had been president of the Swedish Red Cross during World War II, was appointed as UN mediator to supervise the truce and promote a settlement between the belligerents.

Bernadotte spent the summer interviewing representatives of the opposing parties. Throughout his mission Bernadotte consulted the State Department and the British Foreign Office and kept them abreast of his intentions. By late August the mediator informed Marshall about his proposals regarding a settlement of the conflict. He called for the internationalization of Jerusalem, the transfer of the Negev to the Arabs (i.e., to Transjordan) together with Lydda and Ramla, and the conversion of Haifa into a free port. In return, the western Galilee would be assigned to Israel, and the Arabs would be asked to recognize the new Jewish state.

Basically, Bernadotte recommended an imposed peace because both sides found parts of the recommendations unacceptable.

For the Israelis, the Bernadotte proposals would reduce the new state to a mere 2,124 square miles, less than half the size allotted to it by the UN partition resolution of November 1947. To Israel, the Negev figured prominently in the future development of the state and its economic well-being. Moreover, there were already twenty-two agricultural settlements there, and with more irrigation the Negev was destined to become the future home of hundreds of thousands of immigrants. The area also figured to be vitally important to Israel in view of the potential oil and mineral resources to be found there. Its southern tip bordered the Gulf of Aqaba, giving the new state an outlet to Africa and the Indian Ocean. Neither would Israel agree to the internationalization of Jerusalem. While the Arabs, especially Transjordan, went along with the territorial aspects of the plan, they objected to recognizing and living in peace with Israel.[11]

The proposals, submitted to the Security Council of the United Nations on September 16, became public on September 20. But knowing well in advance the contents of the proposals, the United States began planning its diplomatic strategy with Britain for the coming debate over the mediator's recommendations.

On September 1, the president, Secretary Marshall, and Under Secretary Lovett discussed the Bernadotte proposals in the White House. In his own handwriting, the president approved a memorandum detailing the possibility of swapping western Galilee for portions of the Negev. On that basis, Marshall cabled MacDonald in Tel Aviv informing him that the U.S. government felt "that Israel should have boundaries which would make it more homogeneous and well integrated than the frontiers proposed by the November 1947 resolution. Israel might expand into the rich area of the Galilee in return for a large portion of the Negev to be given to Transjordan. Some small area in the Negev, such as that containing Jewish settlers, might still be retained by Israel."[12] On September 8, Marshall cabled Ernest Bevin, the British foreign secretary, about the U.S. decision, urging that Britain and the United States exert pressure on both sides to accept Bernadotte's "reasonable solution."[13]

Before departing for Paris, where the third annual regular session of the UN General Assembly was about to meet in the Palais de Chaillot to debate international problems, including the question of Palestine, Marshall sent a message to the president through the White House Special Signal Center. He inquired whether any changes had taken place in the president's position regarding the Bernadotte proposals and received no reply. Assuming that no change had occurred since the White House meeting of September 1, Marshall upon arrival in Paris on September 21 stated: "The United States considers that the conclusions contained in the final report by Count Bernadotte offer a generally fair basis for settlement of the Palestine question. My government is of the opinion that the conclusions are sound and strongly urges the parties and the General Assembly to accept them in their entirety as the best possible basis for bringing peace to a distracted land."[14]

According to Marshall, the Bernadotte proposals offered a compromise: the state of Israel would be accepted as an established fact by the Arab states but within boundaries considerably modified from the original partition plan of November 1947. Marshall strongly suggested that if Israel and the Arabs would not agree on a solution along those lines it should be forcibly imposed by the United Nations. A day later Bevin, in a show of coordination with the United States, declared in the House of Commons his "wholehearted and unqualified support" for the Bernadotte plan.

Back in the United States, the presidential campaign was in full swing. As on previous occasions, policy on Palestine became intertwined with domestic politics. Marshall's statement drew sharp criticism from Zionist leaders. Rabbi Abba Hillel Silver, chairman of the Zionist Emergency Council, denounced the secretary of state for his support of the Bernadotte recommendations. In a telegram to President Truman he said that the Zionist movement in the United States had "relied on the loyalty of the American Government to the Partition Resolution of last November and on the personal pledge of the Democratic party." American Zionists, he continued, "have been profoundly shocked by Secretary Marshall's unqualified endorsement of the recommendations of Bernadotte which would reduce the area of the State of Israel by two-thirds leaving it a miniature state incapable of large scale settlement of refugees."[15] Similarly, the American Zionist Emergency Council ran full-page ads in metropolitan newspapers condemning the secretary for supporting Bernadotte's conclusions. They urged the president to stick to his party's platform, which stated, "We approve the claims of the State of Israel to the boundaries set forth in the U.N. Resolution of November 29, 1947 and consider modifications thereof should be made only if fully acceptable to the State of Israel."

Political exigencies forced Truman to retreat from his September 1 position. On September 29, Clark Clifford, special counsel to the president, traveling with Truman on a whistle-stop tour in Oklahoma, called Lovett in Washington to express the president's concern over the Marshall statement. "The pressure from Jewish groups on the President is mounting . . . the line of attack was that the position taken at Paris was contrary to that of the Democratic National Platform." A stunned Lovett retorted that a change in policy now "would label this country as violating its agreements with other countries and completely untrustworthy in international matters. The consequences could be absolutely disastrous to us in the U.N. and elsewhere."[16] State Department objections notwithstanding, Truman himself a few days later urged Lovett to see to it that the debate on the mediator's plan be deferred if possible until after the elections by "using any parliamentary procedure available" so as to avoid having the matter thrown again "into political debate here." Marshall received a blunt message from the president: "I request that no statement be made or no action be taken on the subject of Palestine by any member of our delegation in Paris without obtaining specific authority from me and clearing the text of any statement with me."[17]

But U.S. policy in Palestine still became an issue in the political contest for the presidency. John Foster Dulles, spokesman for the Republican party on foreign policy and principal adviser to New York State's Governor, Thomas E. Dewey (the Republican candidate for president), was a senior member of the U.S. delegation at the UN session. Slated to become secretary of state in the event of a Dewey victory, Dulles's inclusion in the delegation was meant to convey to the world a bipartisan approach to U.S. foreign policy. The State Department had arranged separate communication facilities whereby he could inform Dewey immediately of important developments and get the guidance of his views. Dulles distanced himself from Marshall's position. He absented himself from delegation meetings on Palestine, charging a lack of bipartisan approach to the problem. In his view, the boundaries between Israel and her Arab neighbors should be decided by negotiations between the parties and could not be arbitrarily imposed by the United Nations.[18] Dewey for his part attempted to take advantage of the widely publicized criticism of the president among Jewish voters. In a letter to Dean Alfange, chairman of the American Christian Palestine Committee of New York, Governor Dewey condemned administration policy with respect to the Bernadotte plan and reaffirmed his wholehearted support for the Republican platform and its Palestine plank, which pledged "full recognition to Israel with its boundaries as sanctioned by the United Nations and aid in the development of its economy."[19]

Dewey's statement was tailor-made for Truman's "give 'em hell" tactics. In the words of Robert J. Donovan, "Truman was not a belligerent man, but his back went up when he was attacked or put on the defensive."[20] On October 28, in a speech at Madison Square Garden in New York, before a crowd of over 16,000 persons brought there under the auspices of the Liberal party, Truman made the strongest pro-Israel declaration yet. Brushing aside his own political maneuvers, he declared bluntly: "The subject of Israel must not be resolved as a matter of politics in a political campaign. I have refused consistently to play politics with that question. . . . It is my desire to help build in Palestine a strong, prosperous, free and independent democratic state. It must be large enough, free enough and strong enough to make its people self-supporting and secure." The statement sounded the death knell for the Bernadotte plan.[21]

After his election to the presidency in an upset victory, Truman went out of his way to prove that his policy in regard to Palestine had not been dictated by electoral motives. Again and again he expressed a sincere and deep affection for the new state, deprecating the "striped-pants boys in the State Department who are against my policy of supporting Israel."[22] In a reply to a letter sent to him on November 5 by Chaim Weizmann, Israel's first president, congratulating Truman on his victory, he wrote: "The United States deplored any attempt to take it (the Negev) away from Israel." Then he mapped out the future steps to be taken by his administration:

> We have already expressed our willingness to help develop the new
> State through financial and economic measures. As you know, the

Export-Import Bank is actively considering a substantial long-term loan to Israel on a project basis. I understand that your government is now in the process of preparing the details of such projects for submission to the bank. I would like to go even further, by expanding such financial and economic assistance on a large scale to the entire Middle East contingent upon effective mutual cooperation. . . . I am pleased to learn that the first Israeli elections have been scheduled for January 25. That enables us to set a definite target date for extending *de jure* recognition.[23]

This letter indicated that his support for Israel in its political struggle during 1948 had not been an isolated one-time gesture. Truman began to lay the foundations for a growing friendship between the two countries.

On January 19, 1949, the Export-Import Bank announced the authorization of a credit of $35 million to Israel to finance purchases in the United States of equipment, materials, and services connected with agricultural projects. An additional credit of $65 million was authorized to Israel to finance projects in the fields of communication, transportation, housing, and public works. These credits were to be made available until December 31, 1949—all in all a $100 million loan at a time when Israel's exports earnings in the first year of statehood amounted to only $48 million.[24] The United States was in fact providing twice the amount of Israel's foreign currency assets. These measures marked the establishment of an economic link between the two countries that would grow in coming years and provide an important element in Israel's economic viability.

Politically, too, Truman kept his word. After the first elections took place in Israel on January 25, 1949, Ben-Gurion, who headed the moderate Mapai party, assumed the premiership. Soon after, the White House released a statement announcing that as of January 31, 1949, the U.S. government recognized Israel de jure. The U.S. mission in Tel Aviv became an embassy, and James G. MacDonald, until then special representative, was named ambassador to Israel.[25]

On March 3, 1949, the Security Council of the United Nations resumed consideration of Israel's application for UN membership. A day later, Warren Austin, the U.S. representative, submitted a draft resolution to the council: "The Security Council, having received and considered the

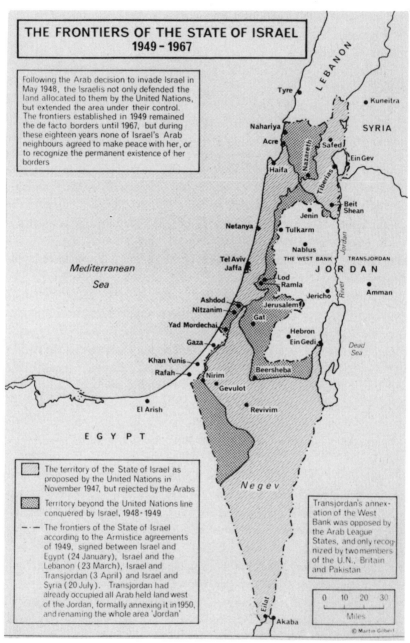

THE FRONTIERS OF THE STATE OF ISRAEL
1949 – 1967

Following the Arab decision to invade Israel in May 1948, the Israelis not only defended the land allocated to them by the United Nations, but extended the area under their control. The frontiers established in 1949 remained the de facto borders until 1967, but during these eighteen years none of Israel's Arab neighbours agreed to make peace with her, or to recognize the permanent existence of her borders

LEBANON

Tyre

Kuneitra

Nahariya

SYRIA

Acre

Safed

Ein Gev

Haifa

Nazareth

Tiberias

Beit Shean

Jenin

Netanya

Tulkarm

Nablus

THE WEST BANK

TRANSJORDAN

Tel Aviv
Jaffa

JORDAN

Jordan River

Lod
Ramla

Jericho

Amman

Ashdod
Nitzanim

Gat

Jerusalem

Yad Mordechai

Hebron
Ein Gedi

Dead Sea

Gaza

Khan Yunis

Beersheba

Rafah

Nirim

Gevulot

Mediterranean
Sea

El Arish

Revivim

EGYPT

Negev

The territory of the State of Israel as proposed by the United Nations in November 1947, but rejected by the Arabs

Territory beyond the United Nations line conquered by Israel, 1948 - 1949

–·– The frontiers of the State of Israel according to the Armistice agreements of 1949, signed between Israel and Egypt (24 January), Israel and the Lebanon (23 March), Israel and Transjordan (3 April) and Israel and Syria (20 July). Transjordan had already occupied all Arab held land west of the Jordan, formally annexing it in 1950, and renaming the whole area 'Jordan'

Transjordan's annex-ation of the West Bank was opposed by the Arab League States, and only recog-nized by two members of the U.N., Britain and Pakistan

Eilat

Akaba

0   10   20   30

Miles

© Martin Gilbert

From Martin Gilbert, *Atlas of the Arab-Israeli Conflict*. Reprinted by permission of Martin Gilbert, C.B.E.

application of Israel for membership in the United Nations, decides in its judgment that Israel is a peace loving state and is able and willing to carry out the obligations contained in the Charter and recommends to the General Assembly that it admit Israel to membership in the United Nations."[26] The resolution came to a vote the same day and was adopted by nine votes to one (Egypt); Britain abstained. On May 11, 1949, Israel became a member of the United Nations. The assembly voted 37 in favor, 12 against; 9 abstained. U.S. leadership and intervention had been indispensable in gaining international recognition for Israel through membership in the world organization.

After having gone out of his way to support the creation of a Jewish state, Truman had realized that political and economic stability in the Middle East was of critical importance to the security of the United States. The president basically concurred with a National Security Council memorandum entitled "Eastern Mediterranean and the Middle East—Basic United States Position," approved on November 24, 1947.[27] The memorandum made the following points:

> The security of the Eastern Mediterranean and of the Middle East is vital to the security of the United States.
>
> It is in the national interest of the United States to have the respect, and insofar as possible, good will of all the peoples of the Near and Middle East, Jews and Arabs alike, and their orientation toward the West and away from the Soviet Union.
>
> The differences between the new Israeli state and the neighboring Arab states should be reconciled at least to the extent that Israel and the Arab states would act in concert to oppose Soviet aggression.
>
> We should provide advice and guidance in the solution of the economic, social, and political problems of the area on an impartial basis, as between Israel and the Arab states, contingent upon the willingness of these countries to apply the maximum of self help.

To achieve those objectives, the Truman administration attempted to promote a settlement of the Arab-Israeli conflict. Three major problems, however, stood in the way: the Arab refugee problem, territorial adjustments, and the internationalization of the city of Jerusalem.

The United States viewed the General Assembly's resolution of December 11, 1948, as a sound basis for achieving the memorandum's goals.

Resolution 194 (III) called for the establishment of a Palestine Concilia-tion Commission (PCC) composed of three members, appointees of the United States, France, and Turkey. The General Assembly instructed the commission to take steps to assist governments and authorities to achieve a final settlement of all questions outstanding between them. It called upon Arabs and Jews to seek agreement "by negotiations conducted either with the Conciliation Commission or directly." Further, an interna-tional regime should be established eventually for the Jerusalem area, including Bethlehem and other outlying towns. Proposals for such an international regime were to be submitted to the September 1949 session of the General Assembly. In the meantime, the PCC was authorized to appoint a representative to cooperate with local authorities regarding an interim administration. Concerning the Arab refugee question, the resolu-tion stated that refugees wishing to return to their homes and live at peace with their neighbors should be permitted to do so at the earliest practica-ble date and that compensation should be paid for the property of those choosing not to return. The assembly instructed the PCC "to facilitate the repatriation, resettlement, and economic and social rehabilitation of the refugees and the payment of compensation."[28] The Truman administra-tion supported the recommendations put forth by the commission to the belligerents. Those recommendations ran counter to Israel's policies and interests, but more than any other issue, the Arab refugee problem placed Truman and Israel on a collision course.

The most poignant tragedy of the 1948 war in Palestine was the fate of Palestine Arab refugees who fled during the fighting. The Israelis placed the blame for their flight solely on Arab shoulders. Had the Arab govern-ments accepted the partition resolution of November 1947 and not engaged in a war of aggression in defiance of the United Nations, that uprooting would not have occurred. Furthermore, the Arab leaders, so the Israelis claimed, encouraged the flight by promising those who fled an eventual return as victors, recapturing not only their properties but also those belonging to Jews—in the meantime, they ought to get out of the crossfire. For their part, the Arabs blamed the Jews for massacring the Arab population (at Deir Yassin, an Arab village located on the outskirts of Jerusalem) and for systematically embarking on a policy aimed at clearing Arab areas in order to use Arab properties and land for future settlement of Jewish immigrants.

As the recent burst of revisionist historical scholarship by Israeli authors clearly shows, the Arab claim is far from baseless. Indeed, many Arabs fled or were driven from Israel in 1948 by military intimidation, economic pressure, and outright violence. This involuntary removal had been privately discussed and advocated by mainstream Jewish leaders, including Ben-Gurion, long before the 1948 war. The aim was twofold: to reduce the presence of a large Arab population in the Jewish state and to make room for the anticipated arrival of hundreds of thousands of new Jewish immigrants.[29]

Estimates of the number of Arab refugees varied. The Israelis set the total at 539,000. The PCC placed the figure at approximately 700,000. It was generally agreed that approximately 100,000 fled to Lebanon, 80,000 to Syria, perhaps 5,000 to 10,000 to Iraq, 115,000 to 150,000 to the Gaza Strip, and between 250,000 and 325,000 to the eastern Hashemite sector of Palestine.

The controversy over the reasons for the Arab flight continued, but none doubted that the refugees' plight was one of unspeakable misery. The first interim report of the UN Economic Survey Mission for the Middle East, issued on November 6, 1949, after an investigation of the problem in the field, stated: "The refugees themselves are the most serious manifestation of economic dislocation created by the Arab-Israeli hostilities. The refugees represent about 7 percent of the population in the countries in which they have sought refuge. About 65 percent of the refugees fled to Arab Palestine and Gaza, almost doubling the population. Resolution of the demoralizing unproductive and costly problem of the refugees is the most immediate requirement conducive to the maintenance of peace and stability in the area."[30]

The U.S. Secretary of Defense, Louis Johnson, expressing the view of the national military establishment, concluded that "the present refugee problem . . . unless rectified, serves to perpetuate and aggravate conditions of insecurity, unrest and political instability, with attendant opportunity for Soviet penetration." U.S. assistance with respect to refugees, the secretary continued, "would be an asset with respect to maintenance and improvement of friendly relations with Arab states, while the withholding of such assistance would add to the trend toward Arab embitterment."[31] Such embitterment would, in the view of the military establishment, endanger the U.S. and Western position in the Middle East and jeopardize access to the valuable petroleum resources essential to the conduct of a future war.

Of course, the same warnings were voiced to Truman during 1948 in order to prevent the establishment of a Jewish state, but the president ignored them. However, with Israel now in place, Truman was cognizant of the importance of solving the Arab-Israeli conflict. His administration did speak with one voice in placing the onus of concession making on Israel.

Mark Ethridge, the American head of the PCC who generally took a pro-Arab stand, had made a series of strong representations to both the Arabs and the Israelis. The U.S. approach to the Arabs had been designed chiefly to induce them to accept the principle of substantial resettlement of refugees in the Arab states. The representations to Israel had been intended to convince it of the necessity of accepting the principle of *substantial* repatriation of refugees and the principle of compensation to the Arab states for any territory Israel had acquired outside the boundaries proposed in the partition resolution of November 29, 1947.

Secretary of State Dean G. Acheson, with the president's approval, sought to pressure the Israeli government. In a meeting with Israel's Foreign Minister, Moshe Sharett, on April 5, 1949, using "serious and straightforward talk," he called upon Israel to declare publicly its willingness to repatriate 200,000 refugees and to comply with the General Assembly resolution of December 11, 1948, regarding the problem of Jerusalem and the territorial question.[32]

Ben-Gurion, however, insisted that any repatriation program must be an integral part of a peace settlement; otherwise the repatriated Arabs would pose a threat to Israel's security. But even if a peace agreement were signed, in Israel's view a "fundamental solution" of the refugee issue would have to be based upon the resettlement of the émigré Palestinians in the neighboring Arab countries. Israel was prepared to reunite separated Arab families based on a formula of close relationships, compensation for loss of land owned and cultivated by Arab farmers, and unfreezing of Arab accounts in Israeli banks. But Israel would not commit to the quantitative and substantial repatriation envisaged by the United States. Regarding Jerusalem, Israel rejected the demand for the internationalization of the entire city but would accept international supervision of the holy places. This attitude stemmed from the failure of the United Nations to protect the city during the war of 1948, when 100,000 Jews lived there. In addition, Jerusalem held a special significance for Israel because it had been the capital city of the Jewish people since the time of King David. In Ben-Gurion's words, "Jerusalem is to Jews, what Rome and Paris are to Italians and French respectively."[33]

As to the territorial question, Israel had no intention of relinquishing any part of the Negev. Transjordan would not be granted a corridor to the Mediterranean, nor would there be a corridor between Transjordan and Egypt. According to Ben-Gurion the territories in Palestine conquered by Israel, beyond those assigned to her by the UN partition resolution of November 1947, were a result of Arab aggression and could not be relinquished in view of the Arab threat to Israel's security.[34]

Israel's policies were at loggerheads with those of the United States and drew sharp criticism from the president. Based on the recommendations of the State Department, Truman on May 28 wrote a "grave note" to Israel's prime minister.

> The Government of the U.S. is seriously disturbed by the attitude of Israel with respect to territorial settlement in Palestine and to the question of Palestinian refugees, as set forth by the representative of Israel at Lausanne in private and in public meetings. According to Dr. Eytan, the Israeli Government will do nothing further about Palestinian refugees at the present time, although it had under consideration certain urgent measures of limited character. In connection with territorial matters, the position taken by Dr. Eytan apparently contemplates not only the retention of all territory now held under military occupation by Israel, which is clearly in excess of the partition boundaries of November 29, 1947, but possibly an additional acquisition of further territory within Palestine.
>
> If the Government of Israel continues to reject the basic principles set forth by the resolution of the General Assembly of December 11, 1948 and the friendly advice offered by the U.S. Government for the sole purpose of facilitating a genuine peace in Palestine, the U.S. Government will regretfully be forced to the conclusion that a revision of its attitude toward Israel has become unavoidable.[35]

The Israeli reply, while expressing the desire to restore the "sympathetic understanding of the United States Government for the problems and anxieties facing Israel," rejected the U.S. demand and reiterated its previous positions. A defiant Ben-Gurion did not flinch. To the Knesset, Israel's Parliament, he declared, "The United States is a powerful country, Israel is a small and weak one. We can be crushed, but we will not commit suicide."[36] But in Washington the Director of the Office of Near Eastern, South Asian, and African Affairs of the State Department, Stuart W. Rockwell, drafted for the Acting Secretary of State, James Webb, a list of measures to be taken should Israel persist in its present attitude. They were submitted to the president and called for:

1. Immediate adoption of a generally negative attitude toward Israel. This would include: refusing Israeli requests for United States assistance, such as for the training of Israeli officials in this country and the sending of United States experts to Israel; maintenance of no more than a correct attitude toward Israeli officials in this country and toward American organizations interested in promoting the cause of Israel; and failing to support the position of Israel in the various international organizations.

2. Export-Import Bank Loan. The Export-Import Bank should be immediately informed that it would be desirable to hold up the allocation of the $49,000,000 as yet unallocated of the $100,000,000 earmarked for loan to Israel.

3. United States contributions to Israel. The time is appropriate to undertake explorations as to whether it is proper, now that a Jewish state has been established as an independent foreign country, for United States contributions to the United Jewish Appeal and to other Jewish fund-raising organizations to continue to be exempt from income tax as having been made for charitable purposes. Such contributions are now of direct benefit to a sovereign foreign state.[37]

There was no indication that the president was prepared to go as far as the draft measures suggested. But he let it be known to a number of Jewish leaders who called on him that "unless they [i.e., the Israelis] were prepared to play the game properly and conform to the rules they were probably going to lose one of their best friends."[38]

This friendly warning was not lost on Ben-Gurion. Israel now expressed a willingness to assume responsibility for the refugees and residents in the Gaza Strip, provided the territory was ceded to Israel. In addition Israel agreed to repatriate members of broken families after a census of such members had been taken. That would have meant the eventual repatriation of some 300,000 refugees.

When the Egyptian ambassador at Lausanne called the Israeli proposal "cheap barter," Israel made a new offer. If the Arabs were prepared to seriously enter into peace negotiations, Israel would make a concrete contribution toward an overall solution by taking back 100,000 refugees. According to the Israeli Foreign Minister, Moshe Sharett, that was the limit that Israel could absorb, because that number would bring the total Arab population in Israel to "well over a quarter million, far beyond the margin of safety by all known security standards." The 100,000 refugees would include returning members of separated Arab families into Israel.

As far as territorial compensation was concerned, Israel maintained that the December 11, 1948, resolution made no mention of it, but rather called upon the parties to reach agreement among themselves without any predetermined territorial formula. According to Sharett, in the debate in the General Assembly at the time the resolution was adopted, Dulles had stated that the boundary settlement should be left entirely to the affected parties to resolve. Regarding Jerusalem, Israel had not retreated from her previous position, favoring an international regime limited to the holy places. Transjordan was only prepared to give the United Nations full guarantees for the protection of and free access to the holy places. However, the United States now believed that the future of the city of Jerusalem could not be decided on the basis of the General Assembly resolution of December 11, 1948, because neither Israel nor Transjordan would willingly agree to the establishment of Jerusalem as a *corpus separatum*, that is, to internationalization as envisaged by the original partition resolution of 1947. Consequently, the United States supported the proposal of the PCC of September 1, 1949, which represented a middle ground between the two extreme positions, that of the UN resolution of November 1947, and the respective positions of Israel and Transjordan. It envisaged a "permanent international regime for the Jerusalem area, with the city itself to be divided into two zones, one Arab and one Jewish, corresponding with the Transjordanian and Israeli sectors." While in each zone the local authorities would be responsible for the administration of the municipal affairs, a UN commissioner would ensure the protection of the holy places.[39]

Even though the PCC failed to achieve any of its goals, in large measure because of Arab intransigence, the State Department, under the "brilliant but frigid Dean Acheson, [still] held Israel in very limited affection."[40] But, fortunately for Israel, the tension with the White House subsided. It was the result of Israel's more forthcoming position on the refugee question, the Arab refusal to sign peace treaties with Israel, and the Arabs' unwillingness to resettle any of the refugees in their own countries. But above anything else, the change in the U.S. attitude resulted from Truman's personal sympathy for the Jewish state. When Abba Eban presented Truman his credentials as ambassador on September 5, 1950, the president decided to forgo the customary speeches and formalities associated with such occasions and instead engaged the new Israeli ambassador in an amicable conversation about his own memorable meetings with Weizmann, his stand on the Negev, and Palestine policy in general. In a move perhaps meant to remind the ambassador where policy decisions were made, Truman remarked that "the striped-pants boys in the State Department are against my policy of supporting Israel . . . they'll soon find out who's the President of the United States."[41]

For its part Israel attempted to convince the Truman administration of Israel's identification with the West in the struggle against the Soviet Union, emphasizing its strategic value to the West in case of a confrontation with the Soviets in the eastern Mediterranean. In a conversation with the U.S. ambassador to Israel, Ben-Gurion explored the possibility of visiting the United States to see the president, the secretary of state, and the secretary of defense in order to convey to them that "America's vital interests would be served by strengthening Israel as the only country other than Turkey in eastern Asia willing to fight Russian aggression to the limits of its strength . . . an equipped and enlarged Israeli army would guarantee Israeli unity in support of the West. . . . If Russia attacked Israel's strategic airfields Israel's new army could and would hold until U.S. and U.K. forces could arrive." According to the Israeli prime minister, with U.S. help Israel could build an effective army of 250,000 capable and anxious to help the United States, Britain, and Turkey resist Russian aggression. Ben-Gurion also praised Truman's policy in regard to Korea as a bold and vital step to block Communist expansion. Russia, according to the prime minister, "was a regime based on fear, deceit, force and repression. It must be stopped if freedom is to live in the world."[42]

Ben-Gurion's comments marked a clear-cut departure from his initial hope of a policy of nonidentification or neutrality in the struggle between East and West. Such a change was the outcome of much soul-searching on the part of Ben-Gurion. He was well aware that Israel's fate lay with the West on both ideological and practical grounds. Ideologically, Israel had become a democracy on the Western model and had found totalitarian communism totally abhorrent. In Ben-Gurion's view, without Western Jewry, Israel could not exist. But on the other hand, Israel could not afford antagonizing the Soviet Union, who had lent its support to Israel's creation, and whose goodwill would be necessary if Russian and Eastern European Jews were to be allowed to emigrate to Israel. Yet affiliation with the West would require a U.S. commitment to help Israel with arms, equipment, and economic aid for the settlement of Jewish immigrants. To what extent would the United States make such a commitment? Because the United States would not send its army to the Middle East just to protect Israel, the question for Ben-Gurion centered on how strategically important to the United States the Middle East was. Would the United States fight for the Middle East? Or would it abandon Israel to the Soviet Union in case of a global war? What roles could Israel and Turkey play in the defense of the Middle East alongside the United States? These important questions, Ben-Gurion believed, would have to be explored with U.S. leaders, the president, the secretary of state, and the secretary of defense.[43]

Ben-Gurion left Tel Aviv on his way to the United States on May 2, 1951. He regretted that he would be absent from his country on its third anniversary day, May 10, but felt that duty preceded festivities and that he had to go. He arrived in Washington on May 3, in the first Israel National Airways plane ever to land in the United States. On May 4, he lunched with the president at Blair House and later conferred with the secretaries of state and defense. In addition he met congressional leaders and labor union leaders, spoke before the Washington National Press Club, visited the Tennessee Valley Authority, launched a $500 million Israel Bonds drive, and conferred with U.S. Jewish leaders, Israel's most important allies in the United States. By all indications Ben-Gurion succeeded in his mission. The president had reaffirmed his commitment to the state of Israel, pledging his support for an Israeli request of $150 million grant-in-aid as well as his firm belief in Israel's destiny as a bulwark of democracy and progress.

While Ben-Gurion's discussions with Dean G. Acheson were less cordial, reflecting the secretary's cool demeanor and general State Department attitudes toward Israel, the discussions with George C. Marshall were heartening to Israeli leaders. Ben-Gurion was gratified to learn how close the Defense Department views were to his own in relation to the urgency of strengthening the defense of the Middle East and the unique and important role that Israel could play in defending peace and freedom in the area.[44] All in all, the prime minister's visit was highly successful— he enjoyed excellent public relations, won praise for his outstanding leadership, and helped cement the relationship between the two countries.

When Foreign Minister Sharett came to Washington on July 1, 1952, President Truman went out of his way to explain the reasons for his positive attitude toward Israel. His attitude was "the result of his knowledge and study of Israel's history from the days of Abraham." In particular, he had "studied very carefully the promises made to the Jewish people in the First World War," and he said to himself, "These promises must be kept." As to the future, the president continued, there must be peace between Israel and the neighboring countries, and something had to be done to raise the standards of living of the masses of people in that wide area. Israel "should become the industrial backbone of the Middle East and should attain the position of economic prosperity and leadership as in the days of Solomon." Israel, he added, "had already been once an example of democracy in antiquity. Were not the judges of Israel the first rulers anywhere in the world to have been elected by the people?" An obviously pleased Sharett expressed his desire to see the president continue occupying his present seat. But Truman felt he had to retire for the sake of his wife. He tried to reassure his Israeli guest: "You need not worry, the Democratic Party is going to win this election and no matter who's elected, it's the Democratic Party's platform that will decide policy, so that the present line with regard to your country will continue." Truman added emphatically, "Mark my word, no Republican will sit on this chair in the next four years."[45]

Perhaps prophecy was not Truman's strong suit. Dwight D. Eisenhower, a man with a public "image of a military hero who is a soldier of peace," rated by polls as the "most admired American," assumed the office of President of the United States on January 20, 1953. A national hero, he lent the presidency his own aura and shunned the controversies that in his opinion had contributed to Truman's low ratings in the polls. To the public, Eisenhower appeared to be a man above politics. In private, however, he employed "reasoning processes that bespoke political skill and sensitivity."[46]

In contrast to the Truman presidency, the new administration would exhibit in private as well as in public a very close cooperation and coordination between the president and the secretary of state. The president greatly admired and trusted John Foster Dulles's diplomatic skills and judgments. Dulles in turn regularly consulted the president; his policy declarations had the full backing of the White House. While contemporary observers believed that the president often took a back seat and allowed Dulles total dominance in foreign policy, in reality Dulles carried out Eisenhower's wishes. In the words of William Bragg Ewald, Jr., the president's speech writer and a member of the small White House Staff, "They were two men who thought like one."[47]

With the intensification of the cold war, both Eisenhower and Dulles viewed the Middle East as a region of great strategic political and economic importance to the Western world because it contained petroleum resources vital to the West's security and economic well being. Should the Soviets gain a Middle East position from which they could restrict this oil supply, "Western Europeans' will to resist communist collaboration would be greatly weakened."[48] Because the establishment of the state of Israel was in Arab eyes a result of Western and especially U.S. support, it was hoped that Arab cooperation against the Soviets could be gained by at least publicly downplaying the relationship with the Jewish state while at the same time maintaining the moral commitment to its existence.

In rhetoric more than in action, the new administration was obsessed with the need to prove how its policy differed from that of Truman. Eisenhower and Dulles defined their approach to the Middle East as "friendly impartiality" toward both Israel and the Arab states, as distinct from Truman's "special relationship" with Israel. Both felt that Truman had gone overboard in favor of Israel because of Zionist pressures and personal preferences. U.S. policy, in their view, should not be influenced by internal considerations. For the sake of balance, "the Arab interest would be upgraded, Israel would be looked after but downgraded."[49] Carrying out such a policy would be easier because Eisenhower had won the presidency in 1952 without the support of U.S. Jewish voters, 75 percent of whom voted for Adlai E. Stevenson.

The talk of change and the absence of the intimacy and consultation that existed between the two countries during the Truman presidency gave the impression that U.S. friendship for Israel had been a "fleeting and accidental circumstance of history" linked with Truman's personal attachment to the Jewish state. The new rhetoric and pronouncements coming from State Department officials caused great strains in the relations between the two countries. In reality, however, continuity rather than change marked the relationship between Israel and the United States during the Eisenhower presidency, albeit in a less friendly atmosphere.[50]

Even the Truman years were not devoid of friction and pressures on Israel on basic questions such as boundaries and the intractable refugee problem. These and other vexing problems would continue to mar the relationship between the two countries, especially during Eisenhower's first term in office, as the United States tried to keep the Arab Middle East outside the Soviet orbit. Nonetheless, the United States of America's basic moral commitment to Israel's right to exist as a state—a Truman legacy— would not change.

The New Administration:
Perceptions and Realities

2

Dwight D. Eisenhower was born on October 14, 1890, in Denison, Texas, the third of seven sons of David and Ida Stover Eisenhower. A year later the family moved to a small, midwestern town—Abilene, Kansas—where Dwight grew up and which to a large extent shaped his world outlook and character. In the words of Stephen E. Ambrose, Eisenhower's biographer, "Ida and David Eisenhower taught their sons the simple virtues of honesty, self-reliance, integrity, fear of God and ambition . . . the Eisenhowers' home life revolved around worship" and Bible reading. In Abilene, people were judged or thought of not in terms of class, rank, or status, but by how hard they worked—success depended on one's effort. Self-sufficiency, personal initiative, and responsibility were highly prized virtues. This kind of environment, according to Eisenhower, provided him with a healthy outdoor existence in a society that more nearly than any other he encountered "eliminated prejudices based upon wealth, race, or creed, . . . maintained a standard of values that placed a premium upon integrity, decency and consideration of others."[1]

In high school he became interested in reading European and U.S. history well beyond the required assignments because "the reading of history was an end in itself, not a source of lessons to guide us in the present or to prepare me for the future."[2] But military history interested him most: Greek and Roman battles, who led the victors and the vanquished. Hannibal, the Carthaginian war hero, and the American Revolution and its hero George Washington excited him.

Sports, especially football, played a very important part in his life. In sports he discovered his talents as a leader and an organizer; he learned the importance of teamwork—a principle he strongly believed in and put into practice as general and as president. According to Eisenhower football perhaps more than any other sport "tends to instill in men the feeling that victory comes through hard almost slavish work, team play, self-confidence and enthusiasm that amounts to dedication."[3]

For Eisenhower, a military career seemed the natural course to follow. In June 1915 he graduated from the U.S. Military Academy at West Point and, after serving at various military assignments, thirteen years later he graduated from the Command and General Staff School. In 1933, as a major, he became an assistant to General Douglas MacArthur, then chief of staff of the U.S. Army. Two years later he went to the Philippines with General MacArthur and remained there for four years helping organize the armed forces of the Philippine Commonwealth against threatened Japanese aggression. Returning to the United States in 1939, he was promoted to the rank of brigadier general and became chief of staff of the Third Army. Eisenhower received national attention for the first time when the press reported him to be the strategist for the winning side in a major defense-preparedness war game. He excelled in his assignment and General George C. Marshall, chief of staff of the U.S. Army, appointed him to the Planning Division of the War Department in charge of formulating strategy in response to the devastating Japanese attack on Pearl Harbor. By February 1942, the first photograph of Eisenhower accompanied by a headline story appeared in the *New York Times*, announcing his appointment to head the Planning Division of the War Department. In June, after careful selection and scrutiny by President Franklin D. Roosevelt and the British Prime Minister, Winston Churchill, Eisenhower was appointed Commanding General, European Theater of War, and Commander of Supreme Headquarters, Allied Expeditionary Forces.[4] His accomplishments commanding Operations Torch, the invasion of North Africa, and Overlord, the June 6, 1944, opening of the Second Front in France, which marked the beginning of the end of nazism, made him a national hero.

In addition to his military skills he also had the diplomatic and political acumen to put together the most astonishingly successful joint command of combined military forces in the world, and furthermore, to hold together such disparate personalities as Roosevelt's, Churchill's, and French General Charles de Gaulle's as each man pursued his own nationalistic political ends. Eisenhower's personality was credited with having reconciled friction and divisiveness.[5]

From November 1945 until February 1948, Eisenhower served as chief of staff of the U.S. Army. In this capacity, he played a leading role in the program for unification of the armed forces. On June 18, 1948, the trustees of Columbia University invited him to become president of the university. In February 1949, President Truman called him back to Washington and appointed him military adviser to James Forrestal, the first secretary of defense under the unification plan. Subsequently Eisenhower served as supreme commander of NATO, the North Atlantic Treaty Organization, a post he held until early June 1952 when he became the Republican candidate for the presidency of the United States.

He had the ideal background for a presidential candidate. He was widely acclaimed for his political as well as his military accomplishments because he had exhibited ability in exercising supreme command under difficult circumstances, and tact and patience under extreme pressures. His affable manner and infectious grin won for him the cooperation of politically diverse groups in support of common aims. As these qualities became widely known, the general's popularity increased and demand grew for Eisenhower to become a presidential candidate. Because both Republicans and Democrats desired him as a candidate in 1948, President Truman was willing even to forgo his own candidacy should Eisenhower accept the offer, but the general declined to run on either ticket. Finally on June 4, 1952, he proclaimed himself a Republican. In his boyhood town of Abilene he declared his candidacy for the presidency of the United States, in his words, "in order to preserve world peace and the social economic system." These were obvious and compelling reasons for him to seek the office.

In the campaign against Robert A. Taft, his conservative Republican opponent for the nomination, and in the fall campaign against Adlai E. Stevenson, the Democratic presidential candidate, Eisenhower was cast in the role of the amateur vis-à-vis the professional politician. Even though he had much to learn about the art of practical politics, his reputation as a war hero, his strength of character, the respect and confidence that he instilled even in many of his opponents, his appeals to national unity against the Communist threat at home and abroad—all these served to offset his shortcomings in political technique. His election as president makes a twice-told tale in the true U.S. tradition—how a typical American raised in a small rural town in the country's heartland, of ordinary heritage and humble parentage, rose first to be a world-famous victorious general and then to the highest office in the world's greatest democracy.

On November 5, 1952, the election results reflected a smashing victory for the general. He received 33,936,234 votes to Stevenson's 27,314,992—55.1 percent to 44.4 percent, 442 electoral votes to Stevenson's 89. Everywhere he ran ahead of the Republican ticket, and he managed to bring a Republican Congress with him to Washington. Eisenhower's victory was more a personal triumph than a Republican one.

In Israel the change in administration was greeted with disappointment and anxiety about the future of U.S.-Israeli relations. Gone was the man whose sympathetic attitudes toward Zionism and Israel had led to the creation of the Jewish state and whose subsequent actions laid the groundwork for the special relationship between the two countries. Given the lukewarm attitude of the State Department toward Israel, the occupant of the Oval Office was Israel's ultimate hope for support. At best the new president was an unknown quantity. What would his policy be in regard to the Arab-Israeli conflict? Who would be his advisers inside and outside the White House?

Among the presidential candidates, Israel had preferred Adlai E. Stevenson. As a Democrat he would more likely be inclined to continue Truman's friendly and sympathetic policy towards Israel. In assessing his candidacy, Eban commented at the time: "Stevenson is a man of vision, an intellectual, eloquent and articulate. His intellectual superiority over Eisenhower is self-evident . . . he is equally charismatic as the General. His fondness for Israel and Zionism runs deep, he understands and is familiar with our case in every detail both in its historical and moral dimensions."[6] Esther Herlitz, the first secretary of the Israeli embassy in Washington, no doubt reflected the views of the ambassador when she wrote that the worst candidate from Israel's perspective was Eisenhower. That was not because there were no friends of Israel in his camp. On the contrary,

Senator Henry Cabot Lodge, Jr., was known for his support of the Zionist cause. There were also influential Republican Jews supporting Eisenhower, and the embassy staff maintained close contact with them. The trouble, said Herlitz, was that Eisenhower as a military man would not view the problems of the Middle East on the basis of justice and moral merit as Truman had, but solely on the cold considerations of balance of power and national interest.[7] The future would show that her assessment had merit. There was, nonetheless, a ray of hope that the situation from Israel's perspective might not take a downturn, thanks to Eisenhower's humane character and most of all because of the circumstances in which his own encounter with the Jewish predicament came about.

On September 27, 1948, Eisenhower was awarded an honorary degree of humane letters by the Jewish Theological Seminary of America in New York City. At the ceremonies he was praised for his role as supreme commander of the Allied Expeditionary Forces in Europe, for having led the fight that ended the terror of the Nazi onslaught. His military accomplishments were acclaimed for the high moral standards they embodied, such as "statesmanship, tolerance and humaneness," and he was praised as "a soldier of intellectual integrity with a love for peace and his fellow man . . . a beloved counselor of our people in peace as in war."

In his speech accepting the honorary degree, Eisenhower affirmed his belief in a future in which Americans would not be described by any "qualitative adjectives" of race or creed. "Our Army," he said, "fights to defend our way of life, freedom for each of us to worship God in his own way." Those beliefs, according to the honoree, emanated from the teachings of ancient Jewish leaders and "gave birth to the doctrines that the American Army fought to defend." In that sense, he concluded, "all the world is the seed of Abraham."[8] Conspicuously absent in his remarks were any references to a most important event in contemporary Jewish history that had occurred only a few months earlier, an event of tremendous significance to his Jewish audience, many of them Zionists—the birth of the state of Israel. That omission was no accident.

It was certainly appropriate for the Jewish Theological Seminary of America, the spiritual and intellectual center of American Conservative Judaism, to honor Eisenhower. His aversion to nazism and anti-Semitism had been clearly demonstrated well before his encounter with the horrors of the Holocaust. In 1938 he served as a young major in the Philippines, where he assisted Douglas MacArthur in training the Philippine army. At a social function held that year in Manila he was outraged upon hearing U.S. businessmen and members of the Spanish community express admiration for Hitler. Impressed by his condemnation of nazism, his Jewish friends asked him to take the job of relocating Jewish refugees from Nazi Germany to China, Indochina, Indonesia, and elsewhere in Asia. The job carried with it a very handsome salary of $60,000 a year plus expenses, with a promise to place the first five years' salary in escrow to be paid to him in full if for any reason he had to leave the job. Apart from the tempting monetary reward, as Eisenhower later recalled, the job offered a challenge. "It would have been a pretty wonderful thing to resettle these poor people who were driven out of their homelands."[9] Despite its advantages, Eisenhower turned it down; the only explanation he gave was that he wanted to continue his military career. Perhaps, as Stephen E. Ambrose suggests, given Hitler's ambitions, Eisenhower might have foreseen as early as 1938 the coming of the storm, with the United States being in no position to stay out of the war. It would be his duty to lend a hand to the military effort needed to end Nazi tyranny.[10]

On May 8, 1945, the war in Europe was over. As the Allied troops converged from the east and west, they captured the showplaces of Nazi horror: Maidanek, Buchenwald, Auschwitz, Dachau, and Belsen. The enormity of the Jewish tragedy and suffering shocked Eisenhower. After visiting some of those sites, he wrote his wife, Mamie, "I never dreamed that such cruelty, bestiality and savagery could really exist in this world! It was horrible."[11] On the same day he dispatched a telegram to George C. Marshall, the chief of staff of the army:

The most interesting although horrible sight that I encountered during the trip was a visit to a German internment camp near Gotha. The things I saw beggar description. While I was touring the camp I encountered three men who had been inmates and by one ruse or another had made their escape. I interviewed them through an interpreter. The visual evidence and the verbal testimony of starvation, cruelty and bestiality were so overpowering as to leave me a bit sick. In one room, twenty or thirty naked men were piled up killed by starvation. George Patton would not even enter. He said he would get sick if he did so. I made the visit deliberately in order to be in a position to give first hand evidence of these things, if ever in the future, there develops a tendency to charge these things merely to propaganda.[12]

Eisenhower invited reporters, British members of Parliament, and members of the U.S. Congress to visit the concentration camps, see for themselves, and convey their experiences to the rest of the world.

After V-E Day Eisenhower was appointed military governor of Germany as well as commander of U.S. troops in Europe. In this role he assisted Jews fleeing from Poland, Rumania, and Hungary, and those who had survived the concentration camps. They were desperately seeking refuge in displaced persons (DPs) camps under Allied supervision with the hope of finding new places to live to avoid returning to their former homelands. Because the Jewish survivors had been treated by the Nazis far worse than had non-Jews and were suffering from malnutrition and disease, Eisenhower ordered that they be placed in separate camps and receive special rehabilitation treatment. The treatment included the end of overcrowding, improved sanitary conditions, sufficient food, and adequate medical services. According to Judah Nadich, Eisenhower's adviser on Jewish affairs in the European theater of operations, the general's personal appearances lifted the morale of the survivors, who saw in him a symbol of hope and a better future.[13] When David Ben-Gurion, at the time chairman of the executive of the Jewish Agency, Israel's prestate government, and later the first prime minister of Israel, visited those displaced persons camps in October 1945, he thanked Eisenhower on behalf of the Jewish people for his role in defeating nazism as well as for his humaneness toward the survivors of the Holocaust.[14]

The overwhelming majority of Jewish DPs, refusing to return to their countries of origin, preferred to emigrate to Palestine. At Ben-Gurion's urging, Eisenhower agreed to provide them with farms for agricultural pioneer training on land requisitioned from the German population. Eisenhower also expanded educational and cultural programs in Hebrew in order to prepare them for a useful life in Palestine. Once a week he dispatched military planes to Palestine to bring Hebrew books, agricultural instructors, and teachers to the camps. The planes also carried mail between the refugees and their relatives in Palestine.

But in subsequent years Eisenhower's humane approach toward Jewish survivors of the Holocaust did not translate into his supporting the creation of a Jewish state in Palestine, the future homeland of many DPs. The reasons for the differences in attitude are not difficult to ascertain. In helping Jewish survivors of the Nazi terror he acted as a humanitarian, in line with his basic decency and tolerance. The questions concerning the future of Palestine and the creation of a Jewish state were controversial political questions closely tied to what he and the military believed to be U.S. interests in the Middle East.[15]

Thus as chief of staff of the army he advised the U.S. Joint Chiefs of Staff against any action that would commit U.S. troops in Palestine or "orient the peoples of Middle East [i.e., the Arabs] away from Western powers, as the United States has a vital security interest in that area." He also stressed the importance from a military point of view of the control of Mideast oil, "this being the one large underdeveloped resource in a world which may come to the limits of its oil resources within this generation . . . a great part of our military strength as well as our standard of living is based on oil."[16] When the Secretary of the Treasury, Henry Morgenthau, Jr., a supporter of the Zionist cause, requested Eisenhower to meet the political adviser for the Jewish Agency for Palestine in order to discuss possible military measures to defend Jews and Arabs in view of pending British withdrawal, Eisenhower shunned any kind of involvement. He suggested to Morgenthau that the adviser should see someone else in the Department of Defense. Such conversations, said Eisenhower, "should be held with someone above me." Presumably he meant James V. Forrestal, whose opposition to a Jewish state in Palestine was well known. A few years later, President Eisenhower in characteristic frankness confided to Philip Klutznick, then president of B'nai B'rith, his doubts as to whether he would have favored the establishment of Israel. But "now that it was done," said Eisenhower, "we'll have to live with it."[17]

In his role as commander of NATO forces in Europe, Eisenhower expressed privately the desirability of winning the friendship of Arab peoples as military allies of the Western world in the struggle against communism. Testifying before the Senate Foreign Relations Committee on July 22, 1951, in regard to the establishment of an Allied Middle East Command tied to NATO, Eisenhower said: "So far as the sheer value of territory is concerned, there is no more strategically important area in the world than the Middle East, the so-called bridge to Africa and Asia. This area is tremendously important in terms of what it could contribute for our whole effort. . . . Turkey is only part of the great Middle East problem. We should bring in the Arab world on our side."[18]

The *Saturday Evening Post* of April 19, 1952, quoted Eisenhower to the effect that "we must support the legitimate aspirations of the Moslem world or else, I don't see how we can hold true to our doctrine that we do not want to dominate anyone." The *Intermountain News* of Denver reported that Eisenhower spoke of the need to win Arab friendship but as in the past avoided all reference to Israel. At a press conference in Denver on June 24, 1952, he urged a NATO type of unification in the Middle East and the Far East. In the Middle East, he said, "you have a problem of just cold hatred to us and there we have got to win friends before we even talk to them."[19] Such statements were in clear contrast to Stevenson's frequent pro-Israel pronouncements, praising its achievements and calling for continued financial support.

With the approach of the national conventions of both parties, Israel's supporters aimed at ensuring the continuation of bipartisan support for Israel in the respective party platforms. While the Democratic platform specifically mentioned continued support of Israel in line with Truman's policies, the going was rough for Israel's supporters when they testified before the Republican platform committee in Chicago. Committee members supporting Eisenhower opposed any mentioning of Israel so as to avoid being tied to any commitment. Those testifying against Israel hoped that the Republicans would accept and exploit their contention that Truman's pro-Israel policy had alienated the Arab world toward the United States.

Dorothy Thompson and her newly established organization American Friends of the Middle East urged the Republican leadership to steer clear of any pro-Israel statement and to oppose declarations favoring any Middle Eastern country. The tendency among the members of the platform committee, even those sympathetic to Israel, was to shun endorsing any Truman policy, of course including references to Israel.[20] Finally, thanks to Dewey and Dulles, who were in charge of drafting the Republican foreign policy plank, a general noncommittal statement regarding Israel was included nonetheless. "The Republican party," the statement read, "has consistently advocated a national home for the Jewish people." By providing a sanctuary for Jews rendered homeless by persecution, "the

State of Israel appeals to our deepest humanitarian instincts . . . we shall continue our friendly interest in this constructive and inspiring undertaking." The Republican party, the statement concluded, would strive to bring about peace between Israel and its Arab neighbors as well as cooperate in bringing economic and social stability to that area.

In contrast to the Democratic plank, the Republican avoided any specific commitment of support for Israel, especially economic assistance to enable the country to absorb the huge number of refugees who poured into the country soon after statehood had been proclaimed. While in general terms the statement committed the Republican party to supporting the sovereignty and independence of the new state, it was also clear that it was written by somebody "who was not thinking just of the election but of having to cash the checks after the elections."[21] Nor could Israel's supporters draw much comfort when Douglas MacArthur in his keynote speech at the Republican convention charged that Truman's policies in the Middle East had lost U.S. friendships in that part of the world.

All in all, the plank dealing with the Middle East in the Republican platform seemed to have been tailor-made for their candidate to the presidency. During the election campaign, the American Zionist Council, headed by Louis Lipsky, was eager to secure a pro-Israel statement from Eisenhower in the context of a general foreign policy speech to a national audience affirming that aid to Israel was an integral part of U.S. policy, not dictated by domestic politics. Some Jewish Republicans who knew Eisenhower, such as Maxwell Rabb, Lodge's campaign chief, Rabbi Judah Nadich, and Congressman Jacob K. Javits, were contacted on the subject—to no avail. Eisenhower would not relent to special interest groups, not in a public speech, anyway.

Nonetheless, albeit grudgingly, Eisenhower began showing a somewhat warmer attitude toward Israel. On August 28, 1952, he lunched at the Commodore Hotel in New York with a group of wealthy Jewish Republicans: Barney Balaban, Sam Hausman, and Dave Kluger. Also present was Walter Williams, national chairman of the Citizens for Eisenhower and Nixon clubs. Eisenhower complained about the general problem of satisfying the demands of pressure groups; he was determined to act only in the broad interests of the U.S. public. The discussion turned to the relationship between the United States and Israel, which according to the Jewish participants was of deep interest to many millions of "our faith in the country." Eisenhower responded that the existence of Israel was no longer a matter for debate but was an established fact and should be recognized as such. Its future depended upon "its ability to make peace with its Arab neighbors." The U.S. government, he continued, must exert every effort to bring about peace in the area. As to the Arab refugees, they lived an entirely different kind of life from the Israeli people; they were content to live in the desert, while Israel was building a modern economy. The refugees should be integrated into the Arab countries.

So far, the candidate's views coincided with those of his listeners. But as far as continuing foreign aid to the area, Eisenhower favored it in principle as long as it was in the self-interest of the United States, but he would make no commitment until he learned more about the needs of the region. In regard to the inclusion of Israel in plans for the defense of the Middle East, Eisenhower was noncommittal. As to the desirability of making a public affirmative statement on the subject, the presidential candidate commented that his position with regard to help for persecuted peoples was so well known that it did not require restatement, but he recognized the practical need for doing so and might act sometime in the future.[22] Compared with his past pronouncements, the participants had a great deal to be satisfied about, even though on important questions he made no promises. That the meeting took place, given Eisenhower's aversion to pressures from interest groups, was in itself important. It was duly reported to Prime Minister Ben-Gurion, whom Eisenhower mentioned having met in 1945 in connection with the fate of the Jewish DPs.

As the presidential campaign gained steam, Eisenhower referred specifically to Israel in his messages to Jewish audiences. On September 17, on the eve of the Jewish New Year when candidates for political office traditionally send greetings to Americans of the Jewish faith, Eisenhower declared: "Here in America we have watched the establishment and development of the modern state of Israel. This too, is part of the miraculous history of the Jewish people. I look forward confidently to the progress of democracy in Israel, to the stabilization of her economy and her growing contribution to the free world." And on October 14 the candidate sent a message to a dinner honoring the Republican Senator from New York State, Irving M. Ives, whose reelection could be helped by a large Jewish vote there. Eisenhower commended the senator for his "magnificent efforts on behalf of the valiant state of Israel. . . . The state of Israel is democracy's outpost in the Middle East and every American who loves liberty must join the effort to make secure forever the future of this newest member in the family of nations."[23]

While these messages were welcome signs of a shift in Eisenhower's position, Israel's supporters were still eagerly waiting for a pro-Israel public statement that would have nationwide appeal. It finally came in the last weeks of the presidential campaign. Dewey arranged a meeting between Eisenhower and Rabbi Abba Hillel Silver, rabbi of Tifereth Israel Temple (The Temple) in Cleveland, Ohio, former chairman of the Zionist Emergency Council, and a lifelong national Zionist leader. The meeting took place at Eisenhower's residence at Columbia University on October 18. During a forty-five minute conversation, Silver familiarized the Republican candidate with Israel's security needs. Soon after, in a reply to a letter addressed to him by Silver, Eisenhower issued to the press the most pro-Israeli statement to date. In fact, the statement affirmed the points raised in Silver's letter. Eisenhower emphasized his role in fighting nazism and expressed his admiration for the pioneers in Israel who were energetically pursuing the work of settlement and land reclamation. Aware of the economic problems confronting the new state, he declared: "Foremost among these is that of establishing peace with the Arab world. Such peace is essential to the free world. Each encouragement should be given to *facilitate direct negotiations between the state of Israel and its Arab neighbors whose independence, freedom and prosperity are equally the hope and wish of the American people*" (italics added).

Then Eisenhower turned to the thorny problem of the Palestine Arab refugees. "In my judgment, both statesmanship and humanity dictate that these unfortunate refugees should, as rapidly as possible, *be assisted with adequate means honorably to reintegrate themselves in the neighboring Arab countries whenever their reabsorption in Israel is not feasible or practical*" (italics added).

In regard to economic aid so crucial to Israel, Eisenhower was equally reassuring. "It is in the interest of the United States and of all peace loving nations that political and economic aid to establish their own security should be extended to Israel and to all countries in the Middle East which are similarly intentioned, to an extent consistent with a sound overall mutual aid program."

The statement must be credited to the successful lobbying efforts of Rabbi Silver. More important, it also marked the beginning of an important relationship between the rabbi and the future president. While in earlier presidential elections Silver remained politically neutral, this time he supported Eisenhower. After the elections, in a show of gratitude, Eisenhower invited the rabbi to offer a prayer at his inauguration. From then on, Silver was one of the few Jewish leaders exerting some influence and had considerable access to Dulles, the president, and his Chief of Staff, Sherman Adams.[24] Often he would serve as a conduit, conveying messages from the administration to Israeli leaders.

Eisenhower's pronouncement notwithstanding, the Israeli press greeted his landslide victory with a restraint bordering on disappointment. On November 6 the independent *Ha'aretz*, reflecting the general mood, preferred to concentrate on Eisenhower's humane character in helping the Jewish DPs in the aftermath of the war but expressed concern that his military background would lead him as president to view the Middle East on the basis of realpolitik rather than on that of moral considerations. Prime Minister Ben-Gurion, in a congratulatory telegram to Eisenhower, accentuated the positive. "When I had the privilege of meeting you in Frankfurt in the aftermath of your great victory, I was deeply impressed by your humane attitude towards the Jewish displaced persons, the victims of Nazism and your willingness to assist them by every possible means." But in private Ben-Gurion expressed doubts about whether Israel would have as easy access to the White House as it had under Truman. "Until now there was only one conduit to the White House—the Israeli, from now on there will be an Arab one as well." Furthermore, "Eisenhower adores his young brother Milton who is close to the pro-Arab group of Dorothy Thompson. Efforts must be made to influence Milton in our direction."[25]

Yet, the most insightful and somber assessment concerning the new administration came from Eban. His comments, a combination of disappointment tempered with realism, withstood the test of time. Expressing the conventional wisdom in Washington, Eban suggested that Eisenhower would rely more heavily on his cabinet for policy guidance than any president in recent times, partly because there were large areas of government in which he had no experience and partly because as a military man he had been accustomed to rely on the staff system. In his view, one should not expect radical or drastic changes in policy toward Israel given that a certain tradition and commitment of friendship toward Israel had already been established.

Nonetheless, for the Israeli embassy in Washington the changes in administration constituted a "total revolution." In the previous five years the staff had succeeded in developing wide-ranging and significant contacts and relationships with the leaders of the Democratic party, in the administration, in Congress, and with the public at large. A new network of relationships would have to be established from scratch. Most troublesome to Israel was the fact that in the new administration, Israel would be hard-pressed to find people as influential as David Niles, Abraham Feinberg, Eddie Jacobson, and Max Lowenthal, friends and Zionists with easy access to Truman who faithfully stood by Israel in the most difficult of times.

Eban also expressed concern that the overwhelming majority of Jews, 75 percent, voted for Stevenson and therefore the Republicans "do not owe much to them." However, according to the ambassador, the Republicans must also think in terms of four years hence, "prefer the future over the past," and could not therefore alienate large blocks of voters. One could assume, Eban continued, that the new administration might limit foreign aid and military assistance as well. In sum, the situation from Israel's perspective was fluid and uncertain, but ingenuity and hard work could produce positive results.[26]

None understood better the challenges facing Israel at this juncture than Eban, and none could answer them better. The Israeli ambassador, who during the 1950s would argue Israel's case most eloquently in the international forum of the United Nations and privately in the corridors of power of the United States, had already served in various diplomatic assignments before coming to Washington. Born in Cape Town, South Africa, he was brought up in England and studied oriental languages and classics at Cambridge University, where he was a research fellow and lecturer in Arabic from 1938 to 1940. During World War II he came to Palestine, and in 1946 the Jewish Agency appointed him political information officer in London. In this capacity he participated in the final negotiations with the British government before the establishment of Israel. In 1947 he was named liaison officer for the Jewish Agency with the UN Special Committee on Palestine. Then he became a member of the

Jewish Agency with the UN Special Committee on Palestine and subsequently a member of the Jewish Agency's delegation to the UN General Assembly instrumental in securing the passage of the partition resolution of November 29, 1947.

When Israel became independent in May 1948, he was appointed as his country's representative to the United Nations and permanent chief delegate in 1949, a job he held simultaneously with his ambassadorship in Washington until 1958. A gifted speaker, his accent reflecting his education at Cambridge, his words those of a juridical poet, Eban became Israel's eloquent voice and symbol for a decade. Aided by the competent staff of the Israeli embassy and prominent U.S. Jewish leaders, he began the hard task of making new friends and influencing policy in the new centers of power. Eban and his staff succeeded in no small measure in preventing a pro-Arab U.S. policy, especially in view of consistent talk emanating from officials of the new administration about changes in domestic and foreign policy.

By early February 1953 the State Department had developed the theme called the New Look. The message: It's time for a change; U.S. policy would not be a continuation of the past. Under a headline of "Dulles Wields Big Broom for Diplomatic New Look," James Reston wrote in the February 2 *New York Times*, "Things are going to be different from now on or at least are going to look different." In foreign policy in general, the Truman premise that the United States should make its plans and intentions on the cold and hot wars crystal clear in order to reassure its allies and make the Communists realize that the United States had no aggressive designs would now be replaced by a reverse course. In Europe, "liberation" and tough talk for unity in face of Communist aggression would replace "containment." Maximum doubt must be created in the Communist mind about U.S. intentions. Secret accords with the Soviets must be done away with, for they only helped the Russians to enslave free peoples. As for the Middle East, the New Look theme relied on a virtuous and moralistic assertion that U.S. policy would not be influenced by internal considerations (i.e., the Jewish vote) and that both Israel and the Arab states would be treated equally, without any preference to the former over the latter as was the case during the Truman administration.

Accordingly, the Associated Press on February 18 quoted top U.S. officials to the effect that the United States was turning a cold shoulder to

Israel's urgent plea for aid, while lining up military and economic help for Egypt. U.S. officials viewed this move as desirable in order to encourage Egypt's strong-man premier, General Mohammed Naguib, to join the proposed Middle East Defense Organization (MEDO).[27] Egypt's membership was viewed by the United States as the key to countering Soviet designs on the Middle East. Therefore, any move to give Israel special military and economic aid at this time would prevent Egypt's membership in MEDO. The premise of this policy rested on the logic that backtracking on support for Israel would make possible arrangements with the Arab states that would strengthen their internal security and make military bases available to the West.

This new approach gained more credence with the March 2 visit to the White House of Prince Faisal Al Saud, foreign minister of Saudi Arabia, aimed at improving what he regarded as deteriorating relations between the two countries. In a statement issued by the White House after the meeting, Eisenhower expressed concern over evidence of a recent worsening in relations between the Arab nations and the United States. The president stated that it "would be his firm purpose to seek to restore the spirit of confidence and trust which had previously characterized these relations and he hoped that the Arab leaders would be inspired by the same purpose."[28] The tone of the White House statement implied criticism of the Truman administration, even though a spokesman denied reports that relations with Arab countries would be improved at the expense of friendship with Israel.

Yet on the eve of the White House meeting top State Department officials briefed reporters and asserted that a new Mideast policy shift was in the offing—specifically, treating all countries in the region scrupulously alike and avoiding any special aid program or privilege for Israel. Under Truman, those officials claimed, the United States gave Israel more financial and technical aid than all Arab states combined. They pointed out that a total of $229,516,000 in loans, grants, and credits were extended to Syria, Lebanon, Egypt, Iraq, and the Hashemite kingdom of Jordan in the last seven years, whereas in four years alone Israel was allotted $276,517,000, much of it in the form of grants appropriated by Congress.

Consequently, the first concrete move in the administration's new policy would be to grant Egypt an $11 million credit so that it could buy

Prince Faisal Al Saud, foreign minister of Saudi Arabia (center), pays a courtesy call at the White House on March 2, 1953. Secretary of State John Foster Dulles (left) inspects Prince Faisal's robe as President Eisenhower looks on. By permission of UPI/Bettmann.

U.S. defense equipment. The gesture was aimed at strengthening the hand of Naguib, who had recently settled an argument with Britain over the Sudan and who was now negotiating over the gradual evacuation of British troops from the Suez Canal area. Once this was accomplished, the United States hoped Egypt would consent to join the MEDO, with other Arab countries following suit, thereby making it possible to thwart Soviet ambitions in the region. As far as U.S. officials were concerned, Soviet ambitions included winning over the Arab nations and eventually seizing the rich oil fields of Iran, Iraq, Saudi Arabia, and Kuwait along with the strategic Suez area.[29] According to Dulles, Naguib was willing to cooperate with the West, and the United States must therefore do whatever possible to see to it that he remained in power. That included granting Egypt immediate military and economic assistance.[30]

To add meaning to the new policy, the Associated Press reported on March 3, Secretary of State Dulles would be making a trip to the Middle East and Southeast Asia in an effort to bolster U.S. prestige in the area. The visit would be aimed at least partly at demonstrating U.S. friendship with Arab governments, which were regarded as the key to combating stepped-up Russian activity. Yet in the first months of the Eisenhower administration the new policy was more rhetoric than reality, but even the talk of change produced anxiety and nervousness within the Israeli leadership and public because it left an impression that U.S. friendship for Israel had been a brief interlude linked organically with the Truman administration. The United States, chiefly for cold war reasons, was about to make a strong bid for Arab support. According to Israeli officials, the New Look theme raised expectations among the Arab governments that the Eisenhower administration would be "pro-Arab" in contrast to Truman's "pro-Israeli" policy. Such expectations, Israelis believed, only stiffened Arab attitudes toward Israel, continuing defiance of efforts to resettle the Arab refugees, reinforcing the economic blockade against Israel, and increasing toleration of the rising tide of infiltration by armed bands bent on smuggling, stealing, and sabotage.[31] In all likelihood Arab policies would have been the same even without a change in administrations, but Israeli leaders thought that the new atmosphere in Washington would fuel Arab belligerence.

Compounding Israeli problems was the Soviet's rupture of diplomatic relations with the Jewish state on February 13. The Soviet action followed a wave of anti-Semitism gripping Russia and the Soviet bloc nations, manifested during the Prague trial of Rudolf Slansky and other Communist leaders. No doubt those moves were also intended to win Arab favor by harassing Israel and condemning Zionism.[32] The rupture in relations with the Soviet Union made Israel more dependent on the West than ever before, particularly the United States. Unlike the Arabs who cultivated both sides in the cold war, Israel had no choice or possibility of bargaining between East and West. Israeli dependence on the United States had become total precisely when Washington seemed eager to woo the Arabs while minimizing its links with Israel.[33]

For the moment, at least, the Israeli embassy staff in Washington had succeeded in forestalling the implementation of the New Look policy. Their success, however, was also facilitated by the fact that the administration talked about change but had not yet thought out the details of the new policy. Israel's diplomatic offensive produced positive results, and that was quite reassuring from Israel's perspective, considering the prevailing atmosphere in Washington.

On February 11, Eban, accompanied by Esther Herlitz, the first secretary of the Israeli embassy in Washington, met General Walter Bedell Smith, now retired from the army and the new under secretary of state.[34] Present, also, was Fred E. Waller of the Division of Near Eastern Affairs of the State Department who was in charge of the office of Israel and Jordan. To Eban's first meeting with a top-echelon official of the Eisenhower administration, he brought with him a number of documents and an aide-mémoire, which he handed over to Waller for Smith's attention.

The memorandum consisted of three main parts. First, a long summary recognized the traditional friendly relations between Israel and the United States and the need to restate U.S. policy in light of Arab hopes that with the new administration there would be a change in U.S. policy in the Middle East. Second, the memorandum called for a renewal of Israel's application for military aid, made in the previous year, as well as the proposed U.S. military aid for Egypt and the question of the defense of the Mideast as a whole. It expressed apprehension that an attempt might be made to establish a MEDO to include all Arab states but exclude Israel. Third, the memorandum presented Israel's claim to be included with those countries entitled to be part of the off-shore procurement program. The thirteen-page document constituted the first formal presentation of Israel's case to the new administration.[35] Based on his record, Israeli leaders viewed General Smith as sympathetic to their cause. Given his close relationship to Eisenhower and the esteem in which the president held him, they hoped that his views would carry considerable importance with the president.

Indeed, the meeting was most cordial. General Smith preferred listening to the ambassador to reading the long memorandum. Eban summarized orally the contents of the written document, adding a new point to illustrate the importance of U.S. backing of Israel in view of Soviet anti-Israeli policy. Doing otherwise "would be a poor way of attracting those who might dare to face Russia by allying themselves with the West." Turkey and Yugoslavia, he added, received U.S. moral and financial support when attacked by the Soviet propaganda machine. Smith listened throughout with great interest. His comments showed genuine understanding, sympathy, and helpfulness. He seemed to be saying, "Why are you telling me all this about Israel, you know that the U.S. Government and I are with you . . . how could we do otherwise?" In fact, Smith at first was taken aback by Eban's implications of a change in policy by the new administration. "You have made quite an indictment against U.S. policy," he said.

The under secretary seemed surprised that anybody should suppose that the new administration would not follow the pro-Israel policy of Truman and implied that the doubts expressed in the ambassador's opening remarks were unnecessary. "There has been a change in the administration," he continued. "There has been no change in United States policy regarding Israel . . . the factor of Israel will never be disregarded, the excellence of your army is well known, both our sentiment and sympathy are with Israel." Having met Ben-Gurion, Israel's prime minister, in Frankfurt in 1945, Smith remarked, "He is one of the grand old men of the world." Repeatedly, he referred to Israel as having "the best military force in the Middle East." As far as he was concerned, "Israel was an important and significant factor in Middle East affairs." If the Arabs were expecting a "volte-face in American policy vis-à-vis Israel they would be disillusioned." But the under secretary also used this opportunity to complain about Israel's actions "raiding neighboring Arab territory" in retaliation for acts of violence carried out by individual Arabs infiltrating into Israel.[36] Before closing the interview, Smith promised to go over the aide-mémoire and the other documents brought by the ambassador, to discuss them with other officials, and to give them sympathetic and friendly consideration.[37]

It was too early for Israeli diplomats to sound the trumpet of victory, nor could they sit idly by and expect the State Department by itself to work out a pro-Israeli policy. Smith's praiseworthy remarks about Israel were not a true reflection of the feelings of others within the State Department bureaucracy. Middle Eastern policy had actually been formulated in the Office of Near Eastern, South Asian, and African Affairs of the State Department headed by Henry A. Byroade and decided upon by the secretary of state in full consultation with the president. The outcome would be a policy of evenhandedness in the Arab-Israeli conflict.

Indeed, Eban's subsequent meeting with Secretary of State Dulles on February 26 was less cordial and more businesslike. Eban did not have to explain to Dulles the background of the problems in the Middle East as he had to Bedell Smith. The secretary, as in so many other areas of foreign policy, was quite familiar with the situation through his work at the United Nations in 1947 and 1948. Eban attempted to impress the secretary with the need for first achieving peace between Israel and Egypt before the establishment of MEDO, as no reliable defense against outside aggression could be assured as long as the countries in the area were in a state of belligerency. He urged that the United States give top priority to the establishment of peace between Israel and Egypt as a prelude to a defense organization in the region. Eban also attempted to impress Dulles with Israel's military capacity as an effective ally in the Middle East. "Israel could put eight divisions into the field. We have airfields which could be enlarged, we have an armaments industry . . . to be used in case of an international emergency. Others [i.e., the Arabs] might be hesitant, but we are prepared to fight along with the West. If the Arabs saw us entering a Mid-East defense organization, they would want to join."[38] The secretary's answer: "You have given me a lot to think about. I have no clear reaction at the moment." In Dulles's view both peace between Israel and Egypt and the creation of an effective defense community ranked high on the administration's agenda. A defense organization would be stronger were it to include the military potential of Israel. Oftentimes, however, according to Dulles, results obtained were a by-product of something else. The secretary shared Byroade's view that Naguib was not strong enough to make peace and remain in power. It would be dangerous to rush him into a peace agreement. The Sudan and Suez problems between Egypt and Britain would have to be settled before one could proceed with any plans for a settlement of the Arab-Israeli conflict. The impression Dulles gave Eban was that neither he nor the administration as a whole had thought out a Middle East policy. As far as the Middle East was concerned, policy was still in the making.[39] That state of affairs in itself was encouraging, for it gave Israel time to prevent the formulation of a pro-Arab policy.

That assessment was reinforced on March 3, when Eban and David

Goitein, an embassy staff member, met with Byroade and Waller.[40] Eban inquired as to the significance of newspaper reports of March 2 proclaiming a change in U.S. policy toward Israel. Byroade retorted that the press was engaging in a guessing game. The U.S. desire to improve relations with the Arab countries did not translate into neglect of Israel. The president, he continued, was concerned about the deterioration in United States–Arab relations, but "we appreciate the friendship with Israel now, not any less than before." As to the White House announcement after Faisal's visit, Byroade turned toward Waller and said, "We did write something for the President, but there was no suggestion of a change in policy." More important, Byroade moved closer to the Israeli view about the need to proceed with the establishment of peace between Israel and Egypt before creating the defense organization.[41]

The visit to Washington of the Israeli Foreign Minister, Moshe Sharett, gave further indication that the New Look policy had at least for the time being no basis in fact, and that Israel's fears at this point were premature, conditions that of course did not preclude some dangerous omens for the future. Sharett held a series of meetings between April 8 and 11 with top U.S. officials and made a short visit to the White House.

He first met Byroade on April 8, with Eban and Waller present. They reviewed the situation in the Middle East as well as United States–Israeli relations. Among the topics discussed: British withdrawal from the Suez Canal Zone, Israel's request for military aid under the Mutual Security Act (MSA), and finally the prospects for peace between Israel and the Arab states. Sharett insisted that British withdrawal from the Suez Canal Zone should be conditioned on an Egyptian commitment to free passage of Israeli ships through the Suez Canal. Byroade, sympathetic to Israel's demands, promised to raise the question in the future with the three Western Powers. In Byroade's view, one had to consider the implications for Israel in case of a British withdrawal from Suez. As to military aid, the foreign minister emphasized Israel's request for such assistance under the nonpayment provisions of the MSA. Here, too, Byroade supported Israel's request as well as the principle of maintaining a military balance between Israel and her neighbors.

But the main problem for the United States still remained: how to achieve peace between Israel and her Arab neighbors. The Soviet Union had exploited the state of war between them to expand its influence in the

Arab world. The conversation turned into a heated exchange and became a major cause of disagreement between the two governments in years to come. Byroade asked the foreign minister point-blank, "What price would Israel pay for peace since it was so crucial to the country?" A surprised Sharett wondered as to the meaning of such a question. Byroade asked, "What are the territorial concessions that you are ready to make?" The only territorial concession Israel was ready to make, retorted Sharett, would be maintaining the present frontiers, despite the difficult and unnatural situation Israel faced on its eastern border with Jordan. Byroade did not find the answer satisfactory. Israel had expanded its territory beyond what had been allocated to it by the partition resolution of November 1947. When Sharett replied that the additional territory acquired by Israel was the outcome of Arab aggression in 1948, Byroade replied, "In that case there will be no peace." Israel, in Sharett's view, should and would hold on to its present frontiers under any circumstances. Sharett warned that the United States ought not to expect any territorial concessions on Israel's part. But the assistant secretary held firm, suggesting that sooner or later the United States would come up with a peace plan that might not be to the liking of either Israel or the Arabs.

As to the Arab refugee problem, Byroade suggested that Israel agree to a symbolic repatriation of refugees. That too was not to Israel's liking. All in all, according to Byroade, Israel was unwilling to make any concessions but wanted peace on its terms. Eban interceded, pointing to the positive implications of peace for the Arabs, such as trade, tourism, and the opening of the port of Haifa to trade with Jordan and Iraq. The Haifa oil refineries could serve Egyptian needs as well. Yet Byroade remained unimpressed.[42]

Later in the evening at a dinner at Eban's residence in honor of Sharett, Byroade apologized for the bitter tone of the day's discussions; he reassured his hosts that his views did not reflect those of the new administration. They were his personal thoughts as a means of finding out the extent of a possible compromise. But his listeners were not sanguine. The direction of his thoughts brought back memories of State Department activity during 1947 and 1948—the attempts to detach the Negev from the Jewish state, and the U.S. trusteeship plan, which aimed at preventing the proclamation of Jewish statehood, both attempts vetoed by Truman. In retrospect, Byroade's apology notwithstanding, his "personal views" were a signal of future official policy.

Fearing that Byroade's attitudes would eventually become U.S. policy, Sharett, in his meeting with Dulles a day later, reiterated that peace between Israel and her neighbors should be arrived at, but only "with an Israel as she is at the present time," meaning no territorial amputations or demographic changes, including the acceptance of Arab refugees. The secretary, as in his interview with Eban, listened carefully without comment. Sharett also reviewed the question of British-Egyptian negotiations concerning the future of the Suez Canal Zone, Israel's stake in the outcome of these negotiations, and the question of MEDO. Here Sharett put forth three possibilities: (1) Establish peace between Israel and the Arab states, which would make it possible for all to cooperate in the defense of the area; (2) since the prospects for peace did not seem very promising at that moment, the United States could enter into separate agreements with Israel and any Arab country willing to cooperate in the defense of the region; (3) in case no Arab country was willing to enter into such an agreement, then the United States could cooperate with the only country in the area eager to do so, Israel.[43] Dulles thanked Sharett for his "monologue," remarking that prospects for peace with Egypt were realistic as long as the moderate Naguib remained in power, a view expounded all along by Byroade.

After meetings with the Secretary of Defense, Charles Wilson, and with the Chairman of the Joint Chiefs of Staff, General Omar Bradley, in which Israel's request for military aid was discussed, Sharett culminated his talks in Washington with a fifteen-minute courtesy call at the White House.[44] There was no time to waste on small talk and generalities with the president; Byroade's comments reverberated in Sharett's ears, and Israel's position had to be made crystal clear at the highest level of the U.S. government. Sharett opened with a statement about Israel's desperate need for a continuation of U.S. economic and military assistance. His country's sympathies and interests, he declared, lay with the West, and Israel would gladly make her military and industrial potential available to the West. As to the question of future peace with the Arabs, he told the president that the U.S. involvement should be confined to exerting pressure on the Arabs, primarily Egypt, to enter into negotiations with Israel. The United States should not submit detailed proposals or conditions for peace, matters properly left open for negotiations between the parties. The president nodded his head in approval. Did he accept the Israeli position on this important issue, or was he politely acknowledging appreciation of having heard it? Only time would tell.[45]

Sharett's assessment of his talks in Washington was publicly upbeat. About his discussions with Eisenhower he told reporters, "I was happy to discover the President's sympathetic interest, he is aware of Israel's problems in the general framework of the Middle East." In a major address before the National Press Club in Washington on April 10, the foreign minister had only praise for the status of U.S.-Israeli relations. Confidently, he went as far as endorsing the concept of U.S. impartiality between Arabs and Israelis by declaring that "friendship towards one side is fully compatible with friendship towards the other." In private, however, Sharett was less sanguine and more cautious. True, Israel's initial fears had not materialized, but the future was still uncertain.

In a letter to Ben-Gurion, the foreign minister summarized his impressions of the Eisenhower administration. They were not flattering. First, he noticed a decline in the "moral and intellectual" level relative to the previous administration. Eisenhower, in Sharett's view, did not measure up to Truman's seriousness of purpose and consciousness. The secretary of state's intellectual ability fell short of Acheson's. As to the man "in charge of the Pentagon, Wilson is his name—a person of limited horizons and slow comprehension." His second impression of the administration was a lack of expertise and an inability to cope with major issues. The president's knowledge of the problems concerning Israel seemed rather superficial. Dulles was altogether groping in the dark. As to Wilson, his major concern was how to save money through cuts in personnel, but he could not yet understand issues of an international scope. All that, Sharett suggested, might not necessarily be to Israel's disadvantage. On the contrary, it offered opportunities for educating U.S. leaders in Israel's direction. That, however, would require a great deal of effort. According to Sharett, the Eisenhower administration seemed to lack a sense of urgency and displayed a tendency to delay planning and decisions, due either to the confusion associated with beginners or surprise at the Soviet aggressiveness and what to make of it.

Under these circumstances, Sharett declared, considerable influence might be exerted on Eisenhower and Dulles by the permanent bureaucracy and career diplomats in the State Department. In this category Byroade must be included. His views regarding an Arab-Israeli settlement

President Eisenhower confers at the White House with Foreign Minister Moshe Sharett (right) and Ambassador Abba Eban (center) of Israel, April 9, 1953. By permission of UPI/Bettmann.

might guide those determining future foreign policy. Consequently, Israel must see to it that no detailed peace plan should emanate from the administration, for such a plan would in all likelihood be detrimental to Israel's interest. Yet at the same time, Israel must constantly explain and propose its own concepts and ideas so that in the worst-case scenario a compromise could be reached between Israel's views and those of the Eisenhower administration. For the moment at least, no clear cut determination had been made by the new administration on whether to proceed with MEDO before the establishment of peace or only after. Both were viewed by the United States as extremely important in order to stem Soviet expansion in the area—a major preoccupation of the new administration that also explained the praises of Naguib sung by administration officials from the president on down as a man of peace and pro-Western, who must therefore be helped. That meant putting pressure on the British to solve the Suez problem to Egypt's satisfaction and most probably ignoring Israel's interest in such a settlement.

Based on these observations, Sharett concluded that the new team in Washington was still something of a tabula rasa as far as Israel was concerned. No basic changes had taken place so far, and no decisions would be reached until Dulles's return from his trip to the Middle East, scheduled to begin in mid-May. That would provide additional time for the Israeli embassy staff to continue explaining Israel's position to influential people both within and outside the administration, especially members of Congress, who were always politically attuned to public opinion in general, and to Jewish opinion in particular.[46]

In an attempt to take credit for his own efforts, Eban's assessment of the situation thus far was somewhat more optimistic than Sharett's. According to Eban, initially the administration had been eager to speak of possible new foreign policy initiatives but had for now settled down and inherited its predecessor's positions. In fact, present United States–Israeli relations, he believed, were not much different from those under the previous Democratic administration—an attitude of general good will and friendliness with some dangers.[47]

Since inauguration of the new administration, the Israeli embassy staff had managed to reach all key personnel in the Department of State, as well as influential members of Congress. Hereafter, it would concentrate on other centers of power: the National Security Council, the Cabinet, the White House inner circle, the Policy Planning Board of the State Department, and, of course, the president himself. In regard to him, a degree of progress was attained as well by leaders of American Jewish organizations.

Soon after his meeting with Prince Faisal of Saudi Arabia, the president told an official delegation representing the American Zionist Council headed by Louis Lipsky, "Our government has only the friendliest feelings for Israel and the Arab states and intends to use its offices to bring about peace in the Middle East." And in a subsequent talk at the White House on April 28 with Dr. Israel Goldstein, the president of the American Jewish Congress, Eisenhower declared that whatever might have been his views in 1948 regarding the establishment of a Jewish state, today "Israel is a fact, a certainty, and it must remain so." The president listened sympathetically to Goldstein's description of Israel's difficult economic condition and need for assistance and pledged that such aid would continue.[48] Byroade for his part informed Eban that the United States was interested in Israel's economic development as well as in the establishment of a defense organization in the Middle East. Israel, he said, would receive close to $70 million in military aid for fiscal 1954 and then added, "We are in the business of supporting the economy of Israel and help it militarily."[49]

Thus, prior to Dulles's trip to the Middle East, Eban in a letter to Ben-Gurion summarized the status of U.S.-Israeli relations during the early months of the Eisenhower administration. "I have been of the opinion since early March that the attempt of our adversaries to change the nature of the American-Israeli relationship has failed. While the President and his advisors do not show a wide philosophical grasp of the problem, I have found a good attitude on all specific issues that we have brought before them."[50]

Although the new administration, according to Eban, was less free than its predecessor with pro-Israeli declarations, it was, however, more forthcoming with pro-Israeli deeds. He listed some of the items for which Israel had pressured the Truman administration for two years with no results that the new administration had provided. Within a single month, Israel secured formal inclusion in the NATO offshore procurement program, received the third grant-in-aid defined at about $70 million, and secured a change in the MSA allowing specifically for military aid to Israel in its own right and not as a residuary legatee of Turkey and Greece. In the economic area, Israel received an assurance of undiminished economic aid and had its wheat allotment raised from 160,000 to 215,000 tons. On the political level, Israel had achieved a fair understanding on the question of peace and regional defense. Also Israel's expression of interest in Anglo-Egyptian negotiations over the future of the Suez Canal Zone had been well received. And Byroade had agreed to warn the press against the "time for a change slogan," which had now ceased as if by magic.

Of course, a danger of a rift with the U.S. government would arise if and when peace talks with the Arabs got under way and it appeared to U.S. officials that "symbolic repatriation of refugees or small territorial adjustments would secure a peace settlement not otherwise attainable." This cloud, however, seemed far removed as long as the Arab position remained so extreme. Eban concluded his remarks to Ben-Gurion with words that are as true today as they were then. "It is a paradox of Arab policy that their refusal to plunge into the peace issue defers their only tangible prospect of creating difficulties between the United States and Israel."

In the first five months of the Eisenhower administration, as far as Israel was concerned, a dangerous situation had developed from the end of January and throughout February when the New Look policy was enunciated. But under the impact of an Israeli diplomatic and Jewish counteroffensive at all levels, the policy remained stalled in its tracks.

The New Look policy was stalled but not dead. The Eisenhower administration had not yet had enough time to formulate new policy. As far as the Middle East in general was concerned, and the Arab-Israeli conflict in particular, the policy was still in the making. U.S. policy on such issues as the Arab refugee problem, the status of Jerusalem, and territorial questions crystallized only after John Foster Dulles's return from his three-week fact-finding mission to the Middle East during May 1953. The lessons he learned and the conclusions he drew from them would be applied throughout Eisenhower's first term and strain the relationship between the two countries. But for now things could have been worse. Israel had received an initial and welcome respite, but difficult days lay ahead.

Dulles's "Listen and Learn" Tour of the Middle East

3

The new Secretary of State, John Foster Dulles, was not a career diplomat in the sense of having spent all of his active life in the State Department or in the foreign service. Rather, he had made a career of diplomacy and was generally conceded to have been the best-briefed man for the post. Thus, when Eisenhower selected his cabinet, his choice for the premier post of secretary of state was without hesitation: John Foster Dulles. Dulles's extensive diplomatic background and knowledge of world affairs, his propensity for hard work, his mastery of detail, and finally his willingness to serve made his appointment all but inevitable.[1]

A serious student of international relations, Soviet communism, and the Bible, John Foster Dulles came from a family of celebrated diplomats. He was the grandson of John Watson Foster, who had served as Benjamin Harrison's secretary of state, and the nephew of Robert Lansing, who had held the same post under Woodrow Wilson. In the same year he gave his class's valedictory address at Princeton University at the age of nineteen, Dulles attended the World Peace Conference at The Hague; at the age of thirty he had advised President Wilson at Versailles. As senior partner in the Wall Street law firm of Sullivan and Cromwell and as chairman of the Internationalist Federal Council of Churches' Commission to study the bases of a just and durable peace, Dulles had met many leading world figures. After World War II he helped organize the United Nations, attended the conference of the Council of Foreign Ministers in London and Moscow and the Paris session of the United Nations in 1948, negotiated the peace treaty with Japan, served for a short period as senator and in between as Thomas Dewey's chief foreign policy adviser in the 1944 and 1948 presidential campaigns. In Eisenhower's words, "Dulles has been training for this job all his life."[2]

To his detractors, Dulles appeared a fanatic anticommunist who exaggerated the threat of communism, a man whose theological inclinations drove him to believe in his own moral rectitude, echoing the dominant cold war attitudes of his time and thus leading the United States to the brink of war.[3] His sympathizers, on the other hand, argued that his crusading anticommunist spirit was in large measure due to a realistic perception of world problems based on his vast diplomatic experience. They saw him as attempting to construct a realistic foreign policy in order to defend U.S. interests in the face of a dangerous Communist threat.[4] Although Eisenhower would sometimes modulate Dulles's strident, bellicose cold war rhetoric, such as that calling for the liberation of the Communist satellites or his concept of "massive retaliation," the president nonetheless found himself in agreement with Dulles's commitment to NATO, foreign aid, internationalism, the Middle East, and the dangers of the Communist threat as a whole. He greatly admired Dulles and regarded him "as the best informed man in international affairs that I believe lives in the world today."[5] He saw him as a dedicated and respected individual, a patriot who passionately believed in the United States, in the dignity of man, and in moral values.

Although many found Dulles impossibly pompous, a prig, unbearably dull (according to a popular saying, "Dull, duller, Dulles"), an unapproachable dour statesman who always seemed to have "one foot on an airplane," Eisenhower actually liked him.[6] So did his associates and those close to Dulles, who found him "warm, possessing a good sense of humor and a pleasant companion [who] inspired not only respect but also genuine affection."[7]

Recent research disputes the long-held traditional view of foreign policy analysts who believed that Dulles's forceful personality and his knowledge of foreign affairs enabled him to pursue a Lone Ranger diplomacy, to dominate and even to manipulate the rather "congenial but bland and passive" Eisenhower. These were appearances rather than realities. In fact, Dulles would never attempt to set his own course or to make foreign policy decisions without full presidential authorization and approval. He was well aware of the fate of his uncle, Robert Lansing, fired by Woodrow Wilson when Lansing pursued policies rejected by the president. Because of his high visibility and frequent statements seeking the limelight, Dulles created the impression that he dominated U.S. foreign policy. That did not displease the president, due in large measure to what political scientist Fred I. Greenstein called Eisenhower's use of the "lighting-rod" effect of delegating authority and allowing associates to take the blame for unpopular administration policy decisions. Yet at the same time Dulles respected Eisenhower and knew who was in command. While flying around the world and giving the appearance of acting on his own, Dulles actually operated under instructions from Eisenhower. Each evening on his foreign trips, he sent a cable to the president informing him of what had transpired that day and what he intended to say or do the next day. Although Eisenhower delegated responsibility for foreign policy to Dulles, he did not encourage independent action. In the words of Eisenhower historian Herbert S. Parmet, "On Middle Eastern policy as on everything else, Dulles and the President worked together, and the secretary, as carefully as in all other matters, deferred to Eisenhower's constitutional role." All important matters were brought directly to the president; less important ones were handled at the staff level but always within the context of general directives set forth by the president. In a letter to his boyhood friend in Abilene, Everett E. "Swede" Hazlett, Eisenhower wrote, "As far as Dulles is concerned he has never made a serious pronouncement, agreement, or proposal without complete and exhaustive consultation with me in advance and of course my approval."[8]

Dulles implemented policies, and that applied to the Middle East in general and Israel in particular. He and the president were in total agreement on policies to be pursued in that region. To them the Arab Middle East was a region of great strategic political and economic importance to the free world because of petroleum resources vital to the security and well-being of the West. Nearly all of the oil used in Western Europe and Japan came from the Persian Gulf through pipelines across Arab countries to the eastern Mediterranean coast or by tankers through the Suez Canal. In Dulles's words, "The North Atlantic Treaty forces in Europe and the Mediterranean fly on Mid-East oil and the ships operate on Mid-East oil."[9] Should the Soviets gain a Middle East position from which they could restrict this oil supply, a National Security Council report concluded, "Western Europeans' will to resist communist collaboration would be greatly weakened."[10] The region was also viewed as important for its global setting, because it contained essential locations for strategic military bases in any world conflict against the Soviet Union. In addition, the presence of the holy places of the Christian, Jewish, and Moslem world exerted religious and cultural influences affecting people everywhere.

In its attempt to block Soviet penetration into the Middle East, the Eisenhower administration soon realized that the Arab-Israeli conflict had given the Soviet Union its greatest opportunity to exploit Arab grievances and win Arab favor. How could Arab cooperation against the Soviet Union be won if Arab eyes were fixed on the "loss" of Palestine and the "menace" of Israel? Furthermore, Arabs viewed the United States as closely associated with those twin problems. Thus, finding a way of stopping Soviet penetration in the Arab world became the main motivating force that shaped Dulles's attitudes toward Israel. From this perspective, he and the president found themselves in full agreement. Gone was the tug of war that characterized the relations between Truman and the State Department on the Palestine question. The Eisenhower administration, as on many foreign policy issues, on the Arab-Israeli conflict spoke with one voice.

Dulles was no stranger to the intractable problems surrounding the question of Palestine. His sympathetic attitude toward the Jews there was reflected in the active role he played in the adoption of a plank in the Republican convention platform of 1944 calling for the establishment of a Jewish commonwealth in Palestine and the protection of Jewish political rights in the area. He also supported and urged U.S. backing of the UN partition resolution of November 1947.

His first direct involvement with the Arab-Israeli conflict had come in the fall of 1948 as acting chairman of the U.S. delegation to the newly formed United Nations, meeting in the Palais de Chaillot in Paris. The U.S. Secretary of State, George C. Marshall, headed the delegation, and Dulles was his deputy. The other delegates included Eleanor Roosevelt, Ben Cohen, an old legal adviser in the Roosevelt administration, and the Assistant Secretary of State, Dean Rusk.

Dulles, in disagreement with Marshall, argued against the adoption by the General Assembly of the Bernadotte proposals, claiming that Israel had fought and won a war imposed on her by the Arabs and that her victory had certain "spiritual and moral implications because of what it proved about the character and resolution" of the Jewish people. Israel, therefore, should not be truncated, and any changes in the November 1947 resolution should be arrived at with her consent. According to Eban, Dulles held strongly to those views, so much so that he ceased to attend delegation meetings that Marshall chaired at which the Bernadotte plan was discussed.[11]

In a speech in the General Assembly on September 28, 1948, Dulles maintained that the Arab-Israeli problem could be settled only by mutual agreement between the parties and that the United Nations must not attempt to draw frontiers. His assistance to Israel at that very crucial moment in its embryonic stage was acknowledged by Israeli leaders and future officeholders. Moshe Sharett, the acting representative of Israel to the United Nations and Israel's first foreign minister, wrote to Dulles on December 17, 1948: "I have nothing but admiration for your personal attitude to our delegation and the cause it had to defend. We have all appreciated deeply your helpfulness and wisdom. We hope to have the benefit of your sympathy and friendliness in the future stages of our struggle for complete and stable peace."[12]

In the few years before Dulles's appointment as secretary of state, Eban maintained contact with him at the law offices of Dean, Sullivan, and Cromwell, briefing him on Israeli positions. Eban was well aware that Dulles's role in U.S. foreign policy had not ended with the 1948 UN sessions. Dulles in return was touched that a "busy ambassador considered him worthy of this investment of time and effort." In July 1952, Dulles sought Eban's advice on the formulation of the Republican party's plank on the Middle East. It included a paragraph written by Dulles himself supporting in broad terms the independence and sovereignty of Israel. Soon after his appointment as secretary of state, in Dulles's first meeting with Eban in late January 1953, the Israeli ambassador could not detect any changes in Dulles's attitude. However, Dulles informed the ambassador of his intention to embark on a mission to the Middle East to study the situation; only afterward would he "formulate the policy of the administration on Israel."[13] Indeed, the trip would change his outlook on the Middle East. Thereafter, policy toward Israel would be determined in large measure within the context of the struggle between East and West over control of that strategic area of the world.

In response to a request by the president, on May 9, 1953, Dulles and Harold E. Stassen, director of the MSA in charge of the foreign aid program, accompanied by Henry A. Byroade and a number of State Department officials, left Washington on a twenty-day fact-finding mission of twelve countries in the Near East and Southeast Asia—Egypt, Israel, Jordan, Syria, Lebanon, Iraq, Saudi Arabia, India, Pakistan, Turkey, Greece, and Libya. The State Department officials were Douglas MacArthur II, a Department of State counselor; Robert E. Matteson, director of mutual security for research, statistics and reports; Lieutenant Colonel Stephen G. Meade, a military aide; Roderic L. O'Conner and Fred L. Hadsel, special assistants to the secretary of state; Athel H. Ellis and Jack A. Herfort, security aides; and W. O. J. Good, a stenographer. In Dulles's words, the aim of the mission was to get firsthand information. "I shall listen carefully to what I am told and consider the problems presented to me with utmost sympathy. . . . I look upon this trip as an opportunity to dispel misunderstandings and to develop close relations between the United States and these friendly nations."[14] By "listening and learning" on the spot about the problems confronting these countries, the secretary hoped to gather the information needed for a new effort to close this 2,000-mile gap in the ramparts of the free world.

Indeed, the secretary of state and his entourage might well have been discouraged by the incredible Pandora's box they were about to inspect. The task of winning the people of the area to the side of the West posed a difficult challenge for U.S. diplomacy. Among the most difficult political problems facing the region were the Anglo-Egyptian dispute over the future of the British military base in the Suez Canal Zone, the Arab-Israeli conflict, the difficulties of Iran and Iraq with their Kurdish minorities, the efforts of Afghanistan to carve an independent Pathan state from Pakistan, and the bitter Indo-Pakistani feud over Kashmir. Hovering over all was poverty and economic decay, making the region a prime and easy target for successful Communist subversion and penetration.

Arriving in Cairo on May 11 on the first leg of his tour, Dulles found the Egyptians brandishing sabers with slogans calling for the unconditional evacuation of the British base in the Suez Canal Zone. The problem represented essentially a conflict between national pride and international cold war strategy. The military base that Britain had controlled for seventy years was irreplaceable in the defense of the Middle East and difficult, therefore, for Britain to relinquish. Egypt, her nationalism reawakened, demanded that the last vestige of foreign domination on Egyptian soil be eliminated. This overriding nationalistic objective, Dulles learned, had utmost priority in the Egyptian scheme of things. General Mohammed Naguib and the junta of army and air force officers who put him in power, among them Lieutenant Colonel Gamal Abdel Nasser, emphatically rejected Western proposals for the establishment of MEDO linked to the West and publicly threatened guerilla warfare against British forces to achieve their end. Any defense organization for the area, the Egyptian leaders asserted, must center on building up the Arab states under the Arab League pact.

On his arrival, Dulles called Naguib "one of the outstanding free world leaders of the postwar period." He met the Egyptian prime minister on May 11 and presented him with a personal letter from the president and with a Colt .38-caliber automatic pistol bearing on the butt plate a silver plaque inscribed "To General Mohammed Naguib from his friend Dwight D. Eisenhower." Their discussions centered on the issues of a regional security alliance and the need for an agreement on the Suez base that would be consistent with both full Egyptian sovereignty and the military needs for the defense of the Middle East. Dulles suggested a phased British withdrawal so that the canal area with its depots of supply and the system of technical supervision would remain in good working order to be used on behalf of the free world in the event of war. Nasser was also present at the meeting, and both he and Naguib stressed that Egypt would settle for nothing less than immediate and unconditional evacuation of all British troops.[15]

In the evening, Dulles met Nasser alone over dinner at the U.S. embassy. At the time a powerful member of the Revolutionary Command Council (RCC), Nasser was viewed by the Americans as the rising star in the constellation of Egyptian future leadership, "the brain and spark-plug" of the RCC, a man worth cultivating even though he held no public post. The two went over the same issues covered earlier in the day with equally futile results. Dulles tried to convince Nasser that the Arabs' real enemy was international communism. To Nasser, however, the real enemies in the region were the Israelis, with whom the Arabs were technically at war, and the British, who occupied their territory. The Arabs, Nasser maintained, did not know anything about the Russians. It was therefore foolish to try to stir them up over a feared Soviet invasion. Colonialism, said Nasser, "is played out and now the match is between two teams—Communism and nationalism." Instead of MEDO tied to the West, Nasser suggested a regional Arab Front that could fight communism within the region.[16] Egyptian leaders persisted in viewing the Suez base problem as a private quarrel between Egypt and Britain without any awareness of its international ramifications. As Dulles later noted in a memorandum, the Egyptian leaders were almost "pathological." "They would rather go down as martyrs plunging Egypt into chaos than agree to anything which the public would call infringement of Egyptian sovereignty."[17]

The Egyptian leaders would consider a peaceful settlement with Israel but only after the question of a British presence in the Canal Zone had been resolved. "At present," said Nasser, "our minds and feelings are aroused against the United Kingdom." Naguib contended that Israel represented a continuing problem but that "something might be done" toward a solution, provided Israel allowed the establishment of land communication between Egypt and the Arab states, that is, if Israel made territorial concessions in the Negev. Dulles kept reassuring his Egyptian hosts that the present U.S. administration, unlike its predecessor, "was trying to work out a Middle East policy on the basis of enlightened self interest of the United States rather than in the self interest of particular groups in America." Although in the past, said Dulles, the United States had "perhaps centered too much of its interest on Israel as a result of pressure groups in the United States, the new administration is seeking a balanced view of the Middle East directed against neither the Arabs nor the Jews."[18]

With the Anglo-Egyptian crisis uppermost in their minds, Dulles and his party arrived an hour behind schedule on May 13 at 1:40 P.M. at the Lydda airport in Israel. The delay resulted from a request by Dulles to fly over the Suez Canal area to view the military base the British were asked to evacuate. Three Israeli fighter planes waited in vain in the air over Eilat to escort the U.S. plane carrying Dulles and his party, which flew in over Gaza from the sea and reached Lydda unescorted. Never before had such elaborate security precautions been taken in Israel. At the airport more than a thousand police formed a cordon around the twelve-mile outer perimeter of the field. Others watched the runways used by the U.S. plane, while over a hundred police guarded the airport building and shoved away all persons not registered on a special list. Telephone communications were halted. Foreign Minister Sharett, in a formal homburg hat, and Israeli officials greeted the straw-hatted visitors and led them to an airport balcony from which Dulles read a brief statement to the press. The secretary was happy to be in Israel on a trip made at the request of President Eisenhower in order to obtain firsthand information and understanding of the situation in the countries that they had visited and were about to visit in order "to show the friendship of our government and people. We know of the great progress which has been made by Israel and the energetic way in which its leaders are attempting to solve the problems which still exist." Then the guests were driven to the residence of the U.S. Chargé d'affaires, Francis H. Russell, for a late lunch. For the next twenty hours they would listen to the Israeli leaders' perspectives on the various aspects of their conflict with the Arabs as well as the role Israel was ready and willing to play in the defense of the region.

Israelis were generally satisfied that for the first time in their nation's short history, a U.S. secretary of state had taken the trouble to come and see the country's problems. In contrast to the Egyptian press, which had been critical of Dulles, the Israeli press almost unanimously welcomed Dulles and his entourage. Editorials carried such headlines as "A day which may be a historic one" in *Haboker* (general Zionist daily). *Ha'aretz* (independent) and *Davar* (Mapai's labor daily) editorially emphasized the help of the U.S. people and government in the building and consolidation of Israel. The one discordant note was struck by the Communist party and the Mapam left-wing opposition party. Through their front organization, Peace League, they made advance preparations for an anti-Dulles mass demonstration that in the end attracted more curious spectators than motivated participants.

The public welcome notwithstanding, Israeli leaders were jittery over the intentions of the new administration, intentions that would become clearer after Dulles's whirlwind tour. As the influential *Ha'aretz* poignantly suggested, those jitters were neither totally surprising nor unjustified. Previous U.S. policy in the Middle East (i.e., under Truman) was

Secretary of State Dulles inspecting a guard of honor upon his arrival in Israel, May 13, 1953. Alongside Dulles is Moshe Sharett, Israel's foreign minister. By permission of Princeton University Libraries.

based on a series of momentary decisions designed to meet ad hoc problems, and that included policy toward Israel. U.S. decisions regarding Israel were taken separately and not within the context of a coherent Middle Eastern policy, which by and large was left for Britain to manage. The lack of a consistent policy in the Middle East suited Israel's interests and made it possible to overcome State Department animosity by turning directly to the White House. The situation was about to change. Dulles, unlike Acheson, would no longer leave the Arab Middle East to Britain, nor would he strengthen the belief among Arabs that the United States was Israel's patron. Because the new administration was in the process of devising a policy for the region as a whole, its attitude toward Israel would be determined within the framework of U.S. interests.[19]

None understood these circumstances better than the Israeli leaders. Weeks before Dulles's arrival the Israeli Foreign Office had begun preparing a set of guidelines and issues to be brought up with the U.S. delegation. On April 30, a summing-up session of Israel's positions in the upcoming talks was held. The participants included Ben-Gurion; Levi Eshkol, the minister of finance; Teddy Kollek, director of the Prime Minister's Office; Dr. Walter Eytan, director of the Foreign Office; Reuven Shiloah, Michael Comay, and Shmuel Bendor, senior officials of the Foreign Office; Shimon Peres, director of the Defense Ministry; and Moshe Dayan, chief of staff of the army. Dr. Eytan summarized the discussions within the Foreign Ministry and suggested the issues to be raised in talks with Dulles.

Given that peace with the Arab states was a remote possibility, Israel should seek instead a nonaggression pact with its neighbors as a prelude to peace. Israel would be willing to discuss financial compensation to the Arab refugees but would need U.S. economic assistance for that purpose. Should Egypt lift its blockade of Israeli ships and allow their free passage through the Suez Canal, the money saved by Israel could be used in helping the refugees. Israel was willing to negotiate with its neighbors in solving the water problems in the region even before a peace agreement was reached. In the absence of a general Mideast defense organization, the United States should help strengthen Israel's ability to defend itself as the only democratic state in the region.

In the ensuing discussion, Eshkol warned against the promise of specific amounts as compensation to the Arab refugees, such as the revenues to be saved by Israel in case of the lifting of the blockade of its ships in the Suez Canal. Instead, he suggested, Israel should offer to participate in the settlement of the refugees in the Arab countries as part of its own domestic economic development. Ben-Gurion, however, had different views, which became the accepted guidelines used with the U.S. guests. He was apprehensive about a nonaggression pact with the Arabs. In his view the armistice agreements already contained the principle of nonaggression, yet they were violated by the Arabs. Israel, he maintained, should concentrate on the following: cessation of all hostilities on the part of the Arabs, good neighborly relations—that is, economic and cultural cooperation between Israel and its neighbors—and Israel's willingness to assist in the resettlement of the refugees in the Arab countries. Peace and stability in the Middle East did not depend on written agreements but on raising the cultural standards of the Arabs, and that required long-range planning and especially an end to the arms race between Israel and its neighbors. Above all, Israel must not appear to be too anxious in its desire for peace. Such a stance would only lead to demands for concessions on Israel's part. Israel, Ben-Gurion continued, was geographically in the Levant but culturally a Western nation. Israel would fight any Communist aggression in order to maintain its democratic system of government. The relations between Israel and the United States should not hinge on U.S.-Arab relations. It was in the U.S. interest to strengthen Israel economically and militarily.[20]

The participants concurred with Ben-Gurion's observations—all designed to support a tough, realistic, noncompromising approach that placed the onus of responsibility for peace on the Arabs. The Israeli approach was also intended to convince Dulles that U.S.-Israeli relations should be based on mutual bilateral interests and not be affected by wider U.S. considerations of the Arab world. All in all, a tall order.

The first high-level political meeting took place a few hours after Dulles's arrival, at 5:15 P.M. at the Foreign Ministry, Hakirya, Tel Aviv. On the Israeli side the participants included Foreign Minister Sharett, Comay, Shiloah, and Bendor. The U.S. delegation included Dulles, Stassen, MacArthur, Byroade, Russell, and Tel Aviv embassy staffers Bruce W. MacDaniel and Milton Fried. The Americans, who came to "listen and learn," gave Sharett the opportunity to present Israel's case. He restated the familiar and long-held Israeli position, the desire for peace and good neighborly cooperation. But achieving this aim, he reiterated, should not mean "territorial changes to our detriment." Israel was ready to make peace on the basis of the present armistice lines, with the possibility of minor adjustments once the principle of peace was accepted by the Arabs. As far as Israel was concerned, the Arab claim to return to the UN resolution of 1947 had no basis in justice or reality. They could

Dulles (right) and Sharett en route to a restaurant at Lydda airport, May 13, 1953. By permission of Princeton University Libraries.

not have it both ways. Having rejected that resolution and declared war on Israel, they now should accept the verdict of that war. For Israel to relinquish the Negev would be unthinkable.

As to the Arab refugee problem, here, too, there was no change in the Israeli position. Fate and the Arab war of aggression, Sharett said, brought about an Arab exodus from Israel that was not unique in recent history, considering Greece and Turkey after World War I, Central Europe in World War II, and India and Pakistan after partition. Nowhere had there been a return to the status quo ante. In Israel the vacuum had been filled by immigrants. Repatriation of the Arabs would destroy the security and economy of the country. In the long-term interests of all concerned, it was better that the refugees be absorbed where they "already had taken up residence"—in the Arab countries. All Arab countries would benefit from an overall plan for the economic integration of the refugees, as they all (with the exception of Egypt) suffered from underpopulation. Israel's obligation, the foreign minister maintained, was to pay fair compensation—fair to those to whom it was owed, fair to Israel in view of its economic position.

In regard to Jerusalem, internationalization of the entire city was out of the question, but Israel was willing to cooperate in the establishment of international supervision of the holy places. Since the main shrines were in Arab custody in the section of Jerusalem occupied by Jordan, that country's consent was essential for any scheme of international supervision to become operative. Then Sharett added that "complete freedom of access to the Holy Places depends upon peace between Israel and Jordan and no amount of international supervision will solve that problem." Sharett informed his listeners that soon Israel intended to transfer the Foreign Ministry from Tel Aviv to Jerusalem. The transfer, he said, was not a political demonstration but a practical necessity; the ministry could not be separated from the body of the government, which was already there. He hoped that foreign embassies would follow the move; if not, lest such a move ran counter to the UN partition resolution of 1947, Israel would provide them full accommodations and facilities in Tel Aviv. But for Israel the transfer of the Foreign Ministry was inevitable because "there is not a single instance in the whole world where a Foreign Ministry is in one town and the other government departments in another."

"Israel can certainly hold out without peace," Sharett continued. Nevertheless, the Arabs must discontinue all belligerent acts, in accordance with the armistice agreements. Sharett specifically emphasized the rising frontier incidents caused by Arab infiltrators from Jordan. Those incidents included large-scale marauding, theft, robbery, murder, and sabotage and led to Israeli reprisals that were often condemned by the world community. Because the "operational initiative" always came from the Arab side, the United States should attempt to influence the Arab states to curb these "acts of aggression." Another form of "aggression," Sharett complained, was the economic boycott imposed on Israel by the Arab states. Moreover, they forced other countries to participate in it. The blockade against Israeli ships in the Suez Canal and the Gulf of Aqaba was still carried out by Egypt in violation of a Security Council resolution. That blockade, according to Sharett, not only cost Israel foreign currency but also was prejudicial to her international rights.

Then the foreign minister turned to issues of a more general nature. In his view there was no country, from Gibraltar to Japan, throughout North Africa and South Asia, in which democracy meant so much to such a high percentage of the population as it did to Israel. The implication, of course, was that the Arabs had no such system. Moreover, Israel was ready to defend its democratic institutions as well as to play its part in defending Western principles and interests in the Middle East. Israel was eager to participate in any plan for the defense of the Middle East, but until that happened the United States should strengthen dependable countries in the area. While it was correct to assume that stability and peace were prerequisites for an effective defense of the area, the strengthening of Israel need not wait for peace. Israel, said Sharett, was in need of additional arms and economic assistance. The U.S. attitude towards Israel, he maintained, should be determined on the basis of Israel's potential benefit to the West rather than in the context of American-Arab relations.

Dulles did not argue with what he called the "illuminating and cogent presentation" of the foreign minister. He and his colleagues came to learn and to seek information because this part of the world had been neglected by the United States in the past. There were policies for Europe, for the Far East, and for South America but none for the Middle East. Dulles was interested in Israel's assessment of whether there had been a change in Soviet policy after Stalin's death. In Sharett's view, the Soviet objective with its "peace offensive" was to "widen rifts in the democratic camp." Dulles agreed "that if there is any relaxation in the common effort of the free world, the differences submerged would come to the top . . . the free world can more easily come apart."

Just before the meeting ended, Dulles turned to a map on the wall and asked Sharett what he thought about a land passage between Egypt and Jordan in the south (i.e., the Negev). Naguib, said Dulles, engrossed in the negotiations with Britain, still found the time to talk about Israel. He had complained that "what was taking place in the area was not the partition of Palestine but the division of the Arab world, into which Israel had driven a wedge." Should Egypt be interested in peace with Israel, Sharett replied, a suitable solution for a link between Egypt and Jordan could be found, provided Israel's territorial integrity remained intact. He clearly implied that relinquishing the Negev was out of the question.[21]

Later, during dinner at Sharett's home, Dulles talked freely with his host about his frustrations with the Egyptian position. He found Naguib to be an honest person but dependent on the goodwill of the group that surrounded him, the military junta. The narrowness of their outlook astounded the secretary. The eviction of the British from the Canal Zone was the only problem that mattered to them. They were completely blind to the far-reaching changes in the balance of strength and to the world-wide repercussions that would follow the transfer of the canal base from Britain to Egypt. Naguib kept repeating the "shibboleths that the British should quit and that was the only way for Egypt to regain her complete independence, etc." The Egyptians were engrossed in their local problems, insensitive to the problems of the region, the world, or communism.

To Dulles and his Israeli hosts the question overshadowing everything else was whether the Judeo-Christian civilization was going to survive, with all the moral and spiritual values for which it stood. Our civilization, Dulles said, was gravely threatened. It was important "that there be people who saw the problem in its broad aspects. Israel did, because the people of Israel had a sense of history . . . from that point of view, the difference between this dinner in the foreign minister's house and the dinner the previous night with Naguib was as between day and night." With the Israelis he felt he had a common language. Sharett appreciated Dulles's remarks and went on to explain why communism was antithetical to everything that Israel stood for, morally, politically, and intellectually.

Although the Anglo-Egyptian dispute was the main topic of Dulles's remarks at the table, he abruptly departed from the subject to talk about Jerusalem. He hoped that if Israel were to move the Foreign Ministry there it would not be done while he was in the region, to save him embarrassment. His advice was that such a move should be coupled with a public statement on the holy places along the lines proposed by Sharett earlier in the day. The foreign minister hastened to reassure his guest that nothing "as precipitate as that was intended" and that Israel would restate its position on that occasion.[22]

So far Dulles's reactions were indeed soothing to his listeners. But then he interjected a few observations on a subject relating to Israel and U.S. Jews that would cause him a great deal of frustration throughout his tenure as secretary of state. He admired the pioneering spirit in Israel, its democratic system, and the building up of the country, but that did not mean he agreed with Israel on all matters. What troubled him a great deal was the idea that "U.S. policy [in the Middle East] had not always been in the best interests of the total situation. It had been affected by political considerations . . . the U.S. government had made mistakes with regard to the situation in the Middle East." He did not elaborate. He was referring to the role played by U.S. Jews who in his view were interfering with the decision-making process of U.S. Mideast policy. This was the single issue that the secretary voiced with anger and frustration, practically lecturing the Israeli leaders.[23]

In his meeting with Ben-Gurion and Sharett the next morning, Dulles brought up the subject again. First he heard the prime minister discuss in general philosophical terms Israel's relations with the United States and the world as well as Israel's role in the region. Israel, Ben-Gurion said, was part of the Middle East before most of its neighbors. But geography was not the only factor. History and spiritual values meant more than geography; the former linked Israel with the West. Because Israel placed high value on human freedom and human dignity, therefore it was part of the free world. If war between the free and unfree were to be averted, preparations had to be made, physical and moral. Two years ago, Ben-Gurion continued, he spoke to the former Secretary of Defense, George C. Marshall, about the role Israel had to play in peace and war. Ben-Gurion doubted whether there was any country in the Middle East except Israel ready to fight for things that the free world held dear—apart from Turkey there was no nation in the area that really cared to fight for freedom or was capable of fighting for it. Consequently, the United States ought to strengthen Israel—a country "with skilled people, a fine army, fine industrial military potential"—for the good of the free world. Strategically, Israel was connected with the Mediterranean Sea and the Indian Ocean. If the Suez Canal fell into the hands of the enemy, Haifa and Eilat would be important not only for Israel but for the whole free world.

Turning to the relations with its neighbors, Ben-Gurion maintained that there was a vacuum in the Arab Mideast because the people were miserable. The United States could render a historic service by helping to improve the lot of the people. What was needed, the prime minister suggested, was a long-range program to raise the cultural and economic levels of the people of the Arab countries. Instead, Arabs requested arms. Whom were they going to fight? The Russians? Nobody believed that.

They required guns only to fight Israel. If the Arabs were not ready for peace, Israel had the right to demand the complete cessation of all hostilities—military, political, and economic. The infiltration from Arab countries into Israel was a kind of war. The blockade on Israeli ships in the Suez Canal must cease. As to the settlement of the refugees, Israel was ready to make her contribution, but the Arab states possessed "fertile lands, water, oil and other resources. They had to show some of the determination and patience which we have shown in reconstructing our country." For her part Israel was ready for cooperation with the Arab states—economic, cultural, and even military. If Dulles and his party in their travels found such willingness, Israel would be pleased and responsive. The prime minister wished them success in their mission, including their goal to win the friendship of the Arabs.

This last remark seemed to be the opening that Dulles needed to elaborate on an issue that he resented: the interference by U.S. Jews in the process of determining U.S. policy in the Middle East. Dulles complained about it at great length. He did not mince words to show his displeasure, implying that it was in the power of Israeli leaders to restrain their coreligionists and apparently forgetting the position he himself held on the subject before joining the new administration.

> The Arabs felt with some justification that prior administrations, those of Roosevelt and Truman, had been subject to Jewish influence and ignored the point of view of the Arabs. And it was known historically that decisions in this matter were taken under direct political pressure by Jewish groups who felt they had a right to exert that pressure because they had contributed to the election of Roosevelt and Truman. The present administration had been elected by the overwhelming vote of the people of the United States. He [Eisenhower] felt a duty to the people as a whole and not to any particular segment. The President believed that U.S. policy had to continue to be one of support for Israel as being a great creative accomplishment which evoked the sympathy of the whole of the people of the U.S. and not only the Jews. . . . But it was also part of his foreign policy to make the Arabs feel that there was concern for them. They had to be helped toward economic improvement and that was the reason why Mr. Stassen was a member of the party. One of the troubles was that there

were some elements in the U.S. who felt that anything the U.S. government did at all which was sympathetic to the Arabs was in some way against the interests of Israel . . . there was a strong feeling in the U.S. that either they had to have a pro-Israel or a pro-Arab policy and that there wasn't any policy that combined the two.

In Dulles's view, the Arabs felt that a change in administration in the United States was an opportunity for better relations. The president saw to it that their visit to the area included the Arab states as well as Israel, "since the Arabs were also important people and not to be ignored." U.S. ability to gain Arab friendship depended to some extent on "whether the Jews in the U.S. had as good an understanding of conditions as we had here. Perhaps the prime minister could help them in this regard."

Ben-Gurion skirted the issue of the role of U.S. Jews but agreed with Dulles that none would benefit from a United States unfriendly toward the Arabs and wished them success from the bottom of his heart in that endeavor—to which Sharett added "if it did not take the course of being harmful to Israel."[24]

The subject of the role of U.S. Jews' influence on U.S. policy took up a great deal of conversation, and Dulles's message seemed to indicate that the new administration would not allow domestic political considerations to impede U.S. policy in the Middle East. Moreover, U.S. policy toward Israel could no longer be determined apart from the general framework of U.S. interests. A fair and reasonable settlement of the Arab-Israeli dispute under U.S. mediation could only be arrived at through a policy of impartiality, thereby alleviating Arab resentment of the United States and bringing the Arabs closer to the West. Without saying so, Dulles provided a hint of things to come. He would later use Ben-Gurion's "endorsement" of the quest for Arab friendship to justify a policy that would not be to Israel's liking. From the U.S. perspective, however, it was not the right time to enter into areas of discord but rather to accentuate the positive and the values that the two countries held in common.

The talks were conducted in a most amiable atmosphere. At the end of a two-and-a-half-hour conference Ben-Gurion presented Dulles and Stassen with copies of the newly published *Jerusalem Tanakh* edited and corrected by the late Professor Moshe David (Umberto) Cassuto—the first edition of a Hebrew Bible prepared by a leading Jewish scholar in recent times and published in Israel. That led to an exchange of Biblical quotations between Ben-Gurion and Dulles. One of the passages in the New Testament that made the greatest impression on Ben-Gurion was the last verse of chapter 13 in the epistle to the Corinthians in which the Apostle Paul spoke of faith, hope, and charity but said the greatest of these was charity. However, said Ben-Gurion, the correct translation from the Greek should be *love* and not *charity*—which would make the passage even more impressive. Dulles, the son of a minister and an avid reader of the Bible himself, replied by citing what was in his view one of the most magnificent bits of history in the Bible—the New Testament recitation of what the Jewish people had accomplished by faith.[25]

All in all, the outcome of the visit pleased Israeli leaders. They had addressed themselves to the major U.S. concern—communism—and had explained Israel's helpful role in stopping it. The secretary had showed understanding and sympathy for Israel's problems.[26] Even Sharett's statements about Israel's intentions of transferring the Foreign Ministry to Jerusalem raised no eyebrows. In fact, Dulles offered advice as to when and under what circumstances the transfer might take place. More important, these official talks were held in Jerusalem despite Arab objections. As to Dulles's complaint concerning U.S. Jews, Eban was not totally unsympathetic. In his view, "the constant demand by individual Jewish leaders to see the President and the secretary of state leads to negative results . . . their frequent intercession harms Israel's interest and is unwarranted. . . . Israeli officials in Washington must be given priority in presenting the country's case before the American policymakers."[27]

After crossing into the Jordanian side of divided Jerusalem, Dulles and his entourage began their short visit to the Arab states bordering Israel—Jordan, Syria, and Lebanon. The sights he saw in those countries would reinforce his views about the need for an impartial U.S. policy in the region. These Arab countries confronted the Arab-Jewish question in the living shape of the unhappy Arab refugees, who numbered more than 50 percent of Jordan and 11 percent of Lebanon. U.S. support for the creation of the state of Israel, Arab leaders lamented, was profoundly responsible for that tragic situation.[28]

The first salvo was fired by the former mayor of the Old City of Jerusalem, who told Dulles on his arrival that the traditional Arab friendship for the United States was seriously weakened by Truman's gift

Dulles (left) holding a copy of the *Jerusalem Tanakh* presented to him by Prime Minister David Ben-Gurion, Israel, May 14, 1953. By permission of Princeton University Libraries.

of arms, money, and general aid to Israel. A surprised Dulles replied, "While we Americans criticize each other at home, we don't do so abroad. . . . I cannot associate myself with criticism of a former American president."[29] Dulles of course would not do so in public.

But on another occasion, in an answer to a complaint of Arab diplomats that U.S. policy concerning the Middle East was dictated by Zionists, Dulles was alleged to have delighted Premier Saeb Salaam of Lebanon by denying that U.S. policy was at present Zionist dictated. Generally, said Dulles, Jews had voted against him in the 1949 senatorial race and against Eisenhower in 1952. He said that the United States wanted to recapture the Arab world's friendship, to which Premier Salaam replied, "You must show us acts, not words."[30] The story created adverse comment at home, and Dulles denied making the statement attributed to him. Whether or not the story was accurate was beside the point. The fact of the matter was that he encountered these complaints in Arab capitals and believed that such charges were not entirely baseless. Although Dulles was primarily interested in stopping Communist penetration, he found that to the Arabs it was Israel, not the Soviet Union, that posed a danger and that the establishment of a defense organization must wait until the United States remedied the "injustices of the past" by restoring "Arab rights" in Palestine.

In assessing Dulles's whirlwind tour, one could ask, Did the Americans learn anything they did not know already? There is no doubt that they might have gained a greater amount of factual knowledge in the comparative calm of a Washington office. The tour gave them a more accurate sense of the intensity of feelings and complexity of issues involved, however, perhaps lessening temptations for overly simple and easy solutions. For Israel the main questions were, What concrete conclusions would the Americans draw from their findings? Would they be disappointed by the Arabs' uncompromising attitudes and reach the conclusion that Israel was a reliable ally, or would they attempt to appease the Arabs in order to diminish their anger and move them closer to the West?[31]

The answers were not long in coming. On May 17, upon arrival in Baghdad, Iraq, Dulles cabled the president his early impressions and his appraisal of the situation after visiting Egypt, Israel, Jordan, Syria, and Lebanon.

Bitterness toward West, including United States is such that while Arab goodwill may still be restored, time is short before loss becomes irretrievable. Find general Arab feeling of hope in you as individual and head of new administration, but basic skepticism as to whether any United States administration can follow any policy not approved by Zionists. Remaining hope will quickly dissolve unless our acts here show capacity to influence British and Israeli policies which now tend to converge in what is looked upon as new phase of aggression to the Arabs.

According to Dulles, it was unrealistic to expect a formal Arab-Israeli peace settlement. Ben-Gurion himself talked of a de facto peace and an end to economic hostilities, not of a formal overall peace settlement. The United States, Dulles continued, "may have to move step by step upon segments of problem that will reduce tension to where it would be politically possible for Arab leaders to agree to a formal peace settlement." Such segments would include a gradual liquidation of the refugee problem, resolution of the status of Jerusalem, assurance against Israeli aggression, and distribution of economic and military aid to show more balance between Arab countries and Israel. He noted that the Anglo-Egyptian problem was most dangerous and if left unsolved would put the Arab world in such open and united hostility toward the West that it would be receptive to Soviet aid. The secretary did not make specific recommendations but thought it useful to inform Eisenhower promptly of his thinking so that "the President and the National Security Council may also be thinking along similar lines with a view to developing readiness for prompt policy decisions upon our return."[32]

In Washington on May 29 Dulles conveyed to the president additional information. Naguib felt that an arrangement with Israel would not be too difficult once he had solved his problems with the British. He would insist on a corridor arrangement linking Egypt with other Arab states. In Israel, Ben-Gurion indicated his hope that "our mission to win friends with the Arabs would be successful." The Israeli leader saw nothing in that mission that was inconsistent with the interests of Israel. He seemed inclined to relax his past position of "total peace or nothing" and was willing to work on a policy of reducing tensions step by step that would create an atmosphere for a final peace settlement. The Israelis, Dulles continued, were jittery over the fact that they did not know the intentions of the new administration and feared that the United States might attempt to impose a peace settlement that they would consider unjust. They were particularly concerned that the United States might attempt to take away some of the territory now controlled by Israel. They were also troubled lest the United States might proceed with water development schemes that would conflict with their plans to bring water down to the Negev from the Jordan. Furthermore, they felt strongly about moving their Foreign Office to Jerusalem, and they would do so regardless of U.S. wishes. But the United States would not move its embassy until a new approach was worked out for the Jerusalem problem. The secretary painted a bleak picture of the Israeli economy, which in his words "is in an acute fiscal" state. Israel, he said, suffered from the Arab economic boycott and the closure of the Suez Canal to its ships. Militarily, however, in his estimation, Israel's strength was greater than the combined military strength of all Arab states.[33]

As for Jordan, its economic backwardness made the refugees an intolerable burden. The Jordanians, concerned over further Israeli expansion, felt a special animosity toward the United States for its support of Israel. Jordan was generally disposed to work with the West because of its dependence and long association with Britain economically and militarily. Jordan's primary interest was in water development schemes such as the Yarmuk Dam project, which the Jordanians felt was being held up by the United States because of Zionist pressures. The Arab Legion in Jordan, according to Dulles, was the most impressive military outfit in the area, but not equal to the Israeli army.

In Syria, Dulles was impressed with its leader Adib al-Shishakli, who seemed to be more aware than other Arab leaders of the Soviet danger. Here, too, however, the Israeli problem dominated all other international issues. Syria truly feared Israeli expansion. Its army could be in Damascus within a few hours.

In Lebanon, Israel was foremost in the minds of officials. Dulles concluded that the U.S. position in the Arab world was precarious and that the loss of respect for the United States varied "almost directly with the nearness of the respective Arab states to Israel."

> The Israeli factor and the association of the United States in the minds of the people of the area with French and British colonial and imperialistic policies are millstones around our neck. . . . The United States must seek every possible means to allay fear in the Arab world over future Israeli objectives and to convince the Arab world that the U.S. is operating upon a policy to true impartiality. We must make the Arabs realize that we accept the State of Israel as a fact and that any

thought of turning back the pages of history is totally unrealistic. We must seek a step by step reduction in tension in the area and an ultimate peace settlement. Any move on our part for immediate total peace would be unrealistic.[34]

Dulles briefed the president and congressional leaders on his and Stassen's impressions from their tour. Then, with Eisenhower's full backing, Dulles went public and for the first time put forth the administration's policy of "true impartiality" in the Arab-Israeli conflict. On June 1, in a radio and television address to the country, Dulles discussed his impressions of the twenty-day tour, focusing on the Middle East. Referring to Israel as a nation he said, "We were impressed by the vision and supporting energy with which the people are building their new nation. Inspired by a great faith, they are now doing an impressive work of building a new nation. They face hard internal problems, which I believe they can solve. Furthermore, the prime minister and other Israeli officials asserted convincingly their desire to live at peace with their Arab neighbors."

After paying this tribute to Israel Dulles turned to his views on specific issues. Here Israel could draw little comfort. On the important question of Jerusalem the secretary studiously avoided the word *internationalization*. "Jerusalem is divided into armed camps split between Israel and the Arab nation of Jordan. The atmosphere is heavy with hate. . . . Jerusalem is above all, the holy place of the Christian, Moslem, and Jewish faiths. This has been repeatedly emphasized by the United Nations. This does not necessarily exclude some political status in Jerusalem for Israel and Jordan. But the religious community has a claim on Jerusalem which takes precedence over the political claims of any particular nation."

Then Dulles described the plight of the Arab refugees, placing the responsibility on both Arabs and Israel but mostly unflattering to the latter.

Closely huddled around Israel are over 800,000 Arab refugees who fled from Palestine as the Israelis took over. They mostly exist in makeshift camps, with few facilities either for health, work or recreation. Within these camps the inmates rot away spiritually and physically. . . . Some of these refugees could be settled in the area *presently controlled by Israel*. Most, however, could more readily be integrated into the lives of the neighboring Arab countries. This, however,

awaits an irrigation project which will permit more soil to be cultivated. [Italics added]

Dulles called for an evenhanded policy.

The United States should seek to allay the deep resentment against it
that has resulted from the creation of Israel. In the past we had good
relations with the Arab peoples. . . . Today the Arab peoples are afraid
that the U.S. will back the new State of Israel in aggressive expansion.
They are more fearful of Zionism than of Communism and they fear
lest the U.S. become the backer of expansionist Zionism. On the other
hand the Israelis fear that ultimately the Arabs may try to push them
into the sea.

Dulles explained that the United States had tried to calm these contra-
dictory fears when it joined Britain and France in a tripartite declaration
on May 25, 1950, pledging to take immediate action against any state in
the Near East that was preparing to violate frontiers or armistice lines.
When the declaration was made, it did not reassure the Arabs, but "the
present administration stands fully behind that Declaration . . . we cannot
afford to be distrusted by millions who could be sturdy friends of
freedom." Ben-Gurion's comment that Israel did not object to the United
States maintaining friendly relations with the Arab states was interpreted
by Dulles as an endorsement of a future impartial U.S. policy in the
region. "The leaders in Israel themselves agreed with us that U.S. policies
should be impartial so as to win not only the respect and regard of the
Israeli but also of the Arab peoples. We shall seek such policies."[35]
Israeli leaders did not respond to the secretary's address with the
sentiments he attributed to them. Although they issued no formal official
statement, reactions were generally critical and in some cases uncom-
monly vehement. In the Knesset, leftist representatives referred to Dulles's
tour and speech as being carried out by "Hitler's helper to power . . . a
chief warmonger, responsible for blood and tears in Korea." They casti-
gated the Israeli government, blaming it for the deterioration of relations
with the Soviet Union while gaining very little from its pro-Western
orientation. On the other end of the political spectrum, right-wing Herut
and even Mapai representatives criticized various parts of Dulles's
speech, united in opposition to territorial concessions, repatriation of

Dulles reports on television, June 1, 1953, to the people of the United States about his tour of the Near and Middle East, which he says he undertook to make sure that the area did "not further swell the ranks of Communist dictators." By permission of UPI/Bettmann.

refugees, and territorial internationalization of Jerusalem. To Arieh Altman of Herut, Dulles had proven the anti-Israel nature of U.S. policy. Sharett's closing speech crystallized some of those views, stressing Israel's opposition to Dulles's observations. The Israeli government, said Sharett, did not regard Dulles's speech as a declaration of U.S. Mideast policy. He was not privy to any communication from Washington indicating a policy change. He would adopt a "wait and see attitude."[36]

The Israeli press, which in large measure had welcomed Dulles's visit, was now unanimous in expressing its disappointment and dismay at the secretary's remarks. Although newspaper editorialists reached various conclusions as to the exact meaning and implications of Dulles's statement, they all expressed a concern for what they viewed as a pro-Arab trend in U.S. policy at Israel's expense. *Davar*, expressing the opinion of the government, took a less alarmist attitude, saying that the speech, "while not a statement of America's Mideast policy is nonetheless indicative of the trend of thought in the State Department which Israel's foreign policy must take steps to change."[37]

Indeed, Israeli officials in Tel Aviv and Washington lost no time in expressing their displeasure with most of Dulles's speech. Especially irksome to them was the secretary's echo of Arab propaganda, particularly in his reference to expansionist Zionism and in his view that the previous administration had erred in its attitude toward Israel vis-à-vis the Arab states. His comments on the repatriation of refugees in areas "presently controlled by Israel" could be interpreted as questioning the legitimacy of Israel's sovereignty or at least as implying that Israel's territory should be reduced. In addition, Israeli officials maintained that suggesting repatriation of refugees was utterly unrealistic and that many of the members of the last General Assembly of the United Nations, including the United States, had accepted this point of view. The reference to Jerusalem and the suggestion that the interests of the world's religions take precedence over the claims of any nation were untimely and bound to incite the Arab states to suppose that something would be done about a problem that the United Nations had for so long been unable to settle. In fact, they maintained, both Israel and Jordan opposed any extensive international control in or about Jerusalem.

The secretary's admission that hopes for MEDO were unrealistic and that the United States would encourage "interrelated defenses" was interpreted by many in Israel as an endorsement of the Arab League Collective Security Pact. It could lead to the arming of Arab states prior to the establishment of peaceful relations with Israel. Finally, while an impartial policy could be justified, there was little hope that it would win "the respect and regard of the Arab people," as the Arabs did not want an impartial policy. They were actually demanding a distinctly partial policy by asking the United States to disregard Israel's interests and its right to exist. The problem was that Israel's encouragement of U.S. impartiality was not matched by any corresponding Arab commitment to be satisfied with a U.S. policy that was both pro-Arab and pro-Israel.[38]

Byroade attempted to allay some of Israel's concerns. On the question of Jerusalem he told Eban that the secretary actually favored a UN authority to exercise control over the holy places and related interests without assuming the administrative or security functions of a sovereign power. Such a solution, Byroade continued, would respect the principle of separation between religious and secular authority and not confuse them, as had the original internationalization formula. Such a solution was of course agreeable to Israel. The only question, however, was a tactical one. Could such a plan be accepted by the UN General Assembly? While the answer was clearly negative, from Israel's perspective Byroade's explanation was encouraging, for it showed no change in U.S. policy on this issue. As to repatriation of Arab refugees in "areas now controlled by Israel," Byroade assured Eban that "no invidious reflections should be read into these words nor should Israel's meager territory be reduced." Nonetheless, Israel should seek ways "of finding room" for Arab refugees within her territory. Byroade explained Dulles's reference to "interrelated defense" by saying that his intention was to strengthen individual countries through bilateral arrangements between each of them and the Western powers. In no way did it imply U.S. recognition of the Arab League or its Collective Security Pact, both of which were directed against Israel. Of course, the secretary had used expressions that Israel might have found offensive, but they were necessary in order to prove to the Arabs U.S. impartiality and evenhandedness in order to induce them to reach a peaceful settlement. Moreover, Byroade maintained, the secretary's address did not attempt to set forth definite and detailed solutions to the problems of the area but rather to indicate lines of approach that would serve as a basis for further discussion.[39]

While Dulles's suggestions for a solution to the Arab-Israeli conflict were no different from those of the previous administration, his choice of words disturbed the Israelis. From their perspective it was neither prudent nor justifiable for the secretary to pay public deference to Arab "resentment" of Israel's existence or to alleged Arab "fears" of "Zionist expansion," for such talk did not accord with the facts. Moreover, it might fuel Arab expectations for a drastic change in U.S. policy, making a peaceful settlement more difficult to achieve.

Dulles's trip and subsequent speech set the stage for an "impartial" policy which would translate into changes more of style, atmospherics, and rhetoric than of substance. To placate Arab "resentment" over the creation of Israel and the U.S. role in it, the State Department would go out of its way to blame Israel for whatever incidents might occur, without paying equal attention to Arab hostility. The outcome would be a long period of strained relations between the two countries. The problem with the policy of "friendly impartiality," however, was not so much whether it was fair or morally right but rather its practicability. Would it rally the Arab states against the Soviet Union? The Arabs would not be impressed with a U.S. policy only of keeping Israel at arms' length. What they wanted was a policy that would reverse the U.S. commitment to the existence of the Jewish state, something that the Eisenhower administration would not even consider. To repeat Dulles's words, "We must make the Arabs realize that we accept the State of Israel as a fact and that any thought of turning back the pages of history is totally unrealistic." The policy of "impartiality" had built-in contradictions, but from the administration's perspective it was worth trying in its cold war with Russia.

"Friendly Impartiality"

4

On their return from the tour, Dulles and Stassen reported to Eisenhower about the economic and political conditions in the Middle East, in the secretary's words "in order to help him determine our future policy."[1] More in its tone than in its content, Dulles's speech set forth a new approach, a new attitude toward the Arab world on the part of the administration.

The driving force behind the new approach was the staff of the Office of Near Eastern, South Asian, and African Affairs (NEA) in the State Department, headed by Henry A. Byroade, assistant secretary of state, career diplomats with long records of involvement in Arab affairs whose pro-Arab views, derailed by the Truman White House, found a more receptive ear in the new centers of power.[2]

Truman had appointed Colonel Byroade to his present post in April 1952, replacing George McGhee, who became ambassador to Turkey. Already Byroade had distinguished himself both in military and diplomatic assignments. A 1937 graduate of the U.S. Military Academy at West Point, he received a Master of Science degree in engineering from Cornell University. In 1942 he was assigned to a battalion of aviation engineers in charge of carrying out wartime construction at Mitchell Field air base on Long Island, New York. Later that year he was sent to India where he commanded a section of the army's service of supply. His duties included supervision of air, rail, and water movement of supplies from the Indian port of Assam by air over the dangerous route across the mountains to China. He was awarded the Legion of Merit and cited for "his resourcefulness, outstanding efficiency, energy and devotion to duty" in directing construction of vital air bases in the region. In 1943 he assumed responsibility for all air force construction in China. In the search for landing sites, he accumulated more than 300 hours of flying time and was awarded the Air Medal. In 1944 he joined the Operations Division, Office of the Chief of Staff, in Washington, D.C., responsible for coordinating all policy relating to operations in India, China, and Southeast Asia. A year later he was appointed military attaché on General George C. Marshall's special mission to China and awarded the Distinguished Service Medal for his accomplishments. Subsequently, he joined the State Department as the director of the Bureau of German Affairs and in that capacity participated in discussions with Eban regarding German reparations to Israel.

Although he had no background in Middle East affairs, Byroade was a fast learner who soon adopted the prevailing views in the State Department, which were promoted by a pressure bloc known as the Arabists, who functioned as State Department representatives in Middle East and displayed a fundamental hostility to Israel. They were a highly definable group of about a hundred foreign service officers who had received intense training in Arabic, most of them at a special language school operated by the State Department in Beirut. These specialists in Arab affairs served in the Middle East or held State Department positions connected with the area. They tended to identify their own concerns with those of the national interests. To them, U.S. support for Israel was a "spoiler pure and simple." As Parker T. Hart, the director of the NE, said later: "The area experts to a man were scandalized by what happened in 1948. We made a tremendous effort to lay the groundwork for good relations with the Arabs, and all of a sudden, when we were in good position, all our hopes were dashed." They felt compelled to counter Israel's influence by expressing the Arab point of view.[3]

Like all newcomers to the post, Byroade toured the Middle East, visiting Israel from May 24 to 26, 1952. The only positive note in his impressions of Israel was praise for the wisdom he discerned in Ben-Gurion and the government as a whole. But Israel's future, in his view, looked bleak. According to the information given him by U.S. ambassadors in Arab countries and the staff of the U.S. embassy in Tel Aviv, Israeli youth were educated to hate the Arabs, and the Israelis were chauvinistic and desired territorial expansion. The Israeli army had to be reduced in size not only because of budgetary problems but also because of the dangers it posed to Israeli democracy, given its militaristic spirit and expansionist aims. Israel, in his view, was not particularly important to the United States. In case of a "hot war," a country with only 200,000 soldiers would not add appreciably to the defense of the region. In the meantime, in the "cold war," Israel had become a negative factor causing instability in the region and disturbing U.S.-Arab relations while providing the Soviet Union with long-awaited opportunities.[4]

On June 4, 1953, shortly after his return with Dulles from their twenty-day trip to the Middle East and Southeast Asia, Byroade spoke before a closed session of the Conference on U.S. Foreign Policy held at the State Department. "The situation of the Arab states vis-à-vis the Israel problem is of great concern to us," said Byroade. The deep-seated emotional problems in the region "are as great as they were five, six years ago when Israel was created and I believe that in some parts of the area they are even greater." In what amounted to an admission of guilt in past U.S. treatment of the problem, Byroade declared: "We must admit that we have a responsibility in this, and it is going to be very difficult for us to set about correcting our position in the Near East. None of us can entertain the thought that what has happened must be undone. That is utterly unrealistic, it is not in our interests, and it is not in our hearts. But we must find some way to ease tensions in this area, taking a problem at a time so that we can make the word peace a fact."[5]

Byroade's input in the formulation of U.S. policy was without doubt of considerable importance. Not only was he in close contact with the secretary of state, but he also channeled information and advice to the members of the National Security Council (NSC) and to Robert Cutler, who headed the Office of Special Assistant to the President for National Security Affairs. Cutler knew very little about Israel or the region in general but viewed Byroade as a very capable official—the expert—who presented persuasive arguments concerning policies for the region.

Periodically Byroade briefed Cutler, who conveyed his views to the NSC. Thus Cutler learned that the Truman administration did not follow a neutral policy in the Arab-Israeli dispute. The Eisenhower administration would attempt to follow a policy of "friendly impartiality" toward both sides in the conflict. Because of oil and the strategic importance of the region, Cutler believed that the U.S. government must also seek Arab friendship. In the long run, Cutler believed that such a policy would also benefit Israel. Should that upset Israel, however, it was nonetheless worth pursuing for the sake of peace. Furthermore, Cutler agreed that the administration should not allow domestic politics to interfere with foreign policy decisions. Of course, "impartiality" did not guarantee a successful solution of the region's problems, but an effort in that direction must be made.[6]

On July 11, 1953, the president approved NSC recommendation 155/1, "U.S. Objectives and Policies with respect to the Near East," calling for a policy of "objective impartiality" between the Arab states and Israel on the lines set forth in Dulles's June 1 speech.[7] Thus the policy had the full backing of the highest levels of government. It was a team approach with the secretary of state an important member and the spokesman.[8] The program, well structured and coherent, favored closer relations with the Arabs, but it was often oblivious to the roots of the Arab-Israeli dispute and at times ignored the underlying causes. Its aim was to achieve regional and global objectives while serving what the administration believed to be not only peace but also U.S. national interests. What the administration viewed as just and impartial, however, Israel and its supporters regarded as a deliberate campaign of discrimination and hostility toward Israel, spearheaded by the State Department. Just as Dulles would later characterize neutrality between freedom and communism as immoral, the Israelis condemned the policy of impartiality because it failed to distinguish between the potential aggressor and its potential victim.[9] It was, unfortunately, a rather harsh and at times wrong analogy born out of the insecurity of a small beleaguered state.

But the call for an impartial policy did not come only from the State Department. The oil industry represented a major vested interest functioning outside the decision-making process. Because of the extensive oil investments in the Arab Middle East and the enormous profits derived by U.S. oil companies, the role of oil interests had a decisive and far-reaching influence on U.S. Middle East policy.[10] The attempts of oil interests to influence U.S. policy in the Middle East was especially acute during the

Truman presidency, when the Aramco Oil Combine used the State Department to undermine the effectiveness of every act of the President of the United States with respect to the partition of Palestine.[11] While under Truman their pro-Arab efforts had little success, such would not be the case with the new administration, for Eisenhower trusted wealth and temporal power, and his close friends were men in industry, oil, and banking.[12] By the summer of 1953 impartiality got its start in rather demonstrative ways.

During Dulles's trip to Israel, Sharett informed the secretary of Israel's intention to transfer the Foreign Ministry from Tel Aviv to Jerusalem. Dulles's reply appeared to be, "Don't do it while I am around." To Sharett, that reply meant that Israel would be free to act once he had left the area. And so it did. On July 10 the Israeli government informed the State Department that it intended to transfer its Foreign Ministry to Jerusalem as of July 12.[13] Dulles reacted as if caught by surprise. He cabled Rabbi Silver: "I had tried to reach you Saturday at the President's request to see if we could concert any measure to halt *abrupt* transfer yesterday of Israel Foreign Office from Tel-Aviv to Jerusalem and thus obviate unfortunate repercussions in Mid-East and elsewhere."[14] The message to Silver, however, was pro forma. Two days earlier, on July 11, the State Department had issued a statement expressing regret at Israel's action and declaring that the United States did not plan to transfer its embassy to Jerusalem. Such a step would be inconsistent with UN resolutions and ran counter to the solution of the Jerusalem problem as set forth in the secretary's address of June 1. Dulles noted that this Israeli action was especially inopportune because it would add to the existing tension in the area.[15] As could be expected the Israeli government viewed Dulles's reaction as unjustified. According to Sharett, the move could hardly have come as a surprise to the United States, as the secretary had been fully informed of Israel's intention during his visit there.[16] Of course, being informed did not necessarily guarantee consent.

In addition, the rising tensions between Jordan and Israel further strained U.S.-Israel relations. These tensions in large measure were a by-product of the Arab-Israeli War of 1948 and the configuration of the boundaries set forth in the armistice agreements. Since the frontiers were only of a temporary nature, pending final peace agreements, they were not clearly marked. Arab villages in Jordan were cut off from their fields and wells located in Israeli territory. Arabs on the Jordanian side often crossed the artificial boundary to reclaim their properties. Once more, large numbers of refugees entered Israel in order to rejoin their families. The Israeli government viewed this situation with great concern.

By late 1951 and early 1952 Arab infiltrators were engaging in theft, robberies, vandalism, marauding, and kidnapping. The extent and scope of the problem could be gauged by the recording between July 1949 and April 1952 of no less than 6,000 cases of Arab raids and infiltration into Israeli territory from all four sectors with criminal intent. During a single twelve-month period ending December 1952, 2,595 Arabs from across the border were arrested in Israel. In 318 cases, marauders opened fire on Israeli citizens with the result that during that period 69 Israelis were killed and 77 wounded. In addition there were 36 kidnappings, 1,198 thefts, and 45 robberies and willful destruction of property. The value of property stolen or damaged during the twelve months was estimated at well over $1 million.[17]

The border with Jordan was most open to infiltration. Although such actions were not as a rule sanctioned by the Jordanian government, they were nonetheless glossed over by the lower-echelon Arab officials and the Jordanian border police. Even though complicity was difficult to ascertain, the Israeli government, responsible for the protection of life and property within its territory, claimed that these wanton acts of individuals took place with the full knowledge and encouragement of the Arab governments. The State Department rejected this interpretation.[18]

Israel's response became more emphatic and retaliation became increasingly harsh. As a routine matter, infiltrators who resisted arrest were shot by border police. In 1952 alone, 394 Arabs were killed and 227 wounded. U.S. officials criticized this policy of retaliation, claiming that the punishment was out of proportion to the crime, more like a "head for an eye" than the biblical "eye for an eye." From Eisenhower's perspective, Israel acted with what seemed like "merciless severity." Dulles warned Israel that its policy of retaliation and the use of excessive force posed a danger to the security and stability of the area. If such actions did not cease, the United States, said Dulles, reserved the right to take appropriate steps under the tripartite declaration and possibly UN procedures. When Israel continued the practice of reprisal raids into neighboring territory, an exasperated Dulles asked, "Is the U.S. government to assume that the Israeli government will continue to flout friendly counsel and take matters into their own hands?"[19] The criticism by the United States turned into severe condemnation when an Israeli military unit raided the Jordanian village of Kibya on October 14–15, causing heavy casualties and adversely impacting U.S.-Israeli relations.

Simultaneously with Israel's harsh reaction to Arab infiltrators another problem developed between Syria and Israel in the demilitarized zone (DMZ) between the two countries.[20] On September 2, Israel began its master plan for diversion to the Negev of a portion of the Jordan River's waters. That plan called for constructing a hydroelectric power plant to exploit the drop in the river's flow between the Hula and Lake Tiberias (Kinneret), thereby driving the waters west and south to irrigate Israel's central plain and the arid Negev. The site of the project at B'not Yaakov Bridge was located in the DMZ close to the Syrian border. Part of the project also included building a water diversion canal, which the Syrians claimed would have affected the flow of the Jordan River in Syria, thus harming Arab villagers whose livelihood depended on the river's waters. In addition, Syria objected to the proposed project because it would give Israel a military advantage.[21] On September 23, General Vagn Bennike, the United Nations Troop Supervision Organization (UNTSO) chief of staff, sustained Syria's objections and ordered Israel to halt construction until it had reached an agreement with the Syrians. Israel saw such a move as caving in to Syria and giving her a veto over Israel's economic development. Refusing to comply with Bennike's order, the Israelis continued digging the disputed canal, whereupon Syria lodged a complaint with the Security Council.[22] The United States supported Bennike's decision. Byroade advised Eban that Israel ought to comply, or the United States would withhold the allotment of aid to Israel under MSA.[23]

On September 25, Eban and Reuven Shiloah, minister plenipotentiary at the Israeli embassy in Washington, took up the issue with Dulles. Dismissing Syria's complaints as invalid, they declared that Israel would appeal Bennike's decision to the Security Council. To the Israeli diplomats, however, the most bothersome problem was Byroade's warning. The Israeli government, said Eban, "has never regarded MSA aid as tied to political action, and it was most unfortunate to make it a counter in this complex issue." He requested the secretary to keep separate the subject of aid and the immediate problem of water development.[24] But to Dulles the technical issues involved were of no importance. To him, Israel's action disregarded UN decisions and created a de facto situation that Israel could no longer abandon. The secretary took issue with Sharett's contention that "what we have we hold." An attitude of fait accompli ran counter to UN principles and legal processes. It could not be condoned by the United States. According to Dulles, "The US was trying to adopt a fair, even-handed policy in the Near East. This was difficult to accomplish if the Israeli government appeared to be disrespectful to UN decisions while we furnish aid which from our point of view was discretionary. The incident of the diversion of Jordan waters had closely followed the move of the Foreign Ministry to Jerusalem which had caused strong protest in Congressional circles. Both these situations will make matters very difficult if there appeared to be defiances of the UNTSO decision by Israel."[25] Israel, Dulles continued, would make a good impression in the United States if it agreed to comply with the UNTSO decision unless and until such a decision was reversed on appeal.

Failing to move Dulles on the aid issue, the ambassador raised the subject of U.S.-Israeli relations. "It could no longer be concealed," said Eban, that a "cloud had fallen over the relationship." While no one issue was paramount, "the cumulative effect of minor issues had caused growing concern in Israeli public opinion." He pointed to the reluctance of U.S. officials to restate publicly the firm friendship between Israel and the United States, while they were most eloquent on the subject of seeking Arab friendship. A recent presidential message to a Zionist group lacked any reference to the cordial relationship between the two countries. This was quite a change from the warm atmosphere manifested during the previous administration. Furthermore, while the State Department objected to the move of the Foreign Ministry from Tel Aviv to Jerusalem, it had not brought to public attention the two governments' general agreement on the question of internationalization of the city. Eban suggested that the administration seemed eager to emphasize publicly differences rather than what the two countries held in common. He hoped that the United States would not continue to be so rigid in "their restrictions of contacts with the Foreign Ministry in Jerusalem and would follow the actions of other countries in this regard." Finally, the ambassador conveyed the "agitation of the Israeli public because of U.S. proposals to supply arms to Arab nations . . . it was incomprehensible to the Israeli public that the U.S. should furnish arms to dictators such as Naguib and Shishakli. Such action was not in the U.S. tradition." Surprisingly, in spite of the above, Eban felt "that relations between Israel and the United States were basically on a sound foundation of public understanding."[26]

Dulles regretted that time did not allow him to respond to the ambassador's complaints, but he would make a full reply in their next meeting, scheduled for October 2. In preparation, the secretary requested the NEA to furnish him an aide-mémoire that would set forth specifically the steps Israel must take before the United States would suspend its embargo on release of economic grant-in-aid funds as well as long-range measures to "put herself back in the good graces of the U.S."

On September 29, Byroade submitted to the secretary a memorandum entitled "Your Forthcoming Meeting with Ambassador Eban: Basic Factors on U.S.-Israeli Relations." Byroade's "talking paper" contained specific charges against Israeli actions. The list included principles that had never been so bluntly and openly stated before in communications with Israel. It deserves to be quoted in full.

Israel should re-examine policy of encouraging large-scale immigration, taking into consideration her economic absorption capacity, political effect on neighbors (i.e., Arab fears of expansion) and inconsistency of this policy with her present attitude toward Arab refugees. Israel should recognize that global defense responsibilities of the U.S. do not permit delay in arming Arab states until they meet Israel's prerequisite for peace. We stand fully behind the Tripartite Declaration of May 1950 and would not tolerate Arab effort to destroy Israel.[27]

As to the short-range actions that Israel should take, Byroade stated:

a. Comply with General Bennike's decision on B'not Yaakov canal. Israel should have stopped work on receipt of Bennike's decision regardless whether appeal to Security Council would set a time limit. Stopping after completion DMZ portion of work would not be in compliance with UNTSO decision. Release of economic aid funds necessarily contingent upon Israel attitude on this matter.

   b. Respect armistice agreements. Cite killing on August 28th by Israeli of twenty-two Arab refugees on Egyptian controlled territory near Gaza; entry of armed Israelis into Egypt-Israel DMZ resulting in decision against Israel by MAC [Mixed Armistice Commission].

   c. Respect personnel and authority of UNTSO (cite Israel's obstruction of General Bennike's inspection of Mount Scopus and threat of fire on chairman Israel-Egypt MAC as latest examples of many instances of disrespect).

   d. Cite deliberate reprisal raids across armistice lines. Latest of series U.S. representation (August 24, unanswered).

   e. Cooperate in a unified development of waters of Jordan Valley in accordance with such plan as U.N. may propose. Unilateral actions such as B'not Yaakov diversion, whether consistent with a unified engineering plan or not, is definitely prejudicial in a political sense since it generates tension.

   f. Bear her share of Arab refugee burden. Compensation not enough and will surely require heavy outside help. Israel owes land to refugees (not to Arab states) either by repatriation or territorial adjustments or both and remains in untenable moral position through present intransigence.[28]

Byroade's suggestions would influence future U.S. policy toward Israel. His charges put the onus squarely on Israel for exacerbating tensions in the area.

But the charges were not totally unjustified. Israel's diversion of water at B'not Yaakov involved its budget, production plans, and relations with Arab states. Yet the diversion of water was done without any notification of, let alone consultation with, the United States, even though the United States was extending grant aid to Israel designed to help that kind of economic development. Byroade's criticism of Israel's indiscriminate retaliation policy was based on the allegation that Israeli newspapers deliberately overemphasized border incidents and that their accounts were more often than not at odds with those received by the State Department from its representatives on the spot and from UN personnel. Israel's water diversion project, if allowed to continue, would scuttle a unified plan for the use of the Jordan River waters by all riparian states.

Such a plan was now in its final stages of preparation under UN auspices with the full backing of the United States.[29]

On the other hand, the assistant secretary failed to fully appreciate Israel's predicament, that of a small country surrounded by hostile and what it believed to be powerful neighbors. His memorandum showed an overindulgence toward Arab provocations, as the United States had not publicly condemned Arab infiltrations into Israel.[30] Furthermore, the charge that large-scale Jewish immigration to Israel fueled Arab fears of Israeli expansion placed Israel in the uncomfortable position of having to explain her refusal to repatriate Arab refugees yet at the same time allowing hundreds of thousands of new immigrants to flood the country. These questions would soon be raised in public by Byroade, causing chagrin in Israel.

In the meantime, the "cloud" in the relations between the two countries was getting thicker in large part due to Israel's policy of massive retaliation, a major component of the country's security policy aimed at protecting the status quo by force if necessary. At the same time, reprisals defended Israel's border settlements and demonstrated to Arabs Israel's military superiority, in the hope of preventing a "second round."[31] But the State Department saw a different motive in Israel's policy of retaliation. According to Byroade and Russell, Israel's actions since the secretary's visit in the area were aimed at coercing the Arabs into peace on Israel's terms, to obscure and provide an excuse for Israel's failure to solve its dire economic problems. Dulles surmised that Israel might calculate that matters could not improve until they became worse. Dissatisfied with the state of affairs—that is, with the armistice agreements—Israel might be prepared to go to open war in order to create a situation from which a "peace settlement rather than armistice will follow." In a conversation with the president on April 21, 1954, Dulles pointed out the "danger that Israel might be deliberately trying to break the armistice open on the theory that that was the only way to get a better arrangement."[32]

The most severe reprisal took place on the night of October 14–15 against the Jordanian village of Kibya. The underlying causes of the attack were quite evident—the accumulated grief and frustration over the deaths of 420 Israelis at the hands of Arab infiltrators from Jordan in the past three years.[33] The immediate cause that triggered the devastating action took place on October 13, when a grenade thrown into a house in

Tirat Yehuda, well inside the Israeli frontier, killed a mother and two children. The Israeli-Jordan MAC concluded that Jordanian terrorists had perpetrated the act, but the Israeli government did not wait for the Jordanian authorities to seek out and punish the guilty.

Ben-Gurion, who by the autumn of 1953 had decided to retire and live in a Negev kibbutz, S'deh Boker, approved a large symbolic raid against the Arabs. The target was the Jordanian village of Kibya, facing Tirat Yehuda across the border and suspected of harboring terrorists. Sharett opposed the raid, but Ben-Gurion disregarded his views and went along with the military, who favored an active policy of reprisals regardless of negative world reactions. A special commando force, Unit 101, under the command of a young flamboyant Israeli Major, Ariel (Arik) Sharon, had been formed specifically for the purpose of carrying out harsh reprisal attacks. The commandos, who wore neither military attire nor badges of rank, used weapons not issued by the army, making it possible for the government to deny any involvement and attribute the action to individuals acting on their own to avenge Arab terrorism.[34] Israeli artillery began shelling the village of Kibya. Then a battalion of 600 uniformed regulars swept across the border and encircled the village. They shot every man, woman, and child they could find and then turned their fire on the cattle. After that they dynamited forty-two houses, a school, and a mosque. By 3:00 A.M. the Israeli force had withdrawn, leaving behind sixty-six dead, including eleven from one family, ten of another. It was the bloodiest night of border warfare since the end of the 1948 war.[35]

The Israeli action met unanimous condemnation from the great powers. General Vagn Bennike deplored the attack and called it "cold-blooded murder." In London, the foreign ministers of the Big Three sent messages to the United Nations in New York requesting an urgent meeting of the Security Council. From Washington came the harshest diplomatic protest ever addressed by the United States to Israel. In a formal statement the State Department described the attack as "shocking," demanding that "those responsible be brought to account and that effective measures should be taken to prevent such incidents in the future." British Prime Minister Winston Churchill, a friend of Israel and a "Zionist ever since the Balfour Declaration," sent a personal protest to Ben-Gurion. Israel decided to lodge a complaint of its own with the Security Council, asking it to consider repeated Jordanian violations of the armistice agreement. Eban, permanent Israeli delegate to the United Nations, was instructed to head the delegation at the Security Council session. Because of the magnitude of condemnation, the Israeli Foreign Office sent Gideon Rafael, Foreign Ministry counselor on UN political and mideast affairs, and Joseph Tekoa, deputy legal adviser to the Foreign Ministry, as well as Brigadier General Moshe Dayan to New York to assist Eban in presenting the Israeli case.

In Jerusalem, three days after the attack, Michael Elizur, the Foreign Ministry spokesman, claimed that the raid had been organized and executed by inhabitants of Israel's border villages, veterans of World War II, who were now farming on the frontier. He said they "lost patience" after continuous attacks on their settlements. A day later, Ben-Gurion repeated the same version, adding that "all the responsibility rests with the Jordanian government which for years had tolerated and thereby encouraged acts of murder and pillage against the inhabitants of Israel."[36] But Sharett, who had opposed the raid, was heartsick when he learned of the death toll. In his diary he wrote, "This reprisal is unprecedented in its dimensions and in the offensive power it used. . . . I walked up and down in my room helpless and utterly depressed by my feeling of impotence. . . . I must underline that when I opposed the action I didn't even remotely suspect such a blood bath." When Ben-Gurion asked him to go on national radio to explain that the army was not involved in the massacre but that it was the work of outraged border settlers, Sharett replied, "None in the world will believe such a story and we shall only expose ourselves as liars."[37] Ben-Gurion, however, believed that under certain circumstances it was permissible to lie for the good of the state and to preserve the good name of the army.

That it took Israel three days to come up with an alibi caused a great deal of confusion and consternation among its diplomats in New York and Washington. They were compelled to defend a policy they believed to be excessive and harmful to Israel's international standing. Eban's diplomatic efforts in Washington were based on the premise of a political relaxation in the Arab-Israeli dispute which would also have a salutary effect on U.S.-Israeli relations.[38]

Just the opposite occurred. The deterioration in those relations continued. Taking advantage of Israel's worsened public image, the State Department went public with a decision that Israel had learned about in private three weeks earlier. On October 20, Dulles announced the suspension of the MSA allocation as a result of Israel's refusal to comply with the request of the UNTSO chief of staff to suspend work on its hydroelectric project on the upper Jordan. Simultaneously, at the Security Council, the United States spearheaded a resolution condemning Israel for its attack on Kibya. Henry Cabot Lodge, Jr., the U.S. representative, maintained that Bennike's report confirmed that the action violated the cease-fire resolution of the Security Council of July 15, 1948, and the Jordanian-Israeli armistice agreement. Eban's retort that Kibya should be seen as a "counter action" fell on deaf ears. On November 18, the Security Council expressed the "strongest censure" of the retaliatory action taken by Israel's armed forces and called upon Israel to take effective measures to prevent such actions in the future.

It was the strongest condemnation in this international forum suffered by Israel since the creation of the state. Gideon Rafael lamented its predicament. In a letter from New York to Walter Eytan, the Foreign Office director, he commented on the Security Council debate. He described how overnight Israel's image changed from that of a young, admired "little country to that of a monster, her friends distancing themselves from her and a cold wind blowing in her face . . . never before had Israel's image in the international arena reached such a low ebb as evidenced during the discussions on Kibya." It was high time, he continued, that the government (i.e., Ben-Gurion and the military) realized that Israel's actions on security problems could not be taken in disregard of world opinion. Should such policies continue, Israel would face consequences detrimental to its existence as a state. The policy of massive reprisals played into the hands of Israel's enemies.[39]

Rafael's letter was a clear reflection of the differences in personalities, character, and views of the world between two lifelong Zionists, Ben-Gurion and Sharett. They both came to Palestine in 1906 and worked together to establish the Jewish state. By the time of the Kibya raid they had grown far apart and held divergent views on how to bring about peace in the Middle East. Ben-Gurion, described by his biographers as the "prophet of fire" or the "armed prophet," had fought for almost half a century for the Zionist cause.[40] Since May 14, 1948, as prime minister and defense minister, in the first five years of Israel's existence he had led the nation by a combination of charisma, mystical Zionism, vigor, and enormous courage against tremendous odds. Adored by many Israelis as a paternal symbol of authority, reverently referred to as the "Old Man," Ben-Gurion was a "wrathful visionary, intolerant of small talk, humorless, hot tempered, and bullying." With a "large head, wreathed by an unruly white mane, and with a gnarled stubby-legged body he looked and often acted like an Old Testament patriarch."[41] Impulsive, impetuous, decisive, and daring, he was also indifferent to external criticism. Courage was his main characteristic.[42]

He believed that in response to any Arab attack or even at the suspicion of a planned attack, Israel must hit with overwhelming force, no matter the international reaction, for it was the only effective way to protect the homeland. He gave two reasons in defense of the policy of massive reprisals: deterrence and education. He pointed to Jewish immigrants who came from countries such as Iraq, North Africa, and Kurdistan, "countries where their blood was unavenged, where it was possible to mistreat them, torture them, beat them, they have grown used to being helpless victims." Now, Ben-Gurion continued, it was time to show them "that the Jewish people have a state and an army that will no longer permit them to be abused . . . that they are citizens of a sovereign state which is responsible for their lives and their safety." Besides, although the Jews were a majority inside Israel, they were surrounded by a sea of Arabs bent on the destruction of the state. The Arabs, he believed, must be taught that Israel was there to stay, and the new immigrants must feel strong and secure in their new country, proud and independent—a new existence entirely different from the one experienced in the countries they left behind. From Ben-Gurion's perspective, the policy of retaliation not only served Israel's security needs but was also morally right. It must be pursued when they were provoked, the diplomatic fallout notwithstanding. As to Israel's "isolation," it was not because of its reprisal policy—"it came about earlier when we were as pure as doves."[43]

Sharett did not share Ben-Gurion's belief in the efficacy of retaliation. Where the prime minister was decisive, tough, a portrait of a new free Jew in Israel prepared to fight for his rights, Sharett was cautious, hesitant, always preoccupied with Gentile attitudes toward Jewish behavior; he sought compromise. They were colleagues for thirty-five years; until the discord of 1956, they worked intimately together in the Jewish Agency, and after May 14, 1948, as prime minister and foreign minister respectively of the state in its formative years. They were not friends, however. In Sharett's words, Ben-Gurion was "a solitary figure preoccupied with himself, his thoughts, his emotions." To Ben-Gurion, Sharett "was the greatest foreign minister of our day in peacetime but not in time of war . . . when it came to an important problem he didn't know how to distinguish words from deeds . . . he was honest and there was great nobility about him."[44]

The raid on Kibya widened the split between them. If Ben-Gurion embodied the voices of "Old Testament militancy," Sharett was the exponent of reconciliation. A mild-mannered intellectual who spoke seven languages, among them Arabic, he always considered the importance of public opinion and the goodwill of the United Nations. Without the UN resolution of November 1947, Sharett believed, Israel would not have come into being. For Ben-Gurion, the United Nations was unimportant in the birth of the Jewish state. The state existed thanks to the daring of its people and primarily thanks to its army. During an argument between them on the merits of world support for Israel's actions, Ben-Gurion declared that "our future depends not on what the *goyim* [non-Jews] say, but on what the Jews do." Sharett responded, "Correct. But it is also important what the *goyim* say."[45] In short, while the two respected each other, each also disdained some of the other's traits and world views. Ironically, on November 24, 1953, Ben-Gurion handed the premiership to Sharett—the successor he did not want. Not by accident were there no major acts of reprisal during Ben-Gurion's "retirement" to S'deh Boker, but the "Old Man" would return with a vengeance to put a halt to Sharett's pacifism.[46]

The cutoff in economic aid and State Department condemnation of the Kibya attack brought about protests from Jewish groups, Zionist and non-Zionist alike. Even though the administration resented and complained about domestic "intrusion" in foreign affairs, the president and, especially, the secretary of state and his assistants found it necessary politically or as a matter of courtesy to receive various delegations requesting explanations about U.S. policy in the Middle East.

On October 22, Byroade saw Joseph Proskauer, president of the non-Zionist American Jewish Committee and a friend of Dulles. He advised Byroade of his attempt "to work out something with Eban to announce stopping the work at B'not Yaakov" and suggesting in turn that the United States would restore the aid.[47] The political pressures in this regard continued. On October 26, Dulles assured Harold H. Riegelman, Republican candidate for mayor of New York, that full economic aid to Israel would be resumed as soon as the dispute over Jordan River waters was settled. Later in the day Senator Irving M. Ives, Republican senator from New York State, and Representative Jacob Javits of New York led a delegation of Jewish leaders to confer with the secretary and asked him to reexamine the decision to cut aid to Israel. The delegation included Bernard Katzen, a consultant for the Republican National Committee; Maxwell Abell, president of the United Synagogue of America; Matthew Brown of Boston, a leading member of the American Jewish Committee; Rose Halprin, president of Hadassah; Philip Klutznick, president of B'nai B'rith; Louis Lipsky; and Bernard H. Trager, chairman of the National Community Relations Advisory Board.[48]

The meeting lasted an hour. Ives and Javits expressed concern about the status of U.S.-Israeli relations. Dulles justified the policy of impartiality and explained that the United States would have no influence if Arabs continued to believe that "we were wholly pro-Israel. . . . If Israel suspended the water project, the United States would immediately allocate economic aid." The United States, he continued, had to support the United Nations and dispel the Arab view that this country supported Israel whatever the circumstance. Dulles faced a torrent of complaints. The United States had done nothing against Egypt's defiance of the UN Security Council resolution concerning free passage of Israeli ships through the Suez Canal; the United States had failed to protest against continuing Arab violation of armistice agreements. Dulles retorted that he had been misunderstood. His efforts on behalf of the establishment of the state of Israel went unappreciated. All that the participants at the meeting wanted was the "policy of the previous administration which had brought no peace but only trouble."[49]

The meeting ended on an acrimonious note, but the pressures by Jewish groups led to a compromise solution. In a series of telephone conversations with Henry Cabot Lodge, Jr., the U.S. representative in the Security Council, Dulles complained about the pressure the "small New York City election brought on the White House and the Congress." Lodge suggested that a tough resolution prepared by the State Department to be submitted for Security Council approval binding Israel never to go ahead with the

B'not Yaakov project would have the effect of giving Syria a perpetual veto. Lodge commented, "We have a number of people in State who live in a dream world." He did not think that "it was possible to please the Arabs anyway, they are childish, all we can do is set a standard of international peace and justice . . . we can't play favorites." Dulles agreed. A deal was struck with Eban. The resolution was rewritten to make it possible for Eban to announce his government's willingness to "temporarily suspend" work on the project for the purpose of facilitating the Security Council deliberations on the question without prejudice to the merits of the case. Such a statement would appear to restore peace and to build up the United Nations and make it possible for Dulles to announce the resumption of aid, The president, Dulles told Lodge, "indicated that we stand firm on this." Lodge suggested that the announcement on aid resumption should be made a day after Eban's statement so that it would not look so much like a "deal." The secretary concurred, but he wanted to get the whole thing over with before the New York mayoral election scheduled for November 3.[50] Accordingly, on October 27, the Security Council unanimously adopted a French resolution (S./3128) stating that the council "deems it desirable that the work started in the demilitarized zone on September 2, 1953 should be suspended during the urgent examination of the question." Eban declared that the Israeli government would suspend the work in question during that examination. A day later, after conferring with Dulles at the White House, the president announced at a news conference the allocation of $26 million under MSA to Israel. He justified the earlier suspension of aid and its resumption as acting in support of the United Nations in all its activities regarding the Arab-Israeli conflict, "exactly as originally planned."[51]

The flurry of activity by Jewish individuals and groups knocking at the doors of the State Department trying to influence policy did not pass unnoticed by the president. He did not appreciate it. Even more important, he advised the secretary to attach little importance to pressures from Jewish groups. In a "Dear Foster" note of October 28, Eisenhower wrote about what a highly respected friend had told him. "The political pressure from the Zionists in the Arab-Israeli controversy is a minority pressure. My Jewish friends tell me, that except for the Bronx and Brooklyn the great majority of the nation's Jewish population is anti-Zion."[52]

But as historian Melvin I. Urofsky correctly points out, this was a highly inaccurate reading of the situation. This comment applied only to two extremes within U.S. Jewry: the ultra-Orthodox and the American Council for Judaism. The former rejected the Jewish state as an abomination, a sinful attempt by humanity to precipitate the coming of the Messiah and redeem the Jewish people. The latter consisted of ultra-assimilationists who feared that a Jewish state would revive the old canard of dual loyalty against U.S. Jews. These two groups, however, minuscule in numbers, stood outside the overwhelming consensus of support for the new Jewish state among U.S. Jews, Zionist and non-Zionist alike.[53]

Marshall Sklare and Mark Vosk's Riverton study in the early 1950s showed that 94 percent of all adults and 87 percent of the children felt positively about Israel and concluded that all Riverton Jews, even "those indifferent to Zionism as an ideological movement feel favorably disposed towards the State of Israel." They saw it at least as a place of refuge for homeless Jews and recognized their responsibility to help their coreligionists even though most had no intentions of ever living there.[54] Similar studies conducted in other Jewish communities showed similar results. Support for Israel was demonstrated regularly by the success of fund raising within the community. In 1947, the United Jewish Appeal raised approximately $170 million, about half of it allotted to Palestine. In the five years that followed, the new state received $416 million from U.S. Jews, two-thirds coming from funds raised by the United Jewish Appeal.

It is true that in the years following the birth of Israel, the enthusiasm of U.S. Zionists declined. According to Will Herberg, the passionate, militant Zionism espoused by groups of U.S. Jews until 1948 "became diffused into a vague though by no means insincere friendliness to the State of Israel."[55] It was quite natural that without the impetus of the dramatic struggle the zeal could not be permanently sustained. Once the state came into being, those concerned with its well-being concentrated their efforts on the economic assistance needed by Israel to absorb immigrants and gain visibility. However disturbing administration actions had been (and they were criticized in the Yiddish and English-language Jewish publications), those actions were not dramatic enough to arouse the large-scale political activism that would erupt in times of crisis such as in 1956 during and immediately after the Sinai campaign. In short, U.S. Jewry was far from being "anti-Zion."

On his trip to the Middle East, Dulles alleged that U.S. Jewry would not exert too much influence on Eisenhower. Because he had been elected to the presidency without Jewish support, he would therefore feel free to pursue a policy he believed to be in the national interest. Israel's traditional constituency (Jews, labor, and liberals) had backed his Democratic opponent.[56] Furthermore, while Truman had close Zionist friends and advisers (Eddie Jacobson and David Niles) who influenced his thinking at critical moments in the decision-making process, no such individuals were among Eisenhower's foreign policy advisers. A check of the roster of Jews serving in the Eisenhower administration revealed the following names: Maxwell Rabb, secretary of the cabinet and liaison between the administration and the Jewish community, but mainly in charge of minority affairs; Arthur F. Burns, chairman of the Council of Economic Advisers; Jack Martin, in charge of relations with Congress; Simon Soboloff, solicitor general; Charles Metzner, executive director to the attorney general; Lewis L. Strauss, chairman of the Atomic Energy Commission; Louis Rothschild, general counsel of the Federation Maritime Board; and Meyer Kestenbaum, member of the Commission on Intergovernmental Relations.[57] In these posts they had no input in foreign policy formulation, nor would they intercede on behalf of Israel knowing the president's aversion to ethnic pressures. Eisenhower made this clear at a cabinet meeting on November 12, 1953, in which Dulles had reported on efforts to promote an Arab-Israeli peace.

> After Dulles had spoken, the President said that since foreign policy so often involves domestic policy as well, he was eager to have the Cabinet talk about it. The best policy at home, he said, was to do the right thing abroad even though this might temporarily alienate extremists in the United States. He cautioned the Cabinet against "playing politics" with foreign affairs. Obviously referring to Israel which Dulles had just mentioned, the President said that he had been told of one case in which the Truman administration had used foreign policy for domestic political advantage.[58]

Thus, although Jewish leaders would make the rounds of the State Department and at times would be received by the president, they were listened to politely but failed to influence the decision makers in moving away from "impartiality." The policy was pursued with consistency from the president down to the lower echelons of the State Department, part of a highly formal system.

In the "talking paper" that Byroade sent to Dulles, he raised two issues about which Israel should be forewarned: first, that its policy of accepting large-scale Jewish immigration placed a tremendous burden on its economy and increased Arab fears of possible territorial expansion on Israel's part; second, that the United States could not wait for a peaceful resolution of the Arab-Israeli conflict before deciding to supply arms to Arab states. The global defense responsibilities of the United States would not countenance such a delay.

By the end of 1953 both issues were taken up by the Operation Control Board (OCB), the agency charged with recommending policies to the National Security Council and supervising the implementation of the council's decisions. On October 29, 1953, the OCB comprising the Central Intelligence Agency (CIA), State Department, and other analysts under the direction of Robert Cutler reviewed "Israel's Fundamental Problems." In their report to the NSC they noted that little attention had been paid to Israel's steadily deteriorating economic and financial situation. The fundamental cause for its economic and financial plight was "that too many people had been admitted too rapidly into a country that possessed almost no natural resources. Whether it will ever be possible to develop a viable economy in Israel is very uncertain." Only 18 percent to 25 percent of Israel's budget was secured from revenues, while the remainder was made up by foreign loans floated by the government, contributions from U.S. Jewry, and aid allocated by the United States. Yet in spite of that bleak outlook, the report continued, Ben-Gurion on October 25 called for the solution of all those problems within ten years and also laid the groundwork for two million more Jewish refugees from the Arab and Eastern bloc countries to enter Israel. That unrealistic approach, according to the OCB,

> can only lead to further economic and financial difficulties and will probably result in additional pressures to expand Israel's frontiers into the rich lands of the Tigris and Euphrates Valleys and northward into the settled land of Syria. . . . There is considerable element in the army, the government and among the people who feel that the only solution to Israel's problem is territorial expansion. As economic

pressure rises, the group is likely to increase in numbers. The situation is serious both for the security of the Near East and for the future of the new state.[59]

The OCB recommended that continued financial assistance from the United States depend on Israel's willingness to "tighten its belt and restrict immigrants." U.S. financial pressure could not, however, go too far without endangering the position of the moderate Israeli leaders who might then be overthrown by "expansionist firebrands. . . . Our best chance of success is a steady pressure for a more realistic Israeli approach to their national problems." The report recommended a slowdown in immigration and a progressive reduction of economic aid to Israel. Accordingly, Israel's share in the technological and economic aid for fiscal year 1954 was set at $54 million, of which $52.5 million was a grant and $1.5 million was in technical assistance. A further reduction for fiscal year 1955 to $41.1 million was recommended. (In fiscal year 1953, Israel had received $73 million.) Even so, Israel did not fare badly if one considers that the administration was diverting funds to Iran, reducing the total amount available to Israel and the Arab states by $100 million. From Israel's perspective, however, such amounts were too small to meet the challenges facing the new state, in view of the need to absorb such large numbers of Jewish immigrants in such a short period of time.

In the eighteen months following its creation, 340,000 Jews arrived in Israel. During the first three years of statehood, the average reached 18,000 a month, and in some months the figure exceeded 30,000. Between May 15, 1948, and June 30, 1953, the population of the country doubled, and by the end of 1956 Israel's population had nearly tripled, reaching 1,667,000. Wealthy nations would have had difficulty absorbing so many. The immigrants came from Eastern Europe, Arab countries, Asia, and Africa. In the words of historian Howard M. Sachar, they arrived "by passenger liner, by rickety dormitory steamer, by plane, and in some instances by clandestine land routes." They kept coming, even though the new state faced possible destruction or bankruptcy. This "Open Door" policy fulfilled a commitment, made by the founders of the state and clearly enunciated in the Declaration of Independence, that "Israel will be open to the immigration of Jews from all countries of their dispersion." The Law of Return passed in 1950 would provide a homeland for all who wished to "forsake the Diaspora and come home." It was the raison d'être of statehood, the bedrock of Zionist ideology.[60]

But beyond the ideological aspect of the unprecedented ingathering there was also an immediate practical reason—the need for an instant population. New inhabitants were needed to replenish the nation's military ranks, to settle the empty spaces in the land such as the Negev, and to create new agricultural border settlements on the exposed frontiers. The new nation required people to create the modern economy necessary to achieve a Western standard of living. Although never mentioned publicly by Israeli leaders, the economic and military factors were undoubtedly the main reasons behind the acceptance of this flood of immigrants. Thus for emotional and practical considerations any attempt to stop the policy of "ingathering of exile" or even to slow down the process, as suggested by the OCB report, in effect meant questioning the need for a Jewish state.

The OCB private observations were made public in an official and most controversial speech delivered by Byroade on May 1, 1954, in Philadelphia before a convention of the anti-Zionist American Council for Judaism. In an address entitled "Facing Realities in the Arab-Israeli Dispute," Byroade focused on the immigration of Jews to Israel as a major source of tension between Israel and the Arab states.

> What spreads like wildfire throughout the Middle East is a series of statements from Israel calling for greatly expanded immigration. A constant fear is that these urging in terms of extra millions will be heeded. Their fears (i.e., the Arabs') are enhanced by the knowledge that the only limitation imposed by statute on immigration into Israel is, in fact, the total number of those of the Jewish faith in the entire world. The Arabs know the capacity of the territory of Israel is limited. They see only one result—future attempts at territorial expansion—and hence warfare of serious proportions.

As a means of lessening some of the tension between these two rivals, Byroade offered the following advice: "Surely it is not asking too much to ask Israel to find some way to lay at rest these fears of her neighbors and remove this specter—which does not seem to be based upon reality—from minds in the Middle East. The tensions in the Middle East, which are translating themselves into almost daily needless loss of human lives, could be considerably less if wise statesmanship could find a way of such accomplishment."[61]

The speech was a sequel to an address Byroade gave on April 19, 1954, before the Dayton World Affairs Council that was more evenhanded.

> To the Israelis I say that you should come to truly look upon yourselves as a Middle Eastern state and see your own future in that context rather than as a headquarters, or nucleus so to speak, of a world-wide grouping of peoples of a particular religious faith who must have special rights within and obligations to the Israeli state. . . . You should drop the attitude of the conqueror and the conviction that force and a policy of retaliatory killings is the only policy that your neighbors will understand. You should make your deeds correspond with your frequent utterances of the desire for peace.
>
> To the Arabs I say you should accept the state of Israel as an accomplished fact. I say further that you are deliberately attempting to maintain a state of affairs delicately suspended between peace and war, while at present desiring neither.[62]

In order to inform the Middle East countries of the impartial U.S. policy toward the area, the United States Information Agency (USIA) press service wired these speeches to all Middle East posts, and the Voice of America broadcast them in English, Arabic, and Hebrew. USIA missions in Cairo, Tel Aviv, Beirut, Damascus, Amman, and Baghdad obtained extensive coverage for the speeches in the local press and distributed copies in translation to government leaders and other influential persons.[63]

But if the administration had hoped to gain Arab goodwill by showing its impartiality through these speeches, the results were mixed at best. Reports from U.S. ambassadors in Arab countries indicated that the press commenting on the Dayton speech focused on Byroade's call to the Arabs to make peace with Israel. This evoked the ultranationalist cry of "Never," while Byroade's admonition to the Israelis went unnoticed. Damascus Radio reported that the Iraqi government had protested the speech. The foreign minister of Jordan was quoted as saying, "We will never accept Israel or its existence." The only favorable comment came from the pro-Western *L'Orient* in Lebanon, which called the speech "nearly" perfect. But if the administration did not score the desired points with Byroade's "evenhanded" speech, the one he gave in Philadelphia was clearly to the Arabs' liking, for it questioned the basic tenets of Zionism. President Camille Chamoun of Lebanon called the speech "constructive," and the Egyptian press gave the address the widest coverage of any U.S. speech in recent years. The U.S. embassy in Cairo reported that Foreign Office and Arab League officials stated privately that the speech represented a "big change in U.S. policy."[64] Based on these reactions the Arabs were not very impressed with an impartial, "evenhanded" policy; they wanted an anti-Israeli policy.

In Israel, Byroade's speeches stirred up a furor quite disproportionate to his utterances. Little attention was paid to his appeal to the Arabs to accept the Jewish state and live in peace with it. The two speeches, nonetheless, epitomized to the Israeli public the new direction of U.S. policy. The U.S. embassy in Tel Aviv reported that the Arab economic boycott and psychological warfare had produced hidden strains in that country. Israel was no longer compensated by the feeling of having the sympathy and support of the U.S. government. The Israeli citizen, irrespective of status, was shocked at the selection of the forum for a speech on immigration policy. In Israel the American Council for Judaism was regarded as a "traitor within the family." Not only was it anti-Zionist but also anti-Israel, and therefore an enemy of the state. Because the immigration question logically lay within the province of Israel, the Jewish Agency, and the Zionist movement, Byroade's selection of such a forum appeared to Israelis an attempt by the administration to drive a wedge between Israel and U.S. Jewry. The implication that limitations should be placed on immigration seemed to challenge the basic tenets of Zionism and to interfere in the internal affairs of Israel. In Israel, European Jews believed that, had not the White Paper of 1939 restricted Jewish immigration to Palestine, "some relative or friend exterminated by the Nazis would be alive today." Many Jewish political and military leaders were convinced that without a population of four million Israel would not be able to survive the Arab threat. In their view, the removal of Arab fears "would not result in the disappearance of the Arab threat." Arab acceptance of Israel's existence would only come through superior Israeli power.[65]

The press in Israel reacted vehemently. Ben-Gurion, writing from his "retirement," stated in *Davar* on May 5 under a pen name that the U.S.

approach to the Middle East was "a danger to Israel," as peace must be bought from the Arabs and Israel would have "to pay the price." The basic theme in the press was that Israel would never give up its ties with world Jewry. The most widely read paper, *Ma'ariv*, was in its May 4 issue the harshest in its denunciation and the most sensational in its appeal to the broad masses. "Official America turns against Israel and against her own Jews . . . Byroade has not learned from his great master Ernest Bevin. . . . He, too, succeeded in uniting the Jewish people around Zionism and liquidating the apathy towards it. . . . Eisenhower and Byroade have now rendered the same service at a time when Zionism is at a low ebb. Bless them."

On the official level, Eban lodged a protest with the State Department and raised the subject of U.S.-Israeli relations with Dulles on May 13. Sharett, now prime minister and foreign minister, in opening the foreign policy debate in the Knesset on May 10 accused Byroade of a "lack of insight into the way Israel was born." In a more moderate vein he conceded that Byroade's speeches were not totally opposed to Israel. "He told the Arabs some truths too. But he did not tell them to cease being themselves, as he did to Israel." But the greatest damage to Israel, according to Sharett, was that the Arabs heard a U.S. spokesman justify their fears of Israeli expansionism.[66]

On May 5, Eban met with Byroade to discuss his comments and to officially protest sections of the speeches dealing with immigration to Israel. A State Department press release issued after the meeting stated that Byroade "felt impelled to speak frankly" on the Arab-Israeli conflict since it affected the security of the Middle East and hence U.S. interests. The assistant secretary regretted that the Israeli government had interpreted his remarks as interference in the internal affairs of Israel.[67]

On May 13, Eban and Shiloah took up the same issue with Dulles. Also present was Parker T. Hart. Eban called Byroade's remarks that Israel should cease "behaving like a conqueror" most undesirable diplomatic language. While Byroade attempted to achieve a certain balance in distributing blame for the current Mideast tensions, he did not advise the Arabs to avoid raiding Israel. But it was the Philadelphia speech that touched a raw nerve and "wounded the feelings of millions outside Israel and hundreds of thousands within that country." The speech, Eban claimed, showed a "lack of scholarship and sensitivity," for it was a reminder of the Jewish wartime experience with the British Mandate. When the Nazi Holocaust against Jews was in progress, the Jews had "no key to a door" that could open for their people. Israel, said Eban, was confronted with a terrible situation. On the one hand Israel "cherished the United States as the sheet anchor of her very life," and on the other hand it appeared that "Israel could do nothing right in American eyes." Dulles did not retract or apologize for Byroade's remarks. He blamed the Israeli press for inflaming the situation and drawing different interpretations than those intended. The press "always seemed to seek out the most disturbing elements of a public address and feature them." The secretary tried to reassure the ambassador and his government that "there was no weakening in the historic friendship between Israel and the United States."[68]

Summarizing the reaction in the United States, the State Department found general approval of the policy of impartiality. The *Washington Post, Dayton News,* and *Christian Century* praised the Dayton speech as a middle-of-the-road appeal to both sides. The *New York Post,* reflecting the views of many of its Jewish readers, found it inconceivable that a U.S. statesman would think that Israel could abandon so basic a policy as unrestricted Jewish immigration. The reaction in the Zionist press was epitomized in a statement by Nahum Goldmann, a veteran Zionist leader and chairman of the Jewish Agency, who stated that the "relationship between Israel and the outside Jewish communities is not the business of the State Department." While editorial reaction in the non-Zionist press was scant, the anti-Zionist reaction of the Council for Judaism, as could be expected, was enthusiastic, calling on all U.S. Jews to support the administration's policies. Although the number of letters to the State Department was not large, the ratio had been almost ten to one in favor of Byroade's speeches. All in all, the administration could feel some satisfaction. Even though the policy of impartiality had not yet scored any points in the Arab world, in the United States, at least, the overall reaction was far from negative. Israel's harsh reaction was expected. Staying the course as initially decided upon remained the order of the day.

Byroade's utterances came on the heels of a State Department announcement on April 26 that the United States had agreed to deliver military assistance to Iraq in order "to enable it to defend its independence" and thereby also contribute to the defense of "the vital resources of the free world."[69] The agreement was an outcome of Dulles's trip to the Middle East. Instead of trying to build a defense organization encompassing all the area linked to the West—something like a Middle East NATO—he suggested doing the job piecemeal, starting with the countries of the "northern tier" closest to the Soviet Union. Gradually other countries would be drawn in. As a means of easing nationalist sensitivities, the indigenous nature of such a grouping was of utmost importance. Therefore, the British and the Americans would not join in. Such an approach would have the advantage of starting an anti-Communist alliance without having to wait for a solution to the Anglo-Egyptian problem and the Arab-Israeli conflict.

The first step toward the realization of the northern tier alliance was taken in February 1954 when the USIA began a cautious low-key effort encouraging Iraq to accept military aid from the United States and to join a pro-Western defense pact—something the Iraqi premier, Nuri es-Said, was most willing to do. The pact would be the launching pad for his ambitions in the Arab world.[70] On April 2, 1954, Turkey and Pakistan signed a mutual defense agreement that received the blessing of the United States, accompanied by a promise of military and economic aid. Iraq and Iran joined and so did Britain, even though Dulles wanted the great powers to stay out. The alliance, known as the Baghdad Pact, came into being in February 1955. The United States was close to the group but not a member, since it wanted to maintain the indigenous character of the alliance. It did not want to alienate Egypt's new ruler, Abdel Nasser, who looked upon Iraq as a stalking horse for Western imperialism in the Middle East.

The granting of military and economic aid to Turkey and Pakistan was of no particular concern to Israel. But when the United States publicly announced the granting of such aid to Iraq in April 1954, Israel protested strongly. Such assistance, Israel claimed, endangered its security, because Iraq participated in the war of 1948 and had not even signed an armistice agreement with Israel. Military aid given to Arabs would lead to an arms imbalance and to renewed hostilities. "Here was an agreement which created a more intimate relationship between Iraq and the United States than that which existed between Israel and the United States," Eban lamented to Dulles. Byroade's pronouncements and the weapons for Iraq generated a feeling within Israel of extreme "isolation, vulnerability and insecurity." This feeling, said Eban, strengthened the hands of those in Israel who believed in the efficacy of self-reliance, and in preemptive wars rather than trust in international friendships and moderation. The ambassador implored Dulles to issue some assurance about Israel's security in order to prevent rash action on the part of Israelis who believed that growing Arab strength called for "preventive" war. Dulles promised to look into making a public statement to that effect and added, "We would also like if possible to embody within assurances to Israel, assurances to Arabs against possible Israeli aggression."

Without going into details, Dulles tried to reassure Eban that the U.S. military agreement with Iraq in the long run "would be found to be in the best interests of Israel." He asked the Israeli government to accept it on faith. The secretary sympathized with Israel's concerns over that important development. He had personally looked into the situation very closely and concluded that at "worst it would not hurt and at best it might help Israel's relations with her neighbors."[71]

Dulles's assurance notwithstanding, Israel's concern over security was sharpened by the simultaneous deterioration of its position caused by the Egyptian-British negotiations over the future of the Suez Canal base. The United States was intimately involved in the negotiations. In order to induce Egyptian flexibility, the president on July 15, 1953, promised Naguib that the United States was prepared to extend economic aid and military assistance once a Suez agreement was reached. At the same time the administration was exerting "friendly pressure" on Britain to be more accommodating and more understanding of Egyptian "national" pride. On March 29, 1954, the United States gave its blessings to a new British proposal involving a complete withdrawal of British troops and the maintenance of the base by civil contracting firms. In return, Egypt would agree to make the base available in case of an attack on an Arab state, Turkey, or Iran. When Winston Churchill and Foreign Secretary Anthony Eden visited Washington in June 1954, the two governments concluded that the United States would begin negotiating the necessary aid agreements once the new British plan had been presented to the Egyptians. Accordingly, the NSC had recommended setting aside special funds for probable future military requirements for Egypt.[72]

All this flurry of activity in pursuit of Egypt by the United States was based on the assumption, skillfully nurtured by Nasser, that after the

Egyptians achieved their "full" independence they would join a Western-sponsored alliance of their own accord. On July 27, Anthony Head, the British secretary of state for war, and his Egyptian counterpart initialed the heads of agreement document spelling out the terms of Britain's withdrawal. Nasser and Anthony Nutting of the British Foreign Office signed the final accord on October 19, 1954, calling for the total evacuation of British troops within twenty months.

In Washington on July 28, both the president and Dulles in separate statements expressed "gratification" at the conclusion of the "agreement in principle." Both hailed the agreement not only for its provision that made the base available to Britain in case of aggression but also for its termination of a dispute that barred unity between the Western allies and the countries in the Middle East. The agreement, according to Dulles, was a step in the evolution of relations between the Near East and the West, and he expressed his hopes "for a new era of collaboration between all the states involved." As planned in their enthusiastic reception of the accord, Dulles and Eisenhower alluded to the inauguration of substantial military and economic aid to Egypt.

Israel had followed the course of the Anglo-Egyptian negotiations with trepidation, hoping that the complex nature of the problems involved might lead to their collapse. The news that an agreement was initialed came as a shock. It raised the specter of an unfettered Egypt, militarily well equipped and no longer subject to the restraining hand of the British. In addition, the evacuation of British troops from the canal base would remove an important buffer between Israel and Egypt and would also place the Egyptians in a better position to enforce a strict blockade of the waterway against Israeli ships and goods. Israel also feared that the settlement of an Egyptian-British dispute would lead to Egypt's joining a U.S.-sponsored alliance without Israeli participation and resulting in her complete isolation. Adding to Israel's disquiet were two specific clauses in the accord. One clause provided for British reentry into Egypt in case of war in the area, excepting a conflict involving Israel. A second clause recognized the Arab League Security Pact, which in Israel's eyes was actually an organization bent on war against Israel.[73] Equally worrisome were elements not included in the agreement: no requirement on Egypt's part to improve its relations with Israel and bring to an end its blockade against Israeli ships, an action in violation of a Security Council resolution of September 1, 1951.[74] Prime Minister Sharett warned that the new situation produced a most important change in the balance of power between Israel and her neighbors. Should the United States now grant arms aid to Egypt after having decided to give arms to Iraq, it would be "an addition of crime upon crime."[75]

Faced with perils to her security, Israel took two actions. Both boomeranged. Prior to the ratification of the Anglo-Egyptian agreement, on September 28 Israel sent a small freighter, the *Bat Galim*, flying the national flag through the Suez Canal in an attempt to test the right of passage through the waterway—a right confirmed by the UN Security Council. This was the first Israeli ship to attempt passage since 1949. Since that time Israeli cargo was allowed passage only in foreign ships. By timing the operation as they did, the Israelis used the *Bat Galim* as a test case to uncover Egyptian intentions before full British evacuation and to emphasize their right to enjoy unmolested transit through the canal. If the Egyptians allowed the ship to pass, Israel would have established a precedent of its right to free transit. If the Egyptians continued to blockade, Israel hoped that the opponents of the canal treaty in Britain would use the incident to prove that Egypt could not be trusted with the physical control of the canal.[76] Perhaps they could marshal enough votes in Parliament to prevent ratification of the agreement.

The maneuver failed. The Egyptians impounded the ship and imprisoned its crew. The Security Council briefly considered the matter but took no action. Neither Britain nor the United States insisted on Egyptian compliance with the previous Security Council resolution. The Anglo-Egyptian accord was ratified, and Israel reaped only the resentment of the British and U.S. governments for seeking to "embarrass them." In the words of Walter Eytan, the two powers "appeared less vexed with Egypt for this violation of Israel's rights, than with Israel for provoking it."[77] Adding insult to injury, even Israeli cargo on foreign ships was afterward prohibited from passing through the canal. Egypt's action was not only politically but also economically damaging.

The additional closure by Egypt of the Straits of Tiran on the Red Sea compounded the problem, for the straits controlled traffic to the southern port of Eilat, the only Israeli opening to East Africa, the Indian Ocean, and Asia. Asia was a potential market for Israeli manufactured goods and the few natural resources she possessed, such as potash and phosphates, which were harvested from the Dead Sea near Eilat. According to Dayan, the newly appointed chief of staff, "the closure of the waterways amounted to a blockade which was not only a political issue for Israel but also a grave blow to her economy and a brake on her development."[78]

The attitude with which the United States and Britain treated the *Bat Galim* test case reinforced Israel's sense of isolation. Its military intelligence, without Sharett's knowledge, decided to launch sabotage operations against U.S. and British installations in Egypt in order to derail a potential Anglo-Egyptian accord and to undermine U.S. trust in Egypt. The aim was to make the sabotage appear to be the work of Egyptian fanatics, thus proving that the Nasser government was so fragile that it could not guarantee the operation of the Suez Canal in the event of a British withdrawal. On July 9, 1954, Avri Elad, Israel's chief operator in Cairo, activated his agents against U.S. and British targets, firebombing U.S. cultural and information centers in Cairo and Alexandria. Damage was slight, but the attacks were numerous enough to draw the attention of the Egyptian security authorities. The operation failed miserably. One of the agents was accidentally caught when the phosphorus bomb hidden in his spectacle case ignited prematurely, setting his clothes afire. His arrest and subsequent questioning led the police to four other saboteurs plus seven other alleged Israeli spies who had no direct connection with the operation. The fiasco wiped out Israel's intelligence operations in Egypt. For years it rocked the political and military establishment in Israel, and it of course failed in its main purpose.[79] That the whole operation was undertaken without the knowledge of Sharett and without the specific orders of the Defense Minister, Pinhas Lavon, only highlighted the extent of Israel's isolation from the great powers and her mounting desperation.

Francis H. Russell, the U.S. chargé d'affaires in Tel Aviv, reported on the mood of the Israeli public. It perceived the moderate leadership of Sharett as "unaspiring and too passive." Articles in the press suggested that solutions to Israel's problems must be "militant," including a "preventive war." Those feelings, wrote Russell, reflected the temperament of the young sabra (native-born Israeli) generation throughout the country.[80]

It would be wrong to assume that the Eisenhower administration, while pursuing a policy believed to be in the national interest, was totally blind to Israel's security needs. Nor were Israel's complaints brushed aside with vague assurances. The State Department had paid more than cursory attention to Israeli concerns about security. The administration, however, considered Israel's fears exaggerated and even misplaced. In the administration's view, the policy of impartiality, although attempting to further U.S. strategic interests, did not endanger Israeli security. Byroade, relying on reports of U.S. ambassadors in the region, saw no remote possibility of an Arab move against Israel. He actually believed that the recent moves diverted Arab attention away from the Palestine question. In response to Israel's claim of isolation and in view of the absence of defensive ties with other and larger powers, Byroade considered formulating a Western guarantee of the territorial integrity of the states of the area—a guarantee "with guts in it." Byroade informed Eban and Dayan that the United States "is determined to prevent any Arab effort to eliminate Israel and that he was certain the United States would employ troops if necessary."[81]

The United States had insisted that Egypt lift the blockade of Israeli ships through the Suez Canal.[82] In fostering a Suez settlement, the administration did not intend to prejudice Israel's position. According to Dulles, a by-product of the settlement might not seem favorable to Israel at present, but anticipated dangers were not immediate. British evacuation would take twenty months. Given the logistical and training problems, any arms assistance would have little immediate effect on Egyptian military strength. "Israel should be aware of United States concerns for her future, the United States would not tolerate that her actions injure Israel—nothing has changed, there is basic American friendship and Israel need not feel alone or abandoned."[83] In a discussion with Philip Klutznick, president of B'nai B'rith, Dulles reiterated what he had already told Eban. The United States was determined "not to let Israel be crushed," and he was giving his personal attention to allay Israeli fears, as evidenced by the frequent lengthy conversations he had recently had with Eban. In fact, said Dulles, U.S. regional defense efforts were distracting the Arabs from their preoccupation with Israel. The reports he was receiving from the region indicated the Arabs were either incapable of attacking Israel or had no genuine desire to undertake such an attack. Dulles did not exclude the possibility of eventually aiding Israel militarily. As progress was made in the political field in developing a satisfactory arrangement for the defense of the area, it would be possible to consider the part that Israel might play. In the meantime, given Israel's preponderance in military strength, arms to Iraq or Egypt would not materially change the power relationship for a considerable time.[84]

But Israel in her predicament viewed Dulles's statements as "arms for the Arabs and assurances for Israel." What concerned Israel was not so much the present Arab strength but the potential strength. Israel wanted a formal defense treaty with the United States, a commitment to maintain a military balance between Israel and all Arab states put together so that Israel's military strength remained superior to any combination of its Arab foes.[85] The demand for a formal U.S.-Israeli treaty was viewed by U.S. officials with extreme apprehension as a move that would strike an "irreparable blow" to the U.S. position in the Arab world. Should that happen, Israel would be placed permanently in a special relationship to the United States—precisely what the policy of impartiality was endeavoring to avoid. As Byroade put it to Nahum Goldmann, "The nature of Israel's demands has made action by the United States next to impossible . . . Israel wants public recognition that it has first claim on the United States as far as the Near East is concerned, grant military assistance and an alliance at a time when there are no grounds for Israel to be concerned over its position vis-à-vis the Arabs as far as American policy is concerned. At some future date the situation might change to the extent that it would be appropriate to consider favorably some of the things she is presently demanding."[86]

Goldmann inquired why the United States could not make a public declaration that whatever security system was eventually established in the Middle East, Israel would not be ignored in any such constellation. That, said Byroade, could easily be worked out. But Israel demanded a lot more, pressing for "treatment equal to that given to all Arab states and this is just not possible." Goldmann concurred.

Officials sympathetic to Israel in the U.S. embassy in Tel Aviv believed that the policy of impartiality had resulted in gains for the United States in the region as a whole. Although they opposed a formal U.S.-Israeli treaty, they nonetheless advised Dulles that assurance to Israel was required to allay its fears. Francis H. Russell recommended a private communication of U.S. policy that would provide Israel with a sense of security and a promise of eventual granting of military aid.

Accordingly, the NEA prepared a statement of U.S. policy in the

Middle East to be relayed to Israel. The statement first and foremost reaffirmed the traditional firm friendship of the United States for Israel. In no way had that friendship diminished by U.S. friendship with the Arab states. The serious threat posed by Soviet imperialism compelled the United States "to assist immediately the efforts of states in the area to increase their ability to resist outside attempts at covert or overt aggression." This course of action, according to the statement, could not await the solution of the Arab-Israeli dispute as demanded by Israel. But the "United States Government does not exclude an eventual program of arms assistance to Israel." The U.S. government attached particular importance to deterring an outbreak of hostilities in the area and to assuring the security of Israel and each Arab state in accordance with the tripartite declaration of May 25, 1950. Should that confidence prove misplaced, and if an "armed attack occurred by an Arab state on Israel or by Israel on an Arab state, the United States in accordance with its constitutional processes and the Tripartite Declaration would immediately take appropriate action to cut off aid to the aggressor and seek to thwart such aggression." Should Israel become the target of aggression, the United States "would take appropriate action to protect Israel's security."[87]

The note fell short of Israel's demand, but it demonstrated that the policies of the Eisenhower administration took Israel's concerns to heart, a far cry from being anti-Israel or seeking to abandon Israel. While U.S. officials, as Byroade's speeches demonstrated, were more often than not insensitive to Israel's problems, by the same token, in demanding a clear-cut pro-Israel orientation, Israel failed to appreciate U.S. regional interests as a whole. Israel naturally refused to admit the impossibility of gaining Arab cooperation against Soviet communism while at the same time demonstrating total friendship toward Israel. Nor could it be argued that the United States did not impress the Arabs with their obligations in regard to Israel. The administration prodded the Arabs to help solve the refugee problem by resettling a large number of refugees in the Arab states, and to work toward the elimination of the Arab economic boycott. The United States resisted Arab efforts to impose a secondary boycott on U.S. trade with Israel and kept reiterating its support for the Security Council resolution calling for the removal of Egyptian restrictions on Suez Canal traffic to Israel. But most of all, National Security Council directives always insisted that the Arabs must be made to understand that the United States would not accept their negative attitude toward proposals involving recognition of Israel and their refusal to work toward an eventual settlement.[88]

Furthermore, while attempting to line up Arab states in a defense organization aimed against Soviet designs in the area, the Eisenhower administration simultaneously searched for constructive approaches that might lead to peaceful cooperation between Israel and its neighbors. A significant step in that direction would be a start toward the permanent settlement of Palestine Arab refugees. Dulles believed that Arab hostility toward Israel could be defused and the plight of the refugees mitigated by an economic scheme that required the joint commitment of Arabs and Israelis. According to Dulles, a Jordan Valley Authority was needed in order to tap and allocate the waters of the Jordan River system along all neighboring riparian states—Syria, Jordan, Lebanon, and Israel.

The Jordan River descended from headwaters in Lebanon, Syria, and Israel. The ensuing streams, the Hasbani, the Banias, and the Dan, merged in Israeli territory where they formed the Jordan River, which enters Lake Tiberias (Kinneret) and then flows southward, ending in a sluggish crawl to the Dead Sea. The Yarmuk River, which flowed through Arab territory (Syria and Jordan), joined the Jordan River below Lake Tiberias (Kinneret). If this water system could be exploited, close to a million and a quarter dunams of arid land (a dunam is approximately one-quarter of an acre) in Israel, Jordan, and Syria could be reclaimed. Even more significant, from the U.S. viewpoint, 200,000 Arab refugees would earn a livelihood on soil irrigated by the Jordan Valley scheme, another 60,000 to 70,000 refugees would find work in the construction project itself, while perhaps as many as 140,000 people would be employed simply in servicing the farming population. The hope of course was that a joint scheme would establish an economic basis for later political Arab-Israeli cooperation. The cost of such a project was estimated at approximately $110 million.[89]

The first steps toward such a possibility were taken in 1952 when the United Nations Relief and Works Agency for Palestine Arab refugees in the Middle East, with State Department encouragement and support, contracted the Tennessee Valley Authority (TVA) for a review and analysis of all past proposals for utilization in the Jordan River.[90]

The resulting study, entitled "The Unified Development of the Water Resources of the Jordan Valley Region," was prepared by Charles T. Main of Boston and made public at UN headquarters in New York on October 19.[91] Known as the Unified Development Plan, or the Main Plan, the project would result in irrigating 416,000 dunams of land in Israel, 490,000 in Jordan, and 30,000 in Syria and provide a limited amount of power to the riparian states. Carrying out such a project demanded decisive U.S. input—diplomatic and financial.

Thus on October 16, two days after Israel's major reprisal raid on Kibya, the president announced the appointment of Eric Johnston, former president of the U.S. Chamber of Commerce, chairman of the International Advisory Board of TVA, head of the Motion Picture Association of America, and an experienced negotiator, as his special representative with the rank of ambassador on a mission to the Middle East. His task—to seek a comprehensive program to develop the Jordan River's water resources on a "regional basis" with Middle Eastern states. The Main Plan of October 19 provided the technical basis for Johnston's initial negotiations. Out of it evolved the Unified Plan, sometimes referred to as the Johnston Plan. At the heart of the U.S. initiative were the lessons that Dulles had learned from his tour of the Middle East—namely, that the Arab-Israeli conflict required a piecemeal constructive approach and not a package deal, and that economic aid and progress toward a solution of the refugee problem would eventually lead to the solution of political problems between the antagonists.[92]

The Johnston mediation effort was carried out in four rounds of negotiations with Egypt, Jordan, Syria, Lebanon, and Israel between October 1953 and October 1955. A genial dynamic public servant with years of successful negotiation experience in business and government, Johnston exhibited extraordinary persistence, given the animosity and state of war between Arabs and Israelis. His closest aide during the mission wrote: "No man worked harder at a job than Johnston worked at this one. On the four separate visits to the Middle East over a span of three years on which I accompanied him as an adviser, I watched him argue and cajole his way through hundreds of weary hours of the most detailed and harassing negotiations it is possible to imagine."[93]

In Johnston's first visit to the area, he arrived in Israel on October 27, 1953, to consult with Israeli leaders about the Main Plan. Coincidentally, on the same day Israel announced its own Seven-Year Plan prepared for an international Jewish Economic Conference meeting at the time in Jerusalem. The plan aimed at doubling the water supply from 810 million cubic meters (mcm) in 1952–53 to 1,730 mcm in 1960–61, tripling the area of irrigated land to meet the needs of an estimated population of two million by the end of 1960. This plan ran counter to and exceeded the water allocation provided by the Main Plan.[94] During three days of discussions, Johnston explained that his proposals were not a "plan" to be accepted or rejected, a take-it-or-leave-it proposition, but a basis for discussion and negotiations. The core of the plan was to use Lake Tiberias (Kinneret) as a natural storage reservoir for the waters of the Jordan and its principal tributary, the Yarmuk. These waters would be released through a system of canals for all-year irrigation in the lower valley. Israel's share would be drawn mainly from headwaters upstream from Tiberias. Tentative yearly allocations were suggested: 426 mcm to irrigate 104,000 acres in Israel, 829 mcm to irrigate 112,500 acres in Jordan, and 50 mcm to water 7,500 acres in Syria. Some 38,000 kilowatts of electric energy could be produced through a power installation on the Yarmuk in Jordan and another 27,000 kilowatts at another plant near Tel Hai in Israel. These figures, Johnston explained to both Israeli and Arab leaders, were subject to discussion and possible revision on the basis of detailed engineering studies and other considerations. Given the political situation in the region, and the impossibility of direct cooperation between Israel and the Arab states, Johnston proposed that the system of waterworks in the valley would require international administration and supervision; some type of valley water authority, probably under UN auspices, would have to be created.[95]

Sharett, who headed the Israeli delegation in the talks with Johnston, realized the potential for regional cooperation in the use of water as a possible breakthrough to a peace settlement. The international financing of the joint plan would also be to Israel's benefit. The Israelis were adverse to the basic themes of the Main Plan, however, namely the use of the water exclusively within the Jordan Valley. They insisted on the right to pipe their water allocation into the Negev desert. Nor did Israel agree to its water quota, claiming it to be less than that allocated to Jordan. Israel was also concerned about the authority of the "supervisor" who, according to the plan, would be responsible for the actual water allocation. A

UN agency for that task might infringe on Israel's sovereignty and control of development plans for the Negev, where most future immigrants would be settled.[96]

In the Arab capitals, particularly in Amman, Johnston encountered a surprisingly friendly attitude, a result possibly of Jordanian anxiety over refugee employment and bitterness. He exploited that concern by hinting that the United Nations (i.e., the United States) would not fund the refugees indefinitely, and, if some wide-ranging irrigation project were not soon adopted, Israel would launch a program of its own. Lebanon, too, was not totally averse to the idea. Given the delicate balance between Christians and Moslems, Lebanon wanted to resettle the refugees outside its own frontiers in order not to upset its internal religious equilibrium. The U.S. proposal for irrigating the Jordan Valley to provide homes for Arab refugees would help meet these problems. Naguib of Egypt gave the impression that he wanted U.S. goodwill in a period when he was about to start ambitious programs of his own. Faced with such prospects, Arab leaders did not reject Johnston's proposals outright. They did, however, object to the large allocation of water provided to Israel under the Main Plan, and they demanded that Israel should be obliged to use the water exclusively within the Jordan Valley basin.[97]

Summarizing the first round of talks, Johnston termed Israel's and Lebanon's responses to his proposals "far from enthusiastic, but slightly interested." As for Jordan, "the door is closed but not locked," for Syria, the "door is ajar," and Egypt "hinted at readiness to influence the Arab League and encouraged it to take an interest in the project."[98] Stopping in Paris on his way back to Washington after three weeks in the Middle East, the envoy declared that there was "possibly a 50-50 chance" of Arab-Israeli acceptance of the Main Plan. When he took the assignment as the president's special envoy, he told Eisenhower that he doubted that he had a better than one in ten chance of succeeding. After he heard what happened at Kibya he revised his estimate downward to "one in a 100." Thus a fifty-fifty chance was at least an "indirect victory" considering the passions dividing Israel and her Arab neighbors. Johnston found public opinion in Arab countries so bitter against Israel that leaders of those countries would run personal risks if they approved a direct settlement with Israel. To overcome that obstacle a UN agency or any other international body would supervise compliance with the terms to be agreed upon in subsequent discussions. Johnston asked the leaders of the five countries involved in the scheme to withhold approval or disapproval but to study the plan and prepare modifications if they so desired.[99]

While waiting for Arab and Israeli formal responses to the U.S.-sponsored plan, in December 1953 the USIA initiated a carefully conceived educational campaign on the subject of Jordan water usage by the Arab states and Israel. The Voice of America broadcast a series of talks in Arabic on the history and geography of the region and the benefits that would accrue to people in the area as a result of the development of the Jordan Valley. Pamphlets in Arabic published by USIA's service center in Beirut extolled the social and economic benefits of the water project. Motion pictures showing large hydroelectric and irrigation projects in the United States were sent to the area for exhibit to government leaders, agriculturists, and engineers. The State Department had pulled out all the stops to popularize the constructive nature of the proposed water plan.

In March 1954, the Arab League set up a special technical committee to study the Johnston proposals. The Arab response emphasized the exclusive in-basin Jordan Valley principle for the use of the Jordan waters. Consequently, Israel would have no right to direct any quantity of water to the Negev. Furthermore, the Arab plan included a reduction of the water quota to Israel from 37.5 percent to 17.4 percent. The three Arab states (Jordan, Syria, and Lebanon) would receive 80 percent, the rest to be utilized by Israel. The Arab plan took exception to the use of Lake Tiberias (Kinneret) for the storage of surplus water from the Yarmuk on the grounds that the lake was entirely under Israeli control.[100] Most significant, however, was the political aspect of the Arab response: the acknowledgment of Israel's status as a riparian state and its entitlement to a share of the waters on which it bordered also implied de facto recognition.

The Israeli reaction was less forthcoming. The main feature in Israel's reply included a demand for more than double the amount of water allocated by the Main Plan, the inclusion of the Litani River in the scheme, seven times the amount of electricity, and an increase in costs from $121 million to $470 million, most of it to be provided by the United States. Israel also insisted on its sovereign rights to use its share of water anywhere within its territory, which, of course, included the Negev. Omitted from Israel's response was any mention of a UN or any other international agency to supervise the whole project. Obviously, the responses by both sides amounted to bargaining postures in preparation for the second phase of indirect negotiations to be resumed during June 1954.[101]

In a memorandum to the president in May 1954, Dulles assessed the replies of both sides, concluding that U.S. efforts to date showed a definite balance of gains over losses. Eric Johnston, asserted Dulles, had made an excellent impression on the Arabs. Although initially unwilling to consider the plan carefully, they were now discussing it in the Arab League. The Arabs realized that their countries would gain from a development of the Jordan basin. But the secretary knew that the issue was not merely a technical one. More than anything the issue was political. In a prophetic comment he stated, "No matter what the problem, we have to face Arab opposition to anything implying recognition of Israel's right to exist. In any event we should not let that attitude deter us from supporting proposals which we honestly consider to be fair and which offer hope of constructive progress toward our goal."[102]

The Arab League committee asked Johnston to visit Cairo in late May–early June for further discussions. He was instructed by the State Department to agree to changes of certain elements of the original Main Plan, taking into account the views of the Arabs and Israelis. Dulles hoped that this trip would lead to indirect bargaining between both sides, ending Johnston's role and leaving the initiative to the United Nations.

In his second visit to the Middle East, during June 1954, Johnston was accompanied by Arthur Gardiner and Oliver Troxell, two State Department specialists; George Barness, a permanent aide; and two engineers. They met an Israeli team headed by the Prime Minister and Foreign Minister, Sharett, and including Eshkol, Pinhas Sapir, water specialists, and engineers. Johnston made a concession to Israel. Despite Arab objections he supported Israel's fundamental demand for out-of-basin use of the Jordan waters. Israel in turn accepted the principle of limited supervision by an international agency. This concession, however, was unsatisfactory from the U.S. point of view, for the United States wanted full supervisory authority to be given to a U.S. agency to operate under U.S. instructions. This was not the only problem. Israel would not relent on the demand for a much larger water quota than that allocated in the Main Plan.

When Johnston left Israel, all that he and Sharett could announce was the common desire on both sides to reach a coordinated development agreement, but that stage had not been reached yet. By contrast, in meeting with an Arab committee consisting of engineering and political representatives of Egypt, Jordan, Syria, and Lebanon, Johnston reached substantial agreement on the division of waters among the interested states, the necessity for neutral control of the waters, and the measures needed to store waters for purposes of irrigation in Lake Tiberias (Kinneret). Arab representatives had not yet agreed to the U.S. position that any nation could use the water allocated to it wherever it wished. Nonetheless, Johnston found greater flexibility on the Arab side. As far as the State Department was concerned, "Johnston came close to agreement with the Arabs, but the negotiations with Israel are liable to prove extremely difficult."[103]

After protracted negotiations and tenacious bargaining during a third visit to the area (January 26–February 29, 1955), Johnston succeeded in reaching a compromise on the quota of water included in a new Revised Main Plan calling for a slight reduction in Jordan's quota, an allocation of water to Lebanon, and an increase for Syria and Israel. Israel received half the amount it demanded initially but nonetheless 15 percent more than in the original Main Plan. Basically, the Jordan and Yarmuk waters were divided 60 percent for the riparian Arab states and 40 percent for Israel. The Arabs consented to Israel's use of the water in the Negev. Israel agreed to compromise on the technical aspect of the project so as not to miss a first-time opportunity to gain political benefits: the possibility of negotiations with neighboring Arab states that could lead to a peace settlement. Based on this understanding Johnston set out on his fourth and last trip to the region (August 25–October 15, 1955) in an effort to eliminate the small margins of difference that still existed.[104] The Arab Expert Committee approved a Memorandum of Understanding previously agreed upon by Israel; in late September the committee recommended approval to the Arab League Council. The memorandum was a remarkable feat for Johnston, all the more so as it was achieved at a time of mounting border violence between Israel and its Arab neighbors and when the Israeli raid at Gaza in February 1955 badly shook the prestige of the Egyptian government. Elated, the envoy expressed "not the slightest doubt that Israel and her Arab neighbors . . . now recognize the Jordan

Valley Plan as the only logical and equitable approach to the problem of developing a river system which belongs in some part to all of them." His optimism was premature. The Arab League Council met on October 7, 1955, to consider the Revised Main Plan. The scheme was debated for four days. On October 11, the council decided to "postpone" it for "further study," thus avoiding the diplomatic onus of an outright rejection. The ever-optimistic Johnston would not concede failure. He still believed that "the remaining minor differences can readily be reconciled. I am sure that they can be."[105]

The ultimate agreement failed to materialize for political reasons. The members of the Arab League realized that the purpose of the plan ran counter to their political objectives toward Israel. If the plan were carried out, it would have resettled the refugees permanently in their countries of residence rather than bring about their repatriation and the fulfillment of what Arab governments euphemistically called "Palestinian rights." Perhaps more important, agreement meant recognition of Israel and extension of economic benefits to that country—precisely what the Arab economic boycott was supposed to prevent. Political considerations finally derailed a constructive approach to the peaceful solution of a major problem in the region.

Dulles must have been disappointed but not surprised. In his May 7 memorandum to the president he had realized the political obstacles to an agreement. He knew that at first the Arabs were suspicious of Johnston because of his past connection with the pro-Israel American Christian Palestine Committee and that acceptance of the Main Plan for the use of the Jordan waters would imply acquiescence in the existence of Israel. The Arabs resented U.S. persistence in pursuit of the plan.[106] An equally disappointed Eisenhower wrote about the failure of the Johnston effort: "Mr. Johnston met with some success and at one time actually obtained the private assurance of the technical and professional advisers representing the two sides that his proposals were satisfactory. However the mission totally came to naught because of the refusal of political leaders to let their respective peoples learn of any project involving cooperative effort among the opposing camps. Apparently they believed that to do so, would bring on revolution and the loss of their power."[107]

True to the principle of impartiality, the president could not bring himself to blame the Arab leaders specifically for defeating a worthwhile constructive plan that could have been a step forward in solving the Arab-Israeli dispute. Nevertheless, the Johnston mission showed that the United States, while attempting to keep the Arab Middle East within the Western camp, had not been oblivious to Israel's interests.

The pattern of U.S. policy was one of deliberate duality. The United States wished to increase its influence in the Arab world, especially in the face of Communist subversion and increasingly active Soviet diplomacy, and at the same time to maintain its commitment to Israel's existence. The decline of British and French influence and the fear of a power vacuum in the region would compel the United States to pursue its quest for Arab favor. But U.S. motives in obtaining its goals in the Arab world were driven not by malice toward Israel but by resistance to the Soviet Union. Israel, however, surrounded by hostile neighbors, saw its security needs to be much greater than those recognized in Washington. Misunderstandings and distrust would continue as the United States attempted to maintain the middle ground between the two sides, believing that such a policy was both morally right and in the U.S. national interest.

Security and Arms

5

Among the strategic regions of the world, the Middle East ranked high in priority for Eisenhower and Dulles. Convinced of Soviet attempts to gain influence in the area, the Eisenhower administration had given increased attention to a U.S. role that would prevent the Soviets from achieving their aims. Economic aid and arms were one way of wooing major Arab states. Thus in April 1954 an arms deal was concluded with pro-Western Iraq. The signing of the Suez Canal agreement between Egypt and Britain in October 1954 removed a major barrier in U.S. willingness to assist Egypt economically, with the understanding that U.S. arms shipments were likely to follow.[1]

But economic assistance and arms were not the only means of containing Soviet influence. Intent upon ringing the Soviet Union with Middle East air bases, Dulles in 1953 won assurances of cooperation from Turkey, Iran, Pakistan, and Iraq. His policy thereafter, in tandem with the British Prime Minister, Anthony Eden, was to seek a new Middle Eastern alliance of an indigenous character oriented primarily toward the Islamic northern tier, thus abandoning the idea of MEDO, an organization more analogous to NATO. Their efforts were crowned with the signing of the Baghdad Pact on February 24, 1955. As this multilateral treaty included not merely Britain (and obliquely the United States) but also Iraq among the four Moslem signatories, the complications of the Arab-Israeli issue were unavoidable. The Israelis were deeply concerned lest Iraq's adherence would evoke broadened military assistance to an enemy nation.[2]

Furthermore, from the Israeli perspective, a network of security and arms agreements involved the Western powers and Arab and Moslem states. Such agreements existed between Britain, Egypt, Jordan, Libya, and Iraq; between the United States, Iraq, Pakistan, and Libya; between Turkey, Pakistan, and Iraq. Yet no security or arms agreement existed between Israel and any of the Western powers. In addition, the agreements already concluded and those envisaged would, according to the Israelis, give the Arab states two advantages: a guarantee by another power of their territorial integrity against an armed attack, and military reinforcement under suitable conditions.[3] Israel lacked any of these advantages. Its sense of isolation and insecurity increased. Israel urgently sought a treaty relationship of its own with the United States in order to equalize the balance between itself and all Arab states. Moreover, the Israelis were convinced that only a security pact with the United States would convince the Arabs that Israel could not be destroyed, leaving them with no choice but to make peace.[4]

On March 3, 1955, the Israeli Foreign Office drafted a document, "Proposed Formulations of Main Clauses in Agreement or Exchange of Notes to be Signed or Exchanged between the Government of the United States and Israel." In it Israel requested that the United States make the following commitments: an armed attack against the territorial integrity and political independence of Israel would constitute a threat to international peace and security prejudicial to U.S. interests; the United States would in accordance with constitutional processes thwart such an attack; the United States would endorse the present territorial integrity of Israel; U.S. military aid and arms sales to the Middle East should be balanced between Israel and all Arab states collectively. In turn, "Israel will use American assistance exclusively to maintain its internal security and its legitimate self defense, will not commit aggression against any state or attempt to alter the present frontiers or armistice demarcation lines by force." Israel also agreed to furnish reciprocal assistance to the United States, "in order to increase its capacity for individual and collective self defense."[5]

On April 13, Eban discussed with Dulles the basic Israeli request for a defense treaty. Since August 1954, said Eban, the State Department has been considering various ideas and proposals to satisfy Israel's security concerns. The time has come, he continued, for the United States to take a stand on this important issue.

Dulles's reply was far from satisfactory. The United States, he said, has been waiting for suitable conditions, such as a relaxation of tension between Israel and its neighbors, before embarking on mutual defense arrangements. Unfortunately, thus far those conditions have not been met. Witness the recent border incidents and, in particular, the Israeli raid on Gaza of February 28, said Dulles. In addition, Dulles continued, the United States had not entered into any security treaty except in the Western hemisphere, unless the treaty was directed against the expansionist threat of international communism. The United States, he maintained, steadfastly avoided involvement in regional controversies. Besides, a security treaty would require the consent of the Senate. Such consent, said Dulles, would be hard to achieve, as many senators would feel that far from guaranteeing stability such a treaty would involve the United States in regional disputes. Thus, in order to obtain the Senate's consent the major issues between Israel and its neighbors would have to be brought immeasurably nearer a solution.[6] In essence, although the United States took Israel's security concerns seriously, it was not about to engage in a bilateral treaty relationship with Israel and thereby antagonize the Arabs. At the same time, according to Dulles, a security pact with Israel would be contingent upon a solution of the Arab-Israeli conflict, in effect giving the Arabs veto power over an issue of utmost importance to Israel.

The State Department, explained Dulles, had been at work on a plan that aimed at achieving a settlement of the conflict. Earnest thought had been given to questions of procedure and timing for the plan to be made public. Although the plan would not completely satisfy either side, Israel, said Dulles, would find in it positive elements. But Dulles had given no indication as to what the United States would do should the Arabs reject the plan.

The plan Dulles referred to had been in the works since late 1954, and it involved close collaboration between the United States and Britain.[7] In late November 1954, Dulles and Eden held informal talks in Paris on ways to bring about an end to the Arab-Israeli conflict.[8] The two countries named the project ALPHA for secrecy, and each established a team to explore various ideas and proposals.[9] Francis H. Russell was appointed by the secretary to head the State Department team. His selection indicated Dulles's attention to Israeli concerns, for Russell had not been known as an Arabist. In addition, his diplomatic service in Israel had acquainted him with that country's problems, and he had been sympathetic to Israel's predicament. Furthermore, his directives from Dulles included a proviso that any plan must take into account the deep friendship existing between Israel and the U.S. people. Every proposed solution must be practical and just. Russell's assignment included not only putting forth solutions, but also suggesting ways on how to bring the parties to the conflict to cooperate in implementing the proposed solutions, a tall order indeed.[10]

The British team was headed by Evelyn Shuckburgh, under secretary for Middle Eastern affairs in the British Foreign Office and favorable to the Arab point of view. During December 1954, he toured the Middle East and held discussions with Arab and Israeli officials. On January 19, 1955, he came to Washington and discussed his findings with U.S. officials. He suggested an Arab-Israeli settlement to be fashioned on the Trieste model. Accordingly, territorial changes—especially a retreat by Israel—were envisaged. On the Jordanian frontier, a series of border modifications would unite Arab villages with their lands, now in Israel; the bulk of the Latrun demilitarized area would go to Jordan, but the Old Jerusalem road would be given to Israel. The most significant territorial change would be in the south, where Israel would be asked to cede a portion of the Negev—a "corridor" providing a link between Egypt and Jordan. In addition, Israel would be asked to repatriate a number of Arab refugees, although the majority would be resettled in Arab lands. In Shuckburgh's view a peace settlement would provide Israel a list of benefits, among them security guarantees, trade opportunities with its neighbors, and an end to the Arab secondary boycott. To obtain these, he felt that Israel must make sacrifices. At this stage, however, the United States had not accepted British ideas of territorial concessions on Israel's part, but Israeli diplomats were aware that Shuckburgh's mission had not been a British initiative alone. Conscious of British ties with the Arabs, Israelis grew uneasy over Shuckburgh's diplomatic activity.[11]

Subsequently Russell traveled to London in February, continuing the discussions he had held with the British in Washington. Upon his return on February 14, in a memorandum to Dulles entitled "Operation ALPHA,"

Russell reported to the secretary about his conversations in London. The memorandum detailed the amounts of U.S. funding necessary to achieve a settlement. Russell inquired whether the president, jointly with the British, would be willing to guarantee the territorial stability of the area once a settlement was reached. In addition, Russell sought presidential approval of an increase in U.S. financial contributions to the Middle East from the present rate of about $100 million a year to $200 million—$1 billion over a period of five years.[12]

Surprised by the enormous amounts of foreign aid requests, the president was noncommittal. He promised to study the plan in detail and seek the views of Treasury and Budget. In the meantime, the president agreed that an all-out effort should be made to reach a settlement, if possible within the next two years.[13]

With the president's encouragement, Russell resumed discussions with the British in London. Agreement had been reached between the State Department and the British Foreign Office on the elements that would constitute an equitable settlement of the major issues between Israel and its Arab neighbors. Those issues included borders, refugee resettlement and compensation, Jerusalem, economic relations, Gaza, and Egyptian rights of transit across the Negev. A vital element in any settlement would include a guarantee by the United States and Britain of the borders between Israel and the neighboring Arab states. Furthermore, funds necessary to compensate the Arab refugees would have to be provided by the United States and Britain. Substantial economic and military assistance to the countries involved would also have to be seriously considered by the two Western powers.[14]

On May 5, the Under Secretary of State, Herbert Hoover, Jr., received a memorandum from Russell detailing the areas of agreement with the British. The same day, the president called Hoover to the White House to review the Russell memorandum known as the "ALPHA PROJECT." Accompanying Hoover were the Secretary of the Treasury, Douglas Dillon, and the Deputy Secretary of Defense, Robert B. Anderson. The president read Russell's memorandum out loud for Anderson's benefit. A brief discussion ensued in which the president discussed the "extreme difficulties" entailed in carrying out the project but became convinced that everything needed to be done to reach a successful conclusion.[15]

The ALPHA Project, a joint British-American plan, became the blueprint for U.S. proposals in solving the Arab-Israeli conflict. Those proposals were made public by the secretary of state on August 26, 1955, in a speech before the Council on Foreign Relations in New York.[16] As indicated earlier, the speech was the outcome of months of discussions with the president, and it had been approved by the NSC.[17] Reminding the audience that he spoke with full authority and approval of the president, Dulles first reviewed the situation in the Middle East since his fact-finding mission of May 1953. He then turned to the various components of the Arab-Israeli conflict. The secretary noted that Ambassador Johnston had been involved in efforts to devise a Jordan River Valley project but that "three problems remained to be solved . . . and if these three principal problems could be dealt with, then the way would be paved for a solution of others."

> The first is the tragic plight of the 900,000 refugees who formerly lived in the territory that is now occupied by Israel. The second is the pall of fear that hangs over the Arab and Israeli people alike. The Arab countries fear that Israel will seek by violent means to expand at their expense. The Israelis fear that the Arabs will gradually marshal superior forces to be used to drive them into the sea and they suffer from the economic measures now taken against them. The third is the lack of fixed permanent boundaries between Israel and its Arab neighbors.

Dulles suggested a multifaceted approach. The solution to the refugee problem should come through resettlement in Arab lands and, to the extent possible, repatriation, to enable the refugees to resume a life of dignity and self-respect. Both resettlement and repatriation, Dulles emphasized, would be facilitated by the creation of more arable land through various practical projects for water development. The necessary funds would be made available partly by the United States, and an international loan would be provided to Israel to compensate the refugees.[18]

Regarding the solution of the two other problems, Dulles was less specific. He suggested that the United States would be willing to assist the parties to the dispute to find a solution to the boundary problems, replacing the existing border fixed by the 1949 armistice agreements. Once a boundary settlement had been reached, the United States would join in formal treaty engagements to prevent or thwart any effort by either side to alter by force the agreed-upon boundaries between Israel and its Arab neighbors. The secretary expressed the hope that other powers under UN sponsorship would join such a security guarantee in providing collective measures to repel aggression.[19]

On the question of a security guarantee from the United States, Israel found little comfort in Dulles's address. Basing security arrangements on agreements that might or might not be reached was obviously another way of announcing that the United States was not prepared at present to enter into security arrangements with Israel alone. The Arabs, by withholding agreement, were in effect granted veto power on any future U.S. security treaty with Israel. According to Eban, Dulles could of course have offered security guarantees to all the states concerned. If some states were not interested in such a treaty and rejected the guarantees offered them, their refusal should not have prevented the United States from implementing its offer to any state interested and willing to enter into such a treaty relation. Or the United States could have guaranteed the present frontiers with automatic application to any subsequent change. The judicial status of a frontier or its alleged provisional character was no bar to treaty guarantees. The United States had treaties with Germany and Korea, although they aspired to far-reaching changes by unification.

Israeli leaders were anxious about the contents of the speech before its delivery. Early on August 26, Maxwell Rabb, secretary of the cabinet, called Reuven Shiloah from the White House, attempting to allay Israel's fears. (Shiloah was director of the Israeli Intelligence Service, MOSSAD, in 1951–52.) Aware of Rabb's concerns in regard to Israel, the president and Dulles conveyed to him that Israel's interests were taken into consideration in the preparation of the speech. Even though Israel objected to any territorial concession in the Negev, the secretary, said Rabb, believed that a solution could be found. Most important, Rabb continued, Israel should weigh very carefully its reactions and refrain from rejecting the proposals out of hand, given the president's personal attention and input.[20] Rabb found the secretary's address reassuring to Israel.[21]

Indeed, Dulles's speech constituted a cautious and moderate approach to a negotiated settlement, as well as a most generous offer to contribute money and assistance toward making peace possible. Israel could find a large measure of comfort in it, especially compared with the June 1953 speech in which Dulles focused on measures to defend the Middle East against outside influence, that is, communism. Now his emphasis was on regional development. In 1953, Dulles sought to allay Arab fears of a U.S. pro-Zionist policy and to downplay the role of the United States in the creation of Israel. Now his statement was far more balanced. It provided more substance in practical terms of U.S. encouragement toward cooperation and development in matters of health, communications, and other human services. In so doing, the secretary stressed the need for mutual recognition, a concept advocated all along by Israel.

What accounted for the change? It was a result in large measure of the departure of Henry A. Byroade to become ambassador to Egypt and his replacement by George V. Allen, who was more sympathetic to Israel. Furthermore, contrary to the conventional belief at the time, because of Dulles's attachment to the Bible and his religious upbringing, he felt a certain sympathy toward Israel and believed in its right to exist as a state. Above all, changes had taken place in the Arab world, especially the coming to power of Nasser in Egypt. His nationalistic policies and strong opposition to the Baghdad Pact had not endeared him to U.S. foreign policy makers.

But Dulles's proposals received little favorable response from any quarter in the Middle East. On August 29, Ben-Gurion, in an interview with the Jerusalem correspondent of the *Times* of London stated: "We can agree to no changes whatever in the present frontiers. We would be prepared to consider minor frontier corrections by mutual agreement, but as the result, not as the condition, of peace. There can only be peace with Israel as it exists geographically today." A few days earlier, on August 25, Sharett informed the U.S. Ambassador in Tel Aviv, Edward B. Lawson, that Dulles's statement contained suggestions of concessions by Israel that Israel was unable to make, leading to negative results both in terms of U.S.-Israeli relations and the prospects for peace with the Arabs. Sharett was "deeply apprehensive."[22]

On October 18, speaking in the Knesset, Sharett replied more specifically to Dulles's proposals. His statement, although more diplomatically phrased, was no more favorable than Ben-Gurion's earlier impromptu rejection. Referring to the positive aspects of Dulles's addresss, Sharett praised the secretary's suggestion of resettling the refugees in Arab countries. He also welcomed the secretary's pledge of U.S. willingness to participate in the resettlement of the refugees by granting a loan to Israel enabling it to carry out such a project. But Sharett found no satisfaction in the secretary's remarks about the borders between the Arab states and Israel. In his view, Dulles's remarks could "be interpreted as aiming at the contraction of Israel's territories in order to satisfy the expansive ambitions of the Arabs, particularly in the Negev including Eilat. We asserted in unequivocal terms that Israel was determined to preserve its territorial integrity from Dan to Eilat and that no unilateral concessions on its part were even conceivable."[23]

Dulles's proposals elicited no better response from the Arab side. The East Jerusalem daily newspaper, *Al Difaa,* gave the reaction typical of Arab opinion. The secretary's statement was a deliberate shift from UN decisions on boundaries and refugees; it was an imperalist attempt to secure Arab acceptance of Israel's existence. In Egypt, the government newspaper, *El Goumhouria,* commented that the Dulles plan was Republican propaganda for the forthcoming presidential elections. No Arab government, the paper stated, would agree to discuss the proposals, which were designed to serve no purpose other than the consolidation of Israel. In private, however, Nasser's reaction had not been totally negative. He did not reject the proposals outright, but found it doubtful whether Arabs would accept the dispersals of the refugees in many Arab states or that Ben-Gurion would be willing to relinquish the Negev or any part of it.[24]

Dulles had called for a peace based on compromise, but neither side in the conflict had been ready for a solution on that basis. Dulles tried to put a positive spin on the belligerents' reactions, stating in a message to the president that "the initial reaction in the Arab states to our Alpha project is not as violent against us as was feared . . . Israel and Jewish sentiment seems more favorable than anticipated. I am more than ever convinced that the move was a good one."[25] To the credit of U.S. diplomacy, the United States kept on trying to achieve what seemed in retrospect an elusive goal. The task proved all but impossible given the upsurge of violence in the region and the emergence of a new ominous development—the Egyptian-Soviet arms deal.

The Israeli raid on Kibya had been a watershed as far as retaliation against Jordan was concerned. In future raids particular care was taken by Israel to avoid killing women and children. As Walter Eytan noted, "Women and children have been killed at Kibya contrary to intention and there was never another Kibya. . . . Care was taken later to attack only police forces, military posts, and other such bases from which the raiders operated."[26] But despite world condemnation for the devastating raid, the defenders of the policy of retaliation could show that it had achieved its aim and that Jordanian authorities took stronger measures against infiltration. The number of Israelis killed in the areas bordering Jordan dropped steadily after the raid to thirty-four in 1954 and to eleven in 1955.[27]

As the clashes with Jordan began to subside, border violence shifted southward to the armistice line with Egypt, as reflected in the following UN report of casualties for the year 1955:[28]

Casualties	Jordan-Israel Front	Egypt-Israel Front
Israelis		
killed	8	47
wounded	30	118
Arabs		
killed	18	216
wounded	7	118

The armistice line along the Gaza Strip had been the scene of intermittent marauding, murder, theft, blowing up of pipelines by Arabs, and Israeli retaliation throughout the fall of 1954. On January 21, 1955, an Egyptian army unit crossed the border and attacked an Israel military outpost, killing three soldiers. The Israel-Egyptian MAC condemned the attack and remarked that the "armistice demarcation line was clearly marked near the place of the attack" and that the "aggressive action" was carried out by an Egyptian military patrol commanded by an officer. Three days later, an Egyptian armed band attacked the settlement of Ein Hashlosha and ambushed its farmers. In early February, Egyptian raiders penetrated thirty miles into Israeli territory, killing a cyclist near Rehovot. The MAC called upon the Egyptian authorities to "terminate immediately these aggressive actions by Egyptian military patrols and the continuous infiltration into Israel."[29]

Adding to the tension, the trial of Israel's eleven alleged spies opened in Cairo on December 11, 1954. It would last until January 5, 1955. Two of the accused were acquitted for lack of evidence, six were sentenced to prison terms of seven years to life, and the two leaders of the spy ring were sentenced to death and hanged. In Israel the trial caused great consternation, anger, and despair. Sharett labeled the proceedings calumnies designed to strike at the Jews in Egypt. A political anti-Semitic farce, cried the *Jerusalem Post*. In the meantime, Egypt continued to detain the Israeli ship *Bat Galim*, claiming a right to interdict ships passing through the Suez Canal flying the Israel flag, a claim in violation of a Security Council resolution of 1951 condemning such actions.[30]

From his "retirement" in S'deh Boker, Ben-Gurion watched these developments with dismay and trepidation. Unable to cope with constant crises, Sharett and top Mapai leaders went off to S'deh Boker on February 1, 1955, to seek counsel from the man who had already decided to return to power. Sharett asked the "Old Man" to return to the government as minister of defense, an offer Ben-Gurion accepted without hesitation, and on February 21, he took up the post. With Ben-Gurion at the helm of Israel's defense, the army would be brought back to the task of fighting. He was no longer prepared to tolerate repeated acts of Egyptian belligerence, including the closure of the Suez Canal to Israel-bound shipping, the ongoing blockade of the Gulf of Aqaba, and particularly the mounting cycle of Egyptian-directed *fedayeen* raids. Hence the biggest retaliatory raid since Kibya, this time against Egypt.

On February 28, a week after Ben-Gurion's return to office, the Israeli army launched a reprisal raid of brigade strength against Egyptian military headquarters in Gaza, blowing up a number of buildings, killing thirty-seven Egyptian soldiers, and wounding thirty-nine. Although the raid was described as a response to a succession of major Egyptian provocations, it was also intended to make plain to Nasser Israel's military superiority. "Israel's restraint has been misinterpreted by the Egyptians as a sign of weakness," Ben-Gurion told the *New York Times* correspondent in Tel Aviv. It was necessary to teach "Egypt a lesson, and indirectly, if possible, strike a blow to the 'ALPHA' project while still in its infancy."[31] But the operation had done more than that, perhaps far more than Ben-Gurion ever imagined. In large measure it set in motion a process that would bring the Soviet Union into the Middle East, creating new challenges for both the United States and Israel.[32]

Nasser was "cool under pressure, and extremely shrewd."[33] The Israeli attack served as an ideal occasion for the Egyptian leader to seek weapons from the United States. Such deliveries had been promised to him the previous November but were not carried out because of opposition from Israel and Britain. Fearing lest these weapons be used against British soldiers in the Suez Canal Zone, Churchill wrote directly to Eisenhower about his misgivings. "You can't give them arms with which to kill British soldiers who fought shoulder to shoulder with you in the war."[34] But the need for such weapons became especially acute for Nasser in view of Egypt's military weakness. Adding to Nasser's embarrassment, Israeli warplanes were flying over Cairo in the winter of 1955 publicly demonstrating Egyptian vulnerability.

Henry A. Byroade, the outspoken assistant secretary of state for Near Eastern affairs, left his post in Washington to become the U.S. ambassador in Cairo. Arriving there a day after the Gaza raid, he found the Egyptian leader in a very angry mood generated by the Israeli operation. When Byroade wanted to discuss regional problems and Soviet aims in the area, Nasser steered the conversation toward his need for weapons. They were indispensable, he stressed, to make it possible for Egypt to stand up to the Israelis and to quiet the growing restlessness in the army. Nor would he make peace with Israel out of fear. Byroade, who took a personal liking to Nasser, sympathized with his arguments and recommended that $27 million worth of weapons promised previously by Eisenhower to Egypt be honored.[35] In the ensuing negotiations the United States offered the weapons to Egypt free of charge, provided a U.S. delegation trained the Egyptians in their use. Furthermore, the United States demanded a commitment that the weapons be used only in self-defense, as well as an Egyptian alliance with the free world in case of Communist aggression. The Egyptians, however, preferred to pay for the weapons rather than accept these conditions. They viewed the supply of weapons as a commercial transaction, while the United States sought to reap political benefits for the West in its struggle with the Soviet Union. Ultimately, the negotiations reached an impasse. Although the Egyptian request was not officially turned down, the United States continued to stall. An exasperated Nasser blamed Jewish and Zionist influence in the United States and gave up any hope of obtaining U.S. arms.[36]

On June 9, Nasser informed Byroade about his talks with the Soviets concerning the purchase of arms. In Washington, the State Department reacted with levity bordering on indifference, believing that Nasser was bluffing, attempting to pit one superpower against the other in order to gain concessions from both. To Eisenhower it seemed suspiciously like blackmail, but with the advantage of hindsight "our attitude . . . appeared to have been unrealistic." Nasser was not bluffing. Byroade, citing the despair the Gaza raid caused in Egyptian military circles, urged immediate approval of U.S. military sales, lest the Soviet Union preempt the United States and achieve a tremendous political victory.[37]

On May 23, the Soviet Ambassador to Egypt, Daniel Solod, had already offered Nasser arms as well as technical and economic assistance, including the financing of the Aswan Dam. If Egypt objected to the presence of Soviet personnel on its territory, the ambassador suggested that the Soviet Union would work through the United Nations. Nasser declined the offer but inquired whether the Soviets would barter heavy artillery for cotton. Solod replied in the affirmative and indicated that shipments might be made within six weeks. Czechoslovakia, he said, would deliver military planes in exchange for cotton.[38]

On June 16, when Dimitri Shepilov, the Soviet foreign minister, visited Cairo, he discussed with Nasser the types and quantities of weapons, terms of delivery, and payments. He offered Egypt hundreds of MIG fighter planes, two hundred tanks, and jet bombers (SC 28s) in exchange for cotton.[39] A tentative agreement was concluded. On July 20, an Egyptian military delegation flew to Prague, Czechoslovakia, to conclude the final details of the arms deal with their Russian counterparts. At the Russians' suggestion, the Egyptians agreed to the fiction that Czechoslovakia was going to provide the weapons, thereby making it possible for the Soviets to deny their role in the arms deal. On the same day, Byroade alarmed the State Department: "Egypt will most probably accept the Russian offer of arms. These purchases made possible as payment acceptable in cotton." He blamed Egypt's move on Israel. "Israeli action in Gaza . . . precipitated Nasser's decision to procure arms."[40]

By mid-September, Nasser's flirtation with the Soviets changed the mood in Washington from indifference to utmost concern. On September 19, Byroade received the following telegram from Dulles: "In your discretion you may advise Egyptian Gov't. that consumation of agreement . . . would create most serious public reaction in United States and greatly complicate our ability to cooperate with him."[41] Byroade cabled back and pleaded for a U.S. counteroffer. Herbert Hoover, Jr., replied that any U.S. credit or arms to Egypt would depend on Nasser's favorable response to ALPHA, that is, peace with Israel.[42] In addition, supplying arms to Egypt might set off an arms race between Israel and the Arab states. Byroade was livid. The free world was about to lose its foothold in the Arab Middle East, and at the State Department they worried about the possibility of peace between Israel and Egypt.

On September 20, Dulles met with the Soviet Foreign Minister, Vyacheslav M. Molotov, in New York, where both were attending the opening of the UN session. With his Russian counterpart, Dulles took up the question of Soviet weapons sales to Egypt. Molotov admitted that an arms deal with the Egyptians had been agreed upon but insisted that "we are doing it on a commercial basis and there are no political implications and no political ambitions in that area." Dulles did not go along with Molotov's explanation. Soviet weapons, he charged, "would change the balance of power. A dangerous situation could be created if the Arabs felt they could destroy Israel or vice versa." It could lead to war, Dulles warned. In such a situation, the United States would not remain an uninterested bystander. Molotov, who did not share Dulles's concerns, repeated his previous assertion. To Dulles, however, Molotov seemed to evade the issue.[43]

In a telephone conversation with the president on September 23, Dulles reported, "We had a little rough time in New York with Molotov . . . they are giving a massive lot of arms to the Egyptians theoretically to be paid for with cotton. It is $100 million worth." Dulles thought the Israelis "would want to attack first because they can lick them easily. We could counter it with a collective security arrangement in advance of any agreement with the Arabs but that would throw the Arabs in the hands of the Soviets." The secretary wondered whether a personal appeal by the president to the Soviet Prime Minister, Nikolai Bulganin, was justified, but he had no final recommendation to make for the president.[44]

On September 27, Nasser announced publicly that he had completed an arms deal with Czechoslovakia after futile attempts to receive weapons from the West. The arms transaction, he said, was a straight barter "on a purely commercial basis by which Egyptian cotton and rice would be exchanged for arms and ammunition." It was a historic breakthrough for the Russians. "We must regard the Egyptian arms deal as a very serious step toward the penetration of the western position in the Arab world. The arrival of Soviet arms with technicians in Cairo . . . would lead to a grave threat to the ultimate security of the Suez Canal and the Middle East as a whole. The United States and British ambassadors in Cairo should protest vigorously," said Dulles.[45]

An outraged Dulles rushed Assistant Secretary of State for Near Eastern Affairs George V. Allen to Cairo with an ultimatum threatening U.S. reprisals should Nasser go through with the deal. Fearing that the ultimatum might backfire and lead Nasser to break off diplomatic relations with the United States, it was not delivered. Instead, Allen tried to convince Nasser about the dangers involved in introducing weapons into the region, pointing to rising tensions and the possibility of all-out war. But the Egyptian leader complained about Israel's military superiority and what he believed to be U.S. partiality toward Israel.[46] Although Allen failed in his attempt to bring about a cancellation of the arms deal, he nevertheless extracted a promise from Nasser that no Soviet technicians or instructors from the Soviet bloc would be allowed to enter Egypt. Nasser did not explain how the Egyptian army would absorb quantities of weapons without the necessary training.[47]

Was there a cause-and-effect relationship between Israel's retaliation policy and Egypt's decision to acquire the massive Soviet armaments via Czechoslovakia? This question remained debatable. Nasser emphasized Israel's role in his decision, but it was no secret that he had requested U.S. arms under the Mutual Security Program even before the Gaza raid. Only after he found the terms offered to him unsatisfactory had he turned to the Soviet Union, something he would have done for another reason—the Baghdad Pact. Iraq's adherence to a Western-inspired military alliance challenged Nasser's leadership in the Arab world. That in itself was incentive enough for accumulating military power, Israel's raid on Gaza notwithstanding. Since the pact had been a Western initiative, resentment toward it provided Nasser with sufficient motive to turn for arms to the Soviet Union, whom he found more than willing to oblige.[48]

The Soviet Union, which looked at the Baghdad Pact as a provocation, naturally found Nasser's consternation an excellent opportunity for exploitation. In fact, the interests of Nasser and the Soviet Union interlocked. Where Nasser viewed the Soviet arms as an answer to Israel's military superiority, the Soviets were far more interested in rewarding him for his opposition to the Baghdad Pact, thereby gaining a foothold in the region and achieving a historic goal. Perhaps the best interpretation for Nasser's move is that the two events—the Gaza raid and the signing of the Baghdad Pact—coming as they did within a few days of each other had a cumulative effect on the Egyptian leader. The Iraqi-Turkish pact was signed on February 24, 1955, and the Gaza raid occurred on February 28. Each event in its own way impacted on Nasser's thinking and subsequent actions. Through the arms deal, Nasser brought the Soviet Union into the Middle East, thus transforming a local conflict into an East-West confrontation. The way had been opened for great power competition in feeding the local arms race because the West could no longer regulate the supply of arms to Arabs and Israelis, as envisaged in the tripartite declaration of May 25, 1950.[49] To the chagrin of the United States, the era of tripartite diplomacy had come to an end.

Furthermore, the Egyptian-Czech arms deal affected the Arab-Israeli power relationship. Until now, both Egypt and Israel lacked allies among the major powers. But by the end of 1955 Egypt could count on the Soviet Union as its ally. Israel's strategy was based on the premise that its own military power was sufficient to face the Arabs alone but not a combination of Arab and outside powers. The entrance of the Soviet Union into the Middle East presented an ominous challenge to Israeli military superiority. The arms to be supplied to Egypt would be sufficient to give Egypt considerable technical superiority in tanks, artillery, and fighter and bomber aircraft. The acquisition of Ilyushin jet bombers was particularly alarming to the Israelis because these aircraft could bomb cities from a height Israel Meteor jet fighters could not reach. And the Meteors would be outmaneuvered as fighters by the MIG 15's that the Egyptian air force would receive.

The danger, however, was not immediate. High-ranking U.S. officers, as well as General Eedson Louis Burns, head of UNTSO in the Middle East, estimated that it would take the Egyptian army at least two years to master its newly acquired weapons and be ready for offensive action. Moreover, the weapons could not compensate for the lack of morale, training, and discipline within the Egyptian army. According to the U.S. Joint Chiefs of Staff, the new Egyptian edge in the quantity and quality of armaments did not eliminate Israel's advantage in training, organization, and morale.[50] Even so, Israel's fears were real enough. The rearmament of

Egypt was seen in terms of how quickly the Egyptian forces, with their superior technical equipment, would be able to launch a war of annihilation against Israel.

The problem facing the Israeli leadership was how to react to the new situation.[51] Given the temporary respite before Egypt fully absorbed the new arms, how best to utilize that remaining time? What choices were open? Although the dangers were not immediate, the public perception in Israel was of imminent destruction by the Arab states. A back-to-the-wall psychology engulfed the entire nation. Thousands of worried and frightened Israelis answered appeals for money needed to buy armaments, donating part of their monthly salaries, jewelry, and other valuables to the government for the purchase of arms. Tens of thousands of volunteers, young and old, took up picks and shovels to dig trenches and prepare fieldworks.

In that gloom-and-doom atmosphere, the government decided on two courses of action, diplomatic and military. First, Israel would demonstrate to the great powers, and especially to the United States, its vulnerability, justifying the delivery of arms and a guarantee of territorial integrity. At the same time Ben-Gurion seriously considered the war option—a preemptive attack on Egypt before it could assimilate the huge quantities of Soviet weapons.

Sharett, in his last days as prime minister, in late October carried the diplomatic torch to Geneva, where the Big Four foreign ministers had convened. His aim was to make a dramatic bid for weapons for Israel in private meetings with Western foreign ministers, and perhaps to succeed in convincing Molotov to cancel the arms deal with Egypt.

In a ninety-minute conversation with Dulles on October 26, and in a subsequent meeting on October 30, Sharett surveyed the situation in the Middle East in light of recent developments and the dangers they posed for Israel, the Middle East, and the world. On a global level, a new factor entered the region with "disturbing effects on its equilibrium." The United States, Sharett advised Dulles, "should reach the conclusion that relaxation of tension is indivisible . . . the Soviets should be confronted with a clear choice, either apply detente everywhere or have the West lose faith in their basic sincerity." As to Nasser, he should be faced with a clear choice: renounce the arms deal or lose Western aid. He should not have it both ways, because, if he did, Nasser and the Arab world would conclude that his rapprochement with the Soviets could be emulated without adverse Western reaction. Israel, Sharett continued, "faced grave perils." For in addition to the earlier Egyptian preponderance in military might, the new arms deal "overwhelmingly will increase Nasser's strength," making all the more possible his goal: the destruction of Israel. Sharett hoped that the situation would not deteriorate to the extent that Israel might feel compelled to preempt an Egyptian attack. To remedy the situation, the Israeli prime minister demanded, first, "arms which we need urgently, and second quick unconditional action on a security treaty with the United States."

Dulles agreed with Sharett's assessment of the implications that Soviet arms might have in the region and the tension they would create between East and West. But he took issue with Israel's contention that the Turkish-Iraqi Pact—the Baghdad Pact—led Nasser to seek arms from the Soviet bloc. In fact, in an earlier news conference held in Washington on October 4, Dulles could not bring himself to condemn the Egyptian action. Alluding to Israel's retaliatory raid on Gaza, Dulles said, "It is difficult to be critical of countries which, feeling themselves endangered, seek the arms which they sincerely need for defense."[52] To Sharett's disappointment, Dulles turned down any idea that pressure on Nasser would bring a change in his policy. "Nasser would not yield and western aid was not sufficiently decisive to make him renounce the deal to which he is committed." But most discouraging to Sharett was Dulles's disagreement with Israel's contention about Egypt's military superiority now or in the future. According to the secretary, "Pentagon and U.S. Intelligence had different figures which do not bear out the belief in Egyptian superiority . . . the new arms deal certainly gave rise to anxiety but whether that would cause decisive Israeli inferiority was not clear." Even if Egypt got all the arms promised and would be able to use them, "how many would be killed flying these planes?" asked Dulles. In short, the secretary did not view the situation as alarming, as did Israel. That meant that Israel's hope for a change in U.S. policy on the two key questions, arms and a defense treaty, was far from being realized. The secretary did not exclude the sale of arms to Israel on a "moderate basis" but nothing in the way of matching the Soviet deliveries to Egypt. "We cannot promote an arms race in the area," said Dulles. The secretary reiterated the longstanding U.S. policy toward Israel: "No attempt to destroy or disrupt Israel would be possible without strong United States reaction." Aware of calls in Israel for a "preventive war," Dulles coupled his reassurance with an implied warning: "Israel should not draw the conclusion that the only security lay in preventive war. Such war could not solve any problems even if Israel won. Any initiative of Israel would seriously embarrass the United States whose policy statements were conceived on basic opposition to any aggression."[53]

The secretary did not wish to threaten, but he had to point out that the United States could not help a country that went against a basic policy principle of nonuse of force. Sharett chose to accentuate the positive. Taking off from Dulles's comment about possible delivery of U.S. weapons of a defensive nature, Sharett stated that during his upcoming trip to Washington he would submit a list of weapons for defense purposes to be purchased from the United States such as antiaircraft, antitank radar, and antisubmarine equipment. Dulles seemed sympathetic but noncommittal.[54] To the secretary, a peaceful settlement of the Arab-Israeli conflict was most urgent. Getting ALPHA off the ground while Nasser had not yet absorbed the new Soviet military equipment was the best answer to the new situation.[55]

If Sharett could draw only limited satisfaction from his conversations with Dulles and Harold Macmillan, the British foreign secretary, talking with Molotov proved to be far worse. Throughout the discussion Sharett attempted to convince the Soviet foreign minister to at least limit the amount of weapons scheduled for delivery to Egypt. Eban, who accompanied Sharett throughout his diplomatic venture to Geneva, commented: "Molotov was unresponsive to the point of rudeness. . . . He obviously regarded Israel's intrusion in Geneva as irrelevant. The issue was not Israel but America and Russia." Besides, the Soviet foreign minister asserted, the arms sale was a pure commercial transaction between Egypt and Czechoslovakia.[56] Molotov later remarked to Dulles, "Sharett was somewhat passionate in his presentation and [I] wondered how strong a character he was."[57] So far it had been a lonely pursuit for Sharett, a hat-in-hand diplomatic journey that gained Israel a degree of sympathy in Western public opinion but little else.

The Israelis had better luck in their discussions with French leaders. The French Prime Minister, Edgar Faure, promised quick delivery to Israel of advanced Mystère IV jets. Antoine Pinay, the foreign minister, was even more forthcoming, informing Sharett that France would fulfill all Israel's requests in weapons deliveries.[58] Pinay did not conceal his aversion to Nasser, who undermined French rule in Algeria by publicly supporting the anti-French rebels with weapons as well as political support. Nasser's support of the Algerian independence movement had alarmed the French, for it aimed at ending the French presence in North Africa, thereby removing once and for all any illusion that France could retain its position as a global power. Even though Israel was admired by large segments of the French public, the enmity that both Israel and France felt towards Nasser bound the two countries in what amounted to a tacit alliance.

Actually, a tacit special relationship between France and Israel could be traced back as far as Israel's inception as a state. French-Israeli scientific contacts began early in 1949, when an Israeli physicist, Israel Dostrofsky, had invented a technique for producing heavy water. No sooner had France acquired the technique, it secretly opened many of its own nuclear installations to Israeli physicists.[59] The same year, Israel began receiving 155-mm Howitzers as well as light arms.[60] In addition, many naval officers and members of the French interior and defense ministries were anti-British and violently anti-Arab. They admired the valor of the Israeli army and were convinced that the Arab defeat in 1948 had delayed an anti-French rebellion in North Africa by ten years. In subsequent years both Israel and the French Right were fearful of the threat posed by rising Arab nationalism. At the same time the French Left had historically maintained a pro-Jewish sympathy dating back to the Dreyfus Affair. That sympathy was transferred to Israel and solidified by the Socialist regimes in both countries.

In late July 1954, Israel's Chief of Staff, Moshe Dayan, was invited to Paris on an official visit by his counterpart General Augustin Guillaume. The agreements signed included the purchase by Israel of Ouragon jet fighters, Mystère IIs (with an option on twelve Mystère IVs), AMX tanks, radar equipment, 75-mm cannon, antitank missiles, and other weapons.[61] Dayan's visit coincided with a deterioration in French-Egyptian relations, as Radio Cairo kept broadcasting effusive praise and promises of support to the rebel Algerian Front de Libération Nationale (FLN). By October 1955 arrangements were completed for the shipment to Israel of additional Ouragons and, for the first time, twelve of the new Mystère IV fighters, which were considered the equal of the MIG 17s the Egyptians were receiving from the Soviets.[62]

This secret alliance was well known to the Pentagon and the Central Intelligence Agency (CIA). In fact, according to the tripartite declaration of May 25, 1950, detailed requests for arms under the terms of the declaration were handled by the Near Eastern Arms Coordinating Committee, composed of representatives of the three signatories, which had monitored the flow of arms to the area since 1950. The signatories customarily kept one another informed about arms shipments to the Middle East. Even though the arms the Israelis received went beyond the type envisioned in the tripartite declaration, the United States preferred to look the other way. The Franco-Israeli arrangement suited U.S. purposes, for it could now turn down repeated Israeli requests for weapons without endangering Israeli security, while at the same time preserving Arab friendship.[63] Dulles summarized that approach in a cable to the president from Geneva.

> I told Sharett in substance that nothing had yet happened that leads us to feel that we had to abandon our basic policies of friendship for both Jews and Arabs, avoidance of an arms race and aggression by each side. Sharett is not happy but the stakes are too high for us to be guided by domestic political considerations. We do not want to lose Arab good will unless the Arabs themselves in conspiracy with the Soviets force this result upon us. I am not without hope that the situation will work out.[64]

On November 10, Sharett arrived in the United States for a prolonged tour for the United Jewish Appeal and Israel Bonds.[65] The visit provided an auspicious occasion to press the Israeli case for U.S. arms and a security guarantee. But Dulles saw the visit as an attempt by Sharett "to go over the heads of our government and my position which I announced to him into a policy of supporting Israel to a degree and manner which will surely antagonize the entire Arab world and allow the Soviet Union to become dominant in the area." From Geneva he dispatched a telegram to Hoover and urged him to contact the president immediately to issue a statement in line with Dulles's approach to the Israeli request.[66] The president, after close consultation with the State Department, issued a statement: "While we continue willing to consider requests for arms needed for legitimate self-defense, we do not intend to contribute to an arms competition in the Middle East because we do not think that such a race would be in the true interests of any of the participants. The policy which we believe would best promote the interests and the security of the peoples of the area was expressed in the Tripartite Declaration of May 25, 1950. This still remains our policy." As to Israel's request for a security pact the president referred to Dulles's speech of August 26: "On that occasion, I authorized Mr. Dulles to state that, given a solution of other problems, I would recommend that the United States join in informal treaty engagements to prevent or thwart any effort by either side to alter by force the boundaries between Israel and its Arab neighbors."[67]

In what must have been more than a coincidence, on the same day, November 9, the British Prime Minister, Anthony Eden, also called on Israel and its Arab neighbors to settle their border dispute and in return offered a British guarantee. During the annual Guildhall speech in London, Eden suggested that the two sides compromise between the borders established by the 1947 UN resolution plan and the larger boundaries claimed by Israel in the 1949 armistice accords following the war. Eden suggested finding a middle ground between the Arab demand for a return to the 1947 borders and the Israeli insistence on maintaining the 1949 status quo. At Geneva, the British Foreign Secretary, Harold Macmillan, showed Dulles the text of the speech before its delivery. Dulles agreed with the tenor of the speech as long as it supported his own August 26 address.[68]

To Israel, Dulles's August 26 address and Eisenhower and Eden's statements of November 9 taken together seemed suspiciously like a joint Anglo-American effort to impose a solution on the Middle East. Lest Eden's proposals assume a life of their own, they had to be rejected by Israeli leaders out of hand. And so they were. On November 15, Ben-Gurion in a speech to the Knesset vehemently attacked the proposals because "they tended to truncate the territory of Israel for the benefit of her neighbors, hence had no legal, moral or logical basis and cannot be considered." Forgotten by Eden, said Ben-Gurion, was the fact that Israel's 1949 frontiers came as a result of a war of annihilation that the Arab states waged on the tiny state and lost. Israel, he stated, was willing to go along with the concept of minor border rectification but not with what amounted to territorial concessions.[69]

Eden's speech highlighted the urgent need for a settlement of the Arab-Israeli conflict in order to stem the Soviet advance in the Middle East in the aftermath of the Egyptian-Czech arms deal. Dulles shared that view and also believed that Nasser could still be steered toward the West, provided Israel did not carry out a preemptive strike, which in Dulles's opinion would drive Egypt further into Soviet arms.[70] Nor was the time appropriate for a commitment to sell weapons to Israel, even though the secretary promised Sharett to give such a request "sympathetic consideration."[71]

The course chosen by the president and Dulles, with British cooperation, had been an intensification of diplomatic activity aimed at achieving a resolution of Arab-Israeli conflict. Dulles's speech of August 26 and the proposals therein became the basis for a major diplomatic offensive.

On November 9, Hoover traveled to Denver to see the president and brief him on the talks at Geneva. They then discussed the status of ALPHA. Hoover advised the president that the State Department had recommended Robert B. Anderson, the former deputy secretary of defense, as an intermediary between Egypt and Israel. His objectives—"to try and bring Nasser back on track" and attempt to bring peace in the area by reviving the ALPHA project. Eisenhower commented on Anderson's selection, "You certainly picked a good one."[72]

In Cairo, on November 17, Byroade met with the Egyptian Foreign Minister, Mahmud Fawzi. The Egyptian welcomed U.S. and British attempts to bring peace. He insisted that the initial moves should be highly secretive through diplomatic channels, with indirect or direct contacts with Israel at a later stage. Byroade was encouraged to note that Fawzi did not insist on Israel's return of the "whole of the Negev" and never mentioned the UN resolution of 1947 as the basis for a settlement. At the same time, Fawzi did not believe that a "corridor" would suffice to bring about contiguity between Egypt and Jordan. From his perspective, the size of territory to be transferred by Israel need not be defined at this stage; only agreement in principle should be sought. Byroade believed that the gap between the Israeli and Egyptian positions could eventually be narrowed. Some middle ground could be found that both sides might "reluctantly" accept.[73]

With Egypt's apparent flexibility assured, the pressure was now turned on Israel. On November 21, Dulles met Sharett at the State Department.

The Israeli foreign minister came to discuss his country's request for arms and a security guarantee, but Dulles wanted none of the above. What he was mostly interested in was launching the ALPHA project. The secretary stated that a settlement of the principal issues of the Arab-Israeli dispute rather than arms was essential to the long-term survival of Israel. The quest for a settlement had become all the more urgent in view "of the apparent intention of the Soviet Government now to seek for its own purposes to implement Arab hostility to Israel." The first requirement in achieving a settlement remained the responsibility of the "governments concerned to do everything in their power to maintain calm along the armistice lines even in face of provocation." Aware of Israeli plans to remove by force if necessary the Egyptian blockade at the Straits of Tiran, Dulles warned Israel "not to seek . . . the settlement of specific issues by force, such as the right of transit in the Gulf of Aqaba." As to territorial adjustments, those might include "concessions in the Negev to provide an Arab area joining Egypt with the rest of the Arab world. These concessions need not, as we see it, involve loss of any appreciably populated land or land of any substantial economic value . . . the position of rigidly standing on the present armistice is not tenable . . . the Arabs will have to retreat some from their positions, so will the Israeli Government." In blunt language Dulles told Sharett: "We must know if Israel is flexible and willing to cooperate, make concessions or not. If 'no' is the last word, then Israel is in peril." Israel, said Sharett, could not make the concessions asked by the secretary. Dulles retorted that "Israel would probably possess less square miles than before, however, this would be compensated, because what Israel might lose in territory it would gain in real security if a settlement were reached." Dulles would not take Sharett's no for an answer. He wanted an Israeli reply in writing within a few days.[74]

Dulles's remarks were immediately conveyed to Jerusalem. When Ben-Gurion read the secretary's proposals, he commented defiantly that Dulles did not suggest any concessions on the part of the Arabs. Israel would not use force in removing the blockade at the Straits of Tiran, provided Egypt did not interfere with freedom of passage of vessels bound for Israel. However, any territorial concession in the Negev, whether populated or not, was out of the question. Concerning peace, Israel was ready to discuss mutual adjustments of the armistice frontiers on the basis of reciprocity. Compensation would be given to Arab refugees, provided they settled in the Arab countries. And, in what was a new demand, Ben-Gurion raised for the first time the issue of compensation to be provided to Jewish refugees who were forced to leave the Old City of Jerusalem, the Etzion Bloc, N've Yaakov, and Naharaim. The Arabs, he said, as a goodwill gesture, must immediately cease the economic boycott and blockades of Israel. Most important: "There is no point in discussing peace now or in the future as long as the United States would not balance the gap in weapons between Israel and Egypt."[75]

On December 6, Sharett presented Dulles an aide-mémoire essentially containing the points made by Ben-Gurion. In face-to-face talks with the secretary, Sharett did not repeat all the conditions Ben-Gurion had set for peace with the Arab states, fearing a rebuff from the United States that might jeopardize any hopes of receiving any kind of U.S. arms. Instead, Sharett focused on the dangers that Soviet arms posed for Israel as well as on the negative impact of relinquishing any territory in the Negev to Egypt. It would mean the abandonment of the southern Israeli port of Eilat, the loss of access to the Red Sea and mineral resources. He accentuated the positive elements that would accrue to the Arab states by making peace with Israel without necessitating concessions on Israel's part—for example, Israel would be willing to contribute substantially to the opening of freer communications between all states in the Near East in order to enhance the economic strength and commercial transactions in the region and to promote political and cultural understanding between the peoples of the area. All of these conditions could be enhanced, according to Sharett, by providing for communication by air and rail between Egypt and Lebanon via Israel and by providing port facilities in Haifa for the kingdom of Jordan, including transit rights by road to and from the port, and a transit arrangement to be agreed to by Israel for communications between Egypt and the kingdom of Jordan, on condition that Israel would not cede territory whether populated or unpopulated in the Negev. On the basis of mutuality, the freedom of transit for Arab traffic between Egypt and Lebanon would entail corresponding freedom for Israeli traffic northwards over Lebanon and southwards over Egypt. Similarly, if Jordan were to have free access to and from Haifa and port facilities therein, it should agree to restore free access to the Western Wall, the Mount of Olives, and Mount Scopus. Israel, said Sharett, would not cede territory. Israel would agree to territorial "adjustments" which would be "mutual, minor, a result of give and take." Sharett concluded his remarks with a familiar demand: weapons for self defense, because without them Arab intransigence and Israeli apprehensions would grow, "thereby making any discussion towards peace futile."[76]

Dulles reiterated his belief in the possibility of an equitable settlement and hoped that Israel would not foreclose it. Sharett persisted in his demand for arms and inquired whether the United States had studied the list of Israel's arms requests, especially jet aircraft. Dulles replied that the arms Israel requested were available and that price tags were put on them. The nature of the reply would have to be studied carefully and would probably be given a week later. Sharett, hoping for an affirmative reply, delayed his departure from Washington so as to receive the "good news" directly.[77]

Despite Sharett's misgivings, Dulles would not give up on ALPHA. The State Department proceeded with attempts to prod Israel toward a settlement. Francis Russell, who together with Shuckburgh authored the ALPHA Project, had a major impact on Dulles's August 26 speech. Sympathetic to the Jewish state, Russell tried to convince Israel of the fairness of the U.S. approach and the urgency of reaching a settlement.

On December 8, Russell invited Reuven Shiloah for a discussion of the overall situation and to present in detail the views of the secretary of state regarding a settlement of the Arab-Israeli dispute. According to Russell, the United States aimed at direct negotiations between Israel and her neighbors. At this stage, however, indirect negotiations would have to be conducted through a mediator acceptable to both sides. The Egyptian-Czech arms deal did not change the secretary's views on how to reach a settlement. On the contrary, the secretary, said Russell, had decided to intensify the process of reaching that goal, for obvious reasons. Russell expressed the opinion that Arab leaders were more amenable to a settlement than ever before. For example, Nuri es-Said, the prime minister of Iraq, had promised the United States to avoid criticizing Nasser should he enter into an agreement with Israel. Such opportunities, said Russell, must not be missed. The State Department, accordingly, had concluded that eight major issues must be dealt with: the refugee problem, Jerusalem, boycotts and blockades, transportation, the Johnston water project, territorial issues, termination of the state of belligerency, and territorial guarantees.

On the question of refugees, Russell asserted that the United States accepted the Israeli contention that the overwhelming majority must be settled in Arab countries where the chances of absorption were the least complicated given the affinity of language, culture, and traditions. But for political reasons and as a matter of principle, Israel too must contribute to the solution of the problem by accepting a certain number, perhaps 75,000 refugees to be absorbed at a rate of 15,000 a year. More important than the numbers would be Israel's readiness to contribute toward a solution of the problem. Israel should assume the responsibility of compensating the refugees for the real property they had left behind. The United States and other countries would assist Israel financially in that endeavor, but Israel and world Jewry would have to contribute their share.

On Jerusalem, the United States actually accepted the Israeli position. It would recognize Israeli and Jordanian sovereignty in the respective parts of the city under their jurisdiction. The part of Jerusalem under Israeli rule would be recognized by the United States as Israel's capital, and the United States would insist on free access for Israelis to the Western Wall and Mount Scopus, now under Jordanian rule. This was a departure from previous U.S. policy on Jerusalem—indeed, a significant step toward the Israeli position.

On the question of boycotts and blockades, the United States would demand from the Arabs a cessation of both and free passage by Israeli ships through the Suez Canal and the Gulf of Aqaba. In other words, the United States accepted Israel's position regarding the principle of free transit and communications as proposed by Sharett. Russell added that Egypt and Jordan would be advised to open to traffic two highways linking Cairo with Beersheba, and Jerusalem with Amman, Jordan.

On the very intractable problem concerning frontiers and territorial adjustments, here too the U.S. position moved closer to that held by Israel. The United States favored abolition of all demilitarized zones between the neighboring countries. Reciprocal adjustments would take place: Jordan would be asked to give up part of the Latrun salient in order to make it possible to reconnect the old Tel Aviv–Jerusalem highway. On the Negev issue, Russell proposed to reconcile Israel's vital interests in maintaining its territorial integrity and hold on Eilat, with the need of providing "an Arab area joining Egypt with the rest of the Arab world." He suggested the idea of triangles of territory in the southern Negev—one to be ceded to Egypt, the other to Jordan—both meeting at a point of intersection through which Israel's communications would run. Russell concluded by emphasizing Dulles's promise of territorial guarantees by the United States once agreements ending the state of belligerency were reached. He reiterated the urgency to reach an agreement because "the Soviet Union increases its penetration into the region hour by hour and we might risk missing perhaps the last opportunity to forestall that process."[78]

But Sharett, in line with Ben-Gurion's directive, would not budge from Israel's stated position. On December 12, before his departure from the United States, Sharett commented on Russell's ideas in a letter to Dulles. Ignoring the important areas in which the United States found common ground with Israel, he again focused on the future of the Negev, rejecting any proposal that might entail territorial concession. Eilat, he declared, even under Russell's suggestion, "would be left hanging at the end of a slender thread, which the Egyptians and the Jordanians would be in a position to snap at any moment from scissor-like position which they would acquire." Communications with the port city would be very precarious. Economic development at Eilat or in the parts of the Negev adjoining the Arab triangles would be discouraged at best and paralyzed at worst, due to the "proximity of these two wedges of foreign territory." Sharett also took issue with any suggestion of accepting Arab refugees, even as a symbolic gesture, for economic and political reasons. He repeated the often-stated Israeli solution to the Arab refugees: resettlement in Arab countries and compensation for properties they left behind in Israel. Sharett concluded by making another appeal for U.S. weapons. The Israeli and U.S. policies thus seemed to be at loggerheads, the former emphasizing military strength and the preservation of the status quo, the latter focusing on diplomacy and mutual concessions by all sides to achieve a settlement.

Even so, the Israeli request for U.S. weapons was given serious consideration by the administration. And, based on his conversations with Dulles of December 6, Sharett had good reason to expect an affirmative answer, he hoped before his departure to Israel. Indeed, on December 8,

1955, Dulles discussed the subject with the president, and they agreed in principle to provide Israel with defensive weapons. To make the U.S. action less subject to Arab criticism, Dulles would at the same time announce weapons for Iraq and Saudi Arabia as well as financial assistance to Egypt in building the Aswan Dam.[79] But on December 11, without consulting the cabinet, Ben-Gurion gave the final order for a devastating attack against Syria, citing Syrian attacks a day before on an Israeli fishing boat. Israeli troops struck Syrian military outposts and civilian homes at Buteiha, Farm, and Koursi on the slopes of Mount Hermon, north of Lake Tiberias (Kinneret). The attack left fifty-six Syrian soldiers and five civilians dead. Thirty Syrians were taken prisoner. Regardless of whether the raid had any justification, its timing had not raised Israel's stock in Washington. Just the opposite. It undermined Sharett's diplomatic effort and confirmed Dulles's long-held view of Israeli military superiority vis-à-vis the Arabs. Moreover, on December 13, Allen informed Eban that the United States could not reach a decision on arms to Israel at this time for a number of reasons, "prominent among them being the recent incident on the Syrian border."[80]

No doubt the ideas put forth by Russell were the most far-reaching and detailed proposals ever submitted by the United States. They were fair and balanced, and they went a long way in satisfying many of Israel's demands. The problem for Israel rested with the request for territorial concessions, perhaps not as painful as described by Sharett, but nonetheless significant, without any tangible evidence that the Arabs or Egypt, in particular, were genuinely interested in a settlement of their conflict with Israel. The West, and particularly the United States, having forgiven Nasser for his arms deal with the Soviets, the Egyptian leader found it to be in his interest to talk settlement in order to get the Aswan loan from the United States and Britain. Moreover, he would also gain time to absorb his new arms in order to achieve military confidence and even superiority over Israel.[81] But even if negotiations began on the basis of U.S. proposals, how could Israel be assured that the Arabs would not demand further concessions? Still, the Israelis found themselves on the defensive, perceived as unwilling—perhaps justifiably—to take any risks for peace and relying only on superior military strength as a means of bringing the Arabs to the negotiating table. In addition, the Israeli hope that the

Egyptian-Soviet arms deal would bring about a shift in U.S. policy toward favoring Israel proved to be illusory. In fact, the opposite occurred. U.S. policymakers viewed Soviet gains in the Arab world not as a result of the Baghdad Pact, but as a direct by-product of the Arab-Israeli conflict. Thus any U.S. tilt toward Israel could only serve Soviet goals.

Sharett's diplomatic ventures both in Geneva and the United States had failed in their basic aims. Israel's position deteriorated even further. The Soviet Union intensified its relations with Egypt. The United States and Britain decided to strengthen the northern tier countries, and at the same time avoid at all costs a crisis with Nasser, hoping to eventually reverse his slide toward the Soviet Union. The United States and Britain had already decided to assist Egypt financially as well as secure for it a $200 million loan from the International Bank toward the building of the Aswan Dam. They hoped that the presence of engineers, technicians, and other peoples from the West in Egypt "would constitute a strong influence in keeping Egypt on the side of the free world."

At the same time Israel had been warned by the United States not to engage in any preemptive war, but given her feeling of insecurity and isolation this was exactly the path Israel would be taking. Ben-Gurion's return to the new Israeli cabinet as prime minister and defense minister assured that Israel would continue its tough border policy. In Washington, Ben-Gurion was viewed by the administration as an activist because of his espousal of firm retaliation on Israel's border. Eisenhower would go a step further in his evaluation of Ben-Gurion. In the summer of 1953, the president told Eli Ginzberg, professor of economics at Columbia University, that although he admired Ben-Gurion for "his dedication, skill and the energy with which he pursued his goal," he was also worried about Ben-Gurion "because he was an extremist who might go the whole way, even to war to achieve his goals."[82]

Yet at the same time, U.S. policymakers considered Ben-Gurion "Israel's ablest diplomat and most experienced negotiator." U.S. officials also accurately assessed the mood in Israel as being one of readiness for war and a closing of the ranks, with Ben-Gurion's decisions enjoying full public and parliamentary support.[83] And, as far as Ben-Gurion was concerned, the Czechoslovak-Egyptian arms deal radically upset the balance of power in the region to the detriment of Israel. For Ben-Gurion, war was all but inevitable. What remained was waiting for the right opportunity to strike.[84]

Still the administration had not given up hope of avoiding the worst and kept urging restraint on all parties as well as attempting to bring about peace between Israel and Egypt. The Anderson secret mission to Cairo and Jerusalem would be the last attempt to sell ALPHA to the belligerents in order to avoid what seemed all but certain—war.

Prelude to War:
Tension and Violence

6

While the Eisenhower administration attempted to re-
solve the Arab-Israeli dispute, it received very little help from the belligerents. On the contrary, tension along the borders between Israel and its
neighbors was compounded by the escalation of raids from one side and
retaliation by the other. The sequence of events following the Gaza raid
was marked by an unprecedented increase in Palestinians infiltrating from
the Gaza Strip into Israel and mining Israeli patrol vehicles. On May 30,
an Israeli military vehicle was fired on from an Egyptian post near kilo 95.
The Israelis returned fire. Small arms and mortar fire spread the length of
the frontier. Casualties were heavy on both sides; four Israeli soldiers and
four civilians were killed, one Egyptian soldier was killed, and four were
wounded. The Israeli border kibbutzim of Kissufim, Ein Hashlosha, and
Nirim were shelled throughout the day. In the words of General Burns,
the UNTSO chief of staff, the aftermath of the Gaza attack of February 28
"showed that the Israelis were sadly mistaken if they believed that the
Egyptians and Palestinians would be cowed by it."[1]

But this was just a prelude to an intensification of the violence. By
mid-1955, the Egyptian-directed guerilla campaign against Israel's territory and population had moved into high gear. The campaign, under
Egyptian sponsorship and training, was carried out by *fedayeen*, an
Arabic word meaning "self-sacrificers" or "commandos." They volun-

teered to fight the battle of the Palestinian refugees against Israel. For the Israelis, however, *fedayeen* was synonymous with marauders, cutthroats, and murderers.

The first of an organized series of attacks by the fedayeen took place during the night of August 25–26. A man riding in a jeep was killed near Yad Mordechai, the nearest kibbutz to the north of the Gaza Strip, followed by an attack on an Israeli outpost near Kissufim. It was the beginning of a week-long series of mine layings, ambushes, and attacks that caused the death of eleven civilians and the wounding of nine. The most serious of these incidents was the wounding of a family of five by small-arms fire near Rehovot deeper into Israel, about twenty-eight miles from the armistice demarcation line. Four workmen in an orange grove near Rishon Lezion, thirty miles from the Egyptian border, were murdered by submachine-gun fire. Repelled by such brutal and indiscriminate action, General Burns commented: "I felt that what the Egyptians were doing in sending these men whom they dignified with the name *fedayeen* to attack men, women and children was a crime."[2] While the fedayeen were Palestinian Arabs, Israel held the Egyptian government responsible for authorizing this campaign. Sharett delivered a warning to Nasser: Israel would use full force if such attacks continued.[3]

The warning was carried out on September 1, when Israel launched the biggest attack since the Gaza raid of February 28. Israel's army unit 101 penetrated into Egyptian territory along the Gaza Strip and attacked a police station at Khan Yunis and the Arab village of Abasan, killing thirty-six soldiers, policemen, and civilians and wounding thirteen. Egypt retaliated on September 11 by tightening its blockade of the Straits of Tiran at the entrance of the Gulf of Aqaba, effectively blockading Israel's southern port of Eilat and cutting off trade from that port with East Africa and Asia. Egypt justified the blockade on the basis that the straits were Egyptian territory and Egypt had been in a state of war with Israel. But Israel viewed the straits as an international waterway through which all nations were entitled to free passage. From Israel's perspective, the Egyptians were engaging in an illegal act prejudicial to peace and security.[4]

In this charged atmosphere of constant tension, Israel conducted a national election campaign. The voting took place on July 26; the results were devastating to Sharett's moderate policies. The Mapai party headed by Sharett lost five seats in the Knesset, whereas Begin's right-wing, hawkish Herut party increased its representation by seven seats. Nonetheless, with the support of labor parties and the National Religious party, Ben-Gurion was able to form a coalition government and become Israel's prime minister again.

The election results marked a shift to a harder line vis-à-vis the Arabs, not surprising since both Ben-Gurion and Sharett promised the electorate a tougher stand toward Egypt and other Arab states. On July 9, during a political campaign rally in Beersheba, Ben-Gurion promised to divert water from the Jordan River to the Negev Desert, an action that would arouse vigorous Arab opposition. He also assured Israeli voters that freedom of passage for Israeli ships from the southern port of Eilat would be restored. This action would entail removing the Egyptian fortifications at Ras Nasrani and Sanapir. From these positions the Egyptians were able to close the Straits of Tiran at the entrance to the Gulf of Aqaba, thus effectively shutting off all ships bound to and from Eilat. The closure of the straits imperiled Israel's trade with the Orient and East Africa. Sharett went a step further by warning Egypt that Israel would assure freedom of navigation by force if necessary, if "our enemies fail to respond to our efforts" and "fail to lift the blockade by peaceful means."[5]

On November 2, in his dual role as prime minister and defense minister, Ben-Gurion presented the new government to the Knesset. He used the occasion to warn Egypt that by its blockade of Israeli ships sailing through the Suez Canal and the Red Sea it had in effect declared a one-sided war against Israel. "This one-sided war," Ben-Gurion announced, "will have to stop for it cannot remain one-sided forever." His warning, however, was coupled with an appeal for peace. Israel, he said, was ready to negotiate a permanent peace with its neighbor based on full cooperation in political, economic, and social spheres. In the absence of a permanent peace, Ben-Gurion would be satisfied with a limited settlement based on full compliance with the armistice agreements, which would include cessation of hostilities and freedom of navigation. He expressed his willingness to meet the Egyptian leader at any time and place of his choosing. Egypt and the other Arab states, said Ben-Gurion, "now have the opportunity to show whether they want war or peace."[6]

But the Israeli prime minister was not about to wait for Nasser to make the decision concerning war or peace. He had already decided that war was the most logical option for Israel. On October 22, two weeks before the premier's "olive branch" speech, Israel's chief of staff, Moshe Dayan, interrupted his vacation in France and was ordered to return to Jerusalem. Ben-Gurion instructed Dayan "to be prepared to capture the Straits of Tiran"—Sharm es-Sheikh, Ras Nasrani and the islands of Tiran and Sanapir—in order to ensure freedom of shipping through the Gulf of Aqaba and the Red Sea.[7]

On November 3, one day after Ben-Gurion's Knesset speech, an Israeli force of battalion strength attacked Egyptian positions in the Al-Auja (Nitzana) DMZ within Israel. In a few hours of intense fighting the Israelis inflicted over one hundred Egyptian casualties, among them fifty dead. The Al-Auja battle was the culmination of a protracted dispute between Israel and Egypt over the DMZ in which both sides had often violated the armistice agreement. The Egyptian action, in occupying positions on the Israeli side, was a flagrant violation of the armistice agreement. But the timing of the Israeli counterattack was bound to diminish the impact and importance of Ben-Gurion's appeal for peace. General Burns, in a meeting with Ben-Gurion a week after the attack, condemned the Israeli military action and rejected the prime minister's argument that Egyptian troops had moved into a restricted area near the DMZ and therefore had to be driven out. According to Burns, Egypt violated the Al-Auja DMZ because Israel acted similarly on previous occasions.[8] Regardless of the arguments, Israel now controlled a very strategic and most important route for a major attack on Egypt, if ever that decision was made.[9]

Indeed, at a cabinet meeting soon after the attack, Ben-Gurion formally raised the issue of a preemptive strike against Egypt. His ministerial colleagues rejected the idea because "the moment was not propitious," but the cabinet did decide in favor of such action at any time Israel deemed appropriate.[10] Dayan protested the delay. In his judgment, the cabinet was procrastinating. Time, he insisted, was working against Israel because the infusion of Soviet weapons into Egypt drastically tilted the balance against Israel. Ben-Gurion concurred with Dayan's assessment. War seemed inevitable. It was only a question of time before the assault would be launched.

In another show of force to intimidate the Arabs and boost morale at home, Ben-Gurion, without consulting the cabinet, on December 11 gave the order for a major military operation on the Syrian border. Israeli troops attacked Syrian positions near the northern shore of Lake Tiberias (Kinneret) at Buteiha, Farm, and Koursi on the slopes of Mount Hermon. Fifty-six Syrians were killed, among them five civilians, and thirty were taken prisoner. In a statement issued the same night the Foreign Ministry claimed that the attack was in retaliation for Syrian shelling of an Israeli fishing boat on the Israeli-held eastern side of the lake.

Previous Syrian violations notwithstanding, the harsh Israeli attack seemed disproportionate to the provocation. Because the attack took place while Sharett was in Washington pleading for U.S. weapons, the action was carried out without his knowledge, let alone approval. It also made his diplomatic mission in Washington all the more difficult. The United States used the attack as a pretext to delay filling Israel's request for arms. Consequently, Sharett returned to Jerusalem empty-handed, angry, and frustrated over the military action. In a meeting with the political committee of the Labor party, he commented on the devastating effect of the Kinneret attack: "Satan could not have chosen a worse timing." Ben-Gurion, present at the meeting, could hardly conceal his anger at Sharett. The incident only widened the rift between them.[11]

The UN Security Council condemned the Israeli attack in strongest terms. But Burns, the UNTSO chief, believed that the Security Council condemnation did not go far enough because it failed to restrain the aggressive Israeli policy that in his view "constituted the greatest danger to peace." He thought that the imposition of economic sanctions on Israel might have diminished its "aggressive policy."[12]

Indeed, the attack had very little to do with the harassment of Israeli fishing in Lake Tiberias (Kinneret). In fact, it aimed at undermining the recently concluded mutual defense pact between Egypt and Syria. The two countries had pledged to place their forces under a single command. Ben-Gurion sent a message to Syria that it would do well not to link itself too closely to Egypt, which did not have the power to defend Syrian territory. The *Jerusalem Post*, in an editorial on December 14, 1955, stated that there was a relationship between the Israeli raid and the military pact and that "Egypt must now be considered as operating out of Syria as well as through the Gaza Strip."

While the winds of war and violence swept the Middle East, the Eisenhower administration continued its efforts to advance ALPHA, a blueprint for peace between Israel and Egypt based on Dulles's August 26,

1955, speech and the subsequent proposals put together by Francis H. Russell. The peace effort involved two parallel moves amounting to the most ambitious scheme ever launched by an administration up to that point. One move was totally secret—the Robert B. Anderson diplomatic mission to Cairo and Jerusalem to bring about a territorial and political compromise between Egypt and Israel. The other was designed to buttress the first—a public offer by the United States to provide financial help to Egypt for the building of the High Dam at Aswan.

The dam would be the largest of its kind in the world—365 feet high, two-thirds of a mile thick at the base, and two-and-a-quarter miles long along the Aswan reservoir. When completed, it would create a 350-mile-long lake whose waters would increase Egypt's cultivable area by as much as one-third and provide electricity for more than half of the country's power needs, as well as needed fertilizers. For a country whose 30 million inhabitants had no fertile land at their disposal apart from the delta and a thin strip along the Nile, the construction of the dam was a matter of survival. But the cost of the High Dam, which had been under consideration since 1924, was extremely high—approximately $1.3 billion, with at least one-third in hard currency.[13]

The decision to carry out an enterprise of such magnitude had been one of the first that Nasser made when he came to power. It was his most cherished domestic program, designed to raise the miserable standard of living of the bulk of the Egyptian people. Not having sufficient capital, he turned to the International Bank of Reconstruction and Development, better known as the World Bank. On September 26, 1955, Egypt applied for a loan of $240 million.

The World Bank's regulations stipulated that loans would be based solely on firm guarantees of repayment. As Egypt had already mortgaged a great deal of its economic resources to pay for Czech arms, its ability to repay the loan could not be taken for granted. In addition, the construction of the dam might flood part of the Sudan. Nasser was asked to obtain prior consent of the Khartoum government, which in turn attempted to impose its own restrictions.

To further complicate the financing problem, the World Bank required that the borrowing country's loan transaction with any third party be subject to its preliminary approval. Nasser, a proud nationalist, saw in those demands an infringement on Egypt's sovereignty. At that point the

Soviet Union, in an attempt to gain further influence in Egypt, stated its willingness to grant Egypt a loan of $200 million to be repaid over thirty years in cotton and rice at a low interest of 2 percent a year. Coming on the heels of the Egyptian-Czech arms deal, this development greatly disturbed Dulles. He told congressional leaders that "Egypt was far from becoming a tool of the Soviets, but it could drift that way if we did nothing to prevent it."[14]

In an effort to block further Soviet inroads into Egypt, Dulles, at the urging of Under Secretary of State Hoover, persuaded Eden to join the United States in financing part of the dam project. Subsequently, negotiations took place in Washington between the Egyptian finance minister, Abdel Moneim Kaissouny, Hoover, the British ambassador in Washington, and officials of the World Bank. In the discussions the participants hammered out the details relating to the financing of such a monumental project.

On December 16, 1955, Dulles announced that a tentative agreement had been reached in which the United States, Britain, and the World Bank would jointly finance the High Dam project at an estimated cost of $1.3 billion. The bank would provide $200 million, Britain and the United States $200 million, and Egypt the rest in local currency.[15]

Such generosity on the part of the United States encountered opposition in Congress from southern senators defending the cotton-growing interests, from Israeli supporters, and from right-wing conservatives. The administration found itself hard-pressed to explain its action, especially after Nasser's arms deal with the Soviets, his recognition of Red China, and his attempts to consider a Russian loan offer while negotiating with the Western powers. In fact, Nasser was trying to play off the Russians against the West, as he had in the Czech arms deal. The United States, however, accepted that fact and decided at least for the moment to play that game, fully aware of the risks involved. The United States could not afford to allow Egypt to be drawn completely into the Russian orbit.

Although in retrospect this strategy seems quite naive, nonetheless Eisenhower, Dulles, and Hoover hoped that Western involvement in Egypt's domestic reconstruction might eventually detach Nasser from the Soviet Union. Moreover, Egypt's own immersion in solving its colossal social and economic problems might lead it to consider making peace with Israel. For if Nasser had complied with the proposed agreement, it would have been impossible for the Egyptian leader to continue buying weapons from Czechoslovakia. Most Egyptian revenues, coming mainly from cotton crops, would have had to be used for economic reconstruction. Dulles's decision to proceed with the loan was aimed not only at preempting the Russians but also at placing Egypt in such a position that it could not afford to spend large sums of money on weapons.[16] Although these expectations did not materialize, they were worth trying.

Eisenhower and Dulles still hoped that Nasser was not yet lost to the West. Despite his arms deal with the Soviets, he was still redeemable. Unfortunately, subsequent events proved otherwise. Early indications to that effect came with the failure of the highly secret and ambitious peace mission to Cairo and Jerusalem undertaken by Robert B. Anderson—the "covert intermediary" between the belligerents.[17]

The idea of a secret mission came from Hoover, who convinced both Eisenhower and Dulles to appoint a highly respected individual to mediate the dispute between Israel and Egypt. The man the president asked to carry out that task in a covert effort was Robert B. Anderson, deputy secretary of defense, and later secretary of the treasury, who had left the Pentagon and returned to private life and business activities. The president's admiration for Anderson was boundless. "He is one of the most capable men I know . . . my confidence in him is such that at the moment I feel that nothing could give me greater satisfaction than to believe that next January 20th I could turn over this office to his hands. His capacity is unlimited and his dedication to this country complete."[18]

Given Anderson's limited expertise in the problems of the Middle East, he would be assisted by the State Department and CIA officials. His mission: to achieve a rapprochement between Israel and Egypt in meetings with Nasser and Ben-Gurion. Should an agreement be concluded, the United States would guarantee the borders of the two countries and extend generous financial help to Egypt in the building of the dam. The United States would also help Israel compensate Palestinian refugees for the properties they had left behind in Israel.

The significance of the mission could be seen in the most unusual manner in which it was carried out. According to William Bragg Ewald, Jr., this most sensitive and secretive presidential mission was put together by the secretary of state and his brother Allen W. Dulles, the CIA chief. The reports about the meetings with the prospective leaders would be delivered through guarded phone calls between the brothers, who would refer to "northerners" for the Israelis and "southerners" for the Egyptians. The U.S. ambassadors in the respective countries would not be involved. Cables about the discussions would be sent to the secretary of state through a special channel of the CIA's most capable officers—Kermit Roosevelt in Cairo and James Angleton in Jerusalem. Both were to report directly to Allen Dulles.[19]

On the afternoon of January 11, 1956, Anderson and Dulles met at the White House to discuss with the president the mediator's approach and the details of the upcoming talks with Nasser and Ben-Gurion. Anderson's mission was to convince both leaders to conclude a peace agreement that would form the basis for peace throughout the region. Generous economic aid to both countries would be forthcoming once belligerency gave way to peace. Anderson carried with him letters of introduction from the president to both leaders. The basically identical letters described the envoy as a "man who fully understands my personal concerns and hopes in the area."[20] As such he would personally represent the president and speak with full presidential authority.

Soon after the White House meeting, Anderson left for Athens and from there in disguise shuttled by small plane to Cairo and Jerusalem. He did not make any contacts with the U.S. ambassador in either country. His only U.S. contacts were the CIA agents stationed in Egypt and Israel.

Anderson held his first meeting late at night with Nasser in Cairo on January 19. Present were Nasser's close confidant, Zakaria Mohyeddin, and Kermit Roosevelt, a CIA agent and Nasser's friend. Anderson opened the discussion by trying to impress Nasser with the economic benefits accruing to Egypt from U.S. aid should Egypt enter into a peace agreement with Israel. Nasser amiably nodded at Anderson's entreaties; the emissary erroneously assumed the nodding meant actual agreement. Anderson left the meeting at 1:30 A.M. satisfied and about to dispatch a buoyant cable to Dulles reporting success. As Anderson was preparing to leave, Nasser asked Roosevelt to stay behind. He told Roosevelt that he did not understand what Anderson was saying. Anderson's thick Texas drawl was an impediment. Roosevelt explained to Nasser that Anderson proposed that Egypt accept as permanent Israel's present frontiers and lead the way to peace between Israel and the Arab countries. Nasser looked stunned with disbelief. Given the current tensions in the area and especially the most recent Israeli attack on Syria, Nasser exclaimed, "You know I couldn't do anything like that, I'd be assassinated. Go stop him. Don't let him send any cable."

Roosevelt rushed to the CIA safe house in Cairo, where Anderson was in the process of dictating his cable to Dulles. Anderson was shocked to learn that his optimism was premature and that Nasser had not understood his proposal. Disappointed, he agreed to delay the dispatch of the cable to await further clarification from Nasser. At a second meeting, Nasser established the rules of the conversation. He told Anderson, "You speak English to Kim and he will speak English to me." Through Roosevelt's "translation" Nasser turned down Anderson's plea for peace with Israel.[21]

Although Nasser did not completely rule out the possibility of a settlement, the problem involved all Arab states and not just Egypt. A "quick settlement," said Nasser, would be impossible since an "atmosphere" conducive to a settlement must first be established and accepted by all Arabs. Such prospects seemed quite elusive, but Anderson did not seem deterred. The solution to the Palestinian refugee problem, said Nasser, must be found first. Even though total repatriation might be impractical, the refugees nonetheless must be given the opportunity to choose between repatriation or resettlement in Arab countries. Nasser also insisted upon Egyptian "territorial contiguity" with Jordan through the Negev as essential to any settlement. When pressed by Anderson to delineate the amount of territory required, the Egyptian leader said that "the line should run from Dhahirya about 10 miles southwest of Hebron to Gaza," practically the entire Negev. According to Nasser, the Negev was absolutely necessary for Egypt in order to establish a territorial link under "Egyptian sovereignty connecting Africa and Asia."[22] Nasser also rejected out of hand the suggestion of holding direct negotiations with Israel and characterized such an attempt as "political suicide or worse." While the envoy cautioned Nasser that a settlement based on Nasser's demands was unfeasible, Anderson nonetheless hoped that they were opening positions for bargaining purposes.

Anderson's task in Jerusalem would not be any easier. Even before his arrival, Ben-Gurion in his diary expressed doubts about the success of the mission. "Nasser's intentions are not directed towards peace, his political ambitions within the Arab and Muslim worlds including his belligerency towards Israel—all point to war. He is only waiting for the appropriate day when he'll achieve military superiority over us."[23]

Arriving on January 23, Anderson met in utmost secrecy with Ben-Gurion and Sharett. Ben-Gurion did not trust Nasser's willingness to reach a settlement, given the conditions he had set regarding the refugees and the demand for the Negev. In fact, the Israeli premier believed that Nasser's ambitions and his alignment with the Soviet Union through the arms deal portended problems for the West and Israel. Ben-Gurion was willing to discuss possibilities for peace with Egypt but only in face-to-face negotiations with Nasser, offering to meet with him at any time and place of his choosing. The Israeli leader seemed prepared to start the negotiations between the two governments at lower levels and suggested that Sharett would represent Israel at the initial stage. Absent such contacts Israel was in no position to discuss questions regarding refugees or territorial concessions. Anderson pleaded for "flexibility" on both sides. In the case of Egypt, flexibility meant that the Egyptians should not be too demanding in asking concessions of Israeli territory, and in the case of Israel, flexibility meant that the Israelis must be willing to give up territory without receiving territory in exchange. The Israeli leaders turned the discussions to Egypt's accumulation of weapons, which posed a grave threat to Israeli security. The emphasis, in their opinion, should be on a U.S. response to that threat—U.S. weapons should be sold to Israel to counterbalance the Soviet supplies to Nasser. In their view, Nasser was not serious about reaching a settlement but merely playing for time, talking until he had absorbed the Soviet weapons and was in a far stronger position than at present. An impassioned Ben-Gurion stated that if the United States continued its embargo of arms to Israel and failed to provide for Israel's safety, it would be "guilty of the greatest crime in our history."[24]

The futility of the mission became apparent. The leaders of the two countries steered the talks in opposite directions. Anderson flew back to Cairo to try to convince Nasser to agree to face-to-face negotiations with Israel. Nasser rejected the idea, citing internal pressures and fears of possible assassination.

At the same time, expecting not peace but war, Ben-Gurion wrote to Eisenhower pleading for U.S. weapons. "No government responsible for the fate and survival of its people can watch with equanimity an enormous accumulation of arms of a neighboring power, which vigorously insists on war, without making every effort to acquire arms, if not in the same quantity, at least of the same quality." Ben-Gurion also hinted that unless such arms were delivered soon, Israel might be placed in a position that necessitated the prevention of an Egyptian attack, that is, preemptive war.[25]

Anderson's first round thus ended in failure. For weeks, he shuttled between the two capitals, with each side demanding what the other could not or would not accept. He returned to Washington on February 10 and reported to the president and Dulles on the dismal situation. But neither the president nor Dulles would concede defeat, as both Israel and Egypt showed a desire to reach a "peaceful settlement."[26] Eisenhower decided to send Anderson back to the Middle East to try again.

On February 27, Eisenhower dispatched separate letters to Nasser and Ben-Gurion. Trying to make the best of what seemed a hopeless task, Eisenhower wrote that Anderson's exploratory conversations "have not advanced as far toward a resolution of the issues confronting us as I had hoped, but a foundation has been laid on which we hope to build." Given the explosive situation in the area, the president continued, the United States wished to make whatever effort necessary to bring about peace. With that desire in mind, "Mr. Anderson plans to return to the Middle East for further discussions within the next few days."

The letter to Ben-Gurion showed goodwill and sympathy but was noncommittal on the most pressing issue on Israel's agenda—arms. "I have taken sympathetic note of your statement of Israel's need for arms. Your request is being given the most careful consideration in light of the need both to ensure Israel's security and to create a situation which will be most conducive to peace in the area."[27]

To Nasser, the president held out the promise of aid in constructing the High Dam at Aswan. "I have followed with interest the reports of the negotiations on the construction of the High Dam at Aswan. I have been pleased to note the progress which has been made. The High Dam represents the finest form of peaceful development of your people."[28]

Judging by the results of Anderson's first round of meetings, there was very little evidence to support Eisenhower's optimism.

Anderson returned to Cairo on March 6 for two secret meetings with Nasser. Present were two close advisers, Zakaria Mohyeddin and Ali

Sabri. Anderson brought up a new proposal concerning negotiations with Israel. As Egypt would not agree to face-to-face negotiations, the envoy suggested a compromise—a meeting in Cairo with a U.S. citizen of the Jewish faith, either under the auspices of the Israeli government or in his capacity as a U.S. citizen who might have some influence in the Israeli government on account of his faith. He and his Egyptian counterpart would be empowered to negotiate the pertinent issues. Final decisions would be left to the top leadership of both countries.

Nasser balked at that suggestion. He could not take the risk of bringing such a person to Egypt, for "he would still be a Jew." Nasser's personal security and that of his government were at stake. Several times during the conversation Nasser mentioned the murder of King Abdullah.[29] "I cannot stake myself and my government on this game," he said. Anderson suggested a face-to-face meeting with Ben-Gurion aboard a U.S. carrier in the Mediterranean. Nasser, however, would only agree to mediation through the good offices of the United States.[30]

On the question of refugees, Anderson proposed U.S. grants to help resettle them outside the Middle East. Nasser replied with a question of his own: "Who would accept them?" Free choice should be given to the Palestinians to decide whether they wanted repatriation or resettlement in Arab countries, said Nasser. He knew that the refugees would only accept repatriation to what had become Israel.

On the question of territorial continuity, Anderson came up with new ideas as well. Knowing full well Israel's adamant refusal to concede any territory in the Negev, especially the port of Eilat, Anderson proposed an east-west corridor across the Negev, with an overpass over the north-south highway to Eilat. That proposal was met with derision by Nasser and his two advisers. Nasser sarcastically suggested that if an east-west Arab corridor were to be built, it might as well be placed farther north, across Israel. The Egyptian leader demanded the return of all of the Negev to the Arabs. In addition, Nasser for the first time declared that in the event Israel accepted his proposals, Egypt would not sponsor a settlement; the United States or the United Nations should offer those ideas to all Arabs as a basis for a peace settlement. Here was a new element underscoring the futility in the Anderson mission. Anderson left Cairo with nothing except a vague promise from Nasser that Egypt would not take part in an aggressive war against Israel.[31]

To a distrustful Ben-Gurion, such a promise meant very little. Meeting in Jerusalem with Israeli leaders on March 9, Anderson reported the minimal progress he had made in Cairo. With no breakthrough on the question of face-to-face negotiations or on the question of boundaries and refugees, the issue for Israeli leaders was no longer how to achieve peace but how best to prepare for war. And so a mission aimed at bringing peace ended up discussing the urgency Israel attached to receiving U.S. weapons.

In blunt language the Israeli premier described the large quantities of fighter planes and tanks streaming into Egypt from the Soviet bloc. He did not believe Nasser's assurance that he would not start a war. After all, Nasser "has told his people that Israel must be destroyed. He will not keep the promise he gave you. Our existence is in danger." Brushing aside the tripartite declaration as assurance that peace would be maintained by the three Western powers, Ben-Gurion forcefully declared: "The only way to prevent war is for Israel to have defensive arms. For that there is no need for a stable government in Syria and Nasser does not need to be afraid that they will kill him. It depends only on you, seeing the danger, can you morally refuse to give us arms?"[32]

The Israeli prime minister outlined the gloomy outlook in a sad epilogue that proved to be prophetic. "If we should get a negative answer or none from the president on our request for arms, after you have submitted your report to him, we will have only one task: to look to our security. Nothing else will interest us. If we get help, good. But we must be prepared to defend ourselves without help from the outside. We will have to devote the last drop of our energy to preparing our people to meet Nasser and his MIGs."[33]

Thus, Anderson's second go-round floundered over the same issues that haunted his mission from the very beginning. Nasser was first of all interested in Israeli concessions on territory and refugees before making peace. Israel would have none of that, insisting on face-to-face negotiations without preconditions, something that Nasser would not accept. When the uncompromising attitudes of both sides became apparent, Ben-Gurion limited the talks to Israel's needs for U.S. weapons. The failure of the mission had little to do with Anderson's inexperience in Middle Eastern diplomacy. The intractable problems in the Arab-Israeli dispute and, most of all, the distrust between the leaders involved caused the mission to fail. Although the outcome could have been anticipated, the attempt in itself was not a mistake. Eisenhower and Dulles wanted to give diplomacy another chance in the hope of arresting the drift toward all-out war.

Late in the afternoon of March 12, Anderson, accompanied by Herbert Hoover, Jr., came to the White House and delivered his pessimistic report to the president. Eisenhower's disappointment was reflected in comments he wrote in his diary. "Nasser proved to be a complete stumbling block. He is apparently seeking to be acknowledged as the political leader of the Arab world. Nasser has a number of fears. First of all he fears the military junta that placed him in power, which is extremist in its position to Israel. . . . The result is that he finally concludes he should take no action whatsoever in seeking peace with Israel, rather he should just make speeches, all of which must breathe defiance of Israel."

To the president, Nasser appeared intransigent. Consequently Eisenhower began considering ways to isolate Egypt, diminish the Soviet influence there, and prevent any concerted Arab action against Israel. Various means of achieving those ends were discussed, including an alliance of Libya and Saudi Arabia with the United States. If Libya and Saudi Arabia were staunch U.S. friends, the president wrote, Egypt could "scarcely continue intimate association with the Soviets and will no longer be regarded as leader in the Arab world." Or perhaps the United States could isolate Nasser and strengthen King Ibn Saud of Saudi Arabia as a counterweight to the Egyptian leader in the Arab world. But the president reached no conclusion on how to proceed except to add the obvious. "It's a very, very sorry situation."[34]

The president's disillusionment with Nasser went beyond the latter's unwillingness to make peace with Israel. On March 12, Eden sent Eisenhower a top-secret message containing evidence gathered by British intelligence about a conference of Egyptian ambassadors in Arab states held in Cairo on January 30, 1956. Nasser opened the gathering and urged them to launch a campaign of subversive activities against Saudi Arabia, Iraq, and Jordan with the aim of overwhelming the pro-Western monarchies and establishing a United Arab State consisting of republics under Egyptian leadership. This antimonarchical policy, said Eden, was receiving the full support of the Soviet Union, which was sending so-called technicians to help organize intelligence services throughout the Arab world.[35] Indeed, the Egyptian leader had engaged in obvious anti-

Western activities, such as broadcasts from Radio Cairo trying to undermine the Baghdad Pact. In addition, Nasser's campaign against pro-
Western regimes in the region had now affected the rule of King Hussein
of Jordan. Under severe pressures from pro-Nasserite elements in Jordan,
the king was forced to dismiss General John Bagot Glubb, the British
commander of Jordan's highly respected army, the Arab Legion. British
military advisers were also dismissed. The action delivered a blow to
British prestige in the Middle East.

By now the president had developed a greater understanding of Israel's
position and sympathized with its plight. "Israel, a tiny nation, surrounded by enemies is nevertheless one we have recognized and on top of
this it has a very strong position in the hearts and emotions of the western
world because of the tragic suffering of Jews throughout two thousand
five hundred years of history." But Israel, the president confided in his
diary, was not totally blameless for the failure of the Anderson mission.
The Israeli officials, the president observed, were anxious to talk with
Egypt, but they are completely adamant in their attitude of making no
concessions whatsoever in order to obtain peace. Their general slogan is
"not one inch of ground, and their incessant demand is for arms." The
president suspected that Israel's clamor for arms from the United States
entailed a quest for something more than weapons. "Of course they could
get weapons at lower prices from almost any European nation, but they
want the arms from us because they feel that in this case they would have
made us a virtual ally in any trouble they might get in the region."[36] And
that was exactly what the United States refused to be dragged into.

On March 28, Dulles submitted a detailed memorandum to the president elaborating upon the actions the United States might take in the
aftermath of Anderson's futile mission. Dulles put forth a series of specific
steps to be taken by the United States in coordination with Britain. The
United States and Britain would deny export licenses covering arms
shipments to Egypt, whether from governmental or commercial sources.
Both countries should continue delaying the conclusion of current negotiations relating to the financing of the High Dam at Aswan. The United
States should hold in abeyance any decision on a CARE (Cooperative for
American Relief to Everywhere) program for Egypt for 1956, amounting
to as much as $100 million. At the same time the United States should
increase its support to the Baghdad Pact without actually joining it. For an

indefinite period the United States should deny export licenses for any major military items to Israel and the neighboring Arab states, except Saudi Arabia and Iraq. The United States, however, should not object if other Western countries wished to sell limited quantities of defensive arms to Israel.[37]

This memorandum was discussed at a meeting at the White House between the president and Dulles on March 28. Also present at the meeting were Herbert Hoover, Secretary of Defense Charles Wilson, and the chairman of the Joint Chiefs of Staff, Admiral Arthur W. Radford. All present agreed with the contents of the memorandum. Once again the president pressed the issue of building up King Ibn Saud as a figure of sufficient prestige to offset Nasser, but no decision was reached on how to achieve that goal. The discussion also centered on ways of giving Israel a security guarantee directed essentially against a possible Egyptian attack. Everyone agreed that should Egypt attempt to liquidate Israel, the United States would have to intervene. Dulles and Radford pointed out "that in such a case the result might be that we'd have to occupy the entire area, protect the pipelines and the Suez Canal."

On the question of arms to Israel, the United States would offer selected types of arms such as radar but would not become a major supplier. On the other hand, the United States would advise other Western countries to sell weapons to Israel. Dulles remarked that Israeli pressure in that regard had subsided somewhat thanks to the fact that the administration was not going to "cave in" to Israel's demands. The Israelis, said Dulles, "are showing a much less arbitrary and truculent attitude in discussions with me."[38] Dulles failed to admit that his proposal to advise other Western countries to sell arms to Israel was quite satisfactory to Israel. From Israel's perspective it marked an advance from his previous negative stance on the subject.

The Israeli clamor for U.S. weapons was a direct outcome of the Egyptian-Czech arms deal of September 1955. Thereafter Israel shifted its emphasis from a security pact with the United States (all but impossible under the circumstances) to demands for arms.[39] First came Sharett's sudden and anguished trip to Geneva in November 1955 and his meetings with the foreign ministers of the Big Four powers lamenting Israel's precarious situation in the aftermath of the Egyptian-Czech arms deal. In December he traveled to Washington where he met with Dulles and other administration officials. The message was the same, an urgent plea for U.S. weapons.

Again on January 16, 1956, in a letter to Dulles, he warned about the critical situation in which Israel found itself in light of Egypt's "menacing superiority" in weapons. Unless something drastic was done without delay, he warned, "Colonel Nasser will be undisputed master of the situation, free to attack whenever he chooses." Dulles's suggestion that arms alone would not solve the problem "is tantamount to telling a starving person that man does not live by bread alone," Sharett said. Arms of the same quality as Egypt "is now getting is our only anchor of safety—the only effective deterrent to Egyptian aggression," Sharett concluded.[40]

Following Sharett's complaint, in a meeting with George Allen, Eban drew Allen's attention to the deep anxiety felt in Israel at the absence of equipment capable of defending the country against the types of fighter planes in the Egyptian arsenal. Eban also raised the possibility of France delivering twelve aircraft of the Mystère IV type to Israel. He hoped the United States would not object to the transaction in view of certain relationships between the United States and France in matters of military procurement. Allen assured his visitor that the "United States would view such a French decision with sympathy."[41] But there would be no promise on American willingness to do likewise.

On January 25, Eban made another unsuccessful plea to Dulles for weapons. But on January 30, Eban went public. In a speech to the Women's National Democratic Club in Washington, he told his audience that "America and Britain should rise to the level of their inescapable moral duty" and provide military assistance to Israel.

By now, Israel's demands for arms had become an issue in U.S. domestic politics, for it was a presidential election year. It was the sort of situation that Eisenhower and Dulles resented most—the intrusion of domestic politics into foreign policy decisions. The Democrats went public, pressuring the administration on behalf of Israel. On January 28, a group of prominent Democrats led by Eleanor Roosevelt issued a statement to the press demanding that the United States counteract every attempt by the Soviet Union to upset the precarious balance of power in the Middle East by providing defensive arms to Israel. The statement was endorsed by the former president, Harry S. Truman, and labor leader

Walter P. Reuther, vice-president of the AFL-CIO. On March 13, George Meany, the president of the AFL-CIO, endorsed the statement, declaring that "the growing imbalance in military strength against Israel would inevitably lead to war."

Not to be outdone, forty Republican House members wrote to Dulles on February 3, strongly urging the administration to match Soviet bloc arms to Egypt with U.S. arms to Israel. Dulles's reply, personally edited by the president, acknowledged that current developments could create a disparity in armed force between Israel and its Arab neighbor. The United States was not convinced, however, that the "disparity can be adequately offset by additional purchases of arms by the State of Israel." Given Israel's small population, two million versus tens of millions of Arabs capable of obtaining weapons from the Soviet bloc, Israel could never win an arms race. Even though the United States had not excluded the possibility of arms sales to Israel, arms alone, said Dulles, were not a deterrent to aggression. The UN Charter and the tripartite declaration of 1950 "are a far more effective deterrent to any potential aggressor than any amount of arms which could be obtained by either side." Referring to his speech of August 26, 1955, Dulles stressed that because part of the fear and tension in the area resulted from "lack of permanent boundaries, it is our belief that the security of states in the Near East cannot rest upon arms alone but rather upon international rule of law."[42]

A disappointed and anguished Eban told Dulles in a meeting on February 6 that his letter to Republican House members was totally negative from Israel's perspective and inconsistent with U.S. assurances of maintaining Israel's security in all its essentials. The UN Charter and the tripartite declaration, said Eban, were no substitute for arms in self defense. Dulles, however, would not budge. The preservation of Israel, he contended, remained a cardinal principle of U.S. foreign policy. Without citing any evidence, Dulles maintained that the danger of aggression against Israel had actually waned in the last few months. For his part, the secretary complained about the political pressures the administration had come under to sell weapons to Israel. He hoped that neither Israel nor the Israeli embassy in Washington encouraged such pressures, for they could only backfire.[43]

Dulles' noncommittal attitude only intensified Israeli demands for a clear-cut decision. In meetings with George V. Allen and Francis H.

Russell, Eban compared Israel's precarious position to that of Britain in 1940. For the first time, he warned, Israel might feel compelled to take "certain actions," hinting at preemptive war. He would report to his government that the United States would not sell arms to his country, in which case none could predict the consequences. Allen dissuaded the ambassador from such a step, as no decision had yet been made. In fact, Allen suggested, the outcome "might actually be positive."[44]

If so, the secretary of state was in no hurry. He was about to leave on a trip to Karachi, Pakistan, where the Southeast Asia Treaty Organization foreign ministers were to meet for three days starting March 6. The secretary wanted to ensure that no decision on the subject of weapons to Israel would be made during his absence. He told the president of his concerns, lest the White House staff "under strong political influence might alarm him on the subject." Eisenhower and Dulles agreed on the need to accomplish a dual purpose—preserving the state of Israel and at the same time avoiding a break with the Arab countries that "would jeopardize the industries of western Europe and the military power of NATO."[45] Furthermore, Dulles was warned by the CIA that providing arms to Israel would result in an immediate end to the Anderson mission and further increases in Soviet supplies of weapons to Egypt and other Arab countries.[46]

In Dulles's absence, Herbert Hoover, Jr., briefed the president on the matter of weapons to Israel and kept the traveling secretary abreast of the situation. On March 16, Under Secretary of State Hoover informed the president about a conversation with Eban. According to Hoover, the Israelis would be putting even greater pressure on the United States to deliver them arms. Eban inquired about twenty-four F-86 fighter planes instead of the original request of forty-eight. He also asked about certain antitank weapons, promising that if these requests were met they would satisfy Israel's needs. While Hoover opposed the sale of airplanes and antitank weapons, he nonetheless recommended giving the Israelis radar equipment. Above all, Hoover insisted that Israel could acquire weapons from Western Europe, especially France. The reason Israel stubbornly pressed for U.S. weapons "was due to their desire to have us morally committed to furnishing them with arms for their own purposes dealing with the Arabs."[47] In other words, as Eisenhower noted in his diary, the

Israelis hoped that with U.S. arms as a start they would eventually coax the United States into an alliance.

As noted earlier the subject was thoroughly discussed at a White House meeting on March 28 soon after Dulles's return from Southeast Asia. The failure of the Anderson mission led the secretary of state to reexamine U.S. policy in the Middle East. Nasser's unwillingness to cooperate in achieving an Arab-Israeli settlement meant that he was no longer entitled to "preferential treatment." Dulles recommended that the United States approve a sale by France to Israel of twelve Mystère IV jet fighters designated for NATO service. The NATO command enjoyed first priority on these jet interceptors, and previously Dulles was unwilling to divert them to Israel. The president went along with Dulles's recommendation. Those "twelve" Mystère fighters, Eisenhower wryly commented, "would display" in coming months "a rabbit-like capacity for multiplication." In addition, Dulles urged the Canadian Foreign Minister, Lester Pearson, to provide Israel with twenty-four F-86 U.S.-licensed jets.[48]

But no amount of pressure would move the president or Dulles to approve the sale of U.S. weapons to Israel. At a White House meeting on April 26, 1956, Eisenhower told Rabbi Silver that the United States wished to exert an influence for peace throughout the area. Silver pleaded with the president to sell Israel the "defensive" weapons necessary to "restore the military balance." Reluctantly, Eisenhower conceded that defensive arms of some kind might be sold to Israel, but only if they served the cause of peace. The president did not want U.S. policy to look as if it had been influenced by the Zionists. He refused to believe that "mass meetings and public appeals helped the situation." Eisenhower was not going to be influenced by political considerations. He would follow his conscience. If that meant he would not be reelected, "that would be quite agreeable to him." Rabbi Silver, taken aback, said, "You can be reelected without a single Jewish vote."[49] That prophecy proved to be correct.

The United States continued to turn down Israeli arms requests. The Eisenhower administration, nonetheless, encouraged other Western countries to sell arms to Israel. In this calculus, Israel's security had to be weighed against other important U.S. interests in the Middle East, such as preserving Western influence and a hold on oil resources and, most important, preventing a Soviet-Arab alliance. Dulles rightly believed that in order to attain those strategic goals, it would be counterproductive for the only Western power that still enjoyed some prestige in the Arab world to jeopardize its standing by selling arms to Israel.

At the same time, however, Dulles realized that Israel could not be driven to despair and hopelessness, hence arms should be delivered to her. Consequently, he approved the sale to Israel of French fighter planes that would otherwise have gone to NATO. He also interceded with Canada for the sale of F-86 Sabre jet fighters. The best way to pursue what Dulles called a policy of friendly impartiality in the Arab-Israeli dispute was to furnish weapons to Israel, but to assure that these did not come from the U.S. arsenal.

The evenhanded policy was clearly on course—preserving Israel's security without endangering Western interests in the Arab world. Such a policy, difficult to pursue at the time, would become increasingly untenable in the future, especially in light of Nasser's ambitions and Israel's plans to carry out a preemptive war against Egypt.

Setting the Stage for
Preemptive War

7

Following the failure of the Anderson mission, another vicious cycle of violence erupted along the Gaza demarcation line. On March 12, the Israelis complained to the Egyptian-Israeli Mixed Armistice Commission about Egyptian troop concentrations including armor and other offensive arms in the Gaza Strip and El Arish areas in violation of article 7 of the armistice agreement. Two days later Israel submitted a protest to the Security Council complaining about 180 incidents between December 5, 1955, and March 9, 1956. Those incidents included firing on Israeli patrols and infiltration by suicide squads, otherwise known as fedayeen, who mined roads and tossed hand grenades, causing civilian casualties. Alluding to Israeli military activities against Egypt, General Burns wryly observed that the Egyptians could have produced a similar list of Israeli aggressions.[1]

By early April the violence further escalated in constant exchanges of fire between Israeli and Egyptian patrols. The killing of three Israeli soldiers and the Egyptian shelling of four Israeli settlements causing scores of wounded and damaged buildings led to severe Israeli retribution. A heavy and relentless bombardment of Gaza on April 4 resulted in 62 Arabs killed and 107 wounded, including men, women, and children.[2]

In turn Nasser unleashed a wave of fedayeen attacks on the Israeli countryside—hand grenades tossed into Jewish settlements and homes, roads mined, water towers, railroad tracks, and bridges demolished with explosives. The daring fedayeen attacks reached the outskirts of Tel Aviv, right in the center of Israel. At Shafrir, during evening prayers, fedayeen burst into a synagogue and machine-gunned the worshipers, killing four and wounding three. A hand grenade thrown into a house at Migdal killed a woman and wounded two children. Similar attacks in other towns left a week's carnage of fourteen Israeli civilians.[3]

The attacks sparked fear, anxiety, and panic throughout Israel. Thousands of high school children began digging fortifications along settlements near the Egyptian frontier. Throughout the country emergency regulations were issued on how to spot and defend against fedayeen attacks. In every settlement civilian neighborhood patrols were organized to guard against such attacks.

Politically, Ben-Gurion came under intense pressure from the right-wing Herut party demanding that Israel launch decisive military action against Egypt. On March 6, in a Knesset debate, Menachem Begin, the leader of the Herut party, introduced a motion of no confidence in the government. He asked for an immediate preemptive war against Egypt. Ben-Gurion, who had already decided on such action and waited only for the appropriate time, used the occasion to pressure the Eisenhower administration to deliver weapons to Israel. At the same time the Israeli premier cleverly concealed his own intentions. Replying to Begin's motion he said: "If war breaks out, we will meet it with armed strength and bring about their downfall. But we do not lust for battle. If the war is not prevented, the responsibility will rest with the U.S. which could have prevented it. We believe that we had a moral and political right to ask for American arms and still think so. If these arms are not given to us within the coming days, America will be shouldering a very heavy responsibility indeed. But we will not start a war."[4]

The escalating violence caused grave concern within the Eisenhower administration. After Ben-Gurion privately warned the United States about the possibility of total war, Dulles pushed for direct UN involvement at the highest level. At the urging of the United States, on April 4 the Security Council met and passed a resolution requesting that the Secretary General of the United Nations, Dag Hammarskjöld, visit the Middle East and report on the situation there. His mandate: to convince the belligerent parties to comply with the general armistice agreements, bring a halt to the violence, cease concentrating troops near the demarcation lines—in short, break the cycle of violence. His mission would not attempt to deal with the underlying causes that brought about the violence in the first place.[5] Achieving that task would involve a whole month of shuttling between Jerusalem and other Arab capitals, primarily Cairo.

An editorial in the Egyptian government-controlled newspaper *El Goumhouria* gave an indication of the gloomy atmosphere under which Hammarskjöld was about to begin his mission. According to the newspaper, "The success of his mission is contingent upon the elimination of Israel." On the other hand, Ben-Gurion and his advisers were suspicious and distrustful of the secretary general as well as of the UN observers on the scene, whom the Israelis regarded as biased in favor of the Arabs.[6] Ben-Gurion was especially piqued over a remark Hammarskjöld made in a conversation with Nahum Goldmann, the veteran Zionist leader, who had played a prominent diplomatic role in the establishment of Israel in 1948. Hammarskjöld had asked Goldmann, "If you had known then, Dr. Goldmann, what you know now, would you still have acted in 1948 as you did?" To Ben-Gurion, Hammarskjöld's remark reflected a belief that the United Nations erred when it voted in favor of the establishment of the Jewish state.[7]

Hammarskjöld began his mission in Cairo on April 10. And as the *New York Times* editorialized the next day, seeing Nasser first was the right approach, as "Colonel Nasser more than any other single leader or government has brought the Middle East to the threshold of war and can bring it back." In his discussions with Nasser and the Egyptian foreign minister, Mahmud Fawzi, the secretary general proposed the withdrawal of rival forces from the demarcation lines, full freedom of movement for UN military observers along those lines, the prevention of future incidents, and prompt detection of any truce violations. During this round of talks, Hammarskjöld obtained assurance from the Egyptian leaders that they would cease fedayeen attacks against Israel and observe a cease-fire along the frontier by the following day, April 11. Nasser's assurances notwithstanding, that same night fedayeen operating inside Israel struck again.

On April 12, the Israeli mission in New York made public a letter that Ben-Gurion sent to Hammarskjöld complaining that despite pledges to the contrary, Egyptian-sponsored suicide gangs carried out eight raids, killing three children and one adult and wounding fifteen others. In addition, the letter cited a flight over Israeli territory by four Egyptian jet fighters.

By the public release of the letter even before it reached the secretary general, Ben-Gurion sought to discredit Nasser and gain public understanding of Israel's predicament. It also reflected deep distrust of the UN role in the Arab-Israeli conflict, which too often had overlooked Egyptian violations of the cease-fire and focused instead on Israel's retaliatory raids.

But Hammarskjöld fired back a response to Ben-Gurion, expressing dismay that the Israeli premier saw fit to make public the letter before the secretary general had read it. More to the point, Hammarskjöld disputed its contents. The UN observers, he maintained, placed the Egyptian planes not in Israeli territory but in the demilitarized zone, where the presence of military aircraft from either side would have been in contravention of the rules applying to that zone.[8] Furthermore, the Egyptian actions did not cast doubt on the sincerity of the assurances given by the government of Egypt that the armistice would be observed. Moreover, according to Hammarskjöld, no such pledges had so far been received from Israel.

Those exchanges did not augur well for Hammarskjöld's stop in Jerusalem because Israeli leaders had little faith either in Nasser's promises or in Hammerskjöld's objectivity. In fact, in an Independence Day speech delivered on April 15, two days prior to Hammarskjöld's arrival in Jerusalem, Ben-Gurion warned Israelis about Egyptian plans "to slaughter" them. He vowed that the Israeli army would deliver "two blows for one." There was no reference in his speech to the secretary general's upcoming visit, in itself an indication of the low priority Ben-Gurion accorded Hammarskjöld's efforts. With more suspicion than confidence, Ben-Gurion awaited the arrival of Hammarskjöld in Jerusalem for three days of talks beginning April 17.

Hammarskjöld, meanwhile, brought a promise from Nasser that Egypt would comply with the cease-fire along the frontier and demanded a similar pledge from Israel. He also demanded that UN observers be given more freedom of movement on the Israeli side of the border to make it possible for them to monitor violations, long a point of contention between Israel and General Burns. To Israel, unrestricted movement by

UN observers did not accord with national sovereignty. Israel also argued that even if General Burns's staff of observers were expanded beyond the present thirty-seven and given complete freedom of movement, it would not halt infiltrations because the frontier could not be hermetically sealed.

Another controversial proposal put forth by Hammarskjöld in his meeting with Ben-Gurion called on both Israel and its Arab neighbors to move their troops back about 500 yards from the demarcation line. Israel had already rejected that idea, when General Burns first proposed it a year earlier. Israel claimed that it could not afford to yield territory and that abandonment of 500 yards along 600 miles of frontier would result in a considerable loss of land for such a small state. Such a proposal, Israel claimed, would expose many settlements to attack by infiltrators. The general tendency of the Israeli government was to diminish the importance of the UN observers and to regard them, in Hammarskjöld's words, as "a hostile power."[9]

Moreover, Hammarskjöld viewed his mission as limited to restoring tranquility along the frontier, especially between Egypt and Israel. Ben-Gurion considered such modest aims mere "palliatives." As far as the Israeli premier was concerned, a temporary cease-fire failed to deal with the roots of the conflict, namely, Egypt's maintenance of a state of war with Israel, its blockade of the Suez Canal and the Gulf of Aqaba to Israeli shipping, the Arab war propaganda against Israel, and Egypt's rapid rearmament. For unless those problems were addressed, the temporary calm the mission aimed to achieve would turn out to be just a "lull before the storm." To Hammarskjöld, however, a cease-fire in itself would be an accomplishment, for at the very least it would permit a breathing space in a highly dangerous situation.

But despite Ben-Gurion's tough line, he nonetheless went along with some measures to restore calm along the border. He agreed to a cease-fire and consented to an increase in the number of UN truce observers as well as granting them more freedom of movement along the Egyptian-held Gaza Strip. Ben-Gurion also agreed to Hammarskjöld's proposals for reducing tension with Syria along Lake Tiberias (Kinneret). The Israeli premier, however, knew full well that neither Egypt nor Israel's other Arab neighbors would comply with the cease-fire arrangements.[10] Consequently there was no reason for Ben-Gurion to appear intransigent and risk world condemnation.

Back in New York, Hammarskjöld reported to the Security Council on the "positive results" he had achieved. In Israel, however, the cease-fire agreed to by Ben-Gurion caused more concern than jubilation, for there was fear that a temporary cease-fire would enable the State Department to resist continued Israeli pressure for defensive arms. At the same time, the Egyptians under the cover of seeming tranquility would be able to absorb the arms they had already received from the Soviet bloc.

To avoid any illusions of peace, Ben-Gurion, in a Knesset speech on April 23, warned his compatriots that the truce did not ease the peril and the dangers of war. Such dangers stemmed from the preparations by Egypt and its allies to wage war on Israel. That, said Ben-Gurion, could be averted only through a restoration of the balance of power between the Arab states and Israel. Only U.S. weapons could bring that about. The U.S. refusal to directly counteract Egypt's military buildup reinforced Ben-Gurion's decision in favor of a preemptive war.[11]

Even though Israel received weapons from France and other sources, from Israel's perspective obtaining U.S. weapons was of far greater significance. U.S. arms would have symbolized the U.S. commitment to the survival of Israel more tangibly than advice to place Israel's trust in the United Nations. U.S. military supplies to Israel would have sent a clear message to Egypt about the futility of accumulating Soviet bloc weapons. Dulles understood the principle involved. Realizing that such a course of action would be inimical to its strategic interests in the Arab world, however, the United States could not and would not play that role.

Ben-Gurion naturally thought of Israel's interests first. The Egyptian army had to be crushed before it could absorb the newly arrived Soviet bloc weapons. In fact, as early as October 1955 the CIA estimated that Israel had been considering the possibility of a preemptive war while she still retained military superiority.[12]

Unable to gain cabinet approval for military action against Egypt in December 1955, Ben-Gurion began to set in motion the necessary machinery to support his future military plans. He became convinced that the government would be faced with the need to make fateful decisions. A unified cabinet under his unchallenged leadership was most urgent.

In December 1955 opposition to war came from the moderate Foreign Minister, Moshe Sharett, and his supporters in the cabinet. A man of deep-seated peaceable sentiments, Sharett, unlike Ben-Gurion, made the pursuit of peace a top priority. He also believed that the possession of arms in itself and the use of force alone were insufficient to ensure Israel's security. On a number of occasions, Sharett succeeded in thwarting the adoption of proposals for military action recommended by the chief of staff and presented by Ben-Gurion to the cabinet for approval. Because of his moral integrity and powers of rational argument, Sharett occasionally succeeded in mustering a cabinet majority against Ben-Gurion. By June 1956, preventive war against Egypt had become a top priority for Ben-Gurion. This time the Israeli premier was determined to prevent Sharett from obstructing such action. Ben-Gurion was bent on cleansing the cabinet of political opposition, and that meant the removal of Sharett.[13]

In a private conversation on June 12, Ben-Gurion bluntly told Sharett that, given the divergence of views between them, they could no longer work together, and that one of them had to leave the cabinet. As expected, the leadership of the Mapai party backed Ben-Gurion. According to Gideon Rafael, the foreign minister had often contemplated handing in his resignation but was nonetheless "flabbergasted by the suddenness of the Prime Minister's blow." Even though the relationship between them was far from harmonious, Sharett never suspected that a twenty-four-year association would end with such painful abruptness.[14]

At a cabinet meeting on June 18, Sharett tendered his resignation. None of the participants attempted to dissuade him. There was total silence. As Sharett noted in his diary, none of his colleagues raised his head or attempted to shake his hand; it was as if all their mental capacities were paralyzed. Indeed, it was shameful and humiliating treatment of a man who had devoted most of his lifetime to the cause of Zionism and the establishment of the state of Israel. Ben-Gurion's handling of Sharett, and the pusillanimity of the Labor party and the cabinet, were a reflection of Ben-Gurion's grip on the country as a whole.

Golda Myerson, later known as Golda Meir, replaced Sharett. A member of Ben-Gurion's cabinet in 1949 as minister of labor and social insurance, she held various jobs, such as minister of housing and subsequently acting foreign minister while Sharett was out of the country. She was a fervent Zionist, and in 1948 Ben-Gurion had instructed her to negotiate a secret peace agreement with King Abdullah of Jordan. With Golda Myerson as foreign minister, Ben-Gurion removed the last political impediment to the eventual preemptive war on Egypt.

By fate rather than by design, a number of significant international developments augured well for Israel's plans against Egypt. First among them was the strengthening of the military relationship between Israel and France. While Israel kept badgering the United States to relent on its arms embargo, the Franco-Israeli connection assumed the character of a virtual military alliance. By mid-1956 three of Israel's staunchest supporters in France were powerful members of the French government: General Pierre-Marie Koenig, Maurice Bourgès-Maunoury, and Abel Thomas. Since 1954 Koenig had been minister of defense. His Zionist sympathies went all the way back to World War II, when he commanded a Free French division in the western desert in cooperation with Palestinian Jewish troops. Bourgès-Maunoury was minister of the interior, and Abel Thomas the ministry's director general. Both were veterans of the Maquis, the French wartime underground; their friendship and sympathetic interest in Israel predated their antipathy to Nasser.

Moreover, after the French elections of January 1956, a new socialist government came to power under the leadership of Guy Mollet, a protégé of Leon Blum and a great admirer of socialist Israel. Mollet appointed Bourgès-Maunoury as defense minister and Abel Thomas as the ministry's director general. The new French premier assured Shimon Peres and Yaa'kov Tzur, the Israeli ambassador in Paris, that he would not be an Ernest Bevin, the British foreign minister who had opposed the establishment of a Jewish state in Palestine. To make good on his promise, Mollet informed Dulles that French-made Mystère jet fighters would henceforth be sent to Israel with or without U.S. approval. To Mollet, the best means of maintaining French influence in the Middle East was by helping the Israelis. Because Egyptian weapons were being shipped to the Algerian FLN, the friendship between Israel and France and their mutuality of interests grew stronger and stronger.

On April 23, Peres and Bourgès-Maunoury signed an agreement for the delivery of an additional twelve Mystère IV fighter planes. A month later, at Peres's suggestion, Ben-Gurion gave his approval to a most far-reaching agreement with France—the conclusion of an unwritten pact against Nasser. The French defense minister responded favorably to the proposed idea. Preparations for joint action began, along with massive shipments of French arms to Israel.[15] On June 22, Dayan and Peres went to Paris on a secret mission. There, during talks with the French high command, they submitted a list of arms requests. It included 200 AMX tanks, 72 Mystère fighter planes, 40,000 75-millimeter shells, and 10,000 SS-10 antitank missiles, all at a cost of $80 million. The French representatives promised to deliver the equipment in total secrecy during the coming months.[16] Both sides agreed to exchange intelligence information and plan military operations up to and including possible war against Egypt.[17]

Parallel to the growing alliance between France and Israel, the relations between the United States and Nasser were worsening. That too did not displease Israel. The Eisenhower administration grudgingly and reluctantly began reaching the conclusion that Nasser's policies were now more than ever at odds with Western interests. Not only had he brought the Soviet Union into the Middle East, subverted pro-Western regimes in the region, and refused to made peace with Israel, now he had committed an unpardonable act. On May 16, 1956, Nasser recognized Communist China, a nation that the United States had kept out of all international organizations and had portrayed as a pariah. The United States feared that other Arab countries would follow suit. On May 17, an irate Dulles complained to Ahmed Hussein, the Egyptian ambassador in Washington, that, by recognizing Communist China, Egypt was turning against the United States. Now it would be even more difficult for the United States to withstand the pressures from the Zionists and Israel in their demands for arms. Moreover, Dulles warned the ambassador, support in Congress for U.S. help in financing the Aswan Dam was slowly evaporating.[18]

Nasser's recognition of the People's Republic of China also triggered a strong negative response from the powerful China lobby and from supporters of Taiwan in Congress. The Republican Senate minority leader, William Knowland of California, the outspoken head of the lobby, informed Dulles that he would oppose the section in the foreign aid bill allocated to the funding of the dam. Even Democratic senators such as Wayne Morse of Oregon opposed funds for the Aswan Dam. He believed that financing several dams in the northwest United States was far more urgent than the giant one in Egypt. The cotton lobby in Congress, representing cotton-growing southern states including Texas and even California, opposed funding the High Dam for fear it would lead to significantly greater cotton export from Egypt and increased competition.[19] Last but not least, Israeli supporters in Congress added their objections. They agreed with Eban's view that U.S. funding of the dam was more than Israel could afford. "Here was Nasser getting arms from Moscow, he would now get the dam from America . . . Nasser would become insufferable through sheer extremity of arrogance."[20]

Thus by early July 1956 a powerful coalition of anticommunist hardliners, southern cotton interests, and Israeli supporters in Congress succeeded in having the Senate Appropriations Committee approve a provision in its foreign aid report to Congress recommending that none of the funds "mentioned in its act be used for assistance in connection with the construction of the Aswan Dam."

The Eisenhower administration had no quarrel with the congressional opposition. In fact, as early as March 28, in the aftermath of the failure of the Anderson mission, Dulles recommended in a memorandum to the president that "the United States and Britain will continue to delay the conclusion of current negotiations on the High Aswan Dam." Eisenhower concurred with the need to weaken Nasser.[21] In view of Nasser's recognition of Communist China, Eisenhower and Dulles agreed to scuttle the Aswan project altogether. In a July 13 meeting with Dulles, the president advised his secretary of state to inform the Egyptians that the United States was no longer interested in financing the dam because of "changing conditions and circumstances." At the same time, the U.S. ambassador to Egypt, Henry A. Byroade, known for his pro-Arab leanings, was replaced with Raymond Arthur Hare, a State Department official involved in a study group on British-U.S. covert actions in the Middle East. The United States had decided to get tough with Nasser. Denying him the dam was an attempt at damaging his prestige in the Middle East and weakening him domestically.

On July 19, the Egyptian ambassador arrived at the State Department for a meeting with Dulles. He expected a U.S. promise to continue the funding of the Aswan Dam. Present at the meeting were Dulles's two senior associates, Under Secretary of State Herbert Hoover, Jr., and George V. Allen. The ambassador, known for his pro-U.S. outlook, wanted the United States to assume the obligation for building the dam. He alluded to a Soviet offer to finance the project, but his attempt at blackmail added further justification to Dulles's prepared message that the United States would withdraw from the whole enterprise.[22]

The stunned ambassador was told that the reasons for the decision had to do with the fact that the project "involves not merely the rights and interest of Egypt but of other riparian states such as the Sudan, Ethiopia and Uganda." Furthermore, such a gigantic undertaking could succeed only in an "atmosphere of international tranquility and with close and understanding cooperation between the Government and peoples of Egypt who provide the internal effort and those abroad who provide the foreign exchange portion of that effort." Accordingly, "in the absence of such an atmosphere the project could generate ill will and success would be impossible." The decision, the secretary continued, in no way involved any alteration in the friendly relations of the government and people of the United States toward the people and government of Egypt. It was rather "designed to avoid embarking upon a vast project when the conditions were not auspicious."[23]

Twenty-four hours later the British announced their withdrawal from the project. It was Eisenhower's first major rebuff to Nasser. It set in motion events that neither the president nor his secretary of state could have predicted. Moreover, Israel's plans for a preemptive attack on Egypt would soon assume dimensions unforeseen by its planners.

Neither the United States, Britain, nor France anticipated Nasser's violent reaction. On July 26, as part of the week-long celebrations commemorating the fourth anniversary of the abdication of King Farouk, Nasser addressed a huge crowd in Alexandria. After describing the negotiations with the United States and Britain and urging the Americans to go "choke on your fury," Nasser dropped his bombshell. The Suez Canal Company was being nationalized, and its future proceeds would henceforth be applied to the construction of the dam. At home and throughout the Arab world, Nasser was hailed as a national hero.[24]

While the act of nationalization won him acclaim in the Arab world, in Britain and France Nasser's action caused outrage and consternation. The British government controlled 44 percent of the company shares, making it the largest shareholder. Nearly one-third of British imports passed through the canal, and more than a third of the ships using the Suez Canal were British. Two-thirds of its oil needs passed through the canal. Tens of thousands of British troops passed through the canal annually, traveling to and from Britain's bases east of Aden. A cutoff in canal traffic, should Nasser decide to do so, would pose a most serious threat to the economy of the British Empire. Finally, Nasser's action struck a blow at Britain's status as a great power and at its prestige in the Arab world. Prime Minister Anthony Eden, who in the 1930s was foreign secretary in the cabinet of Neville Chamberlain, needed no reminder of the fruits of appeasement.[25]

Britain was in an uproar. The press compared Nasser to Hitler and the Suez Canal to the Rhineland. The *Times* reflected the general view of the press, calling Nasser's action "a clear affront and threat to western interests . . . an international waterway of this kind cannot be worked by a nation with low technical and managerial skills such as the Egyptians." The *Daily Mail* referred to Nasser as "Hitler on the Nile" and called for immediate retaliatory action. In the House of Commons, the prime minister condemned Nasser's unilateral action and declared that the expropriation of the Suez Canal Company affected the rights and interest of many nations. The prime minister promised Parliament that he would act with firmness and care. Hugh Gaitskell, leader of the Labour party, supported Eden and called for a firm policy. After an emergency meeting with the cabinet and chiefs of staff on July 27, Eden cabled Eisenhower declaring that only a firm stand by all maritime powers could save Western interests in the Middle East. Force would have to be used, but only as a last resort.[26] Eden urged the president to immediately dispatch a representative to London in order to coordinate common policy against Nasser.

The French reaction was even more militant. Premier Guy Mollet had frequently referred to Nasser as the "Hitler on the Nile" long before the present crisis. He now compared Nasser's book *Philosophy of the Revolution* with Hitler's *Mein Kampf,* the message being that appeasing Nasser would have the same catastrophic results as appeasing Hitler in the 1930s. He detested "Nasserism" and all its implications for French interests in North Africa, especially Algeria. The French Foreign Minister, Christian Pineau, characterized Nasser's action as an act of plunder. Socialists, Gaullists, Radicals, and the press as a whole, with the exception of the Communist daily, were up in arms over the Egyptian leader's action.

For the French, getting rid of Nasser had become an obsession. After all, they were already fighting him in Algeria by virtue of his support for the anti-French rebels. It seemed hopeless to fight in Algeria if Nasser were to simultaneously win a great victory on the canal issue. In short, the

French would rather fight at the center of the trouble, in Egypt, than in the periphery, Algeria. With the exception of the Communist party, the French were united in their determination to take military action against Nasser.

This sudden international crisis found Dulles in Lima, Peru, representing the United States at the inauguration ceremonies of a new president. Eisenhower sent veteran diplomat Robert Murphy, deputy undersecretary for political affairs, to London to assess the situation. The president saw no reason for panic because the situation did not seem to him nearly as serious as the views from London and Paris would have it.

Murphy arrived in London on Sunday, July 29. He dined with Harold Macmillan, chancellor of the exchequer, and with Field Marshal Earl Alexander. "If Britain did not accept Egypt's challenge," said Macmillan, "Britain would become another Netherlands . . . Nasser has to be chased out of Egypt." The next day Eden told Murphy that "there was no thought of asking the United States for anything, but we do hope that you take care of the Bear." For Eden, placing the canal under international control was the ultimate British aim. Far more important was bringing about the fall of the Egyptian government.[27] Conscious of the danger that Nasser might solicit help from the Soviet Union, the British and the French hoped that the United States would neutralize any attempt at intervention by the Soviet Union. After listening to Eden and especially to an even more belligerent French foreign minister, Murphy became convinced that the British and the French meant to use force against Nasser. Immediately, he alerted Eisenhower. The president's previous calm demeanor turned into grave concern. Dulles was recalled from Peru.

On July 31, at 9:45 A.M., an urgent meeting was held in the White House. Present were Dulles; Hoover; Phleger, the State Department's legal adviser; Allen Dulles, director of the CIA; Treasury Secretary George Humphrey; and the Chief of Naval Operations, Arleigh Burke. With them the president discussed the latest developments. He informed them that a message had just arrived from Eden stating that the British "had taken a firm considered decision to break Nasser and to initiate hostilities at an early date for this purpose." The British estimated that six weeks of preparation would be needed for the operation to begin. The president, however, believed military action against Nasser "to be very unwise." First, support for military action by the United States would require congressional approval, and that, the president maintained, would not be forthcoming without "counter proposals" to Nasser. In case of war, Mideast oil would undoubtedly dry up, and western hemisphere oil would have to be diverted to Europe. In addition, Eisenhower believed that in toppling Nasser "they would have to contemplate occupying Cairo." Should the Egyptians, as expected, put up a fight, it would become an impossible task, fighting from house to house, block to block, tying down thousands of troops. "They would probably have to occupy the country and possibly never could get out." In addition, military action against Nasser would be looked upon in the Arab world as siding with Israel, and that, said the president, "would create a situation where you never could live on a friendship basis again with the Arabs."[28]

There was also a moral question. The president felt that attacking Nasser personally was unwise, "for he embodies the emotional demands of people of the area for independence and for slapping the White Man down. . . . It might well arouse the world from Dakar to the Philippine Islands against us." To Eisenhower, Nasser was the symbol of Arab nationalism fighting against European colonialism, a situation with which the president could sympathize. Also, the Egyptian action, however repugnant, did not merit military intervention. As long as he did not close the canal to navigation, Nasser had a legal right to nationalize it. After all, the Suez Canal Company was supposed to revert to the Egyptians in 1968 anyway.

Dulles concurred with the president's assessment. He also believed that the United States could make Nasser "disgorge" what he had seized—not by force, but rather by an agreement to internationalize the waterway. The secretary understood that such a solution, even if it were possible to achieve, would not satisfy the British and the French. The United States, however, should seek an international agreement to achieve that goal and eschew the use of force. War with Nasser, Dulles continued, would result in a cutoff of Mideast oil to the West, triggering oil rationing in the United States and causing a curtailment of automobile production—all in all a severe blow to the United States economy. The secretary suspected that the British were trying to drag the United States into a war in the Middle East. He recalled that the British went into both world wars without the United States, believing that "we would be bound to come in. They are now thinking they might start again and we would have to come in again."

The president reiterated that the United States must let the British and the French know that no matter how much "we sympathized and recognized the intensity of their feeling—specifically the feeling that they have been going down in the Middle East, war, however, would antagonize the American people." It was essential to try other measures. The president decided to dispatch Dulles immediately to London, carrying with him a personal letter from the president to Anthony Eden.[29]

Arriving in London on August 31, Dulles promptly told Eden and Guy Mollet that the immediate use of force would alienate world opinion, as neither France nor Britain had made a case justifying military action. He cautioned the U.S. allies that the United States would regard an immediate resort to force as a violation of their undertakings in regard to the UN Charter and other efforts for world peace. Furthermore, such action would give the Soviet Union unlimited opportunities to exploit the Middle East and Africa. Dulles agreed that letting Nasser have a stranglehold on the canal would reduce Western Europe to an insignificant role in the world, but other options must be tried before military action.[30] What Dulles did not tell the allies was that the U.S. government had already ruled out the use of force. The U.S. strategy now was to come up with proposals designed to reduce the war fever in Britain rather than to convince Nasser to reach a compromise.

Dulles suggested the convening of an urgent conference of maritime powers for the purpose of providing international assurances within the limits of legitimate Egyptian interest that the canal would be operated properly. Consequently, twenty-four invitations were issued, with Egypt and Greece declining to attend.[31] The conference opened in London on August 16, where a week later the participants issued a declaration recognizing Egypt's sovereign right to a fair return on the use of the canal, but insisting on international control of the waterway.

Eden and Mollet had gone along with the idea of a London conference but only very reluctantly. They hoped that Nasser would not accept the plan, and that would permit them to resort to force "with better grace." To them the Dulles plan appeared to be a victory for Nasser. Only military action, they believed, would cut Nasser down to size. Eden and

Mollet hoped and expected that Nasser would reject the proposals of an international authority to regulate traffic in the canal. Their wish came true. The conference proved to be an exercise in futility.[32] Nasser rejected the London declaration.

In fact the British and the French paid little attention to Dulles's diplomatic maneuvering. While the diplomats conferred, they continued with military preparations. As early as August 1, a joint team of British and French staff officers had begun work on a plan to land troops in Egypt. The plan called for launching a joint military operation to seize and hold the Suez Canal Zone, canceling the nationalization order, and restoring British and French rights in the canal authority. The final aim of the operation would be to topple Nasser. The operation, code-named Musketeer, would be commanded by General Sir Charles Keightly, commander of the British land forces in the Middle East. His deputy would be Admiral Pierre Barjot, commander of the French forces.

A combined headquarters was set up in London with branches in Paris, Malta, and Cyprus. Planning for the vast operation was almost as complicated as the planning of the Normandy invasion of June 1944. The plan called for the British to contribute the bomber force and 50,000 troops. The French would assist with several fighter squadrons and 30,000 troops. A combined naval armada of over 100 British warships, 30 French vessels, and hundreds of landing craft would be used to reach Egypt by sea. The ships were to be assembled in Malta and Cyprus for a huge amphibious operation. The bulk of the expeditionary force would reach Egypt by sea on September 15. Following thirty-six hours of air bombardment, British and French paratroopers would be dropped with the aim of capturing Alexandria, and from there the joint allied force would proceed to Cairo. The official aim was "to restore the Suez Canal to International control."[33] D day was set for September 15.

Eisenhower and Dulles were aware of the British and French war preparations. On August 30, in a meeting of the National Security Council with Eisenhower present, the chairman of the Joint Chiefs of Staff presented his views on possible courses of action by the United States in case of an Anglo-French attack on Nasser. He suggested that the United States should provide them with "strong public, political, and logistical support" without direct military intervention "unless a third party intervened in the hostilities." Admiral Radford thus found himself closer to the

British and French position than to that of the president or the secretary of state. The president interjected, commenting that the situation was "so grave that it must be watched hourly . . . the limit of what we consider doing now is to take the necessary steps to prevent the enlargement of the war if it actually breaks out."[34]

Eisenhower's task now was to prevent a war from breaking out. On September 8, he dispatched another letter to Eden. He agreed with the prime minister that "we have a grave problem confronting us in Nasser's reckless adventure with the Canal." But the use of military force against Egypt under the present circumstances might, according to the president, have very serious consequences and even cause a serious misunderstanding between the United States and Britain. As the president put it, "There is as yet no public opinion in this country which is prepared to support such a move; the most significant public opinion that there is there seems to think that the United Nations was formed to prevent this very thing." For those reasons, the president continued, "we have viewed with some misgivings your preparations for mounting a military expedition against Egypt."

The president believed that better results could be achieved by slower and less dramatic processes than military force. For example, the president suggested the formation of a semipermanent organization of the user governments to take charge of the technical problems of the canal, such as pilotage, traffic patterns, and the collection of fees to cover expenses. Other alternatives to the present dependence on the canal should be developed, such as a possible new pipeline through Turkey or some rerouting of the oil, perhaps more oil from the Western Hemisphere. The president hoped that such pressures might "deflate Nasser" and gradually isolate him. But using force would only turn him into a hero. The president did not rule out the possibility of military action. "I assure you we are not blind to the fact that eventually there may be no escape from the use of force," he concluded.[35] Even so, given all the qualifiers, Eden became convinced that the United States had actually ruled out force as an option.

Dulles, however, pursued the diplomatic route as a delaying tactic to further diminish the chances of an Anglo-French attack on Egypt. Following Nasser's rejection of the London declaration, the secretary proposed a new idea, suggesting that a committee made up of the conference participants go to Cairo and personally present the majority view to the Egyptian leader. The group, with members from Australia, Ethiopia, Iran, Sweden, and the United States, and headed by the Australian Prime Minister, Robert Menzies, arrived in Cairo and on September 3 met with Nasser. He rejected the idea of international control of the Suez Canal, claiming Egyptian sovereignty over it. The act of nationalization was legal, and freedom of navigation would be honored. Undaunted, Dulles called for a second conference in London, which convened on September 19. It established the Suez Canal Users Association, a group of maritime nations that would at least partially manage the waterway and collect transit dues. That proposal was as futile as the previous one. Nasser would have none of it.[36]

Exasperated and constrained by U.S. pressure to hold off a military offensive, on September 23 Eden and Mollet brought the issue before the Security Council of the United Nations. The move failed. The Soviets vetoed any meaningful resolution censuring Egypt. Consequently, Dag Hammarskjöld began to arrange for talks between the parties to the dispute. Then Nasser offered to negotiate personally with Eden and Mollet.[37]

These events led Eisenhower to express premature relief, commenting that "it looks like here is a very great crisis . . . behind us." Dulles too was optimistic. He expected the crisis to wither away.[38] Eisenhower and Dulles thought they had achieved their principal aim—preventing the immediate outbreak of war and gaining time for tempers to cool, especially in Britain where public opinion was by now divided on the issue of war against Nasser. The U.S. leaders succeeded insofar as the British were concerned, for there initial militancy gave way to doubts, uncertainty, and even possible retreat from the military option.[39]

The French, however, were determined not to miss what they perceived to be a unique opportunity to topple Nasser. With the British wavering, they turned to the only country that for some time now had similar interests, albeit different objectives. That country was Israel.[40]

The international crisis did not touch Israel directly, even though the Israelis had a stake in assuring free passage for their ships through the waterway, something prohibited by Egypt since 1949. But Israel had other scores to settle with Nasser. Israel's war plans involved achieving aims closely related to its security and existence as a state. Among them was the removal of the Egyptian blockade of the Straits of Tiran at the entrance of the Gulf of Aqaba. The blockade closed Israel's sea lane to East Africa and the Far East, hindering the development of Israel's southern port of Eilat and its hinterland, the Negev. Another important objective of the Israeli war plan was the elimination of the terrorist bases in the Gaza Strip, from which daily fedayeen incursions into Israel made life unbearable for its southern population. And last but not least, the concentration of the Egyptian forces in the Sinai Peninsula, armed with the newly acquired weapons from the Soviet bloc, prepared for an attack on Israel. Here, Ben-Gurion believed, was a time bomb that had to be defused before it was too late.

Reaching the Suez Canal did not figure at all in Israel's war objectives. Nonetheless, British and French problems with Nasser would soon combine with Israel's specific objectives into a common action against a common enemy. Israel had long prepared for a preemptive attack against Egypt; the current international situation would make such an action all the more favorable. In Dayan's words, "Here was an opportunity unlikely to recur, for action against Egypt in cooperation with France and possibly Britain as well. We will not be alone. I thought this called for a supreme effort on our part and in our interest not to miss an historic chance."[41]

The initiative for collusion with Israel came from France because the French were concerned lest Eden, because of U.S. opposition and division at home, lose his ardor for war. Should Britain back out, France in alliance with Israel would do battle against Nasser.

As early as August 1, when Britain and France began planning joint military action against Nasser, the French Defense Ministry asked the Israelis for detailed, up-to-the-minute information on the strength and locations of Egyptian formations—land, sea, and air. A day later, when Dayan met Ben-Gurion, he suggested that the international situation arising from Nasser's action should be exploited by Israel to launch one of three operations: capture the Sinai Peninsula up to the Suez Canal and establish international control of the waterway, capture Sharm es-Sheikh and remove the blockade at the Gulf of Aqaba, or take over the Gaza Strip. Ben-Gurion recognized the auspicious international environment but was more cautious. It was best, he said, to exercise patience. The expected French arms should first be absorbed, then "strengthen our forces and seek another suitable opportunity to nullify the Egyptian threat."[42] Dayan and Peres would convince Ben-Gurion that the timing for military action could not be any better than now.

On September 1, Admiral Barjot contacted Israel's military attaché in Paris, inquiring whether Israel would be amenable to joining a planned military action against Egypt. On September 7, the Israeli chief of military operations began talks in Paris with Admiral Barjot and other French military representatives. With Ben-Gurion's approval, Dayan instructed his chief of operations to relay to his French counterparts Israel's willingness to cooperate.[43] If the French requested the use of Israel's air and naval bases, as well as Israel's active participation in the fighting, the Israeli government would give the requests serious consideration. In the meantime, large quantities of French weapons—fighter planes, tanks, and armor—continued to flow to Israel.

Dayan ordered the various branches of the general staff to reexamine the contingency plans for the Egyptian front with a view to capturing the Sinai Peninsula or seizing the Straits of Tiran or conquering the Gaza Strip. Circumstances would dictate the scope and size of the operation.

Exploratory talks for joint action continued with Peres's arrival in Paris on September 19. The French minister of defense briefed Peres on talks held in London on September 12 between Guy Mollet, Christian Pineau, and their British counterparts. Eden and the British foreign secretary, Selwyn Lloyd, informed the French leaders that because of U.S. pressures and the opposition of the Labour Party, Operation Musketeer had to be postponed. Britain, they contended, had no choice but to accept Secretary Dulles's proposal to set up the Suez Canal Users Association as a possible way of reaching agreement without recourse to war. To the French, the British decision meant a retreat from previously agreed on plans to launch an attack on Egypt on September 15. Bourgès-Maunoury straightforwardly asked Peres for a joint Franco-Israeli military operation without British participation. France wanted immediate military action, whereas Britain in its indecisiveness kept waiting for suitable political conditions to justify offensive operations.

Ben-Gurion, ever distrustful of the British because of their pro-Arab policies, was now inclined to act in concert with France against Nasser. In his diary, Ben-Gurion wrote: "My view was that this was our first opportunity to find an ally. . . . Here is born the first earnest alliance between us and a western power, and under no circumstances must we decline it."[44] Consequently, on September 26, Ben-Gurion decided to send a high-level delegation to Paris to discuss the conditions for joint military action with representatives of the French government. The delegation included Dayan; Golda Meir; the Transportation Minister, Moshe Carmel; and Shimon Peres.

Arriving in Paris on September 29, the Israeli delegation members began secret talks with their French counterparts in an eve of war atmosphere at the home of Louis Mangin, a close aide and political adviser to Defense Minister Bourgès-Maunoury. The French were represented by Pineau, Abel Thomas, and General Maurice Challe, deputy to the chief of staff of the air force. After a review of the international situation, U.S. objections to military action, and British hesitancy, Pineau raised the main point of the discussions—an Israeli-French attack on Nasser's Egypt. He suggested as the most suitable date for military operations sometime before the middle of October, but not later. In his view, the reasons were twofold. One was technical—the Mediterranean would be relatively calm up to mid-October, but stormy later. The other was political—Eisenhower would be very reluctant to oppose an ally on the eve of the presidential elections. Of course, to his sorrow, Pineau would soon learn that his assessment was wrong.

Israel, said Pineau, would go to war against Egypt to defend its interests, without any reference to British-French concerns, that is, the seizure of the Suez Canal Zone. Then, for the first time, the French foreign minister raised the idea of an "Israeli pretext" on which Israel would attack first. Such action by Israel alone would give Britain and France the "justification," or better yet, the excuse, to intervene under the pretense of safeguarding the Suez Canal from the belligerents. According to Pineau, such intervention would accord with the Anglo-Egyptian treaty of 1955, which brought about the evacuation of the British troops from the Canal Zone. Under the terms of the treaty, British troops would be allowed to return if the proper function of the canal was threatened. In other words, an Israeli first strike would not only serve Israel's interests but would also provide the "juridical pretext" for British and French intervention. Should Israel agree to act alone in the first phase of the campaign, that, said Pineau, would immensely improve the chances for

British participation in the entire military venture. In the coming weeks, the idea of Israel being the first to launch the attack would become the core of the joint military campaign against Egypt.[45]

Replying on behalf of the Israeli delegation, Golda Meir said that, although Israel had no qualms about joining France in taking military action against Nasser, Israel, however, did have some misgivings. The Israelis were not as sanguine about the United States as the French were. Would the Soviet Union send forces to the aid of Egypt? If Britain stayed out of the war, would that country invoke its defense treaty with Jordan should the latter attack Israel? Or, in case Israel moved into the West Bank of the Jordan River to counter the entry of Iraqi forces there, would Britain object to such action and come to Jordan's defense? Moreover, Israel was concerned that if Britain did not join the military campaign, France would not have suitable bomber aircraft to destroy Egyptian airfields. That would enable the Egyptians to receive new planes and continue the war.

In particular the British attitude, which the Israelis considered hypocritical, irked them. The British wanted Israel to provide them with a casus belli, but Israel would thereby be branded as the aggressor, the villain in the whole scheme. And yet the British would not even discuss the subject face to face with the Israelis, lest the Arabs accuse them of collusion with their arch-enemy, Israel. Interestingly enough, while the Israelis vented their anger against the British, the "Israeli pretext" idea was not a British idea at all but a French proposal. If Israel accepted the idea, the French would later be able to use it to lure the reluctant British into proceeding with the military campaign by portraying them as rescuers rather than aggressors.[46]

Although Pineau had his own grudge against British indecisiveness, he reassured the Israelis that they had no need to fear a possible British alliance with Jordan against them, provided they did not attack Jordan. He could not predict the Soviet reaction, but he seemed quite certain that the United States would not play a negative role and must not be informed about the unfolding plans.

The next day, October 11, Dayan, accompanied by several Israeli officers, met with the French Chief of Staff, General Paul Ely, and his deputy, General André Martin. Their discussions centered on the military and technical aspects of the planned military operation. Dayan assured his hosts that, from a military standpoint, the operation could be successfully carried out by France and Israel without British participation. Then each side informed the other about the roles of their respective land, sea, and air forces in achieving their objectives. On October 20, Israel would be ready to commence an attack with the aim of capturing the Sinai Peninsula. France, and possibly Britain, would bomb the Egyptian airfields and seize the Suez Canal Zone.[47]

After Ben-Gurion had been briefed on the talks in Paris concerning the proposed joint campaign, he became apprehensive. He worried that without British participation French air power alone would be unable to destroy the Egyptian airfields and air force. As a consequence, Israeli cities would be left vulnerable to Egyptian air attacks. "Conclusions are unfavorable," he wrote in his diary, "assuming that the English will not take part and will not permit the French to operate from Cyprus."[48] Under those circumstances, French aircraft would have to operate from Israeli airbases, and consequently Israel would suffer the main brunt of the Egyptian bombardment.

But Dayan believed that the prime minister exaggerated the capabilities of the Egyptian air force. He prevented a doubtful Ben-Gurion from scuttling the joint military operation.[49] "Three months ago," Dayan told Ben-Gurion, "we would have regarded a situation in which France was prepared to join us in taking military action against Egypt as a dream, and now, when this is happening in reality we are liable to draw back."[50] Although Dayan convinced Ben-Gurion that joint operational planning with the French should continue, the Israeli premier expressed misgivings. "The plan was not to be implemented without Britain's approval," Ben-Gurion said.

On October 14, soon after the Soviet Union vetoed an Anglo-French proposal for the internationalization of the Suez Canal, General Challe and the French Labor Minister, Albert Gazier (acting in place of Pineau), flew to London for an urgent meeting with Eden at Chequers. There, Challe proposed that Israel launch a war against Egypt. The Israeli attack would provide Britain and France with the excuse to intervene under the pretense of ensuring the smooth operation of the canal. According to Challe, Israel would occupy most of the Sinai Peninsula, while France and

Britain would seize the Suez Canal Zone under the guise of protecting it from the warring sides. The British prime minister found the idea of an Israeli first strike ingenious.

On October 16, Eden and Selwyn Lloyd arrived in Paris for talks with their French counterparts. It was a most decisive meeting because the French succeeded in drawing the British back into the military venture.

The leaders of the two countries accepted the idea of an Israeli preliminary attack on Egypt and subsequent British and French intervention in "order to protect the Suez Canal." The British agreed to assure Israel that they would not assist Jordan if the latter attacked Israel, but said they would be forced to intervene if the reverse happened. Reluctantly, Eden agreed to send a high-level representative to the upcoming talks to be held in Paris between the leaders of France and Israel. His reluctance stemmed from the British desire to avoid the appearance of collusion with Israel.

On October 18, Guy Mollet, in a cable to Ben-Gurion, invited the Israeli premier to come to Paris for urgent talks in order to finalize the military plans for an attack on Egypt. Ben-Gurion's departure was scheduled for Sunday night, October 21, but in the meantime, the Israeli prime minister received details from the French of the discussions held earlier between the leaders of the two European powers. The news of the decision to adopt what the French now referred to as a British proposal—Israel to open the attack alone, in order to provide the legal, political, and juridical justification for Britain and France to invade Egypt—shocked the Israeli leader. To Ben-Gurion, such a plan meant that Israel "would fill the role of aggressor, while the British and the French appeared as angels of peace to bring tranquility to the area. . . . Israel [should] volunteer to mount the rostrum of shame so that Britain and France could have their hands in the waters of purity."[51] If that was the core of the joint action, Ben-Gurion would have none of it.

Once again Dayan intervened. He told Ben-Gurion, "To my mind, we'd lose an historic opportunity which would never recur. In our clash with Nasser, we'd have to continue alone without the forces of Britain and France, within the framework of a joint campaign. In such circumstances and from the political point of view could Israel on her own make war to capture Sharm el-Sheikh in order to secure freedom of shipping to Eilat? Would we not be branded as aggressors and be subjected to even greater pressures by the United States and the Soviet Union?" Pointing to the overwhelming air, sea, and land power of Britain and France, Dayan maintained that the two European powers did not need Israel in order to go to war against Egypt. What they needed was a necessary pretext—something that only Israel could provide. Giving it to them "could provide us with a ticket of admission to the Suez campaign club."[52]

On Sunday morning, October 21, a French private plane carrying Generals Challe and Mangin arrived in Israel to take Ben-Gurion and his aides to the meeting in Paris. They knew about Ben-Gurion's objections to the "British proposal" regarding the "Israeli pretext" idea, which the French visitors now referred to as the "scenario." Britain, they told Dayan, insisted on that course of action; the British would not join the campaign on any other basis. They insisted on appearing as "an intermediary, as one who restored order." Challe's mission was to soften up Ben-Gurion and Dayan before their arrival in the French capital. But Ben-Gurion was not mollified. The idea of an Israeli pretext was still unacceptable to him.

On Sunday night, October 22, at 8:00 P.M., a reluctant Ben-Gurion, Dayan, Shimon Peres, and Mordechai Bar-On, an aide to the chief of staff, took off for France for a secret and historic meeting in Sèvres, a suburb of Paris, that would seal the fateful agreement to go to war against Egypt. During the flight Ben-Gurion revealed his apprehension about the entire scheme. He thought there was too much "wishful thinking" on the part of France and Britain. What guarantee did they have that Nasser could be toppled? Assuming that Cairo was captured and the Egyptian army defeated, Nasser could still fight a protracted guerilla war against the invading armies. What would the United States and Russia do?[53]

The air force plane landed on a secret airstrip at Villacoublay southwest of Paris. The Israelis were immediately driven to nearby Sèvres, where a small inconspicuous villa had been placed at their disposal. There talks began later in the afternoon, with Ben-Gurion, Dayan, and Peres on the Israeli side, and Guy Mollet, Christian Pineau, and Bourgès-Maunoury on the French side.

At the outset the discussions were of a general nature. Ben-Gurion opened with his views on the Middle East. His vision of the region went beyond the immediate planned operation, for he wanted a comprehensive settlement of the problems in the Middle East. In his view, Jordan was not viable as an independent state and should be divided. The area east of the

Jordan River should go to Iraq, provided it agreed to settle the Arab refugees. The territory west of the river would become part of Israel. Lebanon should be partitioned. The northern part should be given to Syria, the southern part from the Litani River down would be annexed by Israel, and the remaining territory in between would become a Christian state.

In a newly expanded Syrian state, Ben-Gurion declared, a pro-Western regime would be established. The Suez Canal, he continued, would be placed under international control, whereas the Straits of Tiran would be under Israeli control. In such a Middle East structure, Britain would exercise influence over an expanded Iraq, and France's sphere would be Lebanon and possibly Syria. Such a plan in his view would satisfy the needs of Britain, France, Israel, Iraq, and Lebanon. He stressed that all these goals could be achieved in an evolutionary manner and not in a quick campaign. France should help Israel convince the United States and Britain to support his grandiose plan for the future boundaries of the Middle East.[54]

After expounding on Israel's expansionist outlook for the future, Ben-Gurion finally addressed the matter at hand. He opposed the British plan. If Israel launched the attack first, it would be denounced by the world as the aggressor. Again he described his nightmare—Israel's cities being attacked by Egypt's Soviet-built bombers. The international situation, he argued, was not propitious for immediate war. With more foresight than Pineau, Ben-Gurion saw the possibility that the Soviets might send "volunteers" to fight alongside Egypt. Moreover, Eisenhower, running for reelection on the slogan of "peace at any price," would in all likelihood oppose military action now but feel less inclined to do so after he won reelection. All in all, concluded Ben-Gurion, the operation should be deferred to a later date, after Britain had accepted his overall comprehensive plan for the Middle East and U.S. neutrality had been assured.

The stunned hosts must have wondered why Ben-Gurion went through the trouble of coming to Sèvres in the first place. They listened politely and showed interest in Ben-Gurion's ultimate vision of the Middle East. But to the French, the immediate concern was the campaign against Nasser. They wanted a quick agreement with Israel that would make it possible for the Anglo-French forces to seize the Suez Canal. Pineau, who replied for the French side, kept repeating the need for immediate action.

Now Eden favored a military attack, but as time went by he would face more opposition in Parliament from the Labour party and even his own party and cabinet. In the meantime, Nasser was growing stronger. In addition, in Pineau's view, the international constellation favored military action: Eisenhower's preoccupation with the electoral campaign would prevent him from interfering. Equally important, the Soviet Union, immersed in internal problems in Poland and Hungary, would have little interest in coming to Nasser's aid.

Then came Bourgès-Maunoury's turn. He tried to reassure Ben-Gurion by guaranteeing that French warships would safeguard the coast of Israel and even help with aircraft defenses by stationing French air force units in Israel to protect its cities against Egyptian bombardment.

The discussions reached an impasse. Ben-Gurion would not budge from his refusal to be the first to launch the attack against Egypt. In fact, he was prepared to fly back to Israel the next morning. Bourgès-Maunoury threatened to demobilize the French units that by now had been preparing for the Suez action for over two-and-a-half months unless an immediate decision to proceed with the campaign was taken.

At 7:00 P.M. the British Foreign Secretary, Selwyn Lloyd, and his secretary, Donald Logan, arrived at the meeting while the French and the Israelis were still at loggerheads. Before joining the talks, Lloyd and his aide had been briefed by French officials about Israel's position. According to Dayan, Selwyn Lloyd might well have been a "friendly man, pleasant, charming, amiable. If so, he showed near-genius in concealing these virtues. His manner could not have been more antagonistic. His whole demeanor expressed distaste for the place, the company, and the topic," when he joined the tripartite talks. Indeed, the British found themselves in a most uncomfortable situation. They were conspiring with tiny Israel (whose establishment they had tried to prevent) to attack an Arab state whose capital, Cairo, was the seat of the Arab League, an organization fathered in 1945 by none other than the then British Foreign Secretary, Anthony Eden.[55]

To Ben-Gurion's chagrin, Selwyn Lloyd presented in detail the conditions under which Britain would participate in the campaign. The Israeli army should first invade the Sinai. Its units would reach the Suez Canal within forty-eight hours. In the course of that time an Anglo-French ultimatum would be issued to both sides ordering them to withdraw from the canal. If, as expected, Egypt rejected it, the Anglo-French force would then seize the waterways and topple Nasser. In other words, as Ben-Gurion saw it, for almost forty-eight hours Israel would be left fighting alone, facing the possibility of Soviet intervention and the bombing of Israeli cities by the Egyptian air force. An angry yet restrained Ben-Gurion rejected Lloyd's "scenario" out of hand. Israel, he said, "would not start a war against Egypt now nor at any other stage." Of course, in light of Israel's own plans for a preemptive attack against Egypt, Ben-Gurion's observation was disingenuous to say the least. It did, however, reflect a deep-seated animosity toward the British policy of trying to appear friendly toward the Arabs at Israel's expense. The British, concerned about their interests in the Arab world, were unwilling to be seen by the Arabs as acting in collusion with Israel against an Arab state.

Dayan saved the talks from total collapse. With Ben-Gurion's permission, he presented a compromise. He proposed that an Israeli paratroop unit be dropped in the vicinity of the Suez Canal behind Egyptian lines at 5:00 P.M. on D day. That same evening the British and the French governments would issue an ultimatum to both sides to withdraw their forces in order to maintain the smooth functioning of the canal. Israel, of course, would accept the demand. Once Egypt refused the ultimatum, British and French air forces would begin bombarding Egyptian airfields the next morning. Dayan's plan still envisaged Israel as the first to launch the attack against Egypt, but it shortened the time lapse between the Israeli attack and the beginning of Anglo-French military action. At the same time, it would reduce the risk not only of Soviet intervention but also of prolonged bombings of Israeli cities by the Egyptian air force.

Although he was amenable to Dayan's proposal, nevertheless Selwyn Lloyd wanted the Israeli action to be a "real act of war with the Israeli army advancing in great strength on a broad front in the Sinai peninsula and mounting a heavy attack that would threaten Cairo." Only in a "real war" could the European allies intervene as the saviors of the peace. In addition, the British foreign secretary suggested a slight change in Dayan's proposal. The British and the French would issue their ultimatum on the morning after D day and go into action twelve hours later—thirty-six hours after Israel launched its "real act of war." However, Israel would be left fighting alone for thirty-six hours instead of twenty-four as proposed by Dayan.

The gap between the Israeli and the Anglo-French positions seemed to have narrowed somewhat. But Ben-Gurion was still apprehensive. The atmosphere in which the talks were conducted was bothersome to him. The British did not accord Israel "full partnership" status in the operation. The United States, he believed, would come out against the entire scheme once it was launched. Besides, the British foreign secretary seemed to have lost interest in the operation altogether. He was about to return to London and brief Eden on the discussions. Pineau feared that Lloyd might convince Eden to scuttle the operation entirely because of Ben-Gurion's refusal to attack first.

Consequently, the French foreign minister decided to fly to London the next day, October 23, in an effort to strengthen Eden's resolve to go to war against Nasser.

New developments in the Middle East were helpful in that regard. Anthony Eden had good reason to be in a hostile mood vis-à-vis Nasser. A day earlier, Jordanian elections resulted in a decisive victory for pro-Nasserite elements and the newly elected Prime Minister, Suleiman Nabulsi, a man of Palestinian origin, announced his intention of abrogating the Anglo-Jordanian defense treaty and of joining the already existing Egyptian-Syrian command. Here was the final affront, which convinced Eden that Nasser would not rest until he eliminated all British presence in the Middle East. The stakes for Britain were never higher. The nationalization of the Suez Canal seemed to be only a prelude to the total loss of British influence in the Middle East. In this case, Nasser was the culprit—deposing him was the only recourse left.

Those developments provided the backdrop to the Pineau-Eden discussions. But the French foreign minister wanted more give on the part of the Israelis as a means of enticing the British to launch the operation. Before his departure, Pineau met with the Israeli delegation in the most decisive meeting of the Sèvres talks. Peres suggested sending an Israeli ship through the Suez Canal, which would be stopped by the Egyptians. This action would provide the Israelis with an excuse to go to war, to be followed by British and French intervention. The suggestion did not appeal to the participants as viable.

Again, Dayan rose to the occasion and presented a new detailed plan that lacked Ben-Gurion's approval. Significantly, however, the Israeli premier raised no objection against Pineau's conveying it to the British prime minister. All apprehensions notwithstanding, Ben-Gurion above all was a pragmatic statesman who understood that Israel must not miss such an opportune moment to fight Nasser with British and French assistance, provided that some of his fears could be allayed and Israel allowed to reap the fruits of victory.

Dayan's plan was basically an elaboration of the earlier proposal he had presented to Selwyn Lloyd. It called for dropping a paratroop battalion under cover of darkness at the Mitla Pass, about thirty miles from the Suez Canal. The same night an armored Israeli brigade would break through Egyptian positions in southern Sinai, capture Nakeb, Kusseima, Thamad, and Nakhl, and link up with the paratroopers. Thirty-six hours later the British and French air forces would begin bombing Egyptian air bases. At that point the entire Israeli army would invade the rest of the Sinai. Dayan maintained that the Egyptians would interpret the dropping of the paratroopers and the attack by only one armored brigade column as a large-scale Israeli reprisal action but not as all-out war. The Egyptians, therefore, would have little reason to activate their entire army. Consequently, the danger of Egyptian bombings of Israeli population centers would become less likely. Moreover, the British would have their pretext to intervene. Britain and France, according to Dayan, would have to recognize Israel's right to keep certain parts of the Sinai Peninsula as the prize of victory in order to safeguard freedom of navigation to Eilat. The Straits of Tiran were as important to Israel as was the Suez Canal to the British and the French.

On the evening of October 23, Pineau presented the latest Israeli proposals to Eden, who found them acceptable and urged Pineau to continue the Sèvres talks with British participation. Now the pressure was on Ben-Gurion to make the fateful decision. The success or the failure of the entire nerve-racking conference depended on him. He decided in the affirmative. An entry in his diary of October 24 reads: "This is a unique opportunity in that two powers will try to eliminate Nasser and we will not face him alone as he grows stronger and stronger and conquers all the Arab countries. The operation required of us is on the order of a 'raid' though with larger forces this time—and if it succeeds, we will obtain freedom of navigation in the Straits of Tiran for we shall seize Sharm el-Sheikh and the island of Tiran. . . . And perhaps the situation in the Middle East may change in accordance with my plan."[56]

As to the possible bombardment of Israeli cities, Ben-Gurion hoped that effective measures could be taken until the British and the French destroyed the enemy's airfields.

On October 24 at 4:30 P.M., two British representatives arrived at Sèvres to conclude the talks, Donald Logan and a Foreign Office official, Patrick Dean. The lower level of the delegation no doubt reflected a British desire to minimize its association, or partnership, with Israel. After a brief review of the situation, in which Ben-Gurion declared Israel's intention to capture the Straits of Tiran—"Israel's Suez Canal"—the three delegations began cementing the final details in synchronizing their war against Egypt.

The tripartite agreement stated that on October 29, 1956, Israeli forces would launch a large-scale attack on the Egyptian army with the aim of reaching the Canal Zone. The following day the governments of Britain and France would simultaneously submit "appeals" to the governments of Egypt and Israel. Egypt would be called upon to cease-fire immediately, withdraw its army to a distance of ten miles to the west of the canal, and agree to a temporary occupation of key areas along the canal by British and French forces in order to ensure freedom of navigation. The appeal to Israel would include a demand for a complete cease-fire and the withdrawal of its forces to an area ten miles east of the canal. The appeals would demand compliance within twelve hours. If one of the belligerents should refuse, the two governments would take the necessary measures for the demands to be accepted.

According to the tripartite agreement, Israel would not be required to fulfill the terms of the appeal addressed to it should Egypt refuse. If, as expected, Egypt rejected the appeal, British and French forces would commence their attack in the early morning hours of October 31, that is, thirty-six hours after the start of the operation. In addition, Israel would dispatch forces to seize the western shore of the Gulf of Aqaba and the islands of Tiran and Sanapir in order to ensure freedom of navigation in the gulf. Israel would not attack Jordan in the course of the war. But if Jordan should attack Israel, Britain would not come to Jordan's aid.

The French agreed to dispatch to Israel a squadron of Mystère and a squadron of Sabre F-86 fighter bombers. In addition, French warships equipped with antiaircraft guns would reach their positions off the Israeli coast by October 29, the date set for the attack in the Sinai. Their mission: to protect Israeli cities from possible Egyptian air attacks.[57]

At 7:00 in the evening, in an impromptu ceremony, the agreements were signed by Christian Pineau on behalf of France, Patrick Dean for England, and Ben-Gurion for Israel. Dayan was not wasting time. He sent a "most immediate cable" to his chief of operations in Israel: "Good prospects for Operation Kadesh [code name for the Sinai Campaign]. Mobilize units immediately. Ensure secrecy in mobilization. Activate deception to produce impression that mobilization aimed against Jordan because of entry of Iraqi forces. Leaving midnight tonight, arriving tomorrow morning."[58]

At midnight the DC-4 took off from the Villacoublay airstrip. An entry in Ben-Gurion's diary of October 25 reads: "Yesterday was perhaps a great day. . . . If, on arriving home we find the ratification of the British government, we will face great days in our history. But I am highly doubtful whether London's approval will be forthcoming. In the meantime the Syrian and Jordanian armies are now under Egyptian command. Egypt now is in control of the two countries. The situation is becoming ever more complicated."[59]

A copy of a letter stating London's approval of the Sèvres protocol reached Ben-Gurion in the evening of October 26. Perhaps as an act of snobbery or in an attempt to maintain the fiction that Britain was not colluding with Israel, Eden sent a vague and noncommittal letter to Guy Mollet. To show his dissatisfaction with British hypocrisy, the French premier mailed a photostat copy of the letter to Ben-Gurion. "Her Majesty's Government have been informed of the course of the conversations held at Sèvres on 22–24 October. They confirm that in the situation therein envisaged, they will take the action decided." Ben-Gurion in an angry mood reacted to Eden's communication: "A typically ambiguous British Foreign Office letter. The French by contrast are clearly committed to every word as agreed in our discussions." In his reply to Mollet, Ben-Gurion assured the French premier that "if the conclusions have been ratified by the two governments, they are ratified by the Israeli government as well."[60]

Upon his return to Israel, Dayan issued a revised schedule of orders for Operation Kadesh. The immediate emphasis of the military operation would be on threatening the Suez Canal first; only afterward would the underlying purpose of the campaign develop, that is, Israeli capture of Sharm es-Sheikh, the destruction of the fedayeen bases in the Gaza Strip and the defeat of the Egyptian army.

On October 27, a French naval flotilla carrying military equipment arrived at the Israeli port of Haifa. In addition, a squadron of French Nord-Atlas transport planes arrived from Cyprus with equipment and technicians. Two squadrons of French-piloted Mystère fighter planes withdrawn from French NATO forces landed at Israeli military airfields to assure air cover for Israeli cities.[61] All that activity did not go unnoticed by the United States. The CIA became aware of the unusually large amount of military equipment being transferred by France to Israel without consulting the United States. In a telegram to the U.S. ambassador to Britain on October 26, Dulles strongly hinted that something was afoot. "We have information of major Israeli preparations and suspect there may be French complicity with them and possibly UK complicity with various moves which they think it preferable to keep from us lest we indicate our disapproval."[62]

Israel's preemptive war plans were now bolstered by Anglo-French participation. The involvement of Britain and France would neutralize the Egyptian air force and reduce the danger of Egyptian bombing of Israeli population centers. Moreover, Anglo-French action would ease Israel's burden by securing its eastern flank—Jordan. Otherwise, Jordan might join Egypt against Israel and demand and receive British assistance under the terms of the Anglo-Jordanian defense treaty. The political aspect of the British and French participation was equally important to Israel because both powers were members of the Security Council with a veto power and thus able to defeat anti-Israeli resolutions. (Dayan, Peres, and even Ben-Gurion failed to realize that such action would not be enough to forestall UN intervention.) From all those perspectives, the Sèvres conference must be considered a triumph for Israel. Ben-Gurion's stubbornness, whether tactical or sincere, produced Dayan's compromise formula: British involvement and a more modest role for Israel.

The process for preemptive war, begun with the Egyptian-Czech arms deal of September 1955, reached its culmination with the Sèvres accords. For Israel, a very important element for victory in war included the element of surprise. Egypt had to be caught off guard. Until the last moment, the Israeli government skillfully disguised its intentions. By chance rather than by design, during the month of October 1956 the most volatile of Israel's frontiers was the one with Jordan. There Israel focused its attention and through a campaign of disinformation gave the impression of an impending attack on its eastern neighbor while the real target was its enemy to the south—Egypt. It was a masterful plan of deception that surprised both Eisenhower and Nasser.

Operation Kadesh:
The Sinai Campaign

8

In his book *The War of Atonement, October 1973*, Chaim Herzog, former major general in the Israeli army, comments on Israel's precarious military situation in the aftermath of the 1948 War of Independence. Even though Israel emerged victorious, the new republic comprised less than 8,000 square miles. Its 600 miles of land frontier provided virtually no defense in territorial depth. Israel's "waist" measured scarcely nine miles from the Transjordan bulge to the Mediterranean. From the Golan Heights in the north, Syrian guns were capable of wreaking havoc on the Jewish farm communities of eastern Galilee. The Gaza Strip occupied by the Egyptians was "like a dagger poised against the main centers of population in southern Israel and along the coast." In short, the country's geographic position had become a strategic nightmare, for it lacked strategic depth in which to deploy its troops in case of an Arab surprise attack. Consequently, the Israeli general staff concluded that whenever the danger of war arose Israel must be prepared to preempt an enemy attack by taking the initiative and carrying on the war in enemy territory.[1]

For Israel to implement such a strategy, the element of surprise attack assumed utmost importance. The enemy must be caught off guard; Israeli troops must take the offensive and achieve their objectives in a war of short duration. The shorter the military campaign, the better the chances of avoiding political complications, such as pressure from the United States to cease fighting or, worse, Soviet military intervention before the objectives were achieved. Surprise and speed became the core of Israel's military strategy. Both elements would be shrewdly and successfully employed in Operation Kadesh, the code name for the Sinai campaign. (*Kadesh* was the name of the biblical site where the Israelites sojourned during their wanderings in the Sinai wilderness en route to the Promised Land.)

During September and throughout the month of October 1956 the deteriorating military situation on the Israeli-Jordanian frontier provided Israel with a golden opportunity to skillfully disguise its intentions of mounting an attack on Egypt. While world attention focused on the ongoing violence on its eastern border, Israel, as planned at Sèvres on October 29, would seize the initiative in a surprise attack on its neighbor to the south.

Ironically, while Israeli leaders and their French and British counterparts were colluding in a war against Nasser, Israel's most volatile frontier was the one with Jordan rather than Egypt. Israel launched retaliatory raids against Jordan, with whom Britain had a defense treaty. On September 11, in retaliation for a guerrilla attack that had killed six Israeli soldiers, the Israeli army struck back with full force at a Jordanian military base at Qariya, killing sixteen Arab legionnaires.

On September 22, Arab Legion positions north of Bethlehem opened up with machine-gun fire on a group of Israeli archaeologists who were visiting the excavations at Ramat Rachel on the southern outskirts of Jerusalem. Four of them were killed and sixteen wounded. In retaliation, Israeli troops on September 25 assaulted Jordanian positions at the Tagart police fortress of Hussan, killing thirty-nine and wounding twelve. On October 5, the Israeli Foreign Ministry informed General Burns that Israel would no longer agree to UN observers taking part in the investigation of incidents that might occur inside Israeli-controlled territory. In addition, Israel was withdrawing its representative from the Israel-Jordanian Mixed Armistice Commission.[2] To the UNTSO commander, such action meant "that the Israelis would in the future carry out retaliations or more extensive operations without having to submit any evidence justifying such action." Israel's enmity, he concluded, was now concentrated mainly against Jordan, and "it seemed that an Israeli attack was most likely to fall upon her."[3]

General Burns proved to be right. On the night of October 10–11, in retaliation for the murder of two Israeli workers in an orange grove near Even Yehuda, Israel launched a massive attack against the Jordanian police fort of Qalkilia. It was the largest Israeli reprisal raid since Kibya, on October 14, 1953, and drew worldwide condemnation. Tanks, artillery, and even planes were used in a savage battle approaching full-scale warfare. Forty-eight Jordanian soldiers were killed, and many more were wounded. The Israelis encountered stiff resistance and suffered heavy losses as well—eighteen killed. Moreover, the massive assault led King Hussein to demand British intervention on the basis of the Anglo-Jordanian defense treaty. Thereupon the British consul in Jerusalem warned Israel that unless the attack ceased, Britain's Royal Air Force would go into action in support of Jordan. The attack on Qalkilia strained Israeli-British relations precisely at a time when Israel hoped that Britain and France would join in an attack on Egypt.[4]

The mounting violence also strained relations between Israel and the United States. Eisenhower blamed Israel for the bloodshed. "Ben-Gurion's aggressive attitude," he told Dulles, "was due to his attempt to take advantage of the gradual deterioration in Jordan and to be ready to occupy and lay claim to the West Bank particularly at a time when the Western powers were preoccupied with Nasser." According to Eisenhower, Ben-Gurion might be under the illusion that such action by him would not arouse U.S. objections, as the elections would "keep this government from taking a strong stand against any aggressive move he might make." He instructed Dulles to warn Ben-Gurion not to make any grave mistake based upon the belief that winning a domestic election "is as important to us as preserving and protecting the peace."[5]

The president's anger at Israel was triggered not only by the attack on Jordan. CIA reports indicated that Israel's target was not Jordan but Egypt. On October 15, U-2 flights over Israel revealed the beginnings of Israeli mobilization aimed at an attack on Egypt through the Sinai Peninsula. In addition, information reached the president regarding the presence in Israel of some sixty French Mystère jet fighter planes, well above the twenty agreed to by the United States. The president felt that the French were arming the Israelis in contravention of the 1950 tripartite agreement and lying to the Americans about it. But neither the president nor the secretary of state was able to gauge the significance of the information at hand: the first step in an Israeli-French collaboration to attack Egypt. To them, Jordan was the flash point.[6]

The tension at the Israeli-Jordanian border was compounded by the precarious political situation in Jordan and the instability of the Hashemite kingdom. Those circumstances would be exploited by Israel in confounding both the United States and Egypt. King Hussein faced wide-scale subversive activities sponsored by Nasser and the Soviet Union aimed at toppling him from the throne and bringing the kingdom under Egyptian influence. The British, who had a tremendous stake in Hussein's survival, planned to bring an Iraqi military unit into Jordan in order to bolster Hussein's power during the upcoming parliamentary elections.

Although such a move might strengthen the king and the anti-Nasserite forces in Jordan, it nonetheless faced Israeli opposition. Iraq had not signed an armistice agreement with Israel at the end of the 1948 war. Moreover, the presence of Iraqi troops close to Israel's borders constituted a violation of the balance of power essential to Israel's security. In order to avoid a possible Israeli attack on Jordan, Britain attempted to obtain Israel's acquiescence to the entry of Iraqi troops.

On October 1, under British prodding, the United States through its ambassador in Israel, Edward Lawson, discussed with Ben-Gurion the possibility of Iraqi troops entering Jordan and probed his views on the matter. According to Lawson, the proposed force would be a token one, with the sole objective of strengthening Jordan's internal stability. Its stay would be brief; it would not cross the Jordan River or move close to Israel's frontier. In addition, it would not be equipped with heavy armaments such as tanks or planes. Ben-Gurion replied, "If Iraq sends troops to the other side of the Jordan River we will do nothing. If they send it to our borders, that is different."[7] To Lawson, Ben-Gurion seemed to have acquiesced to the Iraqi move.[8]

But in an interview published in the the the *Times* of London on October 8, the prime minister of Iraq, Nuri es-Said, declared that a settlement of the Palestine issue should be imposed on Israel on the basis of the 1947 UN resolution. To Israel's chagrin, the statement was welcomed by the British Foreign Office, for it contained the elements of Anthony Eden's Guildhall speech of November 9, 1955. At the time, Ben-Gurion had condemned the speech as pro-Arab and unworthy of consideration.

Whitehall's endorsement of Nuri es-Said's statement raised suspicions among Israeli leaders about British motives. To them the entry of Iraqi troops into Jordan took on the appearance of a much larger scheme, that is, British attempts to bring about an imposed settlement of the Arab-Israeli conflict based on the UN resolution of November 29, 1947. Such a settlement would amount to ceding to the Arabs territory Israel had won during the war of 1948. Moreover, rumors emanating from London and Baghdad spoke of a plan on the part of the United States and Britain to unite Jordan and Iraq and to grant political independence to the West Bank, something that might create a new situation prejudicial to Israel. Accordingly, the Israeli government expressed opposition to the entry of Iraqi troops into Jordan. The United States and Britain were informed that the presence of Iraqi troops in Jordan "represented a grave infringement of the *status quo* in the region and a serious threat." Israel was duty bound "to express its strongest opposition to the contemplated action." Israel urged the United States to intervene and prevent the British scheme.[9]

Israel's refusal to countenance the presence of Iraqi troops in Jordan further aggravated the already strained Israeli-British relations. On October 12, Peter Westlake, the British chargé d'affaires in Tel Aviv, informed Ben-Gurion that an Iraqi division was about to enter Jordan in order to help stabilize the country. In the event that Israel took military action, Britain would be obliged to come to Jordan's aid under both the Anglo-Jordanian treaty of 1948 and the tripartite declaration of 1950. But Ben-Gurion remained undeterred. Israel, he told Westlake, objected to the entry of Iraqi troops and reserved to itself freedom of action.

Privately, Ben-Gurion found the British attitude incomprehensible. At a time when Israel and France were preparing for war against Nasser, Britain's arch-enemy in the Middle East, Britain actually might find itself at war with Israel. Dayan, for his part, could not conceal his irritation. "I must confess to the feeling," he noted in his diary of the Sinai campaign, "that save for the Almighty, only the British are capable of complicating affairs to such a degree."[10]

This absurd situation was resolved in a five-hour meeting on October 16 in Paris between British and French leaders, when they met to discuss military plans against Egypt. The British agreed in principle to Israel's participation in a campaign against Nasser. Eden and Lloyd also decided to call off their Jordanian plans, thus eliminating the possibility of having to fight Israel, a potential partner in the war against Nasser.[11]

The British decision notwithstanding, Israel deliberately called attention to the impending entry of Iraqi troops into Jordan, an eventuality, Israel warned, that might compel an attack on its eastern neighbor. By raising tensions on the Jordanian frontier, Israel tried to divert the world's attention from the impending attack on Egypt.[12] While Israel began mobilizing its reservists, the Israeli Military Intelligence Branch spread rumors through the press that the Iraqi army had actually entered Jordan, in order to give the impression that Israel's military preparedness was aimed toward the east. In fact, the deception worked so well that, Dayan jokingly remarked, "the Intelligence began believing their own rumors."[13] In Washington, Abba Eban played along. Following directives from Jerusalem, he innocently told U.S. officials about the sharpening conflict with Jordan.[14]

Eisenhower and Dulles also assumed that Israel was poised to attack Jordan. After receiving reports from Lawson about full-scale Israeli mobilization, on October 27 Eisenhower cabled Ben-Gurion: "So far as I am informed, there has been no entry of Iraqi troops into Jordan. I must frankly express my concern at heavy mobilization on your side. . . . I renew my plea that there be no forcible initiative on the part of your government which could endanger the peace and the growing friendship between our two countries."[15]

The same day, Dulles summoned Eban from the golf course at the Woodmont Country Club near Washington to an urgent meeting at the State Department. The secretary wanted an explanation regarding Israel's mobilization. Accompanied by his deputy, Reuven Shiloah, Eban rushed to the State Department, where he found Dulles surrounded by his advisers with their eyes fixed on a map portraying the Israeli-Jordan armistice line, which nowhere touched the border with Egypt. When Eban began reciting the "great danger facing Israel" and hence the need for mobilization, Dulles retorted: "What have you to worry about? Egypt is living in constant fear of a British and French attack, Jordan is weak. It is now clear that the Iraqis are not going to enter Jordan. On the other hand, if it is Israel that is planning to attack, it is perhaps because your government finds the time suitable."[16]

On October 28, additional reports of Israeli war preparations reached Eisenhower. The president again cabled Ben-Gurion, renewing his plea "that no forcible initiative be taken by Israel which would endanger the peace in the Middle East." The president, referring to the tripartite declaration of May 1950, promised to take up the problems of Israel's security with Britain and France.[17]

Ben-Gurion could no longer ignore the president's appeals. In his reply, the Israeli premier explained the motives behind his country's mobilization. In light of the dangers facing Israel, with Iraqi troops poised in great numbers on the Iraqi-Jordanian frontier, and with the creation of a joint command of Egypt, Syria, and Jordan, Ben-Gurion said, "My Government would be failing in its essential duty if it did not take all necessary measures to ensure that the declared Arab aim of eliminating Israel by force should not come about." Ben-Gurion's reply included a carefully camouflaged hint: perhaps the mobilization was aimed at Egypt after all. He cited Nasser's culpability. His acquisition of vast quantities of Soviet arms, declared Ben-Gurion, has created a "ridge of steel around Israel's borders." Moreover, his sending of fedayeen gangs into Israel, the Egyptian blockade of Israeli ships passing through the Suez Canal, and its extension to the Gulf of Aqaba could not be tolerated, Ben-Gurion concluded.[18] Still, Nasser's provocations were not new, and the Iraqi army had not entered Jordan. Why then the Israeli mobilization, unless Israel was about to launch a preemptive strike? Ben-Gurion left the question unanswered. To his chagrin, Eisenhower would know the answer twenty-four hours later.

Eisenhower's messages were not particularly worrisome to the Israeli leaders. According to Dayan, they were general in nature and could be "swallowed." More important was the fact that Israel's deception in concealing its intentions had succeeded. "From both his signals," Dayan wrote, "it is apparent that he [Eisenhower] thinks the imminent conflict is likely to erupt between Israel and Jordan and that Britain and France will cooperate with him in preventing this. How uninformed he is of the situation! In all its aspects, the reality is the reverse of his assumption. The arena is not Jordan but Egypt, and Britain and France are likely to be found on the same front with Israel against United States opposition and not with the United States against Israel."[19]

On Sunday, October 28, in a regular meeting of the Israeli cabinet, Ben-Gurion received approval for launching war against Egypt the next day. Within the coalition government, only the leftist Mapam faction opposed Ben-Gurion's proposal but nonetheless agreed to share responsibility for the attack if the rest of the cabinet went along. Soon after the meeting, an official announcement informed the public for the first time of the reasons for the reservist call-up. The mobilization, the statement said, was a defensive precautionary measure, "so that we shall not have to face surprise attacks from the south, north, or the east with inadequate defenses, in view of the entrance of Iraqi forces into Jordan and renewed *fedayeen* attacks." The statement was clearly calculated to draw attention to the Jordan border as the likely scene of military conflict.[20]

The same day, at 8:00 P.M., the U.S. ambassador came to Ben-Gurion seeking assurances that Israel planned no hostile actions. The Israeli prime minister again alluded to the "strangle-hold exercised by Jordan and Egypt on the Straits of Tiran." As far as Lawson was concerned, the premier evaded the issue. The United States, the ambassador interjected, "was not concerned over legitimate defensive measures but rather he [the president] was under the impression that non-defensive operations are being contemplated." Ben-Gurion tried to be reassuring. The United States, he said, "had no reason to worry if it succeeded in inducing the Arab states to exercise restraint."[21] As to the safety of U.S. nationals, Ben-Gurion hoped that no harm would befall them but could not be certain; Israel, he believed, had sufficient air strength to intercept possible enemy bombing attacks. He did not think it likely that fedayeen would strike at non-Jewish nationals.

While Ben-Gurion appeared calm, the pressures of the last few weeks weighed heavily on him. He worried about the casualties Israel would suffer, about the possibility of Egypt bombing Israeli cities, about the Soviet attitude, and, most of all, about the reliability of the British. Would Anthony Eden carry out his commitments agreed to at Sèvres, or would his pro-Arab orientation cause him to back down? Those concerns finally took their toll. After his meeting with the U.S. ambassador, the intense strain felled Ben-Gurion; his temperature shot up to 103. Bedridden at his home in Tel Aviv, with some trepidation the Israeli leader would monitor the course of the Israeli army racing against the clock in the Sinai desert.

On October 29 at 3:20 P.M. Israeli time (8:20 A.M. in Washington, D.C.), the Sinai campaign, code-named Operation Kadesh, began. To ensure utmost surprise and confound the Egyptians, four Israeli Mustang planes of World War II vintage flew barely twelve feet over the Sinai desert, cutting the few Egyptian telephone lines with their wings and propellers. Simultaneously, sixteen Dakota transport planes flying in formation took off from secret air bases in Israel, each carrying a paratroop company, totaling 395 paratroopers. In order to evade Egyptian radar, the Dakotas flew at 500 feet, and only when they approached the jump area did they rise to 1,500 feet. At 5:00 P.M. the paratroopers were dropped at the Mitla Pass, about twenty miles east of the Suez Canal. With this initial action, Dayan began fulfilling Israel's obligations under the Sèvres agreement by creating a threat to the Suez Canal, thus providing the pretext for Anglo-French intervention.[22]

With Egyptian communications in disarray, at 4:00 P.M. an Israeli armored force of approximately 3,000 led by Ariel Sharon crossed the Egyptian border along the southern axis of the Sinai Peninsula. Sharon's mission: capture Quintilla and Nakhl and within thirty-six hours link up with the isolated paratroopers at the Mitla Pass. At 10:30 P.M. October 30, his column reached the pass and joined an anxiously waiting paratroop battalion.

Anticipating the successful completion of the first phase of the campaign, from his sickbed Ben-Gurion early on October 30 approved the issuance of an announcement: "Israeli defense forces entered and engaged *fedayeen* units in Ras en Nakeb and Quintilla and seized positions west of Nakhl crossroads in the vicinity of the Suez Canal. This action follows the Egyptian assaults on Israeli transport on land and sea destined to cause destruction and denial of peaceful life to Israel's citizens."[23] With this announcement the veil of secrecy was finally lifted. Israel had carried out the minimum prerequisite, enabling the British and the French to fulfill their obligations.

In the meantime in Washington throughout October 29, Eban received communications from Ben-Gurion and Golda Meir urging him to explain to State Department officials Israel's mobilization as a purely defensive action, a necessary precautionary measure to stave off a possible Arab attack. He was deliberately kept in the dark about Operation Kadesh to avoid any leaks or premature diplomatic complications. Eban would soon learn the truth from a rather unexpected source.

At approximately 3:00 P.M. Eban and Shiloah arrived at the State Department to see William M. Rountree, the new assistant secretary of state for near eastern affairs. Rountree had replaced George V. Allen, who had held this post until July 16. Also present at the meeting was Fraser

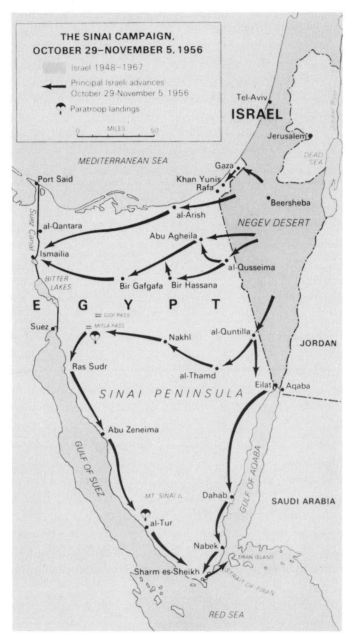

THE SINAI CAMPAIGN,
OCTOBER 29–NOVEMBER 5, 1956

Israel 1948–1967

Principal Israeli advances
October 29–November 5, 1956

Paratroop landings

MILES   50

MEDITERRANEAN SEA

Tel-Aviv

ISRAEL

Jerusalem

DEAD SEA

Gaza

Port Said

Khan Yunis
Rafa

Beersheba

al-Arish

Suez Canal

al-Qantara

Abu Agheila

NEGEV DESERT

Ismailia

al-Qusseima

BITTER LAKES

Bir Gafgafa   Bir Hassana

E G **Y** P **T**

Suez

GIDI PASS

MITLA PASS

Nakhl

al-Quntilla

JORDAN

Ras Sudr

al-Thamd

Eilat   Aqaba

SINAI PENINSULA

Abu Zeneima

GULF OF SUEZ

MT. SINAI

Dahab

GULF OF AQABA

SAUDI ARABIA

al-Tur

Nabek

TIRAN ISLAND

Sharm es-Sheikh

STRAIT OF TIRAN

RED SEA

From Howard M. Sachar, *A History of Israel*. Copyright 1976 by
Howard M. Sachar. Reprinted by permission of Alfred A. Knopf, Inc.

Willkins, a specialist in Arab-Israeli affairs. Eban began by expounding Israel's peaceful intentions as opposed to the utterly hostile attitudes of its neighbors. The mobilization was an attempt to prevent aggression rather than the opposite. Suddenly a secretary came into the room and handed Willkins a note containing the news that had come in on the State Department news ticker: "Israeli paratroop drop deep in the Sinai, Israeli troops crossing the Egyptian frontier." Willkins handed the message to Rountree, who read it aloud and then exclaimed, "War!" Turning toward Eban, Rountree sarcastically commented, "I am certain, Mr. Ambassador, that you will wish to get back to your embassy to find out exactly what is happening in your country . . . this has obviously been an academic discussion."[24] White House and State Department officials compared this encounter to the Japanese delegation's expressing their country's peaceful intentions hours before the bombing of Pearl Harbor.[25] The next day, when Yochanan Meroz, a counselor at the Israeli embassy, attempted to review the war situation with Willkins, the Israeli was rebuffed. "The only matter to be discussed between the State Department and the Israeli embassy," Willkins retorted, "is the evacuation of American citizens from Israel."[26]

The news of the Israeli attack reached the president while he was en route by plane to Florida in the course of the presidential electoral campaign. At the Miami airport, he declared that the United States would do all it could to prevent a war between Israel and the Arab states. When he learned about the widening scope of the Israeli operation, he interrupted his tour and returned to Washington. In the meantime, Dulles summoned the British and French ambassadors to the State Department, in his words "partly to smoke them out to see where they stand." He asked the ambassadors whether Britain and France had any foreknowledge of the Israeli attack and whether their governments would be willing to activate the tripartite declaration and support a UN call for Israeli withdrawal from Egyptian territory. To Dulles, their evasive answers and claims of ignorance were "almost a sign of a guilty conscience."[27]

Eight days before the presidential elections, the Israelis had started a preemptive war against Egypt, not against Jordan as Eisenhower and Dulles had suspected and tried to prevent. On a tactical and strategic level Israel's deception had worked, but at a heavy price: a deterioration in the relations with its most important friend, something Israeli leaders failed to consider, let alone anticipate. According to Ambrose, the president was badly surprised, and "he hated to be surprised," even though experience had taught him to expect surprises.[28] In this case, it was far worse. The president felt deceived and double-crossed. And he reacted accordingly.

At 7:15 P.M. on October 29, soon after his return to Washington, Eisenhower called an emergency meeting at the White House. Present were Dulles; the Secretary of Defense, Charles Wilson; Allen W. Dulles, head of the CIA; Arthur W. Radford; and other senior officials of the State Department and the Pentagon. The president expressed anger at the Israeli action. Until now he had believed that Ben-Gurion's pledges against a preemptive war were genuine.[29] But no longer. The president's early assessment of Ben-Gurion as an "extremist" had just been confirmed. The Israelis, he said, were going to war in order to expand their territory. They wanted more land, but to survive they needed peace with the Arabs.[30] Moreover, through its actions, Israel was doing a great service to the Soviet Union by diverting world attention from resistance to the Soviet repression in Poland and Hungary. The president felt deceived. His personal prestige was at stake. He ordered Dulles to cable Ben-Gurion immediately. "Foster, you tell them goddam it, we are going to apply sanctions, we are going to the United Nations, we are going to do everything that there is to stop this thing."[31]

The president's tirade set the tone for the tense and angry atmosphere permeating the White House meeting. Aggravating the situation were incoming reports describing a buildup of Anglo-French invasion forces around Cyprus. Dulles for some time had strongly suspected a connection between the Israeli attack and Anglo-French intervention against Nasser.[32] Admiral Radford alluded to rumors of the French, British, and Israelis having made a deal to carve up Jordan. In particular the French-Israeli military relationship bothered the participants. Radford pointed out that Israel had obtained fifty to sixty Mystère fighter planes "that we have not heard of . . . and perhaps more." The secretary of state added that such supplies were in violation of agreements whereby "we were supposed to be notified." Moreover, in his view, the British and the French believed that the United States would support them in everything they did. An irate Eisenhower interjected, "We should let the British know at once our position . . . that nothing justifies double-crossing us. If the British back the Israelis they may find us in the opposition. I don't fancy helping the Egyptians but I feel our word must be made good, the Tripartite Declaration must be carried out."

The meeting was interrupted for the president to personally sound out the British ambassador to Washington. In his absence the Chargé d'affaires, John Coulson, was called to the White House. The president and Dulles told him that Britain and the United States must act in unison and support the victim of aggression. The president stressed that the tripartite declaration and subsequent statements committed the United States to come to the aid of the victim of aggression on either side of the conflict. The United States would redeem its pledge on behalf of Egypt. "We must make good on our word," he said. Then the president inquired whether Coulson knew about the large quantities of French weapons that had reached Israel in recent weeks. Also, an inordinately large number of messages had been transmitted between Paris and Israel in the last few days. Coulson truthfully pleaded total ignorance. For his part, Coulson was eager to find out what action the United States would take in light of recent developments. Would the United States call for a meeting of the Security Council? Eisenhower retorted, "We plan to get to the United Nations the first thing in the morning when the doors open, before the USSR gets there."

After a brief recess, the meeting resumed. Eisenhower and Dulles hoped that Britain and France would support the United States in submitting a resolution to the Security Council calling for an immediate cessation of the fighting and the withdrawal of Israeli troops from the Sinai. Eisenhower expected his NATO allies who were signatories of the tripartite declaration of May 1950 to take measures inside and outside the United Nations against any power seeking to alter the present borders between Israel and the Arab states by force. The meeting concluded with Dulles proposing a course of action: to put the matter before the UN Security Council "at the opening of business tomorrow." He would at once contact Henry Cabot Lodge, Jr. the U.S. ambassador to the United Nations, and instruct him to immediately call Hammarskjöld "in order that we may be on record first."[33] That evening, the White House issued a statement in which the president recalled that the United States under both his and the prior administration had pledged itself to assist the victim of any aggression in the Middle East. The president declared, "We shall honor our pledge."

No doubt the president's anger at Israel must be attributed to his belief that the attack on Egypt was an act of aggression that the United States could not and should not condone. Moreover, Israel's action was also a personal affront because Ben-Gurion failed to heed the president's call for peace and Israel deceptively attacked its neighbor to the south.

Still another element influenced the president's negative attitude. He strongly suspected that Israel had deliberately timed the attack close to election day in the belief that political considerations would hamstring the president, preventing him from acting against Israel's interests for fear of losing Jewish votes. That suspicion only increased his rage. In a conversation with his son, Eisenhower lamented, "Well, it looks as if we are in trouble. If the Israelis keep going . . . I may have to use force to stop them. . . . Then I'd lose the election. There would go New York, New Jersey, Pennsylvania, Connecticut at least." Even so he felt obliged to stop Israeli aggression, regardless of the political cost. Otherwise he could not live with his conscience.[34]

In a letter to his boyhood friend, "Swede" Hazlett, the subject of domestic politics and Israel's military action was again on Eisenhower's mind. "The administration had realized that Ben-Gurion might try to take advantage of the pre-campaign period to launch a war because of the importance that so many politicians in the past have attached to our Jewish vote. I gave strict orders to the State Department that they should inform Israel that we'd handle our affairs exactly as though we didn't have a Jew in America. The welfare—the best interests of our country were to be the sole criteria on which we operated."[35]

Did Ben-Gurion choose to attack on October 29 for the reasons mentioned by the president? Neither Ben-Gurion's diaries nor the Israeli archival documents provide any evidence to support such a claim. In fact the evidence suggests the contrary.

At Sèvres Ben-Gurion argued against attacking Egypt before the presidential elections in the United States. He rightly pointed out that Eisenhower, running as a peace candidate, would find it impossible to support a war in the Middle East, even one launched by allies and friends of the United States. He suggested to his French hosts that a better time for military action would be after the presidential elections.[36] In addition, Michael Brecher, quoting Peres, maintains that for Israel the timing of the campaign had no relationship to the U.S. elections. The problem of weather and the situation in Algeria determined the date for the attack. The campaign, according to Peres, had to begin before winter turbulence made sea transport too difficult. Equally, the French expected a nationalist offensive in Algeria before the end of 1956. The war against Egypt must be over before that threat had to be met. In addition, a Nasserite defeat would certainly strengthen the French position there.[37]

At any rate, what mattered most was Eisenhower's interpretation of the timing of Israel's military campaign. And that element turned a negative attitude into outright hostility.

The United Nations would become the area where political pressure would be brought to bear to restore the status quo ante bellum. If necessary, U.S. economic sanctions or the threat thereof would be applied, so that aggression would not succeed in achieving its aims.

On Tuesday morning, October 30, Dulles and his advisers met with the president at the White House to devise strategy for the upcoming emergency meeting of the Security Council, scheduled to begin at 11:00 A.M. The discussions were interrupted by a phone call from Ambassador Lodge reporting that the British had suggested changing the title of the agenda item to the "Palestine Question," thereby eliminating all reference to measures calling for an end to Israel's military operations in Egypt. If the United States agreed to such a change, said Lodge, the British would be willing to join the United States in sponsoring a resolution. Otherwise, they would not. As to the French, they would not collaborate with the United States on this matter under any circumstances.[38]

Dulles for a moment was unaware what lay behind the British and French demur. He thought the attitude of the two Western powers a blessing in disguise. The United States, he said, would be better off "going it alone" than with "our partners who are colonial powers." He had been greatly worried for two or three years over "our identification with powers pursuing colonial policies not compatible with our own." Suddenly, in the midst of the meeting, the president was handed an urgent message from Eden. After reading the message, Eisenhower commented, "Eden says the attitude of Egypt over the past years has relieved the signatories of the Tripartite Declaration of any obligation."[39] In other words, Britain and France did not agree to the proposition that Egypt had been the victim of aggression and, therefore, they would not call upon Israel to cease fire or withdraw its troops from Egyptian territory. The

British and French attitudes relating to the upcoming debate in the Security Council disappointed Eisenhower. Eden's message ran counter to the U.S. position in regard to the military action taken by Israel. Nevertheless, neither the president nor Dulles was able as yet to detect the true motives behind British and French policies, namely, their collusion with Israel against Nasser. Disappointment with the NATO allies would soon turn into outright fury and hostility.

Soon after Israel's public announcement of its attack on Egypt, early on Tuesday, October 30, Mollet and Pineau flew to London for "consultations" with their British counterparts. The main reason for the trip had been the need to coordinate the issuance of the planned ultimatum to Israel and Egypt decided upon at Sèvres.

Accordingly, later in the afternoon, Sir Ivone Kirkpatrick, permanent secretary of the Foreign Office, handed notes separately to the Egyptian and Israeli ambassadors. Those identical notes were actually an ultimatum demanding that the two countries agree to withdraw their military forces to points ten miles west and east of the Suez Canal, "in order to guarantee freedom of transit through the Canal by ships of all nations and in order to separate the combatants, to accept the temporary occupation by Anglo-French forces of key positions at Port Said, Ismailia and Suez." The governments of the United Kingdom and France, the notes stated, "request an answer to this communication within twelve hours." If, at the expiration of that time, one or both Governments have not undertaken to comply with the above requirements, British and French forces will intervene with whatever strength may be necessary to secure compliance.[40] The U.S. ambassador to London, Winthrop W. Aldrich, was called to Whitehall by Ivone Kirkpatrick and at 4:45 P.M. was handed a copy of the ultimatum. A stunned ambassador inquired how Egypt could be expected to accept such conditions. If both sides were to pull back ten miles from the canal, it would still leave the Israelis one hundred miles inside Egypt. He asked if the Israelis were already near the canal. Kirkpatrick had no answer. He referred the ambassador to Eden, who at that moment was informing the House of Commons about the contents of the ultimatums.[41]

With the issuance of the ultimatums, the veil of secrecy concealing the British, French, and Israeli collusion had finally been removed. The United States had been double-crossed, first by Israel and now by its two

NATO allies, in fact a betrayal of the special Atlantic relationship. When Dulles broke the news to the president over the telephone, Eisenhower exploded in anger. In the words of columnist James Reston, "The White House crackled with barracks room language the like of which had not been heard since the days of General Grant."[42] Dulles called the ultimatums "about as crude and brutal as anything he has ever seen . . . it's utterly unacceptable." An exasperated president commented, "They haven't consulted us on anything." The Egyptians, he worried, would most likely turn to the Russians.[43]

The news from London reached New York while the Security Council was debating the U.S.-sponsored resolution calling for an immediate cease-fire and the withdrawal of Israeli troops from Egyptian territory. The draft resolution also implored all member states to withhold all military economic and financial aid from Israel until it complied with the resolution. In light of the new developments, the United States added a paragraph calling on all powers to desist from using or threatening to use force against other countries. This addition was designed to head off an Anglo-French move in the canal area. The British and the French vetoed the resolution, an action that intensified Eisenhower's and Dulles's anger and indignation.

To the United States and to the other members of the Security Council, the ultimatums' intended purpose of separating the belligerents was nothing but a hoax. The two Western powers were ordering the victim, Egypt, to withdraw from its own territory (the Sinai Peninsula) to the west bank of the canal and allowing the invader, Israel, to advance to a distance ten miles east of the canal. Their rationale, "protection of the Canal," sounded hollow and outright insulting. The United States regarded it as a throwback to gunboat diplomacy, a recourse to eighteenth-century methods of settling disputes.

Not surprisingly, at midnight on October 30, Foreign Minister Meir transmitted to London and Paris Israel's reply. It accepted the Anglo-French terms and added, "In giving this undertaking it is assumed by the Government of Israel that a positive response will have been forthcoming from the Egyptian side." As Dayan innocently commented in his diary, "This ultimatum does not worry Israel. We are not within ten miles of the Canal and we have neither interest nor plan to come closer to it."[44]

From Cairo the response was precisely the one Israel, Britain, and

France anticipated. Nasser rejected the ultimatum, which was scheduled to expire at 6:00 A.M. the next day, Cairo time. Immediately afterward, according to the Sèvres script, British and French planes were to start bombing Egyptian airfields. Yet six hours had already passed since the expiration of the ultimatum, and the promised attack had not even begun. That meant that the Egyptian air force remained intact and capable of launching a devastating attack on Israeli cities. Ben-Gurion blamed Eden for the delay. His long-held distrust of the British prime minister had been reinforced. He now viewed Eden not only as the "progenitor of antagonism to Israel, but also as a weak leader whose deeds do not match his declarations." At this point Ben-Gurion did not exclude the possibility even of the British joining the Arab camp at the last moment.[45] If Eden backed out now, Israel would be all alone, exposed to the world as the aggressor.

Ben-Gurion's fears and anxieties grew after eight hours had passed since the expiration of the ultimatum and the Anglo-French bombing raids still had not materialized. Terrified by U.S. and world reaction to the Israeli campaign, Ben-Gurion ordered Dayan to pull out Israeli troops located at the Mitla Pass deep in enemy territory. Dayan, however, insisted that the bombing attacks would eventually be carried out. Even if they were canceled, Dayan was confident that Israel could continue on its own with the campaign. Mitla, he argued, was strategically invaluable as a transit site for reaching Sharm es-Sheikh and removing the Egyptian blockade at the Straits of Tiran—a major Israeli objective. Reluctantly, Ben-Gurion gave in to Dayan's entreaties.[46]

Finally, at 7:00 P.M. on October 31, some twenty-five hours since the ultimatums had been delivered and thirteen hours after their expiration, Anglo-French jet squadrons began the bombardment of Egyptian airfields near Suez. For the next two days 200 British and French fighter bombers operating from carriers and bases in Malta and Cyprus swept back and forth over the delta and canal fields, destroying economic targets in Egypt as well as most of the Egyptian air force on the ground, all preliminary to a landing.

But the British and French expeditionary forces were still several days short of a military capability on the ground, that is, of the occupation of the Canal Zone. Anglo-French ships, with thousands of troops on board, began moving only on November 1 from naval bases in Malta and

Algeria; ahead lay a six-day voyage toward the Suez Canal. D day had been set for November 6. The tardiness of the invasion could not be attributed to geographical distances alone. Eden hoped that the Anglo-French ultimatums and the destruction of the Egyptian air force and airfields would be enough to topple Nasser and thereby obviate the need for an invasion. Such hopes, however, never materialized. Instead of being toppled or surrendering, Nasser remained defiant. Anticipating an allied invasion, he pulled most of his troops back from the Sinai to defend the canal. To further aggravate the allies' predicament, Nasser sank vessels in the waterway, thus effectively closing it to navigation, precisely what the British and French military action aimed at preventing.[47]

The impending allied invasion and the general withdrawal of Egyptian troops from the Sinai to the defense of the Canal Zone made Israel's task easier. Nasser's shift in strategy meant that Israeli military operations could now proceed with greater confidence of success.

If Israel could draw a great deal of satisfaction from the military aspect of the campaign, the diplomatic assault emanating from Washington and running through the United Nations in New York had become a major preoccupation for Israeli leaders. Ben-Gurion and Golda Meir assumed that the Anglo-French veto in the Security Council would stave off any further anti-Israeli moves by the United States. They were sorely mistaken.[48]

The failure of the Security Council to take any action against Israel did not slow Eisenhower and Dulles's determination to punish the aggressor. They now decided to transfer the issue to the General Assembly under the terms of the United Nations for Peace resolution employed by the United States in 1950 during the Korean War.

With Britain and France joining Israel in the war against Egypt, the conflict assumed wider proportions. The president decided to address the nation on radio and television on the crisis in the Middle East and outline the policy his administration intended to pursue. The speech was scheduled for Wednesday night, October 31. Eisenhower's ire toward Israel led to a very unusual situation in the relations between the two countries. For approximately two days following the Israeli attack on Egypt, U.S. officials in the White House and the State Department shunned any contact with the official Israeli representatives in Washington. Instead, the administration used prominent Jewish personalities such as Rabbi

Hillel Silver, Dr. Arthur Burns, Dr. Eli Ginzberg, attorney Philip S. Ehrlich, and businessman James D. Zellerbach as channels of communication with Eban and Ben-Gurion.[49]

Thus, before the president's speech, Sherman Adams, White House chief of staff, contacted Rabbi Silver asking him to convey a message to Ben-Gurion: the president in his upcoming speech would like to refrain from any condemnation of Israel, provided the Israeli premier made a public statement promising that Israel would not retain any of the territory she conquered. As Israel had already accomplished her main goal, namely, the destruction of the fedayeen bases, Adams contended, Israeli troops should withdraw to their previous boundary. The president, he continued, would reciprocate by including in his broadcast speech a statement of deep appreciation of friendship toward Israel. Silver delivered the message to Eban, who in turn telephoned it to Ben-Gurion. The prime minister replied: "The enemy is listening and I cannot possibly tell you now if we will withdraw or not."[50]

A full statement from Ben-Gurion reached Eban early on the afternoon of October 31. The contents were immediately relayed to Silver, who in turn transmitted them to Adams. Ben-Gurion stated that Israel had no territorial ambitions. He would be prepared to withdraw Israeli forces provided "Nasser would sign a peace treaty including clear assurances to abstain from hostile acts against Israel." That would include "the dispersion of the *fedayeen* units, the abolition of the economic boycott, the stoppage of the blockade in the Red Sea and the Suez Canal and the abstention from any military alliance against Israel." Any withdrawal of troops before these conditions were met, according to Ben-Gurion, "would be suicidal." The Israeli leader also stressed the importance of the U.S.-Israeli friendship as "one of the most cherished assets of the Israeli government and people."[51]

Ben-Gurion's conditions for withdrawal could have hardly satisfied the president, who believed that aggressors must withdraw without preconditions. Nonetheless, Eisenhower in his speech on October 31 chose to be conciliatory toward the NATO allies and Israel. The speech included references to Egyptian provocations, thereby indirectly at least placing some responsibility for the present crisis on Nasser rather than solely on Britain, France, and Israel. Eisenhower referred to the three countries as "allies" and "friends," implying a willingness to restore good relations provided certain conditions were met, such as an end to the fighting and the unconditional withdrawal of Israeli troops from Egyptian territory.

The president informed the American people that with the stalemate in the Security Council, the General Assembly of the United Nations, without any veto power, would now become the forum where world opinion "can be brought to bear in our quest for a just end to this tormenting problem," the raging war in the Middle East.[52] As a bitterly disappointed Anthony Eden commented, the United States would now lead the UN General Assembly against Britain, France, and Israel.[53] Israel's only consolation would be the fact that the U.S. wrath would no longer be directed against Israel alone.

While Eisenhower's public address sounded conciliatory toward Israel, in private his anger at the Jewish state had not diminished. In fact, the president had been harsher toward Israel than had Dulles. In an NSC meeting held Thursday morning, November 1, Eisenhower insisted that "it would be a complete mistake for this country to continue with any kind of aid to Israel which was an aggressor." When Dulles enumerated the withholding of certain types of governmental aid to Israel, Eisenhower interjected that "the sanctions outlined seemed a little mild." Dulles promised to add more after the General Assembly condemned Israel for aggression.[54]

The emergency meeting of the General Assembly was scheduled to begin on November 1 at 5:30 P.M. A meeting between Eban and Dulles, the first since the outbreak of the war, was set for earlier that day. Before the meeting, in a telephone conversation with Golda Meir and Shimon Peres, Eban inquired about the military situation and received a glowing report of military success. Israeli forces, Meir told him, were now within ten miles of the Suez Canal. The Gaza Strip had fallen, and the Egyptian army was collapsing in retreat. Thousands of Egyptian soldiers had surrendered, and vast quantities of Russian-made weapons and equipment had been captured. Eban had the unenviable task of trying to extricate his country from an unforeseen and most difficult political situation. The news from the battlefield raised his spirits; it would be very useful for the upcoming meeting with the secretary of state.

By now, some U.S. economic measures against Israel were already in place—for example, the postponement of a scheduled trip to Israel by a team from the Export-Import Bank, which would delay if not cancel a badly needed $75 million loan to Israel. Also held up were negotiations concerning the utilization of grant-in-aid and the Food Surplus Agreement, as well as several technical assistance programs. But Eban wisely decided not to raise those issues with Dulles. He would steer the discussion to a larger context—the future of the Middle East in view of Nasser's apparent military debacle.

The secretary wanted to know whether Israel intended to stay in the Sinai or return to the armistice lines after completing its military objectives. Then came a warning. Should Israel refuse to withdraw, such action "would be bound to affect our relations. We could hardly continue economic aid and all other economic assistance you get from us." Eban, buoyed by Israel's military successes, took up Dulles's challenge regarding Israeli war aims and proceeded to examine the future of the region in light of recent developments. He described the magnitude of Israel's victory in the Sinai and then offered some advice. "The military power of Nasser is in collapse . . . his prestige is sinking. It is possible to bring him down and thereby deal a heavy blow to Soviet influence in the Middle East simultaneous with Soviet troubles in Europe. In this revolutionary situation a crucial hour has been reached. The aim should not be to restore a situation charged with explosiveness but rather to make a dramatic leap forward to peace."

Eban's message: the action taken by Israel, Britain, and France might result in a total change in Middle East power relations to the benefit of the West and Israel. Such an opportunity ought not be scuttled. Broad strategic considerations and a lasting solution were far more important than short-term moral gains. Eban's message was not lost on the secretary. Dulles paced his office for several minutes and then replied:

Look, I'm terribly torn. No one could be happier than I am that Nasser has been beaten. Since Spring I have only had good cause to detest him. . . . Yet can we accept a good end when it is achieved by means that violate the Charter of the UN. . . . If we did that the UN would collapse. So I am forced to turn back to support international law and the Charter. I have to work on the basis that the long term interests of the United States and the world are superior to these considerations of self-benefit. Another thing . . . if the invaders do not evacuate and go back behind the armistice frontier Secretary General Hammarskjöld will resign.[55]

In short, for Eisenhower and Dulles, all that mattered now was peace, the integrity of the United Nations, the rule of law, and the principle that aggression would not succeed. Justice must prevail, with the United States leading the way to peace. The United Nations would become the forum where the issues would be debated, fought out, and decided. Its decisions ought to be the law for all nations. In fact, the United States began leading a moral crusade against Britain, France, and Israel.

In his speech to the General Assembly, Dulles argued that "the resort to force, the violent armed attack by three of our members upon a fourth, cannot be treated as other than a grave error, inconsistent with the principles and purposes of the Charter and undermines [*sic*] this organization."[56] He admitted that there had been Egyptian provocations. Israel had a just grievance because Egypt had never conformed to the Security Council resolution of 1951 recognizing Israel's right to use the Suez Canal. But all that, in Dulles's judgment, did not justify recourse to force.[57]

Eban delivered a hastily prepared speech, probably the most brilliant speech of his decade at the United Nations. It was heard and seen by millions on radio and television. He defended Israel's action on the basis of article 51 of the UN Charter, which, he declared, accorded any nation the "inherent right of self-defense." On October 29, "the Israel Defense Forces took security measures in the Sinai Peninsula in the exercise of our country's inherent right of self-defense." Israel's objectives were "to eliminate the bases from which armed Egyptian units under the special care and authority of Colonel Nasser, invaded Israel's territory for murder, sabotage and the creation of permanent insecurity to peaceful life."[58] Eban cleverly disassociated Israel's motives from those of the British and French. In doing so however, he also laid the basis for Israeli withdrawal once those aims were accomplished.

Eban's impressive address notwithstanding, at dawn on November 2, by an overwhelming vote of sixty-four to five (Britain, France, Israel, Australia, and New Zealand) and six abstentions, the General Assembly approved a U.S. resolution for an "immediate cease-fire and withdrawal of all occupying forces from Egyptian territory as soon as possible." Twenty-four hours later, Dulles, afflicted with severe abdominal pains, was taken to the hospital and diagnosed as having cancer. For about a week, the president would be assisted chiefly by Herbert Hoover, Jr., and

Henry Cabot Lodge, Jr. In essence, Eisenhower, now alone at the helm, determined to restore peace and to see the withdrawal of the invading forces from the Sinai.[59]

The debate in the United Nations and the subsequent resolution increased the political pressures on Israel. But Ben-Gurion, for the moment at least, had good reason to be cheerful. The military campaign had been proceeding at full speed, sometimes even ahead of schedule. On November 2, Dayan came to see him at his home in Tel Aviv to report on the situation on the battlefield. The prime minister had fully recovered both from the flu and from his trepidation of forty-eight hours earlier; he was now in high spirits, so much so that he found the UN debate totally irrelevant. When alarmed officials kept informing him about the barrage of anti-Israeli speeches delivered there, Ben-Gurion calmed them. "Why are you so worried?" he asked. "So long as they are sitting in New York and we are in the Sinai the situation is not so bad!"[60] Ben-Gurion's demonstration of confidence was premature, for a tough political struggle still lay ahead. Nonetheless, he could draw satisfaction from the manner in which Israel had executed its military plans.

And the credit for that must first and foremost go to Dayan. From the beginning of the Sinai campaign, he was aware that the political clock was running against Israel. By October 30, the United States led the diplomatic assault on his country. Joining the United States were the Soviet Union (which found the occasion propitious to divert world attention from its brutal suppression of the Hungarian revolution), the Afro-Asian countries, and Dag Hammarskjöld, who saw the British, French, and Israeli actions as a threat to the world organization he headed. Dayan became convinced that mounting international pressures could force Israel to halt military operations before its objectives were achieved.

The strategy, therefore, was not to destroy the enemy forces, as is customary in most wars, but rather "to confound the military array of the Egyptian forces and bring about their collapse." That meant seizing crossroads and key fortifications and compelling the enemy to surrender rather than getting bogged down in battles with no end in sight. It was a strategy calculated to achieve specific objectives in the shortest possible time. With such a strategy, speed was of the essence.[61]

After the parachute landing at the Mitla Pass, Israel launched a three-pronged assault across the Sinai Peninsula. By late afternoon of October

30, Israel had completed the first phase of the entire military campaign, conquering Quintilla, Thamad, Nakhl, and the Mitla Pass. In so doing, Israel secured the southern axis and outflanked all the Egyptian positions in the northeastern Sinai. Also, by the morning of October 30, the Fourth Brigade overran the vital crossroads of Kusseima near the Negev-Sinai border, opening an additional gateway into the Sinai from the east.

On October 31, the Seventh Brigade carried out the most spectacular and most difficult armored battles of the campaign, capturing Abu Ageila, the Kuafa Dam, Bir Hassna, Jebel Livni, and Bir Hama. By crushing the Egyptian forces in those strongholds in northeast central Sinai, Israel had achieved virtual control of the three southern routes across the peninsula. Throughout November 1, while the UN General Assembly had been debating the issues of the cease-fire and Israeli withdrawal, the Israeli army conquered the northern sector of the Sinai with attacks on the powerful defense position of Rafah at the southern end of the Gaza Strip, thus leaving the strip totally defenseless. From there the Israeli troops pushed ahead to El-Arish on the Mediterranean coast in pursuit of the enemy fleeing toward Kantara on the northern part of the Suez Canal. That completed the battle for the northern axis across Sinai. On November 2, the Gaza Strip, the base for fedayeen attacks against Israel, was captured. In sum, by the time the United Nations had passed the U.S.-sponsored resolution calling for a cease-fire and immediate withdrawal, Israel had only one more objective to accomplish, albeit a very important one—the capture of Sharm es-Sheikh. Its capture on the morning of November 5 would break the Egyptian blockade at the Gulf of Aqaba, a primary aim of the campaign. But in order to achieve that goal, Israel first had to defeat the Egyptian army in the whole of the Sinai. And that was already accomplished by November 3.[62]

While the Israelis were quick, the British and French were slow. In contrast to Israel's speed and effectiveness, Operation Musketeer was still 500 miles off the Egyptian coast. November 6 would still remain their D day.

In the meantime, at the United Nations, frantic efforts were under way to devise a solution that would prevent the allied landing on Egyptian soil from taking place. When the General Assembly resumed its deliberations on November 3, Hammarskjöld declared that Britain, France, and Israel had failed so far to comply with the UN resolution. And, when Soviet tanks were preparing to enter Budapest in their drive to crush the Hungarian revolution, its delegate at the United Nations was demanding immediate compliance by the "three aggressors" with the UN resolution. The convergence of the crisis in the Middle East and the events in Hungary created an atmosphere of doom—a fear that the world was teetering on the brink of atomic cataclysm.[63] In that crisis-laden atmosphere, the General Assembly overwhelmingly voted for a resolution inspired by the United States but submitted by the Canadian Foreign Minister, Lester Pearson. It called for the establishment of a UN Emergency Force (UNEF) to be stationed between Israeli and Egyptian troops and for the restoration of freedom of transit in the canal as soon as possible. Such a force would obviate the need for the British and French invasion purportedly "to separate the combatants along the Suez Canal." The assembly also renewed its demand that Britain, France, and Israel immediately declare their acceptance of a cease-fire.

An awkward situation had been created. Israel, now under severe U.S. pressure and with its objectives all but accomplished, accepted the cease-fire resolution "provided that a similar answer is forthcoming from Egypt." Eban correctly assumed that by the time Egypt replied, Israel would have already captured Sharm es-Sheikh.[64]

The British and the French, however, were aghast at Israel's decision. What justification was there for their intervention at the canal "in separating the belligerents" if a cease-fire was already in place? For Anthony Eden, who by then faced a rebellious Parliament, the loss of support within his own Conservative party, and worst of all U.S. pressures to cease all operations, the Israeli move only increased his difficulties.

The British sought French help in persuading the Israelis to retract their announcement of agreeing to a cease-fire. When the French approached Ben-Gurion on the matter, he fumed. "Why haven't the British and the French planned their landings earlier than November 6, say any time between October 29 and November 4 when fighting raged near the east bank of the Canal?" he asked. "Now when the United Nations called for a cease-fire, Britain was asking Israel to reject it for the sake of her political convenience." Had Israel acted on its own without the allies, said Ben-Gurion, it would not find itself in such a difficult political position.[65] Of course, with Israel now in a favorable military situation, Ben-Gurion had forgotten the benefits that had accrued to his country as a result of its collaboration with the Western powers.[66]

The Israeli premier reluctantly acceded to the French entreaties. An urgent message reached Eban from the Foreign Ministry in Tel Aviv. His earlier announcement should be "amended." Hammarskjöld should be immediately notified that Israel's acceptance of the cease-fire was contingent on Egypt's renunciation of the state of war with Israel, cessation of economic boycotts, and lifting of blockades on Israeli shipping. Eban wryly observed: "This was the only occasion in my experience in which other powers ever have objected to Israel ceasing fire too soon."[67]

Finally, at dawn on November 5, a wave of British and French paratroopers dropped on the outskirts of Port Said and Port Fuad. By that afternoon the Anglo-French troopers had surrounded the two cities. At dawn on November 6, British and French commandos made an amphibious landing, linking up with the forces already there. Both cities surrendered late in the afternoon. Thereafter, Anglo-French troops captured El Cap and set off for Suez City at the southern exit of the canal. The conquest of the entire length of the canal was only forty-eight hours away when Britain decided to accept a cease-fire. The Anglo-French invasion force stopped its advance before achieving its major goal: control of the Suez Canal and the possible overthrow of Nasser. Operation Musketeer had been stopped in its tracks because Anthony Eden and senior members of his cabinet were no longer able to withstand the intense political and economic pressures.

The opening of the allied air assault on the Egyptian cities along the Suez Canal had coincided with the Soviet troops crushing the Hungarian revolution. As a result, the Soviet leadership was free to tackle the Middle East.[68] On November 5, the Soviet Prime Minister, Nikolai Bulganin, dispatched sharply worded letters to the leaders of Britain, France, and Israel. In the letters to Eden and Mollet, he characterized the Anglo-French attack on Egypt as premeditated aggression and indirectly threatened to employ Soviet nuclear missiles against the two Western countries.[69] At the United Nations, news of the imminent outbreak of world war spread like wildfire.

Although Eden was not too concerned about the Soviet threat, Eisenhower used it as a means to further pressure the British to cease fighting. Twenty-four hours before the presidential election in the United States,

Eisenhower called Eden imploring him to cease fighting and implying that Britain would have to face the Soviet Union alone.[70]

U.S. economic pressures also weakened British resolve to continue fighting. On November 4, Eisenhower refused a British request for oil shipments to make up the losses caused by the closing of the Suez Canal. To further aggravate Britain's economic predicament, on November 6, the Secretary of the Treasury, George Humphrey, informed Chancellor of the Exchequer Macmillan that Britain's urgent loan application for $1 billion from the International Monetary Fund, money needed to help arrest the decline of the pound sterling, would not be approved unless Britain ceased military operations immediately.

Anthony Eden could no longer face the mounting pressures. Physically sick, nervous, depressed, and deserted by close associates, his resolve to continue the battle finally cracked. On November 6, in an emergency meeting of the cabinet, he told the ministers that a cease-fire was essential and could no longer be delayed. They did not need much convincing. Macmillan, who two days earlier had voiced doubts about the entire operation, now spoke about the run on the sterling pound threatening Britain's economic well-being. Other members expressed doubts about the wisdom of continuing military operations. In the face of such dire economic difficulties, the cabinet accepted a cease-fire.[71] Immediately after the end of the meeting, at 1:00 A.M., Eden phoned Mollet. Pineau was also present in the room. The British prime minister pleaded with them to go along with the British cabinet's decision. He told Mollet: "I am cornered! I can't hang on. I'm deserted by everybody, my loyal associate Nutting has resigned as Minister of State. I can't even rely on unanimity among the Conservatives. The Archbishop of Canterbury, the Church, the oil businessmen, everybody is against me. The Commonwealth threatens to break up, Eisenhower phoned me. I can't go it alone without the United States. . . . No, it is no longer possible."[72]

Pineau, recalling the telephone conversation, said, "I heard a broken voice, that of a man who has exhausted the limits of his own resistance and is ready to let himself drown."[73] Mollet pleaded for another forty-eight hours in order to complete the seizure of the canal. Eden would only consent to delay the cease-fire announcement until midnight, November 6. Bitterly disappointed, believing that victory was only two days away, Pineau and Mollet reluctantly went along with the cease-fire decision.

The French were unable to carry on alone because of British leadership at every level of the operation.[74]

At 5:00 P.M. General Charles F. Keightley, the commander in chief of the allied operation, was informed by the British defense minister that a UN force would replace his troops. He was ordered to cease fire at one minute before midnight that day. All military action must cease after midnight. Israel had already announced its agreement to the cease-fire twenty-four hours earlier with the conquest of Sharm es-Sheikh.

In retrospect, Eden's loss of nerve deprived the allies of the opportunity to change the nature of the Middle East by regaining control of the Suez Canal and possibly toppling Nasser. The pressures from the United States and the Soviet Union notwithstanding, once the allied forces had landed and the operation was proceeding well, it was an act of folly to call off the operation before the entire canal was captured.[75] Winston Churchill commented on November 26: "I cannot understand why our troops were halted. To go so far and not go on was madness."[76]

On November 18, Selwyn Lloyd came to Washington to see Dulles. In a moment of disingenuousness the secretary of state asked his British counterpart: "Lloyd, why did you stop? Why didn't you go through with it and get Nasser down?" Lloyd replied, "If you had so much as winked at us we might have gone on."[77]

Eden was told about the comments made by Dulles and other senior U.S. officials. He doubted their sincerity.[78] And rightly so, for the U.S. pressures had been genuine. Still, that did not justify the lack of courage and inconsistency exhibited by the British leadership throughout the crisis.

Having succumbed to U.S. pressures in accepting a cease-fire, Eden now hoped to gain some concessions from Eisenhower, among them U.S. support for British and French participation in the UNEF slated to be stationed at the canal upon allied withdrawal, or bargaining their withdrawal against a settlement of the original dispute with Nasser that had triggered the whole military operation—or perhaps U.S. support for the idea that the canal must first be cleared for navigation before any withdrawal took place. But Eisenhower would have none of it. Having brought the two NATO allies to their knees, he now insisted on unconditional withdrawal.

To achieve that aim, the United States used two instruments of coer-

General Moshe Dayan (center), commander of Israeli forces during the Sinai Campaign, celebrates the cease fire, somewhere in the Sinai desert, November 7, 1956. By permission of UPI/Bettmann.

cion: refusing of financial support for the ailing pound and denying Britain and France emergency supplies of oil. Those supplies became imperative following the closure of the canal and the blowing up of oil pipelines in the Middle East.[79] Facing gasoline rationing and possible economic disaster, they capitulated. On December 22, the last British and French troops left Port Said. For the allies, Operation Musketeer, better known as the Suez war, came to an ignominious end. The canal had not been taken, Nasser had not been overthrown, and British and French influence in the Middle East was all but gone.

For Israel, the pressures would have been the same but the outcome quite different. Israel had not gone to war to preserve vital interests, as had Britain and France. Because Israel had fought for survival, surrender under pressure was out of the question. Eisenhower himself came to realize the difference between Israel's motives and those of the British and the French. He eventually showed more understanding for the former, whereas he viewed Britain and France as attempting to maintain colonial possessions in an age when nationalism was sweeping the entire Middle East. He distinguished between wars for survival and "colonial" wars.[80]

Even so, while the pressures from Washington were serious, Ben-Gurion did not flinch but continued the well-thought-out battle until all goals were accomplished. He also knew that the U.S. pressures were mainly economic, and that the United States was not about to send troops to stop the Israelis.

But Bulganin's letter to Ben-Gurion and the Soviet attitude in general were far more ominous. Bulganin's letter was brutal, scornful, and menacing. It expressed "unqualified condemnation of the criminal acts of the aggressors" against Egypt and called on Israel to stop operations and withdraw from Egyptian territory at once. And then it continued: "The government of Israel is criminally and irresponsibly playing with the fate of peace and the fate of its own people, *which cannot but leave its impression on the future of Israel and which puts a question mark against the very existence of Israel as a state* [italics added]. Vitally interested in the maintenance of peace and the preservation of tranquility in the Middle East, the Soviet government is at this moment taking steps to put an end to the war and to restrain the aggressors."[81]

For Ben-Gurion, the Soviet threat was military and far more worrisome than that from the United States. On October 1, when French and Israelis held talks concerning joint military actions against Nasser, he had remarked to the visiting French generals, "We must not forget that the Soviet Union is a nation of 200 million . . . a gigantic global factor . . . we must not ignore the possibility of volunteers being sent from Russia, and their support of Nasser against Israel."[82] At Sèvres, Ben-Gurion raised the possibility of a Soviet aerial attack on Israel. The French tried to allay his fears by claiming that the Soviets were so bogged down in Budapest that they would not even think of bombing Tel Aviv. Ben-Gurion was not convinced. Only after the French promised to send a squadron of French fighter planes to patrol the skies of Israeli cities did he agree to the planned military operation.

Throughout the military campaign, the nightmare of Soviet military intervention had always been with him. On November 2, Eban sent Ben-Gurion a cable describing the Pentagon's fears of possible Soviet intervention. Isser Harel, the head of the MOSSAD, advised Ben-Gurion that the United States would not come to Israel's defense should the Soviet Union take military action against Israel.[83]

And now with Bulganin's threatening letter came reports of massive shipments of Soviet weapons to Syria accompanied by "volunteers."[84] But despite his anxiety, Ben-Gurion did not panic. In his answer to Bulganin he stressed Egypt's belligerency vis-à-vis Israel's quest for peace. The Israeli premier was mostly angered by the vitriolic content of Bulganin's message. In his diary he wrote: "If [Bulganin's] name were not appended [to the note], I could think it had been written by Hitler, and there is no great difference between those hangmen."[85] What particularly infuriated Ben-Gurion were the differences between the letters sent to Eden and Mollet and the one sent to him. Although Britain and France were threatened with ballistic missiles, the letters to them were devoid of the calumny and scorn that characterized the one to Israel. Nor was their right to political independence questioned. Fortunately for Israel, Bulganin's letter arrived late on November 5, twelve hours after the last shot had been fired in the Sinai campaign. Had such a letter arrived before October 29, chances are that Operation Kadesh might not have been launched.[86]

All in all, Operation Kadesh was a brilliant eight-day campaign. Israel's losses were relatively light: 171 killed and one prisoner taken, twenty planes lost, and some 2,000 worn-out vehicles destroyed. By contrast, the Egyptians had lost between 1,000 and 3,000 dead. Nearly 6,000 troops were taken prisoners. Israeli forces captured vast quantities of Egyptian armor and war materiel valued at over $50 million. Included in the war booty were 7,000 tons of ammunition, half a million gallons of fuel, 100 Bren carriers, 200 artillery pieces, 100 tanks, and over 1,000 vehicles.[87]

The military campaign had been successful because it was well planned and meticulously executed with clearly defined objectives: the removal of the Egyptian blockade at the Straits of Tiran, which threatened Israel's shipping in the Gulf of Aqaba, an end to fedayeen incursions into Israel by conquering the Gaza Strip, and, finally, neutralizing the Egyptian threat of a sudden attack on Israel. Such a threat had become more and more ominous with the signing of the Egyptian-Soviet arms deal in September 1955.

The Israeli nation rejoiced in its victory. Ben-Gurion joined the jubilation. Recalling the anxieties and misgivings before the onset of the campaign, he still could not believe its victorious outcome. On November 7, he wrote in his diary, "At first, the military outcome looked like a daydream, then like a legend, and finally like a series of miracles."[88]

But the rejoicing would be short-lived. With the British and the French having withdrawn from Egyptian territory in humiliation, a difficult diplomatic struggle lay ahead as Israel tried to obtain maximum gains from its military victory. Eisenhower, Dulles, Hammarskjöld, and the Soviets would keep up the pressure for total Israel withdrawal without any preconditions. The diplomatic struggle with the United States and the United Nations, while not exacting human lives, would test Ben-Gurion's tenacity even more than had the military campaign.

Israel's Withdrawal from the Sinai and Gaza: The Diplomatic Struggle

9

Ben-Gurion, carried away by the resounding military success against Egypt, on November 7 delivered a victory speech from the rostrum of the Knesset that would place Israel on a collision course with the United States and the United Nations. The speech marked the beginning of a four-month-long difficult uphill diplomatic struggle culminating in Israel's withdrawal from Egyptian territory under conditions far less palatable than those envisaged in the premier's victorious address.

A triumphant Ben-Gurion told the packed to capacity Knesset audience that the Sinai campaign "was the greatest and most glorious in the annals of our people." It restored, he said, King Solomon's patrimony from the island of Yotvat (Tiran) in the south to the foothills of Lebanon in the north. "Yotvat," he proclaimed passionately, "will once more become part of the Third Kingdom of Israel!" He made an oblique reference to his intention to annex the Sinai Peninsula. "Our army," he said, "did not infringe on Egyptian territory. . . . Our operations were restricted to the Sinai Peninsula alone." Then, in language couched in biblical analogies, he put forth Israel's basic policy principles. The armistice lines with Egypt, he asserted, had no more validity; they were dead and could no longer be restored. Under no circumstances would Israel agree to the stationing of a foreign (UN) force in its territory or in any area it occupied.[1] For the moment at least, Ben-Gurion, a statesman well known for his sober realism, took flight in dreams of grandeur.

But the prime minister and his countrymen enjoyed only one happy day of uncompromised triumph. The speech with its harsh arrogant tone was a tactical error because it caused anger and antipathy not only among Israel's enemies but among friends as well. Lester Pearson, the Canadian foreign minister and a friend of Israel, remarked to Eban, "The speech must have been as offensive to the British, the French and Americans as it was to the Arabs . . . if you people persist with this, you run the risk of losing all your friends." According to Eban the general reaction at the United Nations to Ben-Gurion's speech was "confusion and consternation . . . much of the understanding that we had acquired after October 29 was now dissipated."[2]

The pressure increased on Israel to withdraw its troops immediately. On the night of November 7, the General Assembly of the United Nations by a vote of 65 to 1 (Israel) called on Israel to withdraw forthwith from Egyptian territory. The following morning, Hammarskjöld blamed Israel for endangering world peace. He would not discuss any guarantees or assurances with Israel until it agreed to withdraw.

The Soviet Union used Ben-Gurion's address to further intensify its threats against Israel. On November 7, the CIA informed the French that based on a report it had received from the U.S. ambassador in Moscow, the Soviets intended to "flatten" Israel the next day. The French leaders duly conveyed the message to Ben-Gurion. Adding to the atmosphere of doom and gloom was the news that the U.S. ambassador in Paris had assured Mollet that a Soviet missile attack on Britain and France would lead to a U.S. response, a reassurance that conspicuously omitted Israel.[3] An entry in Ben-Gurion's diary of November 9 speaks of his concern about the Soviet threat. "It was a nightmarish day. From Rome, Paris, Washington there is a succession of reports on a stream of Soviet planes and volunteers to Syria on a promise to bomb Israeli airfields, cities and so on. . . . There may be a great deal of exaggeration in these reports, but Bulganin's note to me, and the Soviet tanks' campaign in Hungary testify what these Communist Nazis are capable of doing."

U.S. pressure was now added to the Soviet menace. To Eisenhower, Ben-Gurion's speech declaring that Israel refused to withdraw from

Egyptian territory was "terrible" news. In an urgent message to the Israeli leader the president minced no words in describing his displeasure.

> I must say frankly, Mr. Prime Minister, that the United States view these reports, if true, with deep concern. Any such decision by the government of Israel would seriously undermine the urgent efforts being made by the United Nations to restore peace in the Middle East and could not but bring about the condemnation of Israel as a violator of the principles as well as the directives of the United Nations. . . . It is in this context that I urge you to comply with the resolutions of the United Nations General Assembly dealing with the current crisis and to make your decision known immediately.[4]

On November 8, Herbert Hoover, Jr., called Shiloah to an urgent meeting at the State Department. In a harsh and uncompromising tone he warned Shiloah that Israel's attitude would inevitably lead to most serious measures, such as the termination of all governmental and private aid, UN sanctions, and eventual expulsion from the international organization.

Ben-Gurion's immediate reaction to Eisenhower's message and Hoover's warning was to ask Eban to arrange a secret meeting with the president in which Ben-Gurion could explain Israel's position. But Eisenhower would consider such a meeting only after "the Israelis dropped out of Egyptian territory."[5] The president in his punitive mood was not about to award Ben-Gurion with the prestige of a summit meeting. In a telephone conversation with Rabbi Silver, the president wondered "whether Ben-Gurion's reputation for balance and rationality was really well founded."[6]

Ben-Gurion and the Israeli government now faced the gravest challenge since the beginning of the Sinai war. Surprised at the intensity of opposition from both super powers, from the United Nations, and even from respected U.S. Jews, Ben-Gurion and his colleagues were forced to plan a respectable retreat. A formula had to be devised that would mollify Eisenhower without renouncing the basic objectives Israel wanted to achieve as a result of victory. After consulting Bedell Smith, the under secretary of state, as well as Allen Dulles and the secretary of state, Eban advised Ben-Gurion to declare Israel's "willingness to withdraw from the Sinai when satisfactory arrangements were made with the UNEF about to enter the Suez Canal Zone."[7]

The Israeli cabinet went into continuous emergency session on November 8, from 5:00 in the afternoon until after midnight. The combination of U.S. and Soviet threats, one economic, the other military, turned the stormy cabinet meeting into one of the most fateful in the nation's short history. The sobering mood of a possible world war and another Holocaust permeated the meeting. The existence of the state hung in the balance. The debate was no longer over the need for withdrawal but rather the circumstances under which it should be carried out. In the words of Ya'akov Herzog, the director general of the prime minister's office and a close aide to Ben-Gurion, the Israeli premier "courageously bowed his head to realities and consented to withdraw without a peace treaty" with Egypt.[8]

The ultimate decision was left to Ben-Gurion, who decided in principle on withdrawal from the Sinai. He was frightened by Soviet threats, but it was to the Americans that he decided to capitulate. An urgent message went out to Eisenhower late on November 8. The message contained Eban's suggestion, and as such it constituted an honorable retreat from Ben-Gurion's boisterous position of just over twenty-four hours before. In the message to the president he declared: "Your statement that a United Nations force is being dispatched to Egypt in accordance with pertinent resolutions of the General Assembly is welcomed by us. We have never planned to annex the Sinai Desert. In view of the United Nations resolutions regarding the withdrawal of foreign troops from Egypt and the creation of an international force, we will upon the conclusion of satisfactory arrangements with the United Nations in connection with this international force entering the Suez Canal area, be willing to withdraw our forces."[9]

A half hour after midnight on November 9, a weary and dejected premier delivered a radio broadcast to an anxiously waiting nation.[10] Agonizing realism replaced the victorious mood of only twenty-nine hours earlier. He tried to reassure the soldiers. "There is no power in the world that can reverse your great victory. . . . Israel after the Sinai Campaign would never be the Israel that existed prior to this mighty operation." The people got the message—the army would withdraw from the Sinai. What remained was to negotiate the conditions under which such a withdrawal would take place.

On November 9, Eisenhower cabled Ben-Gurion, congratulating him for his decision to withdraw. "This decision," said the president, "will be warmly welcomed not only by the United States, but by all other nations which are striving to restore peace and security for all nations in the Middle East."[11] Ben-Gurion did not share Eisenhower's enthusiasm. Angrily he wrote in his diary, "Can I send him a cable of appreciation for his behavior during the crisis?"[12] Hammarskjöld expressed "tremendous relief" at Israel's decision to withdraw. The head of the Soviet delegation at the United Nations, however, was less charitable. He wanted to know exactly when withdrawal would take place.[13]

For now, Israel's promise to withdraw had achieved its purpose. It ameliorated the immediate crisis and borrowed time for Israel to explain its views in the United States in order to gain the sympathy of public opinion there and, it was hoped, to steer the administration's policy in Israel's favor.[14] Israel's strategy was one of procrastination, withdrawing gradually under pressure but using the withdrawals as bargaining chips to gain security guarantees from the United States—the only power whose guarantees had any validity. Protracted and at times acrimonious diplomatic negotiations took place in Washington and at UN headquarters in New York from mid-November 1956 until March 1, 1957. Aided by a team of such experienced diplomats as Shiloah in Washington, Rafael and Mordechai Kidron at the UN in New York, and Herzog in Jerusalem as liaison between Ben-Gurion and Eban, Abba Eban and Golda Meir fought Israel's case under most trying circumstances. The final decision maker of course was Ben-Gurion.

Indeed, by mid-November, after a series of talks that Abba Eban and Golda Meir held with foreign ministers at UN headquarters in New York, Israel's diplomatic situation had improved. Lester Pearson was sympathetic to Israel's demand for guarantees that the Straits of Tiran would remain open to the free passage of Israeli ships and that the Gaza Strip would not become a springboard for fedayeen raids against Israel. Henri Spaak, Belgian foreign minister, supported Israeli demands not to return to the status quo ante. The U.S. Deputy Secretary of State, Robert Murphy, promised Eban that the United States would oppose any attempt to prohibit free passage through the Straits of Tiran. Even Hammarskjöld remarked on November 21 that, although Israel must withdraw from Egyptian territory, it should not do so precipitously lest a sudden void be created. Those expressions of goodwill notwithstanding, the Afro-Asian

Israeli Foreign Minister Golda Meir (right) is greeted by Israel's Permanent United Nations Representative, Abba Eban, on her arrival at Idlewild airport in New York, November 14, 1956, to attend the UN session. By permission of UPI/Bettmann.

bloc of countries and the Soviet Union introduced another resolution calling for Israeli withdrawal without preconditions.

At Eban's urging, Ben-Gurion approved an Israeli announcement that by December 3, Israeli troops would pull back thirty miles east of the Suez Canal. Israel's partial withdrawal, however, did not prevent the General Assembly from passing another resolution on November 24. By a vote of 63 to 5 the General Assembly reiterated its previous calls for immediate Israeli withdrawal.

Now, with Israeli withdrawal well under way and external pressures mounting for total withdrawal, Ben-Gurion had to decide what could be salvaged from Israel's great victory. By mid-December his thinking about Israel's ultimate objectives began to crystallize. In a cabinet meeting on December 23, he presented his views on Israel's goals. As to Gaza, he did not favor its annexation. Israel, he argued, could not digest 300,000

Arabs there, nor should the Egyptians be allowed to return. In addition, Israel could not rely on a UN army in the Gaza Strip because such an army could not prevent Egyptian agents from organizing fedayeen anew and activating them against Israeli border settlements. The best solution for Gaza: to maintain an Israeli presence and to provide services such as police protection, health, education, and transportation. Israel should co-opt the United Nations in caring for the inhabitants.[15] In short, Ben-Gurion's standard position was for effective Israeli rule in cooperation with the United Nations without formal annexation of the strip, lest Israel should find itself flooded with a huge Arab population.

As to Sharm es-Sheikh, in a meeting with his senior military advisers on December 29, Ben-Gurion came out against its annexation, but he ruled out Israeli withdrawal until Israel was assured freedom of navigation through the Straits of Tiran. What Ben-Gurion wanted was a firm U.S. commitment to that effect. "A United Nations resolution, or an Egyptian promise would not be sufficient to get us out." Israel would withdraw from the rest of the Sinai Peninsula and would seek but not insist on the demilitarization of its eastern part.[16]

Accordingly, on January 10, 1957, Israeli troops retreated to the El-Arish line in the eastern Sinai. By January 13, Israeli troops pulled back to the line from which Ben-Gurion vowed no further retreats without firm security guarantees. The army deployed along Palestine's mandatory borders, leaving Israel in possession of the Gaza Strip. Sharm es-Sheikh on the western coast of the Gulf of Aqaba along the southern extremity of Egypt's Sinai Peninsula, also under Israeli control, would guarantee free passage of Israeli shipping through the Straits of Tiran. Since 1951 Egyptian artillery batteries at Sharm es-Sheikh had prevented ships bound for Israel from passing through the waterway. On January 13, 1957, the Israeli cabinet adopted Ben-Gurion's proposals. Israeli troops would remain at Sharm es-Sheikh until free passage in the Straits of Tiran was assured, Israel would administer the Gaza Strip together with UN observers, and neither Egyptian nor UN forces would be allowed to enter Gaza. This was the only way to prevent the recurrence of fedayeen raids against Israeli border settlements adjacent to the Gaza Strip.

Meanwhile, in Washington, the Israeli embassy embarked on an extensive information campaign aimed at influencing members of Congress, newspaper editors, and influential policymakers about the justice of

Israel's demands for security guarantees. In speeches, memorandums, and meetings with influential friends of Israel such as Arthur Dean (Dulles's former law partner), Chester Bowles, Paul G. Hoffman, General Lucius D. Clay, Bedell Smith, and others, Eban recounted the illegality of Egypt's blockade of the Straits of Tiran and the nightmare of the possible return of the fedayeen to the Gaza Strip. He found a sympathetic response, more concerning guarantees for freedom of navigation through the Gulf of Aqaba than for Israel's demand to remain in the Gaza Strip. Herman Phleger, Dulles's legal adviser at the State Department, and Robert Murphy recognized the merit in Israel's case against the possibility of restoring an illicit blockade. Dulles too was sympathetic on the question of the straits.[17]

But at UN headquarters in New York, Hammarskjöld and Henry Cabot Lodge, Jr. opposed any guarantees prior to a full and complete withdrawal from Egyptian territory. Viewing the problem in strictly legalistic terms, they contended that the British and the French surrendered to the United Nations unconditionally. They had withdrawn their military forces from the Suez area in accordance with the basic UN principle that armed force could not be used to gain political objectives. That same rule must also apply to Israel.

Disillusioned by Hammarskjöld's rigid legalistic approach and having little faith in UN assurances altogether, Ben-Gurion requested guarantees from the United States as a condition for withdrawal.

On December 29, Golda Meir and Abba Eban were scheduled to meet Dulles for a comprehensive review of the situation. On December 28, in preparation for the meeting, Ben-Gurion instructed them on Israel's ultimate objectives. There would be no Israeli withdrawal from Sharm es-Sheikh without firm U.S. guarantees of freedom of passage through the Straits of Tiran. Although Israel did not intend to annex the Gaza Strip, they wanted to insure that fedayeen attacks would no longer emanate from the area. Only an Israeli presence there could guarantee against a return of Egypt to Gaza or the stationing of a UN force there.[18]

Before their meeting with Dulles, Meir and Eban saw Arthur Dean, a friend of Israel who had been a partner of Dulles for many years in the law firm of Dean Sullivan and Cromwell and who had maintained a close relationship with his former colleague. Eban often consulted and sounded out Dean on various issues, hoping to use his influence to soften up Dulles.

In turn, Dulles used Dean with exactly the opposite aim in mind—to convince Eban that Israel should be more amenable to U.S. entreaties.[19]

At a breakfast meeting on December 28, the Israelis discussed with Dean their proposals for guarantees before withdrawal from Sinai. In addition they discussed Israel's plans for building an eight-inch and subsequently a thirty-inch oil pipeline from the Gulf of Aqaba to the Mediterranean port of Haifa. The pipeline would carry oil from Iran and would, therefore, offer an alternative to the Suez Canal. Whatever they did, Dean advised his guests, they must first inform the secretary of state and obtain his support so that the secretary should not wake up some morning and find that shooting had taken place, a reference to Israel's surprise attack on Egypt, which greatly disturbed Dulles and the president.[20]

In their meeting with Dulles, Golda Meir put forth a number of questions in accordance with Ben-Gurion's directives. Would the secretary pledge "today" that he favored freedom of navigation in the Straits of Tiran and the Gulf of Aqaba and would guarantee any further settlement on that basis? Would the United States do all it could to prevent an Egyptian return to the Gaza Strip? And finally, would the secretary use his influence on Hammarskjöld to bring the United Nations to accede to Israel's requests? Dulles replied that the United States was "immutably" committed to the principle of free navigation for Israeli ships in the Suez Canal and the Gulf of Aqaba. He agreed that the Gulf of Aqaba must remain an international waterway. On the question of Gaza, the secretary was less specific. He did not know yet what would constitute an "equitable solution." The Gaza problem, he asserted, needed further study. Regardless of the U.S. position on both questions, Israel, said Dulles, must deal with Hammarskjöld. The United States could not reach an agreement with Israel behind his back. The United States, said Dulles, would of course use its influence in the United Nations but would not replace the international body in reaching a bilateral agreement with Israel on those issues. The secretary's message: first withdraw, then guarantees.

Dulles wanted to use the opportunity for a heart-to-heart talk with his Israeli counterpart. He began by pointing to the friendship between the two countries and, like a parent admonishing an errant child, plunged into a monologue that criticized Israel's general policy vis-à-vis the Arabs as devoid of vision and long-term planning. Ever since he came into office, he complained, Israel had always demanded from the United States help in dealing with ad hoc problems—weapons, loans, now support on Sharm es-Sheikh and Gaza. The United States, according to Dulles, had tried to be forthcoming. But he and the president wondered "whether you [Israelis] know where you are going?" When, he inquired, would Israel think about its long-term existence as a state and try to win the acceptance of its Arab neighbors? When would Israel admit that its policy of force and massive retaliation against her Arab neighbors would not bring peace any nearer? In fact, Israel's reliance upon force was the real threat to its long-term security. The United States, continued Dulles, would like "to align itself with policies which would assure Israel a broad progress and make her a safe and prosperous land for a hundred years." But, unfortunately, he could not discern on Israel's part any pattern of serious thinking about long-term accommodation with its neighbors.[21] The implications of Dulles's remarks were not lost on his visitors. Dulles hinted that once again Israel was thinking of short-term advantages, refusing to withdraw without preconditions and thereby further alienating its Arab neighbors and the member states of the United Nations. There was very little understanding on Dulles's part about the motives that had led Israel to attack Egypt in the first place. Hence, whatever guarantees Israel wanted, no matter how justified, they would have to come after withdrawal.

The Israeli visitors could draw little satisfaction from Dulles's overall impression of Israeli policies.[22] They found, however, some consolation from the meeting in the secretary's positive attitude on the immediate problem relating to freedom of navigation through the Straits of Tiran and the Gulf of Aqaba. But his noncommittal attitude on Gaza was a harbinger of future disagreements between the two countries on that important issue. Moreover, Dulles's insistence that Hammarskjöld and the United Nations play the main role in solving the crisis did not bode well for Israel. In talks that Eban held with the secretary general and Ralph Bunche, the under secretary of the United Nations, on January 2, 5, and 12, they persisted in their demand for prompt Israeli withdrawal.[23]

Ben-Gurion was equally adamant against any withdrawal until Israel's demands were granted by the United States. On January 7, he wrote to Eban: "I shall suggest to the Cabinet that we consent to any arrangement in Sinai if we are forced to, but under no circumstances to give in over the Tiran Straits and the islands which incidentally do not belong to Egypt, nor the Gaza Strip. . . . They are vital to us and we will accept death rather than surrender."

Israel, Ben-Gurion argued, would be prepared to go to the bitter end. He was well aware of the consequences of such a stand: the United States might embargo all monetary allocations to Israel, including contributions from U.S. Jews. "A nation that's unwilling to struggle for its basic rights could not survive." His only concern was a cutoff of the supply of oil.[24]

By early January, Ben-Gurion was preoccupied with the financial hardship and military sanctions against Israel. In a conversation with Abel Thomas, Ben-Gurion estimated that total economic sanctions would cost Israel $200 million. There was one sanction that he feared most: oil. In that event Israel would need fuel from France, itself an oil-importing country. On January 7, he asked Israel's Finance Minister, Levi Eshkol, how long Israel could withstand sanctions. "Three months," answered Eshkol. After meeting with Treasury officials, Eshkol was more optimistic. Israel, he said, could survive even if the United States imposed a complete financial embargo.[25] But a report presented to Eisenhower about Israel's economy told a different story: "They [the Israelis] are going close to bankruptcy." In a telephone conversation with Dulles on January 12, Eisenhower insisted, "Israel has got to get out of the Sinai."[26] There was no mention of security guarantees.

Israel fared better in the United States in the arena of public relations. During the month of January, the Israeli public relations campaign succeeded in mobilizing official and public support for guarantees of freedom of navigation in the Straits of Tiran. Editorials in the *New York Times*, the *Washington Post*, and other prestigious papers ridiculed the idea of unconditional Israeli withdrawal from Sharm es-Sheikh, an action that in all likelihood would lead to the restoration of the Egyptian blockade.

On January 23, 1957, seventy-five Democratic members of Congress joined in a letter to Dulles opposing UN pressures on Israel to evacuate its positions along the Gulf of Aqaba. They also called for concessions to be obtained from Nasser to assure freedom of passage of Israeli ships in the Suez Canal. On January 25, forty-two members of Congress sent a telegram to Dulles calling on the U.S. delegation at the United Nations to support measures assuring the stationing of a UNEF in the Sinai to prevent the Egyptians from returning to their bases in the Sinai, the Gaza

Strip, and Sharm es-Sheikh. On January 29, a joint resolution sponsored by eight senators was submitted to the Senate calling on the United States to guarantee that there would be no resumption of border raids or of the blockade of vital international waterways. All those expressions of support for Israel notwithstanding, the Eisenhower administration was still committed to solving the crisis within the framework of the UN Charter.

Israel's public relations success did not extend to the United Nations. On January 19, 1957, the General Assembly passed another resolution, the fourth, reiterating that the Israelis must evacuate the remaining positions they held in the Sinai and Gaza Strip and withdraw beyond the armistice demarcation line. The vote was 74 to 2 (Israel and France). The significant fact in this vote was that Western countries that previously had supported Israel's demands for security guarantees now for practical reasons endorsed the call for immediate withdrawal. Their economies were critically dependent upon the passage of oil through the Suez Canal. Nasser shrewdly refused to allow clearing operations in the blocked waterway until Israel withdrew.

In response to the UN resolution on January 23, Ben-Gurion, in a speech to the Knesset, for the first time presented in public Israel's position on the question of Sharm es-Sheikh and Gaza. Israel, he said, would evacuate Sharm es-Sheikh only after receiving specific guarantees for the free passage of its shipping through the Straits of Tiran. Gaza, he maintained, was never part of Egypt, and a UNEF there by its very nature would be unable to prevent the organization of fedayeen by the Egyptian authorities or prevent their incursion into Israel. Consequently, an Israeli presence there would be necessary to administer the area in cooperation with the United Nations. Ben-Gurion hoped that Israel's administration of Gaza would be a pilot plan of general cooperation with the Arab world. The overwhelming majority of the Knesset greeted his remarks with wild cheers of approval. The government's policy as outlined in the premier's speech was approved by a vote of 54 in favor, with only 11 legislators voting against any withdrawal.[27]

Ben-Gurion's speech was a far cry from the triumphant one he delivered on November 7, 1956. But scaling down Israel's objectives was not enough to mollify Hammarskjöld or for that matter the U.S. administration. For his part, the secretary general on January 25 responded to Ben-Gurion's address in a report to the General Assembly in which he rejected the idea that an Israeli administration should remain in the Gaza Strip. The Gaza Strip, he argued, had been placed under Egyptian control by the armistice agreements of 1949. Any changes in that arrangement could only come about with Egypt's approval. He proposed that a UNEF should be deployed on both sides of the demarcation line. As for the Gulf of Aqaba and the straits, a UNEF would be stationed there after Israel's withdrawal from Sharm es-Sheikh. Hammarskjöld did concede that international law guaranteed freedom of passage through the waterway. But that was as far as the secretary general was willing to go in meeting Israel's demands for "firm" guarantees of free passage. On January 28, in a speech before the General Assembly, Henry Cabot Lodge supported Hammarskjöld's report. Israel, he said, "must withdraw its forces without delay."[28]

The lack of movement on Israel's part produced two additional UN resolutions, sponsored by Brazil, Colombia, India, Indonesia, Norway, Yugoslavia, and the United States. The resolutions were passed by the General Assembly on February 2. The first deplored Israel's failure to complete its withdrawal behind the armistice lines and called for the implementation of the UN resolutions without further delay. The second resolution for the first time took notice, however slight, of Israel's demands for security. It recognized that "withdrawal by Israel must be followed by action which would assure progress toward the creation of peaceful conditions" such as the stationing of UNEF on the Egyptian-Israeli border. Henry Cabot Lodge, Jr., the principal speaker sponsoring the resolutions, declared: "In all seriousness and solemnity, I cannot predict the consequences which can ensue if Israel fails to comply with the will of this Assembly as expressed in the resolutions." For the first time since the onset of the crisis, the United States had strongly hinted to Israel that sanctions might have to be applied if Israel refused to comply with the UN resolutions.

Lodge's thinly veiled threat of sanctions received the full backing of the president. In a sharply worded letter to Ben-Gurion on February 3, Eisenhower reminded the premier that three months had passed since Israel had promised to withdraw its forces upon "the conclusion of satisfactory arrangements with the United States in connection with the international force entering the Suez Canal area." But while British and

French forces had been withdrawn from Egypt, Eisenhower complained, "Israel's withdrawal to the General Armistice line has not yet been completed." The resolutions passed by the United Nations on February 2, said the president, "lay a sound foundation for the establishment of peaceful conditions in the former area of hostilities, the prevention of further outbreaks and the solution of the problem of Gaza and Sharm es-Sheikh." Accordingly, Eisenhower continued, Israel should proceed with its withdrawal behind the armistice lines without further delay. And then came a warning of possible imposition of sanctions should Israel refuse to comply with the UN resolutions. "Such continued ignoring of the judgment of nations as expressed in the United Nations Resolutions would almost surely lead to the invoking of *further United Nations procedures* [italics added] which could seriously disturb the relations between Israel and other member nations including the United States."[29]

Reiterating the president's harsh message on February 5, Dulles told a press conference that the United States would give serious consideration to a UN call for sanctions against Israel to support its resolutions calling for Israeli withdrawal. He said, however, that the United States would not take unilateral action.

No doubt Eisenhower's strongly worded telegram to Ben-Gurion was also intended to impress King Ibn Saud of Saudi Arabia, who arrived on an official visit to Washington on January 29. The king demanded that the administration exert maximum pressure on Israel to evacuate the entire Sinai Peninsula and the Gaza Strip. He warned that U.S. interests in the Middle East would suffer as long as Israel troops had not withdrawn. U.S. interests could not be forfeited. One of them was the U.S. air base in Dhahran, Saudi Arabia. The Saudi monarch promised that the United States would be able to use the facility, provided it supplied his country with arms and secured Israeli evacuation. In addition, the administration for some time now had tried to shore up the king as a counterweight to Nasser's leadership in the Arab world.[30]

But Ben-Gurion would not retreat. In his reply to the president he restated Israel's position: no withdrawal from Sharm es-Sheikh without firm guarantees of free passage through the straits and a civil Israeli administration in Gaza. As to the possibility of "procedures," that is, sanctions against Israel, Ben-Gurion remained defiant:

No such "procedures" were ever invoked against Egypt which for eight years past has violated resolutions of the Security Council and provisions of the Charter and continues to do so. At a time when public opinion in most of the free countries has come to acknowledge the justice of our stand, is it conceivable that the United States the land of freedom, equality and human rights should support such discrimination and that the UN "procedures" should be invoked to force us back into a position which would again expose us to murder and blockade?[31]

The threat of sanctions against Israel led to an avalanche of criticism of administration policy. The chorus of protests, led by members of Congress, senators, and leading public figures, condemned the policy of sanctions as unbalanced and unfair. Jewish pressure through demonstrations, letters to Congress, and strategy meetings played an important role in arousing congressional opposition to sanctions. Leading the charge against administration policies was none other than William F. Knowland, Republican senator from California and Senate minority leader. On February 5, in a statement to the press, he criticized the "double standard" of the United Nations in applying sanctions against a small country while sidestepping the question of sanctions against the Soviet Union. Dulles, very displeased by Knowland's statement, complained to the president that such statements harmed the administration's policy to bring about Israeli withdrawal. "If the President should now follow Knowland's thesis," said Dulles, "it would make it almost impossible for Israel to comply."[32] Alexander Wiley, a Wisconsin senator and ranking Republican on the Foreign Relations Committee, declared that sanctions against Israel would not be fair, justified, or an effective answer to the Mideast dispute. Israel, he maintained, was entitled to reasonable guarantees that its citizens would not be attacked and that its freedom of navigation in international waterways would be safeguarded.

For some time before the administration's threat of sanctions, the Democrats had been strongly opposed to administration policy. Vocal support for Israel's stance was expressed by such figures as Eleanor Roosevelt, Harry S. Truman, and Lyndon B. Johnson, Senate majority leader. Eisenhower and Dulles could not easily ignore the criticisms of their policy emanating from Congress, for the issue was not only moral but political. Congressional displeasure would now affect the administration's general Mideast policy. The question of sanctions against Israel had become intertwined with a general program, the Eisenhower Doctrine for the Middle East, which the administration submitted for Senate approval on January 5, 1957. The Eisenhower Doctrine was undergoing skeptical and scathing hearings before the Senate Foreign Relations Committee. The Democrats threatened to vote against it if the administration insisted on pursuing a policy of sanctions against Israel.[33]

By early February the administration found itself in a difficult dilemma. On the one hand, Eisenhower and Dulles believed that Israel must withdraw without preconditions in accordance with UN resolutions. That stand was not only an attempt to preserve the prestige of the United Nations, but it was necessary in order to maintain U.S. influence in the Arab world. The longer Israeli troops remained in the Sinai, the more influence the Soviet Union gained in the Arab world by blaming the United States for not exerting sufficient pressure on Israel to withdraw. Moreover, Nasser would obstruct the clearance of the Suez Canal until Israeli troops withdrew from Egyptian territory, thus depriving Western Europe of oil from the Persian Gulf. On the other hand, Israel would not withdraw unless strong measures such as sanctions were applied. But sanctions, Dulles learned, were highly unpopular. Congressional and public sympathy for Israel made such a policy all but impossible to carry out. In addition, the Eisenhower Doctrine for which the administration lobbied so hard in the Senate would be doomed unless the administration took a more favorable attitude toward Israel.

Caught between conflicting pressures, Dulles, with presidential approval, decided to break the deadlock by partially conceding to Israel's demands for guarantees outside the context of the United Nations. That marked a significant shift in U.S. policy.

On February 11, Dulles met Eban and Shiloah at the State Department. Dulles began by reading the text of an aide-mémoire explaining the U.S. position on the questions of Aqaba and the Gaza Strip. With respect to the former, "the United States believes that the Gulf constitutes international waters and that no nation has the right forcibly to prevent free and innocent passage" and access thereto. The United States, Dulles continued, "is prepared to exercise the right of free passage of vessels of U.S. registry and join with others to secure general recognition of this right."

The passage of pilgrims on religious missions would be fully respected.[34] Those assurances would be given by the United States to Israel on the understanding that Israel would first agree to withdraw its troops in accordance with the UN resolutions of February 2, 1957.

As to Gaza, Dulles acknowledged that the area had been a source of armed infiltration by fedayeen into Israel. But in his view neither the United Nations nor the United States had the right to require Egypt to modify the armistice agreement of 1949, which "gives Egypt the right and responsibility of occupation." According to the secretary, "Israeli withdrawal from Gaza should be prompt and unconditional, leaving the future of the area to be worked out through the offices and efforts of the UN." Finally, according to the aide-mémoire the UNEF would be stationed in both Sharm es-Sheikh and Gaza following Israeli withdrawal.[35]

All in all, the U.S. position moved closer to Israel on the question of free passage through the straits but remained unchanged on the future of the Gaza Strip. Dulles rightly assumed that Israel would ultimately be flexible on the question of Gaza provided it received ironclad guarantees concerning access to the Gulf of Aqaba, vital to its national and economic interests.[36]

After the meeting with Dulles, Eban and Shiloah lunched with Robert Murphy, who had always been more sympathetic to Israel's concerns than anyone else in the State Department. He wanted to impress upon the Israelis the urgency for a favorable reply on the part of the Israeli government to the U.S. proposals. The United States, he said, would ask other maritime powers to join in securing free and innocent passage to the Gulf of Aqaba. He implied that each power, including Israel, would have the right to protect its own shipping. Murphy implored the Israelis to view the U.S. assurances with utmost seriousness and accord them careful consideration. Dulles's memorandum, he explained, must be regarded as a "sensational development." The United States expected a favorable Israeli reply within three days.

Eban agreed with Murphy's assessment. Immediately, he cabled Ben-Gurion the contents of Dulles's aide-mémoire and then added, "A propitious turning point has come . . . we should do everything to keep the UN General Assembly out of the picture and in order to achieve this we should give our assent to Dulles in principle."[37] Eban saw in Dulles's proposals a very important breakthrough. After long months of confrontation with the United States, Israel could finally look forward to negotiations and cooperation with its most important friend.

But Ben-Gurion was far less enthusiastic. In fact, he decided to continue procrastinating in the hope of securing better terms. On February 12, he informed Eban that while the U.S. memorandum showed a desire to achieve a positive solution, it did not go far enough and could not be accepted by Israel. Ben-Gurion rightly pointed out that the memorandum did not include specifically the provision for free passage of Israeli ships through the straits and the gulf. Furthermore, no guarantees were given concerning the nonreturn of the Egyptians to Gaza. Ben-Gurion insisted on an Israeli civilian authority in Gaza to administer the area in cooperation with the United Nations. He reiterated his previous decision: Israel would make no further concessions, even if sanctions were imposed.[38]

Dulles eagerly awaited the Israeli reply. At the United Nations, the Afro-Asian bloc was about to introduce another resolution, this time calling for sanctions against Israel. But sanctions would be ineffective and would not be voted upon unless the United States were to participate. Consequently, Lodge kept postponing the vote, hoping that a U.S.-Israeli agreement would obviate the need for it.

On February 15, a disappointed Eban accompanied by Shiloah met with Dulles. Also present were Wilkins; the Under Secretary of State, Christian Herter; and Rountree. Eban tried to put the best face on his effort to disguise a most difficult situation. Israel, he said, appreciated Dulles's declaration that "the United States would take a heavy responsibility if Israel were to withdraw and the blockade were to be renewed." A peace agreement with Egypt would, of course, obviate such prospects. In its absence, said Eban, Israel insisted on "effective" guarantees regarding the role of the UNEF guarding the straits at Sharm es-Sheikh. How long would its presence there be maintained? What could be done so that Nasser would not renew the blockade once the Israeli troops were withdrawn? Eban insisted on conditions prior to an Israeli withdrawal: a public U.S. declaration, preferably by Lodge, before the General Assembly of the United Nations containing U.S. pledges of free passage of Israeli ships through the straits, and a U.S.-Israeli agreement concerning the roles of the UNEF in the evacuated areas. On Gaza, Eban repeated the standard Israeli position.

Dulles could not contain his irritation over the Israeli position. Exasperated, he told Eban: "I am afraid that Israel did not understand the spirit of the U.S. initiative and did not respond as the United States anticipated. The fact is that the UN called for Israeli withdrawal to the armistice line without conditions. The United States hoped that if Israel would be assured of our position concerning the two major questions raised by Ben-Gurion in his letter to the President it would make it easier for her to withdraw." The U.S. guarantees included in the February 11 aide-mémoire, according to Dulles, were predicated on Israel's agreement to withdraw first. Instead, Dulles asserted, Israel intended to engage the United States in long-drawn-out bilateral negotiations in an attempt to circumvent the United Nations entirely. As a member of the United Nations and as a maritime power, the United States could use its influence and declare publicly its policy in regard to the straits as a national policy. "To our sorrow Israel demands a bilateral agreement with the United States, this is impossible, the United States could not replace the UN," concluded Dulles.[39]

Dulles called the president in Thomasville, Georgia, vacationing at the plantation of the Secretary of the Treasury, George Humphrey. The Israeli reply, he said, "is extremely unsatisfactory and seems completely to misapprehend the nature of our aide-mémoire." The president replied: "Make clear to Eban that we are trying to be helpful and if they don't want it we will have to go along and see what the UN does."[40]

Early the next day, Dulles and Lodge flew down to Thomasville to brief the president and Humphrey on the Mideast crisis. Dulles was in an angry mood. Ben-Gurion, he reported to the president, would not agree to withdraw Israeli troops unless Israel retained civil administration and police power in Gaza. Israel also demanded from the United States a guaranteed right of free passage in the Gulf of Aqaba. The United States, the secretary continued, "had gone just as far as was possible to try to make it easy and acceptable to the Israelis to withdraw." Any further guarantees "would almost surely jeopardize the entire Western influence in the Middle East and make it almost certain that virtually all of the Middle Eastern countries would feel that United States policy toward the area was in the last analysis controlled by Jewish influence in the United States." The Arabs would surely turn to the Soviet Union.

Eisenhower concurred with Dulles's assessment. He would step up the pressure on Israel. Lodge urged immediate action, for he could not delay much longer a UN vote condemning Israel and calling for sanctions. They discussed various options. The president approved U.S. action in support of a UN resolution calling on member states to suspend not only governmental assistance to Israel (which the United States had already done) but also private assistance. The United States would also introduce a resolution for prospective sanctions against Egypt if it interfered with Israeli shipping in the Gulf of Aqaba. Humphrey, after consulting treasury officials, reported that Israel received about $40 million a year in private, tax-deductible gifts and about $60 million worth of Israel bonds sold each year in the United States. Eisenhower thought that the threat to stop the flow of that money should be enough to force Israeli compliance. He advised Humphrey to "get in touch with one or two leading Jewish personalities who ought to be sympathetic to our position and help to organize some Jewish sentiment."[41]

But Eisenhower and Dulles, to their chagrin, would soon learn that there was no sentiment, Jewish or otherwise, for sanctions against Israel, a circumstance that further weakened U.S. leverage on Israel.

In a telephone conversation with Lodge on February 12, Dulles mentioned a letter he had just received from Lyndon B. Johnson objecting to sanctions. The secretary worried about a unanimous vote in both houses for a resolution against sanctions. If that happened, "we are going to be in very serious trouble and indeed may lose our authority to impose sanctions . . . we did not want the Israelis to know we were weak on this thing at all." The secretary complained to Lodge about the "terrific control the Jews have over the news media and the barrage which the Jews have built up on Congressmen."[42]

On February 16 at 6:40 P.M., Dulles received a phone call from Knowland, who had already been briefed about the contents of the February 11 aide-mémoire. He wanted to know if the president was still considering sanctions against Israel. Answered Dulles, "Unless the Israelis go we will probably go along with sanctions." Knowland objected. "I have gone along as far as I can go and this will mean the parting of the ways . . . sanctions are pretty serious. I would like to know the timing. . . . I want to send in my resignation as a U.N. delegate before the delegation votes on sanctions." Dulles pleaded with him to reconsider. "We cannot have all our policies made in Jerusalem . . . if we can't get the Israelis out of Egypt the Russians will get them out and in the process we will lose the Middle East."[43] Knowland was not convinced.

Dulles, angry and frustrated over the constraints on U.S. Middle East policy, invited Eban to his home for another review of the situation. This was the second meeting with Eban in twenty-four hours and came soon after Dulles's return from Thomasville. The secretary, visibly irritated and impatient, wanted to know if there was any change in the Israeli position. Eban had no news to report. Dulles was both firm and conciliatory. He sympathized with Israel's predicament and Israel's fears, based on unfortunate experiences of hostile Arab acts and Arab unwillingness to recognize Israel. He understood that Israel might have to fight in case of Egyptian violations and a return of the blockade at the Straits of Tiran. He confessed that he was no "pacifist" and approved of "just" wars. The president, said Dulles, "is aware of the solemn and grave choices facing Israel." If Israel accepted the U.S. proposals and withdrew from Gaza and Sinai, the United States and all humankind would owe a great debt to Israel. Dulles promised "that the debt will be paid." But if Israel rejected the U.S. initiative, it better try its "luck elsewhere."[44]

The U.S.-Israeli negotiations had reached a stalemate. Again it was left to Eban to prevent an open rift with the United States. He felt that the diplomatic gains Israel had made with Dulles were about to dissipate. Israel, he rightly believed, was about to forfeit its best chance of attaining most of the objectives for which it had gone to war with Egypt. The ambassador lamented to Ben-Gurion that, because of Israel's rejection of the February 11 aide-mémoire, the nation was now viewed by its erstwhile supporters as unreasonable and intransigent.[45]

Eban decided to buy time. Without consulting his prime minister, he told Dulles that he expected to be asked by Ben-Gurion to return to Jerusalem and report to him directly about the status of the negotiations and try to bridge the gap between the U.S. and Israeli positions. In the meantime, he asked Dulles that the United States should hold off any UN vote on sanctions.

Eban's expectations were realized. Early on February 17, Ben-Gurion formally asked him to return home for consultations. The indefatigable ambassador saw Dulles and told him that he would leave for Jerusalem tomorrow. Eban had nothing new to report regarding any change in

Israel's position. He thanked the secretary for his efforts. But Dulles was uninterested in platitudes. Although he appreciated the ambassador's sentiments, they were not of much use, "since the government of Israel had apparently decided not to accept the U.S. proposal, not even in principle." He had done all he could to stave off a UN debate and doubted if more could be done.[46] The secretary hoped that Eban would convey to Ben-Gurion the gravity of the situation.

On February 18, the day before his departure for Israel, Eban met Arthur Dean in New York and asked Dean to inquire whether Dulles would agree to some modifications in the February 11 aide-mémoire—for instance, specifically defining the role of the UNEF, its length of stay, and whether the UNEF would leave at Egypt's request. Eban also suggested that perhaps Dulles could send a letter to Ben-Gurion promising that, if Egypt reinstated the blockade, "the United States would feel a deep sense of responsibility and would feel it incumbent upon them to take such steps as might be necessary to bring about a lifting of the blockade."

As to Gaza, Eban had been told by Lester Pearson that the United Nations would never accept an Israeli administration there. Eban conceded to Dean that an Israeli administration in Gaza was not absolutely essential and that he believed that Israel would agree to a UN administration provided it did not merely mean a return of Egypt to the Strip, "because in that event Egypt would close all roads, all water and electrical facilities and Israel would be faced again with an enemy at its border." In other words, Eban was now willing to accept a formula for Gaza that would entail UN control, provided the Egyptians were kept out. That of course was a significant departure from the previously stated Israeli position. According to Eban, if the secretary would agree in principle that a solution along those lines would be satisfactory to the United States, then the ambassador had good reason to believe that the Israeli government would accept and agree to withdraw. Eban was very anxious to work out something along those lines and was confident "he could sell it to his government." Dean telephoned the content of his conversation with Eban and asked the secretary whether some agreement along those lines was feasible before Eban's departure for Israel.[47]

Dulles immediately returned Dean's call and noted that Eban was personally in favor of accepting the February 11 aide-mémoire, but Ben-Gurion and Golda Meir were adamant against it. On Gaza, Dulles saw a possibility that, "while recognizing the ostensible Egyptian right of occupation, there will be in effect a UN administration. . . . Hammarskjöld is working on it, and it is likely there will not be a reversion to a total Egyptian administration." When Dean mentioned to Dulles that Eban was pleading for something to take back to Ben-Gurion, the secretary interjected: "I told Eban several times that if they want some slight modifications and tinkering with the text of our declaration that was something we could consider on the assumption that this would be acceptable. But merely to get into it and have it turned down again is something we will not do. We could put in a sentence that we hope there would be established in accord with Egypt some administration of the area under U.N. auspices. Perhaps strengthen the words." But Dulles would not go into details unless he knew in principle that Israel would withdraw. "We are willing to spell out hopes and expectations and what our policy would be, perhaps a U.N. practical administration in Gaza to be mutually agreed upon by Egypt."[48]

Thanks to Dean's intercession, only hours before Eban's departure, Dulles and the Israeli ambassador hammered out detailed points of agreement between the United States and Israel on the question of Gaza and the Straits of Tiran. The agreement overcame the vagueness of the February 11, 1957, aide-mémoire. In fact, Dulles did something that a few days ago he vowed he would not do: negotiate a bilateral agreement with Israel. Eban had something more tangible to take home. It was an important breakthrough and came in large part thanks to Ben-Gurion's stubbornness, Eban's diplomatic skill and, most important, Dulles's realization that sanctions against Israel would be highly unpopular and in all likelihood unworkable.

Indeed, the Special National Intelligence Estimate (SNIE) on the probable effects of sanctions questioned their effectiveness in bringing about Israeli withdrawal. Even with the active implementation of sanctions by the United States, NATO countries might be reluctant to carry out such a policy. Canada had already indicated it would not cooperate. Germany stated it would not suspend reparation payments, and France not only would not take part in such a policy but would actually increase shipments to Israel. The SNIE report concluded that sanctions would obviously be harmful, but Israel could sustain the pressure for three to twelve months.[49] Dulles decided to go as far as he could to avoid the imposition of sanctions.

Thus, before Eban's departure for Jerusalem, Dulles and the ambassador agreed on Israeli withdrawal and the demilitarization of the Gaza Strip, the entrance of the UNEF (its authority and length of stay to be discussed later), and the nonreturn of the Egyptian army to Gaza. On the questions of the Straits of Tiran, Israeli withdrawal, and U.S. recognition of Israeli's right to free passage, the United States would invite other maritime powers to join in declaring the international character of the Gulf of Aqaba and freedom of navigation for all countries including Israel. They also agreed that the UNEF troops would enter Sharm es-Sheikh, and that the United States and other countries would send ships destined for the port of Eilat through the gulf. Israel would declare publicly that any attack on its ships in the gulf would be viewed as an attack on Israel proper, thus giving Israel the right to act in self-defense in accordance with article 51 of the UN Charter. Additional U.S. promises included a letter from the president of the United States to Ben-Gurion stating U.S. responsibilities if the principle of freedom of navigation was violated, as well as U.S. support for Israel to build an alternative to the Suez Canal, that is, an oil pipeline linking the Red Sea with the Mediterranean. In addition, the United States would seek free passage for Israeli ships through the Suez Canal and remove the economic sanctions it imposed on Israel at the start of the Sinai campaign on October 29, 1956.[50]

Because Dulles was uncertain as to whether Ben-Gurion would be satisfied with the latest U.S. modifications and agree to withdraw, he decided on a twofold approach: hold off UN action on sanctions as much as possible and at the same time step up the pressure on Ben-Gurion to go along with the U.S. proposals.

In the hope of turning congressional and public opinion against Israel, the president issued a statement from Thomasville on February 17 making public the aide-mémoire of February 11, thereby justifying U.S. pressure on Israel to withdraw. The president also declared that the United States was aware that Israel had "legitimate grievances and should in all fairness see a prospect of remedying them."[51] The implication was that the aide-mémoire did just that, and now it was Israel's turn to withdraw. In addition, Eisenhower and Dulles scheduled a meeting at the White House with congressional leaders for February 20, intending to convince them to pass a resolution endorsing the administration's opposition to Israel's occupation of the Sinai.

Twenty-four hours before the meeting Lyndon B. Johnson interrupted the debate in the Senate on the Eisenhower Doctrine to announce that the Senate Democratic Policy Committee unanimously endorsed Johnson's letter to Dulles of February 12, opposing sanctions on Israel. Johnson told the senators that he would convey the same message to the president in the upcoming White House meeting. Jacob Javits, Republican senator from New York, concurred with Johnson and remarked that the issue "has always been bipartisan . . . the minority leader [Knowland] has also spoken to the same effect."

On February 20, a group of twenty-six bipartisan legislative leaders met with Eisenhower, Dulles, and Lodge at the White House. The president reviewed the situation in the Middle East and lamented that Israel's refusal to withdraw despite U.S. assurances "would lead to increased influence of Russia in the Arab world, a threat of economic crash in Britain and France because of the closing of the Suez Canal and finally the possibility of a general war." He agreed that nobody liked the idea of sanctions, but how else could Israel be convinced to withdraw to the 1949 armistice lines?

Dulles briefed the legislators about the bilateral negotiations that had taken place with Eban, which "attempted to assure the Israelis that the ultimate outcome would be a better situation for Israel than it was prior to the attack." Israel, claimed Dulles, would withdraw if convinced that Congress stood behind the administration policies, showing the world that in crucial moments Israel did not control U.S. policy. Sanctions could be avoided if the legislators were willing to go along with the administration policy, "showing that the Executive branch policy is also the policy of Congress." Johnson and Knowland repeated their stated objections to sanctions or Israeli withdrawal without firm guarantees. Richard Russell, senator from Georgia, summarized the feeling of all present, declaring that he could not see any possibility of unanimous agreement by "this group backing the President's policy."[52]

The president failed to get a unified statement from the congressional leaders in support of immediate Israeli withdrawal. It seemed to him that Israel had more influence with Congress than had the President of the United States. In disgust, he wrote in his diary, "As I reflected on the pettiness of much of the discussion of the morning, I found it somewhat dismaying that partisan considerations could enter so much into life or death, peace or war decisions."[53]

Dulles was even more furious than the president. In a telephone conversation with his old friend Dr. Roswell Barnes of the National Council of Churches he lamented: "I am very much concerned over the fact that the Jewish influence here is completely dominating the scene and making it almost impossible to get Congress to do anything they don't approve of. The Israeli embassy is practically dictating to the Congress through influential Jewish people in the country. The non-Jewish elements of the community have got to make themselves more felt or else there will be a disaster here. It was impossible to hold the line because we got no support from the Protestant elements of the country. All we got is a battering from the Jews."[54]

The absence of congressional support did not deter Eisenhower from pursuing a tough and unyielding course toward Israel. Soon after the meeting with the congressional leaders, he cabled Ben-Gurion, warning him that the United States might vote for sanctions at the United Nations and that such sanctions might include not only governmental but private assistance to Israel, such as individual contributions and sales of Israeli bonds in the United States.[55] And in the evening of February 20, Eisenhower delivered an even stronger message to Israel. In a televised broadcast to the nation he reiterated the point that the United Nations had no choice but to exert pressure on Israel to comply with the withdrawal resolution. A nation that attacked and occupied foreign territory in the face of UN disapproval had no right to impose conditions on its withdrawal, the president asserted. But the administration knew that the Achilles' heel in the threat of sanctions was the total lack of support in Congress and the public at large for such action.

The Eisenhower administration decided to try to convince leading U.S. Jews to support U.S. policy and thereby help change Israel's position. On February 21, Dulles met with a group of prominent U.S. Jewish leaders headed by Barney Balaban, motion picture magnate and a friend of Dulles, and including Irving Engel, president of the U.S. Jewish Committee; Philip Klutznick, president of B'nai B'rith; and Bill Rosenwald, Samuel Leidersdorf, Mendel Silberberg, and Jacob Blaustein, all distinguished figures in the world of business. To Dulles's astonishment, these assimilated U.S. Jews strongly objected to Eisenhower's speech of the previous night threatening sanctions. One member of the group spoke for all when he said: "I don't know anything about politics or diplomacy. But I do know that for our country to try to bludgeon Israel against its own vital interests is morally wrong." Dulles offered to take them to the White House to speak to the president, but in light of the president's harsh speech, they declined the honor and dispersed.[56]

The same day, the president used another channel to pressure Ben-Gurion. General Walter Bedell Smith, a close friend of Eisenhower and a supporter of Israel who enjoyed Ben-Gurion's confidence, was called to the White House. The president asked him to contact the Israeli prime minister and advise him that U.S. guarantees included in the February 11 aide-mémoire constituted a strong moral obligation that the administration intended to fulfill. Smith in an urgent letter to Ben-Gurion asked the Israeli leader to place his trust in the president and give "some flexibility" to Eban, who was "perfectly capable of reaching an agreement which would ensure stability for many years."[57] Simultaneously, additional pressure on Ben-Gurion emanated from the United Nations. On February 22, six Moslem countries, trying to force the United States into making a decision, introduced a sanctions resolution calling on all states to deny Israel "all military, economic and financial assistance or facilities." A spokesman for the group threatened that the Arabs would turn to Moscow if their demands were not satisfied.

All these pressures and activities coincided with Eban's attempts in Jerusalem to convince Ben-Gurion and the cabinet to be more "flexible." In cabinet sessions on February 21 and 22, Eban explained the points of agreement he had reached with Dulles that would ensure free passage in the Straits of Tiran, prevent a return of the Egyptian army to Gaza, and guarantee U.S. promises for a secure Israel. While in a public speech in the Knesset on February 21, Ben-Gurion remained defiant and uncompromising, in private, his position began to change.[58] Eban's presentation of the gains accrued to Israel in his negotiations with Dulles as well as the pressure from Washington clearly had an effect on Ben-Gurion. He instructed Eban to return to Washington to continue the negotiations and obtain from Dulles clear detailed clarifications on the two main issues—the straits and Gaza. In a cable to Eisenhower on February 22, Ben-Gurion stated that Eban would bring with him new instructions. He asked the president that the United States seek a further delay on a vote on sanctions in the United Nations until Eban had a chance to present Israel's position to the secretary of state.[59]

Among the new instructions had been a careful retreat on Ben-Gurion's part concerning the future of the Gaza Strip. He no longer insisted on any Israeli presence there, military or civilian. Israel's interest in Gaza, he told Eban, was security against fedayeen attacks and could be assured by a nonreturn of Egypt to the area in any form. An Israeli presence there, he confided to Eban, would mean that Israel would have to absorb 250,000 refugees or rule over them and face world condemnation. But the more likely explanation for Ben-Gurion's change of heart is that all along he never intended to maintain Israeli rule in Gaza. His insistence on the Gaza issue was aimed at improving Israel's negotiating position on the question of the straits and the Gulf of Aqaba, the waterway linking Israel with Africa and Asia and the route of vital supplies of oil from Iran to the Israeli port of Eilat.[60] Ben-Gurion's about-face on Gaza now opened the possibility for a resolution of the crisis.

Eban arrived in New York early on February 24. He briefed Golda Meir on his discussions in Jerusalem. He also telephoned Arthur Dean to ask for his assistance in convincing Dulles to be more amenable to Israel's proposals. Dulles received advance word from Dean about his conversation with Eban. The Israeli ambassador then proceeded to Washington. Accompanied by Shiloah, he met the secretary at his home for what became a crucial discussion. Also present on the U.S. side were Under Secretary of State Herter; Herman Phleger; Francis O. Wilcox, assistant secretary of state for UN affairs; and Rountree.

The participants drew up a memorandum containing Eban's questions and Dulles's replies so that Eban could send Ben-Gurion a verbatim account of U.S. commitments and assurances. Eban began by asking Dulles a number of questions that had been carefully prepared during the discussions in Jerusalem. On the question of the straits, Eban asked: Would the United States encourage its ships to pass regularly through the Straits of Tiran for trade purposes as well as for the shipment of oil to the port of Eilat? Dulles replied in the affirmative. Did "free and innocent passage" mean passage of all ships, commercial ships as well as warships, provided their conduct caused no injury? Dulles accepted the definition and elaborated. Passage "would be considered innocent provided a ship did not use the sea for committing any acts prejudicial to the security of the coastal state." In other words, what counted was the conduct of the ship and not its type, flag or cargo. Could the UN force at the straits include naval units and remain there until peace or any other suitable arrangement was concluded? Dulles supported the idea of a UN naval presence but only with Hammarskjöld's concurrence, as such an arrangement needed UN approval. Next, Eban wanted to know whether the United States would publicly declare Israel's right to protect its ships in the gulf against attack? The United States, replied Dulles, would recognize such a right in accordance with article 51 of the UN Charter as an exercise of the "inherent right of self-defense." In answering additional inquiries, Dulles promised to encourage other maritime powers to join, although the matter must still be cleared with Hammarskjöld. Dulles also promised that the president would write a letter to Ben-Gurion reaffirming U.S. commitments. Israel, the secretary declared, would have no reason to regret its trust in U.S. assurances.

Regarding the Gaza Strip, Eban pointed out that Israel was no longer insisting that either its troops or its civil administration remain there. It accepted the presence of a UNEF. The only point on which Israel insisted was that civil administration must not revert to Egypt so it could resume belligerency in the Gaza Strip area as it did before October 1956.

On the question of Gaza, Dulles was equivocal, something that Israeli leaders—Ben-Gurion, Meir, and Eban—chose to overlook and that would cause a minor crisis later on. Couching his words in diplomatic nuances, Dulles replied:

> The United States fully understands your objections to an Egyptian return to the Strip. On the other hand, legally speaking, Egypt according to the Armistice Agreement of 1949 has rights that the General Assembly has no authority to abrogate. The United States believes that it would be impossible to force Egypt to concede their rights there publicly, but it is possible to convince Egypt not to exercise that right in practice. The United States advises Israel to clarify this question as soon as possible with the Secretary General of the UN.[61]

All in all, the United States gave Israel the assurances it wanted regarding the Gulf of Aqaba. The future of Gaza and the certainty of non-Egyptian return remained ambiguous. On February 22, in a report to the General Assembly, Hammarskjöld had already declared that the Egyptian government agreed that the takeover of Gaza from the military and civilian control of Israel would be "exclusively by the UNEF in the first instance." There was no definition of how long "the first instance" would last. Dulles hoped that the Egyptians could be persuaded to stay out of the area permanently and allow the UNEF to be deployed between the armed forces of Egypt and Israel, thereby preventing incursions and raids on either side. The Egyptians and Hammarskjöld went along with the role envisaged by Dulles and Israel for the UNEF. But neither the Egyptians nor Hammarskjöld ever promised that no Egyptian administrative personnel would reenter the strip, despite Israeli efforts to obtain such assurances.[62]

Dulles wanted Hammarskjöld to give the Israelis "reasonable" assurances that Egypt would not return to Gaza. The secretary felt that Israel had gone so far that he did not think that the United States could ever vote for sanctions. All they now wanted was to put Ben-Gurion in a political position where he could say that he had gotten the Egyptians out of Gaza.[63] Dulles concluded that because of the Israeli concessions, Ben-Gurion's government was not secure, and right-wing politicians were demanding Eban's resignation. In his conversation with Dulles, Eban demanded that no leaks or suggestions be made to the press that Israel had withdrawn its absolute conditions, lest it might cause the fall of the government before arrangements could be concluded.[64]

But Hammarskjöld was not about to give Eban "reasonable" assurances on Gaza. Never a friend of Israel, Hammarskjöld now displayed great irritation over the U.S.-Israeli agreement. He felt left out. On February 25, he told Eban that he could not promise the nonreturn of the Egyptians to Gaza. "As regards Gaza, Egypt has her rights. What you arranged with Dulles does not suit me or Egypt." He also refused to send a ship bearing the UN flag through the Gulf of Aqaba. A disappointed Eban told Dulles, "I am less optimistic now than yesterday! The Gaza proposal is not working out. I thought that would be okay."[65]

Surprisingly, the impasse was broken by Mollet and Pineau. The two French leaders, in Washington on an official visit, presented their views to both Eisenhower and Dulles on how to end the deadlock. Dulles went along with their proposals and urged Eban to take up the problem of Gaza and the general question of Israeli withdrawal with Pineau. After all, the French leaders were staunch allies of Israel and would not steer it wrong.[66]

At 4:00 P.M. on February 26, Eban met Pineau at the French embassy in Washington. According to Pineau, Israel, would announce its readiness from the UN rostrum to carry out a complete withdrawal of its forces in accordance with UN resolutions, on the "assumption" or "understanding" that:

> 1. Upon Israel's withdrawal, the UNEF will be deployed in Gaza as contemplated by the UN General Assembly Resolution of February 2, 1957 and . . . *the initial take-over will be exclusively by the UNEF* [italics added]. The UN accepted full responsibility for the security and administration of the Strip.
>
> 2. If the "assumptions" were violated and Egypt would create conditions which failed to comply with its international obligations and indicated a return to the conditions of deterioration which has previously come about, Israel would reserve its freedom to act to defend its rights.

The role of the United Nations in the administration of the strip "will continue for a transitory period until there is a peace settlement." Until then there would be strict compliance by both parties with their international obligations.[67]

According to Pineau, soon after the Israeli announcement, the representatives of the United States, France, and other maritime powers would declare from the UN rostrum that they took note of the Israeli statement, the legitimacy of Israel's assumptions, and its right to self-defense. This scenario had a very important advantage. It removed the crisis from the sphere of the General Assembly by avoiding a vote in an organization where the Soviet bloc and Afro-Asian countries comprised a majority likely to derail the proposed agreement. Pineau rightly predicted that the world body would acquiesce in these proposals because Israel would have agreed to withdraw.

Significant in the Pineau proposal was the wording that the "initial" takeover of Gaza from Israeli control would be exclusively by the UNEF. In fact, Pineau's suggestion did not differ much from Hammarskjöld's position on the future of Gaza. Both left open the possibility of an Egyptian return to Gaza.

Ben-Gurion was aware of the ambiguity in the French proposal, but as he saw it, Israel had no choice but to accept it. On February 28, he told Dayan that "we must accept the French proposal because of our complete isolation and the possibility that France also would move away from us and that will place us in great jeopardy because we will not receive arms for defense." At first, Dayan was unconvinced. He believed that Israel had enough arms for at least one year, but nonetheless, he went along with Ben-Gurion's acquiescence to the French suggestions.[68]

Ben-Gurion instructed Eban to negotiate a resolution of the crisis with U.S. officials based on Dulles's latest assurances and the French proposals.

On February 28 at the State Department, Eban, Shiloah, and Rafael met a U.S. team of officials consisting of Phleger, Rountree, Wilcox, Wilkins, and Donald Bergus, head of the Palestine desk, to iron out the details of an agreement and its implementation. By late afternoon, Dulles, Pineau, and Eban had agreed on a text that would be proclaimed before the General Assembly by Israel's Foreign Minister, Golda Meir. Her speech would subsequently be endorsed by Lodge, followed by the French and representatives of other countries.[69] At a special meeting held late on the afternoon of March 1, the Israeli cabinet approved the statement that Golda Meir was about to deliver before the UN General Assembly.

On the evening of March 1, Golda Meir walked to the rostrum of the General Assembly and made the long-awaited fateful declaration. Israel, she announced, would withdraw from Gaza and the coastal strip between Eilat and Sharm es-Sheikh on the basis of the following "assumptions" and "expectations":

1. That on its withdrawal the UN forces will be deployed in Gaza and that the takeover of Gaza from the military and civilian control of Israel will be exclusively by the UNEF.

2. It is, further, Israel's expectation that the UN will be the agency to be utilized for carrying out the functions enumerated by the Secretary-General, namely . . . safeguarding the life and property in the area by providing efficient and effective police protection; as well as guarantee good civilian administration.

3. It is, further, Israel's expectation that the aforementioned re-

sponsibility of the UN in the administration of Gaza will be maintained for a transitory period from the takeover until there is a peace settlement, to be sought as rapidly as possible, or a definite agreement on the future of the Gaza Strip. It is the position of Israel that if conditions are created in the Gaza Strip that indicate a return to the conditions of deterioration that existed previously, Israel will reserve the freedom to act to defend its rights.

Meir also declared Israel's expectations that the Gulf of Aqaba and the Straits of Tiran would be open to free navigation for all nations. Any reinstatement of the blockade would entitle Israel to act in self-defense in accordance with article 51 of the UN Charter. Finally, Golda Meir stated that her government expected that any proposal for removing the UNEF from the Gulf of Aqaba would first be referred to the Advisory Committee of the General Assembly to ensure that no precipitate changes were made that could have the effect of increasing the chances for blockage and belligerency.[70]

By prearrangement, Lodge succeeded Golda Meir on the rostrum, but to Israel's consternation, Lodge's speech deviated from the Dulles-Pineau-Eban agreement. Instead of confirming Israel's assumptions and expectations as "legitimate," he substituted a half-hearted phrase calling Israel's conditions for withdrawal "not unreasonable." Far worse, from Israel's perspective, was his reference to the future of Gaza. Not only did he fail to mention the nonreturn of Egypt but went out of his way to emphasize the importance of the 1949 armistice agreements (which gave Egypt the legal right to control Gaza) and the UN secretary general's role in the area.[71] All in all, Lodge did not exclude an Egyptian role in the governing of Gaza.

Golda Meir was outraged. An angry Ben-Gurion summoned the cabinet for an unprecedented extraordinary meeting on Saturday, March 2. Two parties within the coalition government, Achdut Ha'avodah and Mapam, threatened to withdraw from the coalition if the Israeli forces came out of the Gaza Strip without an ironclad guarantee that the Egyptians would not be permitted to reenter. The cabinet decided to delay the Dayan-Burns meeting designed to hammer out the details for Israel's final withdrawal. Ben-Gurion instructed Eban to see Dulles at once and to demand an explicit written statement containing a U.S. pledge that Egypt would not return to Gaza and acknowledging Israel's right of self-defense.[72]

Eban's remonstrations to Dulles produced ardent professions of good faith but no official statement. According to the secretary, Lodge introduced "small" corrections in order to ensure Hammarskjöld's consent to the U.S.-Israeli agreement. U.S. policy, explained Dulles, had not changed; it favored freedom of navigation and an international regime in Gaza. The United States, he continued, remained faithful to the assumptions contained in Golda Meir's speech. In Eban's presence, Dulles wrote down the contents of a letter that Eisenhower was about to send to Ben-Gurion. Minutes later Dulles called James Hagerty, the president's spokesman, and read to him the proposed message to Ben-Gurion. "Can I put Ike's signature on this?" asked Dulles. The answer was "Yes!"[73]

The "president's" message to Ben-Gurion expressed his gratitude at Israel's decision to withdraw promptly and fully behind the armistice lines and then added the following assurances:

> I know that this decision was not an easy one. I believe, however, that Israel will have no cause to regret having thus conformed to the strong sentiment of the world community as expressed in the various UN resolutions relating to withdrawal. Hopes and expectations based thereon were voiced by your Foreign Minister and others. I believe that it is reasonable to entertain such hopes and expectations and I want you to know that the United States, as a friend of all the countries in the area and as loyal members of the UN will seek that such hopes prove not in vain.[74]

Ben-Gurion was not assuaged. In the words of Gideon Rafael, Eisenhower's message "was a textbook letter on noncommittal diplomatic correspondence, adding anger to Israel's other anxieties."[75] On March 3, Ben-Gurion again instructed Eban to demand from Dulles a guarantee in writing recognizing Israel's rights to self-defense should her "expectations" remain unfulfilled both in regard to the Straits of Tiran and the Gaza Strip. Dulles agreed to exchange letters on the former but not on the latter. In Gaza, he argued, no matter how much the United States would object to a de facto Egyptian presence there, it could not prevent it because legally and politically the armistice agreements accorded Egypt that right. All the United States could do was hope that Egypt would not exercise that right, and this had been the U.S. position all along.[76] An exasperated Eban wrote back to Ben-Gurion that the president's letter and Dulles's oral assurances were the maximum that could be obtained from the U.S. administration. Mollet and Pineau, who were contacted by Eban, advised that Israel trust in the U.S. assurances and proceed with the withdrawal as planned. With that, Israel's persistent struggle for further guarantees came to an end. Despite all the misgivings, there was no going back on the promise to withdraw, for doing so at that point would have spelled disaster.

On March 4, Israel announced in the General Assembly its final decision to withdraw. The same day, in a meeting between Dayan and Burns, agreement was reached on a complete withdrawal from Gaza to take place on March 6–7. A UNEF unit arrived at Sharm es-Sheikh on March 8. The last Israeli unit was withdrawn from the area on March 12.

In Israel, the rejoicing in the aftermath of the great military victory had now turned to anger, sadness, and uncertainty. The somber mood of the nation was expressed by Ben-Gurion in a speech to the Knesset on March 5. Reflecting on Eisenhower's letter and the U.S. assurances, the Israeli leader added: "I must state that there is no certainty and no clear and authoritative undertaking that the Egyptians will not return or be restored, whether as a civilian administration or through military occupation relying on the excuse of the Armistice Agreement. My heart is with the border settlements . . . in the South and the Negev who listened with fear to the evacuation decision."[77]

Ben-Gurion's comments were prescient. Late at night on March 5, Golda Meir received a confidential report informing her that the UN Secretariat was discussing arrangements with the Egyptians for their return to Gaza. She urgently called Eban and Rafael to her suite on the twenty-seventh floor of the Savoy Plaza Hotel in New York. In a state of extreme agitation, she showed them the secret report. She demanded that Eban contact Ben-Gurion immediately and ask that he cancel the orders for the evacuation of the Gaza Strip now in progress. Eban refused. Israel, he contended, "could not go back on its solemn pledge without causing itself irreparable harm . . . its position in the world would be demolished." He advised the foreign minister to write to Dulles and warn him about the consequences of the Egyptian action. Whereupon Golda Meir vented her anger and frustration on the ambassador. "Now you want me to repair the mess . . . after you have confronted me with a *fait accompli?*" She lashed out at Eban for his failure to report to her and consult her personally on all the stages of his negotiations with Dulles and Hammar-skjöld. Again she demanded that he cable Ben-Gurion at once to postpone the withdrawal. Eban again refused. When Golda Meir raised her voice and ordered him to do so, the visibly shaken ambassador got up, marched out of the room, and slammed the door loudly behind him.[78]

Eban of course had the full backing of Ben-Gurion, whom he constantly kept abreast of every development, as the prime minister was the main decision maker. That did not mean that the foreign minister was kept in the dark throughout the negotiations. She resented the fact that an ambassador was allowed to exercise such tremendous authority, at times overshadowing the foreign minister. In an interview, Eban recalled the incident and characterized Golda Meir's behavior throughout the crisis as emotional, "hysterical, and devoid of sound political judgment."[79]

Despite her anger at Eban, Meir took his advice, and early in the morning of March 6, she dispatched an urgent letter to Dulles. The foreign minister thanked Dulles for the long hours he had devoted to a resolution of the crisis and then issued a warning: "The abandonment to Egypt by the UN of any part of its responsibility or the civil and military administration of the Gaza area would create in the view of my government a situation which would compel it to defend its rights as envisaged in my statement at the General Assembly on March 1, 1957. This is a situation which I hope will not arise. . . . We agreed that an arrangement for a *de facto* exclusion of Egypt would meet the very vital security problems of the area and it was this that my Government had in mind when it took its decision."[80]

By March 7, the Israelis had evacuated Gaza completely. At once, the UNEF under the command of General Burns took over the area. Soon after, local Palestinian leaders issued vehement demands for the return of the Egyptian administration. For reasons of prestige, Nasser decided to risk Israeli retaliation and meet these purported demands of the local population. On March 11, Nasser dispatched a civil governor with an administrative staff to the strip. However, no Egyptian military units entered Gaza. There was no protest from the United Nations. As General Burns put it, "I knew that the take-over was to be exclusively by the UNEF in the first instance." The only question in his mind was, How long was the first instance to last? Hammarskjöld had supplied the answer to General Burns a few days before the Israeli withdrawal, when he told the commander that the future of the strip would be decided within the framework of the UN resolutions. The UNEF authority would thus be based on Egyptian acquiescence.[81] As far as Hammarskjöld was concerned, Gaza belonged to Egypt even though Egypt had seized it by force in 1948 in violation of UN resolutions.

The United States expressed regret over the Egyptian action, but not surprise. On March 14, Christian Herter, in response to Golda Meir's letter of March 6, reaffirmed the U.S. commitment to free passage in the Gulf of Aqaba. But on Gaza, he continued, "there are as you know points on which we hold differing views: As the Secretary told Ambassador Eban on March 2, we would not feel that the mere presence of Egyptian personnel in territory which under the Armistice Agreement Egypt is entitled to occupy would give Israel the right to act." Nonetheless, the United States, said Herter, believed that the UN should remain in the area pending an agreement on the future of Gaza or a permanent settlement.[82]

Dulles, for his part, regretted very much that not all U.S. "hopes and expectations" were fulfilled. But the game, he told Golda Meir, "is not over yet," and the United States would do all in its power to prevent further deterioration of the situation. Israel, however, should not act abruptly and engage in any action without first notifying the United States. He intimated that Israeli retaliation against Egypt would not be justified, as Egypt had not yet engaged in any acts of aggression against Israel.[83] Ben-Gurion, despite his deep disappointment, reluctantly agreed with Dulles's assessment. So far, Nasser's action was not worth another military confrontation.

Israel's remonstrations to the United States and its disillusionment and anger over Egypt's return to Gaza were understandable. But in fairness to Dulles, throughout his negotiations with Eban he had never guaranteed the nonreturn of Egypt to the area. He always maintained that Egypt had legal rights in Gaza based on the 1949 armistice agreements. He hoped, perhaps in vain, that Egypt in its eagerness to bring about Israeli withdrawal would not exercise that right, even though he knew that was a remote possibility at best.

The charge by Golda Meir and Gideon Rafael that Israel was duped or tricked by Dulles is out of place and unfair.[84] One can honestly disagree with his policy without questioning his integrity.

Ben-Gurion was certainly not duped. He saw the loophole in the French proposal on Gaza as allowing the Egyptians to return to the area. He was surprised by the swiftness and the timing of the reentry but not by the action itself. Nonetheless, he accepted the French proposal. On March 10, he wrote in his diary, "The French effort to find a solution in large measure tipped the scales. . . . In rejecting the French proposal I saw a great danger to our future though not immediately." According to Ben-Gurion, the consequences of a rejection would have meant world ostracism for Israel, with or without sanctions. That would not have been so terrible, with the exception of one type of sanction—oil. But more ominous to Israel would have been an Egypt rearmed with Soviet weapons preparing an attack against an Israel without friends and, most important, without French weapons. He feared that under such circumstances Israel could be defeated in the battlefield. Therefore, he concluded, "in order to hold on to Gaza I am not willing to take upon myself such a grave eventuality."[85]

Thus, Ben-Gurion's fears of international isolation, including an arms embargo by France, finally persuaded him to go along with a proposal that did not at all guarantee the nonreturn of the Egyptians to Gaza. Furthermore, his previous insistence on the retention by Israel of Gaza or merely of a decisive role in its administration was a negotiating ploy to obtain better assurances on the freedom of navigation in the Gulf of Aqaba. Israel's future economic development depended on trade with Africa and Asia, making free passage through that waterway imperative. As he told Dayan on February 19, "If our enemies were smart they would let us have Gaza. The danger in staying there is both economic and political. Economically, we will have to feed 250,000 refugees. But still greater is the political danger. There can be no doubt that the refugees and others will carry out terrorist attacks against us. Will we be able to suppress them like the English do in Cyprus or the French in Algeria?" Maybe militarily, said Ben-Gurion, that would not be a problem, but surely morally Israel could not withstand such a situation.[86]

The withdrawal of Israeli troops from Gaza and Sharm es-Sheikh, and especially the immediate reentry of Egypt into Gaza, left a bitter taste throughout the country, a feeling that Israel had won a great victory on the battlefield but lost the diplomatic struggle. The anguish was greatest among the Israeli officer corps and the army in general for what seemed to them an Israeli retreat, taking place without sufficient assurances that the war's objectives had been met and that peace would prevail. They were particularly worried about the implications of the withdrawal from the Gaza Strip, fearing a resurgence of fedayeen attacks.

Ben-Gurion shared those apprehensions. On March 1, shortly before Golda Meir was scheduled to make the fateful speech before the General Assembly in New York, he invited a number of Israeli generals to his home for what amounted to a pep talk. He knew the risks involved and confided to the officers:

> I told the Cabinet that this is a gamble, but it is a known risk. We may have to fight again, the whole of the UN will not back us. But we will have the backing of enough states sufficient to enable us to do so with greater peace of mind. . . . Tomorrow, there won't be dancing in the streets. I can imagine that in the army itself there will be great sorrow. But I am sure that in six months time . . . ships will come, tankers . . . work will begin on constructing a railway, U.S., French, English, Italian and Ethiopian ships will come and there will be rejoicing.[87]

This assessment of the situation proved to be prophetic. True, the Sinai campaign had not brought Israel formal peace with Egypt. On the debit side of the ledger, Israel's "collusion" with Britain and France only reinforced its negative image in the Arab world and parts of the Third World as a Western imperialist enclave in the Middle East. Nonetheless, the positive consequences of the campaign more than outweighed the negative.

The Sinai campaign brought Israel rich dividends, foremost among them eleven years of relative tranquility at its frontiers with the Arab states in general and Egypt in particular. The fedayeen did not return to Gaza, and a type of de facto peace descended on the border between the two belligerents. Israelis in the outlying border settlements now could work and live in peace for the first time in seven years. The Gulf of Aqaba was opened to free navigation, and Ben-Gurion's vision of Eilat as the southern gateway to Israel became a reality. Thanks to the new conditions, Israel established trade relationships with the Orient, laid an oil pipeline from Eilat to the Mediterranean coast, and developed an industrial infrastructure that launched the country into a period of impressive economic growth. Its military and political position in the region had strengthened, gaining respect and extending its influence and cooperation to countries at the periphery of the Middle East, such as Turkey, Iran, and Ethiopia.[88]

And, despite dark predictions about Israel's "isolation" and "ostracism" by the world, Israel's international relations flourished and expanded. African and Asian countries who had roundly condemned Israel in the United Nations now regarded the nation as a symbol and a model. African, Asian, and South American delegations came to Israel to request technical, agricultural, and military assistance and training.

But most important, U.S.-Israeli relations assumed a new character. The Sinai campaign and the subsequent actions by Nasser made U.S. leaders aware of the dangers of Soviet penetration of the Middle East. During the next decade, Egypt, Syria, and Iraq became identified with the pro-Soviet camp, while Israel's political stability as a modern democracy and an obstacle to Soviet influence further strengthened U.S.-Israeli relations. Eisenhower kept his word when he promised that Israel would have no reason to regret placing its trust in U.S. assurances. On April 24, 1957, the SS *Kernhills,* loaded with thousands of tons of crude oil, docked at the port of Eilat, symbolizing the U.S. commitment to freedom of navigation in the Gulf of Aqaba as well as the new friendship between the two countries.

As Ben-Gurion predicted, Israel would have to fight again over the same terrain but under different circumstances. When Nasser ordered the withdrawal of the UNEF from Gaza and Sharm es-Sheikh and reinstated the blockade at the Straits of Tiran, President Lyndon Johnson condemned the action as a violation of international law and sympathized with Israel's decision to go to war—a situation far different from the U.S. position of October 1956.

All in all, Israel had to withdraw under conditions far less desirable than those put forth by Ben-Gurion on November 7, 1956, or in mid-January 1957, that is, the retention of Gaza and Sharm es-Sheikh. But sobriety and pragmatism finally won the day for Israel, who achieved the objectives it set out to achieve in October 1956 before the outbreak of the Sinai war. But Israel did not endure the political humiliation that befell

Britain and France through their ignominious swift withdrawal. Moreover, the stubbornness with which Israel resisted an evacuation deprived of guarantees ended all efforts by the Western powers, notably Britain and the United States, to impose a political settlement inimical to Israel's security.

Eisenhower and Dulles failed to achieve their erstwhile goal of pushing Israel back without security guarantees on the premise that "aggressors" should not set conditions for their withdrawal. And despite Eisenhower's pronouncements that domestic political pressures would have no impact on his foreign policy decisions, the facts proved otherwise. If it were not for congressional opposition to sanctions, Israel would have been forced to withdraw without guarantees. Congressional opposition to the administration policy on sanctions was generated in large part by U.S. Jewry, which despite its diversity stood behind Israel in time of crisis. Ben-Gurion's tenacity and Eban's diplomatic skills, backed by a united U.S. Jewish community, had finally produced a resolution to the crisis beneficial to Israel's security as well as to the future strengthening of U.S.-Israeli relations. The most difficult period in those relations had come to an end.

U.S. Jewry and
the Sinai Campaign

10

The successful lobbying efforts by U.S. Jewish organizations enabled Israel to withstand administration pressures for immediate withdrawal from the Sinai and Gaza despite the threat of sanctions. The overwhelming support for Israel exhibited by U.S. Jews, in turn, generated congressional and public sympathy for Israel's case, so much so that even Eisenhower, who vowed not to allow domestic political considerations to influence foreign policy decisions, found it difficult to resist the constant pressures emanating from Jewish organizations, Zionist and non-Zionist alike.

Although most U.S. Jews were not Zionists, support for Israel and its welfare bound virtually all U.S. Jewish organizations into a strong pressure group.[1] Dulles often expressed his irritation to the president and administration officials about the "terrific" control the Jews had over the media and the pressures they had exerted on members of Congress against the administration policy of sanctions. Of the mail received at the White House opposing administration policies toward Israel, 90 percent came from Jews.[2] Indeed, a very well-organized campaign in support of Israel's goals by U.S. Jewish organizations aroused congressional and public opposition to the administration's policies of demanding Israeli withdrawal without U.S. security guarantees, let alone the imposition of sanctions should Israel refuse to withdraw. As a result the administration finally relented, and Israel did withdraw, but only after its legitimate security demands were guaranteed.

By the early 1950s U.S. Jewry had begun a process of organizational consolidation, making it a potent pressure group. In 1954, the American Zionist Council (AZC) set up an official lobby for Israel in Washington. The agency was legally registered with Congress that year as the American Israel Public Affairs Committee, known since 1959 as the Israel Public Affairs Committee (AIPAC). Headed by a very able former journalist, Isaiah "Si" L. Kenen, the lobbying group maintained intensive daily contacts with members of the Senate and the House of Representatives through personal meetings and through the distribution of informational materials. These included reprints of editorials, articles, and background information about Israel and the Middle East, all in attempts to stimulate congressional efforts in favor of increased U.S. economic aid to Israel, arms sales, and security guarantees. Its activities would be especially influential in gaining congressional backing against the administration's intentions to impose sanctions on Israel. AIPAC has since gained a reputation as being "the most powerful, the best run, and effective foreign policy interest group in Washington."[3]

The next step in the process of organizational consolidation came with the establishment in 1955 of the Conference of Presidents of Major Jewish Organizations, usually referred to as the Presidents' Conference. It was born out of a need to centralize and organize the Zionist and non-Zionist response to administration policies concerning Israel. The Presidents' Conference served as an umbrella organization for some sixteen national organizations, one of which was AIPAC. Among its most important member organizations are B'nai B'rith, Hadassah, the Jewish War Veterans, the American Zionist Federation, and the American Jewish Congress. While AIPAC concentrated its efforts in Washington, the Presidents' Conference became the chief public voice and link between executive decision makers and the Jewish community on major issues. The main strength of the Presidents' Conference lay in its ability to speak with one voice for the overwhelming majority of U.S. Jews, whenever a consensus could be reached among the disparate organizations.[4] Ironically this consolidation came in the wake of a complaint by none other than Henry A. Byroade, who told Nahum Goldmann that he had been receiving representatives of Jewish organizations "five times in five days during one week."[5] Goldmann subsequently urged Jewish leaders to form an umbrella organization to speak with one voice for the maze of groups representing U.S. Jews.

Another national Jewish organization established during the 1950s was the National Jewish Community Relations Advisory Council, an umbrella group for organizations operating in each community. In effect it was a public relations body coordinating the activities of the Jewish communities on the local level. Adding to all these organizations was the American Jewish Committee, founded in 1906 but not part of the Presidents' Conference. Sociologically, the American Jewish Committee identified with the German Reform, non-Zionist, upper crust assimilated U.S. Jews of German extraction.[6] Its leaders, such as Judge Joseph Proskauer, Jacob Blaustein, and Irving Engel, had access to the president and the secretary of state. The American Jewish Committee developed a style of activity that focused on independent action through the use of discreet encounters with governmental leaders in contrast to the more vocal and belligerent methods employed by the majority of U.S. Jewish organizations.

Thus, with the exception of the relatively small anti-Zionist American Council for Judaism, by the mid-1950s U.S. Jewish organizations were well positioned to take a unified stand in support of Israel. They had at their disposal a trained staff, adequate financing from membership fees, and the personal wealth of their leaders. They maintained an elaborate internal communication network capable of exerting political pressure in furthering Israel's objectives. According to Goldmann, "All through the years the State Department's pro-Arab policy was hindered by Jewish organizations making their views known and their influence felt."[7]

During the Eisenhower presidency they succeeded in gaining for Israel generous U.S. economic and technical assistance as well as funding of cultural and educational exchange programs; a total of $508.1 million of aid in various forms in outright grants.[8] But they were less successful in the diplomatic strategic sphere, that is, in the delivery of U.S. weapons to Israel or in the formation of a formal alliance with the United States that would guarantee Israel's security. Neither did Jewish pressure bring about U.S. insistence that Arab countries cease their boycott of Israel and allow Israeli ships to pass through the Suez Canal. In addition, they could not prevent the Eisenhower administration from providing some Arab countries with economic and military aid, despite Israeli protests.[9]

Even so, Jewish leaders through their intercessions with governmental leaders and members of Congress succeeded in preventing the U.S. policy of evenhandedness in the Arab-Israeli conflict from turning into an outright pro-Arab stance. For in addition to economic and technical assistance, the Eisenhower administration did not renege on its moral commitment to the legitimacy and survival of Israel and did not impose any solutions that would have endangered Israel's existence, despite cold war calculations and Arab pressures to do so. The Eisenhower administration continued to uphold the U.S. commitment to resist any attempt to alter by force the territorial and political status quo between Israel and the Arab states as well as the "integrity and independence" of all states in the Middle East.

But the real test of Jewish political strength would come during the Sinai campaign and its aftermath, a period of major crisis in U.S.-Israeli relations. Israel's invasion of the Sinai had been roundly condemned by Eisenhower and Dulles. U.S. public opinion in general supported the administration policy of action by the United Nations and wanted no U.S. involvement in the Middle East.[10]

Israel's action was particularly embarrassing to organized U.S. Jewry because it came one day after Eban had personally assured Dulles that his government planned no attack against any Arab country. Consequently, U.S. Jews were confronted with a political dilemma they had never had to face before. As a result, a conflict of interest arose, pitting specific Zionist Jewish interests against the broader strategic concerns articulated by the administration. Zionist and para-Zionist groups found themselves in the most unenviable position of having to choose between Israel's security needs and U.S. policy based upon regional neutrality and world stability.

On October 30, 1956, less than twenty-four hours after Israel's invasion of the Sinai, the Conference of Presidents of Major Jewish Organizations convened in New York for an emergency meeting. Eban sent Shiloah to the meeting to brief the heads of leading Jewish groups in the United States. Their solidarity with Israel in the face of mounting criticism from the administration was of utmost importance. Instead of unity, Shiloah found the Jewish leaders shocked, confused, and in a quandary over Israel's military action against Egypt. Many of them had been led by statements of the Israeli government and the State Department to believe that a preventive war was most unlikely, that Israel had been receiving arms from France and Canada and economic aid from the United States. The leaders had been transmitting these reassuring developments to their followers in the Jewish community. This positive theme was also emphasized in a report published on September 24 by the AZC entitled "Israel Gains Strength" and widely distributed among its members throughout the United States. The publication stressed the positive turn of events in Israel's favor and the Western resolve to stand up to Nasser.

Suddenly, Israel's attack seemed to contradict the confident assurances Jewish leaders had made to their constituencies in previous weeks. Some of the leaders participating in the meeting felt deceived and in their anger suggested that the conference issue a public statement disassociating itself from Israel's action. Moreover, some leaders were thinking of organizing an anti-Israeli demonstration in front of Israel's consulate in New York. For the first time since the creation of the state of Israel, U.S. Jewry was about to disagree strongly with Israel in a time of major crisis.[11]

After considerable debate, cooler tempers prevailed, and in Eban's words the conference gave "reluctant endorsement to what the Jewish leaders considered a reckless adventure on Israel's part."[12] In a statement issued the following day the conference, chaired by Philip Klutznick, who had access to Dulles, issued a statement avoiding any criticism of administration policy. The statement blamed Nasser as the culprit, describing him as a threat to Israel and the free world. Israel's attack was explained as a defensive measure in light of the nation's dangerous situation as a result of the signing of the Egyptian-Syrian-Jordanian military pact.

The Presidents' Conference met sixteen times between October 30, 1956, and March 7, 1957. It convened national and regional conferences, took out advertisements in major newspapers, and sent delegations to Washington to meet with members of Congress and officials of the administration. But throughout, it refrained from any sharp condemnation of the administration, and at the same time it refrained from totally identifying itself with Israel's own position. While on the one hand it supported Israel's demand of the nonreturn of Egypt to Gaza and Sharm es-Sheikh, the conference at the same time avoided any statement that might have been construed as encouragement to Israel not to withdraw from those areas should such withdrawal become necessary. In short, the

Presidents' Conference would not side with Israel to the extent that it might find itself in open conflict with the administration or public opinion at large.

In line with this strategy, the Presidents' Conference in its emergency meeting on November 17–18, 1957, urged that direct peace negotiations between the belligerents be launched without delay and called on the United States to "assume the role as leader of the coalition of free peoples" and to seek to "lay the basis for a durable peace."

Among the national Jewish organizations affiliated with the Presidents' Conference, B'nai B'rith, the Central Conference of American Rabbis, the American Jewish Congress, and the Jewish Labor Committee each issued individual statements designed to focus on the role of the United States as a peacemaker rather than to criticize the administration or to justify Israeli actions.[13]

The American Jewish Committee, although acting independently of the Presidents' Conference, in effect followed the same middle-of-the-road strategy. Although mildly justifying Israel's "incursion" into Egypt, it focused on developing models for the peaceful resolution of the conflict, thereby placing itself as mediator between Israel and U.S. policymakers. On November 3, Irving M. Engel, the president of the American Jewish Committee, together with the two prestigious honorary presidents, Jacob Blaustein and Judge Joseph Proskauer, sent a letter to Dulles expressing their views on the Mideast crisis. Explaining Israel's attack as a result of continuous Arab provocation, they emphasized the constructive possibilities inherent in the UN cease-fire resolution as a means of achieving permanent peace. U.S. policy, they suggested, should now be directed against a return to the status quo ante; they submitted a three-part program for achieving a durable peace in the region. They advised Dulles that the United States should call upon the United Nations to urge the Arab states to enter into direct negotiations with Israel in order to achieve peace. Refusal by any of the parties to do so should be branded as incompatible with the UN Charter. The United States and other nations, they asserted, should guarantee the treaties reached.[14] The letter was well received by the public and by newspapers around the country editorializing against a return to the situation that preceded the Israeli action.

When a cease-fire came into effect followed by Ben-Gurion's victory speech, the American Jewish Committee advised Ben-Gurion to renounce expansionist plans and to begin withdrawing Israeli troops from the Sinai in accordance with the UN resolutions. At the same time, it used its influence with Dulles and Eisenhower to prevent the imposition of sanctions against Israel and instead to grant security guarantees as a condition for withdrawal.[15]

In contrast to the moderate conciliatory tone of both the Presidents' Conference and the American Jewish Committee, the AZC—the executive body of the Zionist Organization of America (ZOA)—took a more militant stand. It launched a propaganda campaign calling for total identification with Israel and sharply criticizing U.S. policy.[16] In a nationwide broadcast over the NBC network on November 4, the ZOA president, Emanuel Neumann, noted that, in going to war against the "Hitler of the Nile," the Israelis were continuing "an old war launched eight years ago by the Arab states." Neumann criticized the administration for its denial of weapons to Israel by stating that Israel "had no military alliance and no security pact of any kind to fall back on." Rabbi Silver was even more blunt: "When the Suez Canal was seized by Nasser, . . . Mr. Dulles made sure that nothing would be done about it, the administration gave Israel neither the security pact it had granted to some forty other countries, nor did it grant the imperiled young state the right to acquire arms in this country to defend itself."[17]

As the presidential elections drew to a close, the Zionists clearly sided with Adlai Stevenson by stating in their propaganda leaflets, "If John Foster Dulles had inherited the wisdom from Harry S. Truman we might conceivably have peace between Israel and the Arabs today."[18] Calling for the support of those who "cherish Israel and its dream," the Zionists denounced the "shocking record of Nasser, Nixon, and Dulles . . . what they have done to Israel only Stevenson and the Democrats can repair."[19]

But the propaganda campaign by the Zionists against the administration and the raging war in the Middle East had actually helped Eisenhower in his reelection as president. In all likelihood Eisenhower would have been reelected no matter how he handled the current crisis. In fact, his policy of condemning the British, French, and Israeli attack on Egypt gained him votes, and the turmoil in the Middle East actually weakened Stevenson. The outbreak of fighting in the Mideast alarmed the U.S. public, which feared a new Korea or perhaps World War III. Americans were thankful that the president was the leader who got them out of

Korea and managed to preserve the peace for four years. But should the United States become involved in fighting, they wanted a president who had already demonstrated military capacity. Hence the public was ready to accept Eisenhower's judgment on any course he might take, particularly if the course did not involve U.S. military intervention but resorted to the United Nations.

Making the Zionist case even more difficult was the fact that Israel's standing in U.S. public opinion had suffered, less because of Israel's aggression against Egypt than because of its alliance with "colonial" powers, Britain and France. Israel was no longer viewed by the U.S. public as fighting for survival but perceived as using force for the sake of territorial aggrandizement, in this case the conquest of the Sinai. Ben-Gurion's arrogant November 7 victory speech only reinforced such suspicions.[20]

In an early November 1956 Roper survey of 598 U.S. respondents, only 18.5 percent replied in the affirmative when asked, "Do you think Israel was justified in sending troops to Egypt?" While 49.6 percent had no opinion on the matter, 31 percent felt that the Israelis were not justified in attacking Egypt. A Gallup poll released on November 14 showed similar results. Editorial opinions in newspapers of major U.S. cities showed widespread disagreement with Israel's policy and supported the administration's demand for immediate Israeli withdrawal from the Sinai.

But as soon as Ben-Gurion, under heavy pressure from the United States, the Soviet Union, the United Nations, and U.S. Jewry, agreed in principle to withdraw provided Israel received U.S. security guarantees regarding freedom of navigation in the Straits of Tiran and special arrangements in the Gaza Strip, Israel's image in the United States began to improve.[21] Those who had previously perceived Israel as using force in collusion with Britain and France for the sake of self-aggrandizement now saw a small, beleaguered, democratic state fighting for legitimate security interests.

In addition, a more supportive atmosphere for Israel began to emerge when the Israeli government succeeded retroactively in focusing public attention on the circumstances that led to Israel's attack on Egypt. It accomplished that goal by tenacious insistence on guarantees against the repetition of Arab raids and blockades. Moreover, the brilliance of the Israeli military action, contrasting with the vacillation and fumbling of the British and the French, won Israel the admiration of many military brass in the Pentagon. Even Eisenhower, although condemning the Israeli attack from a political standpoint, praised its military execution. Once the crisis had subsided and in a calmer atmosphere, he told Philip Klutznick, "You know, the one thing I learned from that lesson watching the way Israel's forces performed and the way Britain and France performed is perhaps we've got the wrong allies."[22]

Yet despite these changes in Israel's attitude, the Eisenhower administration persisted in its demand for unconditional Israeli withdrawal. This uncompromising stance now galvanized Jewish organizations in support of Israel's demands for security guarantees. They viewed the administration policy as unfair, a sentiment widely shared in Congress and among the public at large.[23] The issue was no longer whether or not Israel should withdraw but the conditions under which such withdrawal would take place.

The strategy of the Jewish organizations now was aimed at convincing members of Congress to urge the administration to prevent the return of the Egyptians to Gaza and Sharm es-Sheikh, preferring a UNEF presence there instead. On December 20, the AZC sent a letter to 3,500 local Jewish leaders urging them to seek meetings with their respective members of Congress and impress upon them the need for preventing a return to the conditions that prevailed prior to the outbreak of the October 29 war. Indeed, influential members of Congress began to speak out critically about the administration's Middle East policy. Strong statements endorsing Israel's demand for security guarantees were issued by Senators Hubert H. Humphrey of Minnesota and Mike Mansfield of Montana. By late December 1956, the sentiments of most members of Congress ran in Israel's favor, and they were demanding that a UNEF should be dispatched to Gaza and Sharm es-Sheikh.

Thanks to Kenen's lobbying efforts, on January 25, 1957, forty-two Republican members of the House of Representatives sent Dulles a strongly worded telegram in which they opposed any further one-sided UN resolutions calling for unconditional Israeli withdrawal from Egyptian territory. In addition, on January 29, 1957, four Republican and four Democratic senators—Republicans Javits and Ives of New York, William Langer of North Dakota, and John Beal of Maryland, and Democrats Humphrey, Allen Sparkman of Alabama, Paul Douglas of Illinois, and

Richard Neuberger of Oregon—sponsored a resolution calling for UN forces to take up positions between Israel and Egypt in the disputed areas to guarantee against recurrence of raids and blockades.[24]

Congressional criticism of administration policy came at a time when Eisenhower and Dulles were seeking a joint congressional resolution in support of the president's doctrine authorizing him to use economic aid and military force if necessary as a means of stopping Soviet penetration or aggression in the Middle East.[25]

On January 5, 1957, before a joint session of the Eighty-fifth Congress, the president informed Congress of an imminent danger of Communist aggression in the region and urged the immediate passage of his program, lest the Middle East come under the sway of international communism. The program, known as the Eisenhower Doctrine, in fact formalized direct U.S. interest and involvement in the region rather than total reliance on the United Nations. In effect, it provided the basis for U.S. diplomacy in the area during the post-Suez period.

The doctrine consisted of three main points. First, the commitment of U.S. military force to assist any nation in the Middle East requesting aid against armed aggression from any country controlled by international communism. Second, U.S. economic assistance free from the usual limitations imposed by Congress in the Mutual Security Act for special military and economic projects in the Middle East. Third, a U.S. offer of $120 million in economic and military assistance to all states in the region who subscribed to the doctrine.[26]

The AZC, aware of the administration's eagerness for speedy approval of the doctrine by both houses of Congress, began lobbying the lawmakers for changes in the language of the resolution to make it compatible with Israel's interest in its conflict with the Arab states. Although the AZC welcomed the Eisenhower Doctrine in principle as marking an end to U.S. isolationism in the Middle East, it left out important elements pertaining to the Arab-Israeli conflict. The doctrine, the AZC claimed, offered no solutions to intraregional problems, remained silent on the issue of freedom of navigation, and referred such problems to the United Nations, where there was no prospect of securing a solution. In short, while the doctrine focused on U.S. aid against overt armed aggression from any nation controlled by international communism, it failed to address the main issue concerning Israel: What would U.S. policy be should the Arab states launch a war against Israel with Soviet concurrence but without direct involvement? From the Israeli perspective, Israel had been the only country in the Middle East threatened with direct armed aggression from nations controlled by international communism, because Egypt and Syria were receiving large quantities of weapons from the Soviet Union. Yet the doctrine failed to address one of the main issues disrupting the peace in the region.[27]

Accordingly, AIPAC lobbied members of Congress to correct that omission in the doctrine. Kenen, its director, met with congressmen, including Democrats John Dingell of Michigan, James Roosevelt of California, Emmanuel Celler of New York, and Brooks Hays of Arkansas, Republicans Hugh Scott of Pennsylvania and John Marrow of New Hampshire, and Senator Frank Church, Democrat of Idaho. Hays relayed the Zionists' criticism of the doctrine to J. William Fulbright, Democratic senator from Arkansas and a member of the Senate Foreign Relations Committee. On January 12, 1957, Fulbright offered a resolution in the Senate favoring free passage of shipping through the Suez Canal and efforts to bring about an Arab-Israeli peace.

Rabbi Philip S. Bernstein, representing the AZC, testified before House and Senate Foreign Relations committees and urged that the administration's resolution be supplemented by a seven-point course of action, among those points a call for direct Arab-Israeli peace negotiations, security guarantees for any nation ready to commit itself to the West, and strong international action to stop sea blockades.[28] The same points were reiterated by Dr. Israel Goldstein, president of the American Jewish Congress, in a statement he submitted to the Foreign Relations Committee and the Armed Services Committee of the Senate. The main lacuna of the doctrine, he argued, was its failure to "come to grips with the regional conflict" between Israel and the Arab states.[29]

This approach was strongly supported by a number of members of Congress who testified before the House Foreign Relations Committee and urged that the doctrine focus on the internal problems of the region as well as the Soviet threat in the area. Thus, when Dulles appeared before the Senate Foreign Relations Committee urging swift passage of the doctrine, he was challenged about the U.S. position in upholding the sovereignty of the state of Israel. In response he said: "I can assure the Committee that we shall not in any application of this policy or any of our discussions with the Arab countries do anything whatsoever that would detract from the statements so often made by this administration and others and by Congress that the preservation of the State of Israel was a vital part of United States policy."[30]

As a result of Lyndon B. Johnson's intervention, Dulles agreed to support an amendment to the doctrine proposed by Senator Mike Mansfield that tried indirectly to allay Israel's security fears. The amendment, attached to section 2 of the doctrine, stated that the United States viewed with utmost importance the connection between U.S. national interests and world peace on the one hand, and the preservation of the independence and sovereignty of countries in the Middle East. The amendment was a gesture toward supporters of Israel and indirectly strengthened the U.S. commitment to Israel's security.[31]

Yet the administration's insistence upon unconditional Israeli withdrawal without any security guarantees complicated quick congressional approval of the Eisenhower Doctrine. Thanks to strong Jewish lobbying efforts, on January 25, 1957, seventy Democratic members of Congress, in a letter to Dulles, asked that Israel be provided with security guarantees prior to the withdrawal of its troops from the Sinai and Gaza. In the letter, they announced their opposition to UN pressures on Israel to evacuate positions along the Gulf of Aqaba. Moreover, they demanded that the status quo ante not be reinstated and that concessions be obtained from Nasser regarding freedom of passage of Israeli ships through the Suez Canal.[32] Congressional consent to the doctrine now hinged on a quick resolution of the administration rift with Israel over the withdrawal of its troops from Egyptian territory.

Dulles's statement to the press on February 5, that the United States would give serious consideration to a UN call for sanctions against Israel should it refuse to withdraw immediately, further complicated the administration's efforts to gain congressional approval of the doctrine. Moreover, for the first time since the outbreak of the crisis, Dulles's statement galvanized and united all Jewish organizations (with the exception of the anti-Zionist American Council for Judaism) in public criticism of administration policies as unfair and immoral.

On February 6, Zionist leaders, in an emergency meeting in New York City, agreed that the Presidents' Conference would publish a statement in the form of an advertisement condemning the administration's position on sanctions. They also decided to issue an appeal to Jews throughout the country to dispatch letters and telegrams to Congress against any sanctions proposals. Kenen telephoned Jewish leaders, Zionist and non-Zionist, in Alabama, Iowa, Arkansas, Louisiana, Wisconsin, and Vermont to come to Washington and lobby key lawmakers against administration policy.[33]

In this atmosphere of threats to Israel, "a popular revulsion of feeling against unfairness to Israel" erupted throughout the country.[34] The *New York Times* and the *Washington Post* in editorials on February 9 and 12 reflected the strong support for Israel's demand for security guarantees. Both papers insisted that Israel's stance had not been unreasonable. The State Department's insistence that Israel must withdraw first before any guarantee could even be negotiated was, according to the *New York Times*, unrealistic and even dangerous. Congressional and public disapproval of administration policy of sanctions served as important supportive ingredients to the Jewish organizations in their efforts to counter the use of financial and economic pressures against Israel.

Congressional opposition to sanctions erupted at once. First and most important was an angry and unexpected retort from William F. Knowland, the Senate minority leader, who described the proposed move against Israel as both immoral and in good conscience unacceptable. He called the sanctions a "double standard by the United Nations that would apply one law to a small country . . . while sidestepping the question of sanctions on a larger aggressor," the Soviet Union. Knowland's reaction was spontaneous and did not need any prodding from the pro-Israeli lobby. The senator was in the process of preparing a speech on the weaknesses of the United Nations; when he read Dulles's statement about sanctions on the ticker, he saw it as proof of the correctness of his thesis. Knowland's statement was most significant, for it gave the green light to influential Republican senators—Style Bridges of New Hampshire, chairman of the Republican Policy Committee; Leverett Saltonstall of Massachusetts, ranking Republican on the Armed Services Committee; and Alexander Smith of New Jersey, the chief Republican voice on foreign policy—to come out in opposition to the administration policy. As a follow-up to Knowland's statement and Zionist pressures, seventy-five Democrat and forty-one Republican House members called on the administration to desist from any sanctions against Israel.[35]

Yet Lyndon B. Johnson, the powerful Senate majority leader, had so far not spoken out against sanctions. Kenen and Nathaniel Goodrich, the representative of the American Jewish Committee, arranged a meeting with George Reedy, Johnson's press aide and director of the Democratic Policy Committee. They discussed ways of getting Johnson to join Knowland and call on the president to abandon any thought of sanctions. The Jewish lobbyists impressed Reedy with the fact that the Republicans had taken the initiative and that the Democrats should have reacted more quickly and more vigorously.

Soon thereafter, at Reedy's suggestion, Kenen called Zionist and non-Zionist Jewish leaders in Dallas, Houston, Waco, Fort Worth, San Antonio, and Austin, urging them to orchestrate a flood of letters and telegrams to Johnson's office in Washington denouncing the imposition of sanctions. Rabbis, in sermons delivered at Saturday synagogue services throughout Texas, urged their parishioners to register their opposition to administration policy in letters and telegrams to Johnson. Over the weekend more than 5,000 telegrams poured into the office of Johnson and Sam Rayburn, Speaker of the House.

Two days later, on February 11, Reedy mailed Kenen a copy of a letter Johnson had sent to Dulles condemning the sanctions proposal. On the Senate floor, Johnson urged the administration to break the deadlock without reviving "the talk about sanctions or other methods of coercion." He advised the secretary of state to order the U.S. delegation at the United Nations to oppose any proposal for sanctions "with all its skills."[36] And, like Knowland, Johnson contrasted the United Nations' cavalier attitude toward Soviet actions in Hungary with its threats against a small country like Israel. Moreover, he insisted that no action would be taken by the Senate on the administration's much-desired Eisenhower Doctrine until an agreement was reached between the United States and Israel regarding withdrawal from Egyptian territory.[37]

During February 16–17, on both sides of the Senate chamber, members rose to speak in opposition to the administration's policy of sanctions and its demand for Israeli withdrawal without security guarantees. Their message to Dulles could be summed up in two sentences: The United Nations could not have one rule for the strong and another for the weak. Israel's request for security guarantees was justified. The crisis came to a head when the president invited party leaders to meet with him at the

White House on February 20. Unable to move congressional leaders to exert pressure on Israel for immediate withdrawal, the president addressed the nation that evening. He repeated his demand for Israeli compliance with the UN resolutions and implied that strong measures would have to be taken by the United Nations and the United States should Israel refuse.

But the president's speech to the nation had not swayed congressional opinion in the administration's favor. In fact, Johnson, Knowland, and Javits, in telegrams to the White House, criticized the speech as unfair and totally one-sided. Simultaneously, the ZOA telephoned leaders of sixty major Jewish communities and asked them to send urgent messages to the White House condemning the president's speech. The Jewish leaders were also urged to convince Christians to sign messages critical of administration policy. In addition, Zionist leaders in New York sponsored a Madison Square Garden demonstration in which 20,000 people participated in denouncing administration policy.

Significantly, Senate debate on the Eisenhower Doctrine slowed to a snail's pace. On February 24, Senate leaders told Dulles that the doctrine would not win Senate approval if the administration proceeded with sanctions. In the House of Representatives, members warned of a delay in the vote on the doctrine until the crisis with Israel was resolved satisfactorily without the need for sanctions.

The news of an agreement between the United States and Israel under French auspices calling for Israeli withdrawal based on "assumptions and expectations" of U.S. security guarantees came as a welcome relief to members of Congress and especially to U.S. Jewish organizations, whose lobbying efforts had staved off a most dangerous threat to the existence of the Jewish state.

Still, the Presidents' Conference, after the tough fight with the administration, did not issue any statement crediting Secretary Dulles for any contribution to the settlement reached. But a delegation of top Jewish leaders, Zionists and non-Zionists, came to Washington to meet with Senate and House leaders and other lawmakers to thank them for their support of Israel throughout the crisis. The Jewish leaders were well aware that the attitudes of both houses of Congress in their opposition to sanctions and demand for security guarantees to Israel played a major part in changing administration policy. But that would not have taken place without the strong lobbying efforts of the various Jewish organizations, Zionist and non-Zionist alike.

Needless to say, the successful outcome of those efforts must also be attributed to the fact that Israel's demand for security guarantees prior to withdrawal found a large degree of sympathy among the U.S. public at large. In short, U.S. Jewry's impact on the country's policy toward Israel depended on the extent to which it could convince national public opinion that support of Israel accorded with U.S. moral and strategic interests. By portraying Israel as a small democracy fighting for survival against an Arab country supported by the Soviet Union, U.S. Jews succeeded in their task. A popular president who vowed many times not to allow domestic politics to influence his foreign policy decisions had to yield to a basic fact: in a democracy, foreign policy is always impacted by domestic politics.

With the crisis over Israeli withdrawal now resolved and the Eisenhower Doctrine approved by Congress, U.S. Jewish organizations would concentrate their efforts on the restoration of normalcy in U.S.-Israeli relations by pressing the administration to resume aid to Israel and lift the travel ban to the Middle East. Achieving those objectives would now be much easier, for Eisenhower and especially Dulles came to realize that Nasser's Egypt had become the threat to peace in the Middle East. The Egyptian leader had failed to show any gratitude toward the United States despite its efforts to pressure Israel, Britain, and France to stop their attacks on Egypt and withdraw from Egyptian territory. On the contrary, Nasser pursued a policy that enhanced the Soviet position in the region at the expense of the West. The inclusion of Israel in the Eisenhower Doctrine marked a clear departure from the previous U.S. policy of detachment from Israel. From now on, U.S. leaders would view Israel as a country that might after all serve the strategic interests of the United States in the region.

Indeed, a decade later Eisenhower would regret the manner in which he handled the Suez crisis. On an October afternoon in 1965, the former president hosted Max M. Fisher, a prominent national Jewish leader, general chairman of the United Jewish Appeal, and a Republican party fund-raiser, a man referred to by many as *the* Jewish Republican. At the end of their conversation Eisenhower said, "You know, Max, looking back at Suez, I regret what I did. I should have never pressured Israel to evacuate the Sinai." Richard M. Nixon, a friend of Max M. Fisher, confirmed Eisenhower's remarks. "Eisenhower," said Nixon, "many years later, in the 1960s told me—and, I am sure he told others—that he thought that the action taken [at Suez] was one he regretted. He thought it was a mistake."[38]

From Confrontation
to Cooperation

The withdrawal of Israeli troops from Egyptian territory brought an end to the strain and confrontation between the United States and Israel. A period of relative tranquility in bilateral relations ensued. U.S. and Israeli interests were in basic consonance thanks in large part to the administration's shift of attention from an immediate solution to the Arab-Israeli dispute to the Communist threat to the independence and integrity of the states in the Middle East. In the administration's view, countering Communist penetration and radical Arab subversion of pro-Western regimes in the region became top priority. Success in that endeavor would in the long run also contribute to a resolution of the Arab-Israeli conflict. Such a policy coincided with Israel's own interests.

The adoption by Congress on March 9, 1957, of the Eisenhower Doctrine inaugurated a major U.S. commitment to diminish Soviet and Nasserite influence in the region and at the same time maintain stability in the Middle East by attempting to prevent an Arab-Israeli war. Israel's cooperation in achieving both objectives marked a turning point in U.S.-Israeli relations.

Israel's inclusion in the Eisenhower Doctrine was in itself an indication of how much matters had changed since the beginning of the decade. In 1951, when the Allied Middle Eastern Command was established by the Western powers, Israel's inclusion was not desired lest it prevent Arab participation. But now, when Eisenhower's envoy to the Middle East, James P. Richards, visited the region in order to seek support for the doctrine, Israel was included in his itinerary. The United States was no longer shying away from Israel in order to please the Arabs.[1]

On May 3, 1957, Richards arrived in Jerusalem to explain the main points and objectives of the Eisenhower Doctrine to Israeli leaders and to urge them to join the president's initiative. Yet despite the changing circumstances in Israel's favor, adherence to the doctrine did not win unanimous cabinet approval. Cabinet ministers representing the two Socialist parties, Mapam and Achdut Ha'avodah, were against any association with the doctrine. Citing their parties' pledge of September 1955 not to join in any "aggressive purpose or alliance directed against any power whatsoever," they warned of a Soviet negative reaction should Israel become part of a U.S.-led campaign against the Soviet Union. Such action by Israel, they warned, would jeopardize the chances of large-scale Jewish immigration from the Eastern Bloc countries and involve Israel in the cold war struggle between East and West.[2] Ben-Gurion, however, disagreed. He did not regard the Eisenhower Doctrine as aggressive, nor was Israel asked to join in an alliance with the United States.

After weeks of discussions, on May 21 the Israeli government issued a statement declaring its attitude on the subject. In the statement the government welcomed the support of the United States for the preservation of the independence of Middle Eastern states and for the development of the economic strength necessary to maintain that independence. Sensitive to Soviet reaction, however, the government explicitly renounced any aggressive intentions and omitted any reference to "international communism." The emphasis was on peace and cooperation, national independence, and loyalty to the UN Charter. After consultations with the Israeli embassy in Washington, the State Department issued a communiqué taking note of the Israeli government's expressed "support of the purposes of the Middle East policy set forth by President Eisenhower." The communiqué added that "the United States shares and supports the principles and objectives outlined in Israel's statement relating to American policy under the Doctrine."

On June 3, the government sought the Knesset's approval for the May 21 statement. In the ensuing debate Ben-Gurion defended the government's decision. He pointed out that Syria, Israel's enemy to the north, had intensified its relationship with the Soviet Union, receiving large quantities of Soviet weapons and military advisers. Likewise, Nasser had become the beneficiary of Soviet military assistance and was now in the process of reviving his military supremacy. In light of these developments, Ben-Gurion found great promise in the doctrine's stipulation that the United States would help militarily any country attacked by a Communist-backed aggressor. "Let us say," he continued, "that Syria helped by Russian flyers attacked us. . . . I am sure that not one member of Mapam or Achdut Ha'avodah would oppose any help we can get rather than die from Russian bullets." If Israel were attacked by Soviet pilots aiding Syria, Israel's air force would have little chance of defeating them, said Ben-Gurion. But a warning to Syria that such a provocation might be countered with U.S. intervention would surely act as a deterrent to Syria's plans. According to Ben-Gurion, the practical importance of the doctrine lay not so much in what would happen if war broke out but in the probability that a U.S. warning would prevent aggression altogether. In reply to Soviet condemnation of Israel's association with the Eisenhower Doctrine, the premier stressed that his country harbored no aggressive designs against any other country and certainly not against the Soviet Union. In view of the fact that immigrants from the Eastern Bloc countries had begun trickling into Israel, Ben-Gurion went out of his way to ensure that the flow of immigrants would not be interrupted by Israel's adherence to the doctrine.

But perhaps the best argument for Israel's association with the doctrine was the U.S. attitude of including that nation for the first time in a pro-Western program together with several Arab states. Had Israel been left out, the message to the Arabs and the Soviet Union would have been that the United States was not interested in its fate. Given the fact that, with the exception of Egypt and Syria, most of the Arab countries had joined the doctrine, Israel's noninvolvement would have placed her, in the words of Abba Eban, in a position of a "leper colony."[3] Ultimately, Ben-Gurion's pragmatism won the day. The government's statement was adopted by the Knesset by 59 to 5 (Communist members); 39 abstained. The Socialist Mapam and Achdut Ha'avodah abstained so as not to forfeit their membership in the government. Also abstaining were members of the right-wing opposition Herut party, though supporting the doctrine would not support the government.[4]

Relations with the United States continued to improve as the two countries' objectives became more compatible. During 1957–58, under the guise of Arab nationalism and with Soviet support, Nasser embarked on a campaign aimed at subverting pro-Western regimes in the region. Nasser's drive forced the United States to develop a policy designed to contain his influence, which also created harmony between U.S. goals and Israeli interests.

By August 1957, Syria was moving closer and closer to the Soviet camp. Large quantities of Soviet arms were unloaded at the Syrian port of Latakia. Soviet military experts, sent to train the Syrian army in the use of those weapons, began arriving in Damascus. Ben-Gurion warned Dulles about the growing danger that Syria would become a base for international communism. He urged Dulles to take firm and immediate steps to encourage rebellious elements in Syria to topple the pro-Soviet regime there. Indeed, the United States planned a coup in Syria with the help of Turkey, Iraq, and Jordan. With Israel's encouragement, the United States dispatched the Sixth Fleet close to Syrian shores while Turkish, Iraqi, and Jordanian army units concentrated on Syria's borders. But the coup failed.[5]

Soviet successes in Syria, coupled with Nasser's subversive activities and expansionist ambitions, aroused great concern not only in Washington and Jerusalem but also in states at the periphery of the Middle East: Ethiopia, Iran, and Turkey. Emperor Haile Selassie of Ethiopia, anxious about Nasser's Pan-Islamic and Pan-African expansionism, was eager to receive Israeli military help and to cooperate with Israel in the economic field and in the establishment of joint projects. Iran, likewise greatly concerned with the rise of Nasserite and Communist influence in the region, explored the possibility of secret cooperation with Israel in such areas as agriculture and scientific development, including strategic cooperation. Turkey, too, alarmed over the alliance between the Soviet Union (Turkey's northern neighbor) and Syria (Turkey's southern neighbor), was looking for any ally in the region to block potential threats.

In characteristic fashion, Ben-Gurion sensed the opportunities now open to Israel. For the first time since its establishment, Israel stood a good chance of breaking through the isolation imposed by its Arab neighbors. Israeli emissaries in secret and clandestine missions to the capitals of Turkey, Iran, and Ethiopia eagerly concurred with their leaders about the common threat facing them. Israel now spearheaded a movement that would soon make Israel the linchpin of a group of states opposing the alarming trends in the region. The result was the emergence of a "periphery alliance" consisting of a bloc of states around the edge of the Middle East: Turkey and Iran to the north and Ethiopia to the south, linked to Israel in an unofficial alliance. All eventually collaborated with the United States to foil Nasserite and Soviet designs.[6]

With this secret and prospective alliance in hand, Ben-Gurion pressed for U.S. political and financial backing of the "periphery pact." In a letter to Eban, Ben-Gurion wrote, "If America adopts this plan a link between Iran, Turkey, Israel and one should add Ethiopia—something important may grow out of it."[7]

The upheavals that shook the Middle East during the spring and summer of 1958 lent further urgency to Ben-Gurion's strategy, as well as to Israel's willingness if not eagerness to serve Western interests in the region.

In February 1958, Egypt and Syria proclaimed the merger of their two countries in a United Arab Republic. Disjointed as the political hybrid appeared, it nonetheless formed a major pro-Soviet nationalist Arab bloc in the Middle East. In May, civil war broke out in Lebanon between Christians and Moslems. The Moslem armed uprising began as a domestic conflict, but fanned by propaganda emanating from Cairo and Damascus, the rebellion threatened to topple the pro-Western government of President Camille Chamoun. The Moslems demanded Lebanon's integration into a Nasserite-led bloc.

In an effort to counter Nasser's United Arab Republic, Iraq and Jordan, with Western blessing, announced in May the formation of an Arab Union. Even though such a union was unpalatable to Israel because it could affect its security should Iraqi troops enter Jordan, Israel did not interfere with the pro-Western anti-Nasser scheme.

But the fast-moving events in the region brought the union between Iraq and Jordan to naught. On July 14, officers of the Iraqi army led by General Abdul Karim Kassem revolted and murdered King Faisal and the pro-British Prime Minister, Nuri es-Said. The new government consisted of a military junta, ostensibly pro-Egyptian in orientation. The bloody events in Baghdad dealt a terrible blow to U.S. and British interests in the region. Overnight, Iraq, formerly the key to the Baghdad Pact, was now about to turn into a Soviet satellite. Moreover, Iraq's neighbors, Iran and Turkey, watched in dismay and trepidation as the Soviet noose tightened around them.

The events in Iraq coincided with a worsening situation in Lebanon, where the Chamoun government faced imminent downfall. It looked as though all Western strongholds were collapsing in succession. The president of the United States activated the Eisenhower Doctrine. On July 15, Eisenhower announced that in response to a request by the president of Lebanon, the United States would send 15,000 marines to Beirut. Simultaneously, the Strategic Air Command and aircraft carriers in the Middle East were placed on emergency alert. In addition, U.S. troops from the Gulf of Okinawa were rushed to the Persian Gulf, and still others were dispatched to bases in Turkey. Eisenhower hoped that opponents of the coup in Iraq would invite the United States to intervene, but no such call came.[8]

The chain of tempestuous events had now reached Jordan. King Hussein, a longtime target of pro-Nasser elements, found himself in far greater danger following the collapse of his royal allies in Iraq. Facing assassination or overthrow, King Hussein remained a prisoner in his palace, protected by British soldiers flown in from bases in Cyprus. Simultaneous with U.S. marines landing on the shores of Beirut, Britain, in response to a request from Hussein, sent planes loaded with troops and military equipment to Jordan. Because the planes flew over Israeli airspace, the overflights caused consternation in Israel. The British had not bothered to ask Israel's permission for the overflights, and the Soviets had issued threats against Israel for colluding in an imperialist plot to occupy Jordan.[9]

To further complicate matters, on July 24, in a meeting with Eban, Dulles requested Israeli clearance for U.S. tanker planes to use Israeli airspace in order to replenish Jordan's exhausted fuel reserves. In addition, Dulles wanted Israel to allow U.S. giant transport planes to fly over its airspace to deliver military equipment to the Hashemite kingdom. Dulles estimated that the operation would last about two weeks. Eban saw no difficulty in acceding to the U.S. request. Mindful of the Soviet threats, however, he explained Israel's dilemma to Dulles. "The root of the problem," he said, "is that Britain and the United States come to us with demands as if we were allies. We indeed are willing to take risks, but we do not have the security guarantees granted by the United States to an ally." The ambassador demanded that the United States and Israel open discussions leading to U.S. weapon deliveries to Israel and direct security guarantees.[10]

Indeed, in subsequent days Israel's wishes would be partially fulfilled, thanks to the continuing deterioration in the Western position in the region and Israel's usefulness in stemming the pro-Soviet Nasserite tide.

In the meantime, Ben-Gurion's idea of a periphery pact gained further momentum. With Syria in the Soviet camp and Iraq on its way to becoming a Soviet satellite, Turkey decided to strengthen its ties with Israel—a most welcome development from Ben-Gurion's perspective. Elated, he wrote in his diary on July 20 that the Israeli emissary in Ankara was informed by the Turkish foreign minister about the country's willingness to coordinate political action with Israel. According to Ben-Gurion, "We have entered historic times, and the opportunity for such action will not return."[11] The premiers of both countries agreed in principle to meet and to discuss ways of stopping Soviet penetration in the area, particularly in Iran and Ethiopia.

A confident Ben-Gurion was eager to prove to the United States Israeli reliability and benefit to the West. After consultations with Golda Meir on ways of "tightening links with Iran, Turkey and Ethiopia with the aid of America . . . and American assistance to those countries," he sent a letter to Eisenhower outlining for the first time Israel's plans of becoming the keystone in a pro-Western alliance. "Our object," he wrote, "is the creation of a group of countries not necessarily a formal public alliance, that will be able to stand up steadfastly against Soviet expansion through Nasser and might even be able to save the freedom of Lebanon and perhaps in the course of time Syria too. . . . We can carry out the mission since . . . it is a vital necessity for us as well as a source of perceptible strength to the West in this part of the world."[12] Ben-Gurion asked for U.S. political, financial, and moral support to the countries involved, but most of all to convey to Turkey, Ethiopia, and Iran that Israel's efforts had the approval of the Eisenhower administration.

On July 25, Ben-Gurion received Eisenhower's reply: "I am deeply impressed by the breadth of your insight into the grave problems which the free world faces in the Middle East and elsewhere." Referring to U.S. intervention in Lebanon, the president noted his concern "for the integrity and independence of Lebanon which was so demonstrably threatened from without." Eisenhower went on to reassure Israel. "The integrity of the nations of the Middle East is vital to world peace and to the United States national interest . . . and since the Middle East comprehends Israel you can be confident of U.S. interest in the integrity and independence of Israel." Furthermore, said Eisenhower, "I have discussed your letter with the Secretary of State who will be writing to you in more detail."[13]

On August 3, Ben-Gurion received a letter from Dulles in which the secretary expressed full support of the idea of the peripheral pact and pledged U.S. assistance to it. But most important from Israel's perspective was Dulles's reference to Israel's security. "As it pertains to Israeli security," said Dulles, "the President already wrote to you about the implications of our actions in Lebanon . . . we believe that Israel must be in a position of being able to deter any attempt of aggression by regional forces, and we are willing to discuss the military implications of such a problem."[14]

Although both Eisenhower's and Dulles's statements were greeted with a great deal of satisfaction in Israel, Ben-Gurion could not ignore a Soviet demand of August 1 that Israel immediately stop British and U.S. over-flights to Jordan. Concerned about the possibility of a Soviet attack, Ben-Gurion declared that the overflights would stop immediately. Washington reacted with anger at Israel. Dulles informed Eban that the Israeli action constituted a surrender to the Soviets, a violation of a commitment to the United States, and a bad example for countries willing to stand up to Soviet expansionism. Eban immediately cabled Ben-Gurion informing him about the adverse reaction to his statement in the United States. He urged the premier to issue an immediate clarification of the Israeli position to Washington's satisfaction.

While Eban tried to assuage Dulles by stating that the press overplayed Israel's position on the question of the overflights, he also pressed Dulles to issue a public statement that the United States would respond in kind should the Soviet Union attack Israel. Israel, said Eban, found itself at a great disadvantage in comparison with countries who were threatened by the Soviet Union such as Greece, Turkey, and Italy—all members of NATO. "We are not defended by an American guarantee and the Soviet Union is able to wipe us out in five minutes." Dulles replied: "The President had decided based on the Congressional Resolution [the Eisenhower Doctrine] that if Israel would be attacked by the Soviet Union, the United States would come to Israel's assistance . . . the Soviet Union is well aware of that fact. The United States is committed to Israel's existence and would fight for her should an attack by the Soviet Union compel her to do so."[15]

The rift with the United States regarding the overflights was immediately patched up when Ben-Gurion informed the U.S. ambassador in Israel that, contrary to reports, Israel had no intention of stopping the overflights and would not buckle under the Soviet threat. Lawson promised that the flights would be discontinued within forty-eight hours, perhaps by August 6 or August 8. Eban informed Dulles that no interruption in those flights would take place and that Israel would answer the Soviet complaint of August 1 upon the termination of the Anglo-American campaign to help Jordan.

With that minor crisis in U.S.-Israeli relations resolved, Ben-Gurion turned his attention to a subject dear to his heart. With the blessings of the United States he proceeded toward the consolidation of the periphery pact.

Late on August 29, Ben-Gurion secretly flew to Ankara where he met with his Turkish counterpart, Adnan Menderes. They agreed on political, economic, and scientific cooperation as well as on the sharing of intelligence information between the Israeli Intelligence Service, MOSSAD, and the Turkish Security Service. At the same time, secret commercial and military agreements were concluded with Iran. The MOSSAD agreed to exchange intelligence information with Iran's intelligence agency, Savak. Among their common interests were the activities of Soviet spies in the Middle East. Ethiopia also further strengthened its ties with Israel. Emperor Haile Selassie had for many years proclaimed himself a descendant of the ancient Hebrew tribe of Judah and used its symbol, a majestic lion, as his emblem; he admired the Jewish state. Israel for its part trained his security forces and intelligence personnel and provided agricultural advisers. In turn, Israel was permitted to build a powerful listening post in Ethiopia that monitored Arab radio traffic.[16]

Israel's role in stemming Nasserite and Soviet influence had now won the wholehearted support and recognition of the United States. Sensing Israel's strategic importance to the West, the United States for the first time agreed to supply Israel with 1,000 recoilless guns and with electronic

President Eisenhower, Prime Minister Ben-Gurion (left), and Under Secretary of State Douglas C. Dillon (right) in the president's White House office, March 10, 1960. By permission of the Dwight D. Eisenhower Library.

and aircraft-detection equipment. In addition, Dulles consented to provide secret financing for Israel's purchase of tanks from Britain.[17] The magnitude of that offer in financial terms was six to ten times larger than any previous U.S. military transaction with Israel.[18]

The improvement in relations culminated in a meeting between Ben-Gurion and Eisenhower. On March 8, 1960, Ben-Gurion came to the United States to receive an honorary Doctor of Law Degree at Brandeis University. He used the occasion for an unofficial visit to the White House, where he met with Eisenhower on March 10 for a discussion that lasted two hours. The unusual length of the conversation was a reflection of the improved relations between the two countries and a personal triumph for Ben-Gurion.

The prime minister approached the discussion philosophically and globally, analyzing the threat to the Middle East stemming from Soviet designs and Pan-Arabism fanned by Nasser. He focused on Israel's efforts in developing commercial and strategic links with countries in Africa and Asia, and especially with those countries at the periphery of the Arab nations. Ben-Gurion did most of the talking, emphasizing the values Israel shared with the United States, such as democracy and the pioneering spirit that helped build both countries. Eisenhower reiterated that the United States would never allow the destruction of the state of Israel. But he refused Ben-Gurion's request for the delivery of U.S. arms, especially the Hawk surface-to-air missiles. The United States, Eisenhower said, would not be the main supplier of weapons to the Middle East, leaving that task to France and other countries. Facing reporters after the meeting, Ben-Gurion was asked whether he was encouraged by his discussions with the president. Ben-Gurion replied: "One is always encouraged after meeting a man like the President of the United States."[19]

Eisenhower was equally impressed with his visitor. In the words of the new Secretary of State, Christian Herter, "the discussions with the Prime Minister were profitable for us also. We were impressed by his breadth of vision, his faith in the destiny of his people and his dedication to the great moral verities shared by free men all over the world. We concluded that with such vision, faith and dedication Israel can assuredly make significant contributions to a better world."[20]

Conclusion

Between 1953 and 1957, in an attempt to entice the Arab countries (especially Egypt) into a closer relationship with the West and in an effort to maintain control of the very important oil resources vital to Western economies, the United States minimized its relationship with Israel, hoping to avoid alienating the Arabs. The pursuit of Arab goodwill was not a result of malice toward Israel, but it stemmed from what seemed to be a cold war imperative. Even so, the policy of even-handedness, or what Dulles preferred to call "friendly impartiality," in the Arab-Israeli conflict did not diminish U.S. commitment to the existence and survival of the state of Israel.

Despite serious reservations about the wisdom of Truman's policies, among them recognizing Israel in 1948, Eisenhower never considered backtracking from Truman's basic commitment. He firmly supported the commitment to the legitimacy, existence, and survival of the Jewish state. Continuity rather than change marked the relationship between the two countries during the Eisenhower presidency, though there were periods of stress and times of trouble in the relationship. After all, the Truman years had not been devoid of friction and pressures on Israel regarding basic questions such as boundaries and the intractable Arab refugee problem. These and other vexing problems continued to cause strains and tensions between the two countries as the United States desperately tried to keep the Arab Middle East out of the Soviet orbit.

But the basic moral commitment to Israel's right to exist as a state, a Truman legacy, had not been tampered with by the Eisenhower administration, rhetoric notwithstanding. A good argument could be made that if the Eisenhower administration was less free with pro-Israeli declarations, it was more forthcoming with pro-Israeli deeds. Indeed, contrary to the conventional belief at the time, Dulles, the son of a minister and himself an avid reader of the Bible, despite his cold demeanor had a hidden affection for the Jewish people, and his support for the Jewish right to statehood predated his appointment as secretary of state. Zionist critics failed to acknowledge that fact. Eisenhower and Dulles did take Israel's concerns to heart. They did not, as Zionists charged, abandon the Jewish state. The critics failed to understand the difficult circumstances in which U.S. policy in the Middle East had to operate: on the one hand, preserving Western strategic interests in the Arab world and, at the same time, maintaining the U.S. commitment to Israel's existence in face of Arab enmity. It had been a difficult balancing act, but the United States never compromised its basic principles, despite Arab pressures and cold war considerations.

The Eisenhower administration, in an evenhanded approach, attempted to bring about peace between Israel and its neighbors. Those attempts included the ALPHA Project, the Jordan Valley Authority Plan, and the most ambitious of all, the secret Anderson mission to Cairo and Jerusalem. They all failed because Israel had been asked to make territorial concessions and accept the repatriation of Arab refugees. Israel had been asked to do these things without a clear-cut commitment from the Arab side to recognize and live in peace with Israel.

What was missing in the relationship between the two countries during the Eisenhower years was the public demonstration of sympathy, warmth, and support that Truman exhibited toward Israel. At times, Dulles and State Department officials publicly demonstrated a lack of sensitivity to Israel's needs and predicament. But the change from Truman's attitude was more in tone than in substance. Neither Eisenhower nor Dulles ever tried to impose any solutions that would endanger Israel, despite cold war calculations and Arab pressures to do so. The administration continually upheld the commitment to resist any attempt to alter by force the territorial and political status quo as well as the integrity and independence of all states in the Middle East. Furthermore, economic aid and grants to Israel actually increased during the Eisenhower years.

The hard-line approach toward Israel during and in the aftermath of the Sinai campaign, right or wrong, should not be seen as a deliberate anti-Israel policy; rather it should be seen as part and parcel of the general attitude of an administration that viewed the attack on Egypt as both legally and morally unjustifiable. In retrospect, maintaining those principles did not in the long run serve U.S. interests in the Middle East. The policy might have been naive, it might have been unwise, but it was not wicked. Indeed, it represents a rare case in modern history, where moral principles overrode strategic interests.

Still, Israel's withdrawal from the Sinai came only after its legitimate security interests were guaranteed by Eisenhower and Dulles. Those guarantees might not have come about in the way they did if it had not been for Eban's diplomatic ingenuity, Ben-Gurion's tenacity, and, last but not least, the successful lobbying efforts by Jewish organizations. These groups effectively pressured members of Congress and the administration against an unconditional Israeli withdrawal from the Sinai and the Gaza Strip. Their success was especially significant in view of Eisenhower's repeated vow that domestic political considerations would not influence foreign policy decisions. In reality they did. But whatever the reasons, the security guarantees demanded by Israel were granted, and they served Israel well when faced with the possibility of annihilation in June 1967.

But, although the United States saved Nasser from total humiliation, the Egyptian leader did not respond in kind. He rejected the Eisenhower Doctrine, and, with Soviet support, he began a campaign aimed at undermining Western interests in the region.

Ironically, in doing so, Nasser elevated Israel's importance to the West as the only country in the region willing and capable militarily of standing up to Nasser's challenge. Israel became a player of importance in the deadly games of Mideast politics. Eisenhower and Dulles became aware that Israel, through its commercial and military links with non-Arab countries at the periphery of the Middle East, was serving not only its own interests but also furthering Western goals in the Middle East—hence the marked improvement in U.S.-Israeli relations towards the end of the Eisenhower presidency.

Generally speaking, the attitudes of Eisenhower and Dulles toward Israel were devoid of sentimentalism. Their attitudes were rooted in practical interests, in how support for Israel served U.S. national interests in the context of the cold war competition with the Soviet Union. From their perspective, morality went only as far as keeping the commitment for Israel's existence, but it did not require supporting Israel's case in the dispute with its Arab neighbors. The difficult period of strain and confrontation during Eisenhower's first term in office gave way to cooperation and even coordination, thanks to a shift in the balance of power in the region threatening the Western position.

Since then, Israel's usefulness to the West has become more apparent to policymakers in Washington. Israel's victories over the Arab states in the Six-Day war of June 1967 and the Yom Kippur war of October 1973 were in a sense also a defeat for the Soviet Union, who armed and supported both Egypt and Syria. The Camp David accords of 1979, which led to peace between Israel and Egypt, were brokered by the United States and marked a significant decline in Soviet influence in the Middle East. Egypt, the largest Arab country that was hostile to the United States for almost three decades, had become a U.S. ally in the Arab world.

The Persian Gulf war, the latest example of the strengthened relations between the United States and Israel, contrasts sharply with the situation during the Sinai campaign and the Suez war of 1956. In 1956, the United States was heavily involved diplomatically and determined the outcome of the war against Nasser. In 1991, the United States led a military campaign in the Persian Gulf to liberate Kuwait, defeat and humiliate Hussein, and defend Israel against the Scud attacks. In 1956, the United States viewed Israel as part of the problem and a hindrance to U.S. interests in the region. In 1991, Israel remained a U.S. ally in the region. By showing restraint and forgoing retaliation, despite Hussein's incitement, Israel spared the U.S.-led coalition fatal strains.

There are similarities and differences between the Sinai-Suez war of 1956 and the Persian Gulf war of 1991 apart from the Scud missile attacks on Tel Aviv and Israel's restraint. In 1956, the United States, by pressuring Britain, France, and Israel for a cease-fire in the war against Egypt, prevented U.S. allies from gaining a clear-cut military victory. That outcome proved detrimental to U.S. and Western interests in the Middle East. The reasons the United States acted in that manner are well known. The United States opted for morality and legality over realpolitik. And, of course, the Soviet Union and most member states of the United Nations condemned the attack on Egypt.

In 1991, the Soviet Union tried to do for Hussein what the United States did for Nasser in 1956. The Soviet Union suggested a cease-fire and withdrawal of Iraqi troops from Kuwait. In a sense, the United States found itself now in the same situation as Britain, France, and Israel in 1956, but with a very important difference. In 1956, the United States had the power to impose its will on the allies. In 1991, with the end of the cold war, the Soviet Union, facing internal disintegration and economic collapse, had neither the will nor the power to stand up to the West. Consequently, the United States could politely disregard Moscow's entreaties and decisively pursue a ground war in order to achieve a military victory. With that victory achieved, the United States had used its leverage with both Arabs and Israelis in an attempt to build a system of peace and stability in the region. The new international order formed a matrix for a solution to the Arab-Israeli conflict.

With the United States playing a leading role, for the first time in history Israeli, Arab, and Palestinian representatives have begun a process of face-to-face negotiations that might lead to the end of a seemingly endless conflict. Thanks to the end of the cold war and the demise of the Soviet Union, the United States has emerged as the only world superpower. It finds itself in the enviable position of being sought after by the warring parties as the only force capable of helping them achieve peace. That is quite a change from the 1950s, a change Eisenhower, Dulles, and Ben-Gurion prayed for but did not live to see.

Notes

Abbreviations

DK	Divrei Ha-Knesset, Israel Parliamentary Proceedings
DS File	Record Group 59, General Records of Department of State Central Decimal File, National Archives, Washington, D.C.
DSB	*Department of State Bulletin*
Dulles History	John Foster Dulles Oral History Collection, Seeley G. Mudd Manuscript Library, Princeton University
Dulles Papers	John Foster Dulles Papers, Mudd Library
FRUS	U.S. Department of State, *Foreign Relations of the United States: Diplomatic Papers, 1948–1957*
ISA	Israel State Archives
JCS Records	Records of the U.S. Joint Chiefs of Staff, 1954–56: JCS Chairman Radford's Files, National Archives
JTA	*Jewish Telegraphic Agency*
WHCF-DDE	Dwight D. Eisenhower Papers (White House Central File), Eisenhower Library
Whitman File	Dwight D. Eisenhower Papers (Ann Whitman File), Eisenhower Library

Preface

1. See Bernard Reich, *Quest for Peace: United States-Israeli Relations and the Arab-Israeli Conflict;* Nadav Safran, *Israel: The Embattled Ally;* Donald Neff, *Warriors at Suez: Eisenhower Takes America into the Middle East;* David Schoenbaum, *The United States and the State of Israel;* and Steven L. Spiegel, *The Other Arab-Israeli Conflict: Making America's Middle East Policy from Truman to Reagan,* among others.

Chapter 1. The Truman Legacy

1. *Jewish Week*, May 13, 1983.
2. Ben-Gurion, in a series of taped interviews with Israeli journalist Moshe Pearlman, in *Ben-Gurion Looks Back in Talks with Moshe Pearlman*, 116. See also Clark M. Clifford with Richard Holbrooke, *Memoir: Counsel to the President*, 25.
3. Record Group 59, General Records of Department of State Central Decimal File, National Archives, 867 N01/5-1148 (hereafter DS File).
4. *New York Times*, May 16, 1948.
5. Jorge Garcia-Granados, *The Birth of Israel*, 289–90 (also in Joseph B. Schechtman, *The United States and the Jewish State Movement: The Crucial Decade, 1939–1949*, 302–3).
6. Harry S. Truman, *Memoirs*, 2:164.
7. A great deal of literature has appeared on this controversial subject. Among the important works emphasizing the diverse elements determining the president's decisions, see John Snetsinger, *Truman, the Jewish Vote, and the Creation of Israel;* Zvi Ganin, *Truman, American Jewry, and Israel, 1945– 1948;* Michael J. Cohen, *Palestine and the Great Powers 1945–1948;* Keith Bein, *March to Zion: U.S. Policy and the Founding of Israel;* Clifford, *Memior*, 5–25. Michael J. Cohen, *Truman and Israel*, provides insights about the significant role played by Max Lowenthal in Truman's decision to recognize Israel. See also David McCullogh, *Truman*, 618–620.
8. James G. MacDonald (*My Mission to Israel, 1948–1951*, 110) writes that he always maintained close contact with Clark M. Clifford, as the State Department "technicians continued to ostracize me . . . for after all I was a Presidential appointee, not a Foreign Service career man, and moreover known for his sympathies for Jews and Israel." Additional detailed information about Clifford's crucial role in Truman's decision to recognize Israel as a state can be found in Clifford, *Memoir*, 5–25.
9. U.S. Department of State, *Foreign Relations of the United States: Diplomatic Papers*, vol. 5, part 2, Memo of telephone conversation by Under Secretary of State Lovett, June 22, 1948, 1131 (hereafter *FRUS*).
10. Isaiah L. Kenen, *Israel's Defense Line: Her Friends and Foes in Washington*, 57.
11. For more details on Israel's attitude toward the Bernadotte proposals, see MacDonald, *My Mission to Israel*, 66–67; 86–87.
12. *FRUS*, vol. 5, part 2, Sept. 1, 1948, 1368; see also Assistant Secretary of State to MacDonald, Oct. 13, 1948, 1473.
13. *FRUS*, vol. 5, part 2, Secretary of State to Embassy in the United Kingdom, Sept. 8, 1948, 1382.

14. Ibid., Sept. 21, 1948, 1415; *New York Times,* Sept. 22, 1948.

15. *New York Times,* Sept. 23, 1948.

16. *FRUS,* vol. 5, part 2, Sept. 29, 1948, 1430.

17. Ibid., Oct. 18, 1948, 1473. Accordingly, in the Political Committee of the UN General Assembly, where the Bernadotte proposals were debated, the United States backed an Iranian resolution postponing the discussions until after the elections.

18. Ibid., Secretary of State to Acting Secretary of State, Oct. 1, 1948, 1463; see also 1448–49. See also Abba Eban, *Personal Witness,* 177–78.

19. *New York Times,* Oct. 23, 1948.

20. Robert J. Donovan, *Tumultuous Years: The Presidency of Harry S. Truman, 1949–1953,* 202.

21. The Bernadotte proposals became a dead letter. On Dec. 11, 1948, the UN General Assembly by a vote of 35 to 15 with 8 abstentions passed a resolution establishing a Palestine Conciliation Commission composed of representatives of the United States, France, and Turkey to carry out three major tasks: bring about peace between the Arab states and Israel, facilitate measures to repatriate and resettle the Palestine Arab refugees, and formulate a plan to organize a permanent international regime for Jerusalem. The mediator's recommendations, for which he paid with his life, went unmentioned in the resolution.

22. Abba Eban, *An Autobiography,* 156.

23. *FRUS,* vol. 5, part 2, President Truman to President of the Provisional Government of Israel (Weizmann), Nov. 29, 1948, 1933–34. Truman often expressed his warm admiration for Weizmann the man and the leader since they met in November 1947 and later in March 1948. The personal tie they established enabled Weizmann to express his views in personal letters to the White House with a directness that the Israeli foreign minister might have hesitated to use in his communications with the State Department.

24. *Department of State Bulletin,* Feb. 6, 1949, 173 (hereafter *DSB*).

25. Ibid., 205.

26. UN Security Council, *Official Records,* 4th year, no. 16, Mar. 3, 1949, 8.

27. *FRUS,* vol. 5, Nov. 24, 1947, 485.

28. UN General Assembly, 3d Reg. Annual Sess., Dec. 11, 1948, 479.

29. For some of the "revisionist" works on this and related subjects dealing with Israel's early history, see Simha Flapan, *The Birth of Israel: Myths and Realities;* Tom Segev, *1949: The First Israelis;* and especially Benny Morris, *The Birth of the Palestinian Refugee Problem.*

30. *FRUS,* vol. 6, Nov. 6, 1949, 1473.

31. Ibid., Secretary of Defense (Johnson) to Secretary of State, June 14, 1949, 1134; see also 677.

32. Ibid., Memo of conversation by Secretary of State, Apr. 5, 1949, 890–94.

33. Ben-Gurion's statements were made in a meeting with the members of the PCC in Jerusalem. See *FRUS,* vol. 6, 1949, 952.

34. The Israeli representative, Walter Eytan, presented those positions to the PCC during April 1949 in Lausanne, Switzerland. Before that, the three members of the commission spent three months in a leisurely and disorganized tour of Middle Eastern nations. For more details on the subject see Walter Eytan, *The First Ten Years: A Diplomatic History of Israel,* 52–54.

35. *FRUS,* vol. 6, Acting Secretary of State to Embassy in Israel, May 28, 1949, 1072–74. James MacDonald, whose sympathy and admiration for Israel were well-known, made the following critical observations concerning Israel's attitude towards the refugee problem: "I doubt that during this first hectic year of Israel the top officials ever took the time to concentrate on the refugee problem. I had the distinct impression that this was being left primarily to the technicians. No one of the big three, Ben-Gurion, Weizmann or Sharett, seemed to have thought through the implications of the tragedy or of Israel's lack of complete helpfulness." *My Mission to Israel,* 175–76. See also Itamar Rabinovich, *The Road Not Taken,* 26–27, 163.

36. Howard M. Sachar, *A History of Israel from the Rise of Zionism to Our Time,* 439–40.

37. *FRUS,* vol. 6, Memo by Department of State to President, June 10, 1949, 1110.

38. Ibid., Memo by Assistant Secretary of State, meeting with the President, June 10, 1949, 1109.

39. Ibid., Memo of conversation by Acting Secretary of State, June 17, 1949, 1148–53; Ambassador to Israel (MacDonald) to Secretary of State, July 28, 1949, 1265; Sachar, *A History of Israel,* 443.

40. Eban, *An Autobiography,* 155.

41. Ibid., 156.

42. *FRUS,* vol. 7, Ambassador in Israel to Secretary of State, July 31, 1950, 960–61.

43. David Ben-Gurion Diary, Ben-Gurion Research Institute and Archives, S'deh Boker, Jan. 20 and 30, 1950; Uri Bialer, *Between East and West: Israel's Foreign Policy Orientation, 1948–1956,* 211.

44. Israel State Archives, 2467/3, May 31, 1951; June 7, 1951 (hereafter ISA).

45. ISA, 388/15, July 1, 1952.

46. Fred I. Greenstein, *The Hidden-Hand Presidency: Eisenhower as Leader,* 25.

47. William Bragg Ewald, Jr., *Eisenhower the President: Crucial Days, 1951–1960,* 194–99.

48. Dwight D. Eisenhower Papers, Ann Whitman File, Dwight D. Eisenhower Library, National Security Council Series, NSC, 5428, box 12, July 23, 1954, 34 (hereafter Whitman File).

49. Eban, John Foster Dulles Oral History Collection, Seeley G. Mudd Manuscript Library (hereafter Dulles History); Herbert S. Parmet, *Eisenhower and the American Crusades*, 476–77; Bernard Reich, *Quest for Peace: United States-Israeli Relations and the Arab-Israeli Conflict*, 25.
50. Author's interview with Eban, New York City, April 8, 1990.

Chapter 2. The New Administration: Perceptions and Realities

1. Stephen E. Ambrose, *Eisenhower*, 1:13, 27. Eisenhower's ancestors were Pennsylvania Dutch who came from the Rhineland in the middle of the eighteenth century. In Pennsylvania, the family joined the Brethren in Christ sect of the Mennonites known as the River Brethren. Dwight's parents, David and Ida, were students at Lane University in Lecompton, Kansas, which was characterized by pacifism and strong faith in the Bible, both highly prized in the Eisenhower home.
2. Ibid., 32.
3. Dwight D. Eisenhower, *At Ease: Stories I Tell to Friends*, 42–43; Ambrose, *Eisenhower*, 1:34–35.
4. Greenstein, *The Hidden-Hand Presidency*, 11.
5. Parmet, *Eisenhower and the American Crusades*, 9.
6. ISA, 2400/28, July 31, 1952.
7. *ISA*, 2479/1, Feb. 20, 1952.
8. *New York Times*, Sept. 28, 1948.
9. Whitman File, Diary Series, box 9 (file 2), Jan. 15, 1958. For a more complete account of this episode see, Eisenhower, *At Ease*, 229–30.
10. Ambrose, *Eisenhower*, 1:113–14.
11. Dwight D. Eisenhower, *Dwight D. Eisenhower: Letters to Mamie*, 248.
12. Dwight D. Eisenhower, *The Papers of Dwight D. Eisenhower: The War Years*, Doc. 2418, 4:2615–16; see also Harry Butcher, *My Three Years with Eisenhower*, 815–16. Eisenhower conveyed to Churchill his shock and horror; see Gilbert, *The Holocaust*, 790; Abraham L. Sacher, *The Redemption of the Unwanted*, 4, 9; Dwight D. Eisenhower, *Crusade in Europe*, 408–9.
13. Judah Nadich, *Eisenhower and the Jews*, 41; Abram L. Sachar, *The Redemption of the Unwanted*, 164.
14. Pearlman, *Ben-Gurion Looks Back*, 114.
15. Eisenhower, *Papers*, Memo by Eisenhower to Joint Chiefs of Staff, June 18, 1946, 7:1137–38. For the crucial role of oil in U.S. diplomacy see Robert A. Divine, *Eisenhower and the Cold War*, 71–77.
16. Eisenhower, *Papers*, Letter from Eisenhower to Lauris Norstad, June 14, 1947, 8:1178–79.
17. Ibid., Eisenhower to John Hersey Michaelis, Dec. 8, 1947, 9:2122. Regarding his remarks to Klutznick, see Howard M. Sachar, *A History of the Jews in*

America, 724. The information relating to Eisenhower's experiences with the Holocaust DPs and actions as chief of staff of the army had appeared in Isaac Alteras, "Dwight D. Eisenhower and the State of Israel: Supporter or Distant Sympathizer?" 237–39.

18. Nadich, *Eisenhower and the Jews,* 11, and interview with author, New York City, Nov. 28, 1986.
19. Kenen, *Israel's Defense Line,* 90.
20. ISA, 2414, July 8, 1952.
21. Eban, Dulles History.
22. ISA, 2381/22, Aug. 28, 1952; also in David Ben-Gurion Correspondence, Ben-Gurion Research Institute and Archives, S'deh Boker, Nov. 11, 1951.
23. *New York Times,* Sept. 18, Oct. 15, 1952.
24. Marc L. Raphael, *Abba Hillel Silver: A Profile in American Judaism,* 197–99. Silver's action angered Ben-Gurion; see Ben-Gurion Correspondence, Nov. 25, 1952.
25. Ben-Gurion Correspondence, Nov. 6, 25, 1952.
26. ISA, 2414/23, Nov. 6, 1953.
27. For complete documentation concerning the establishment of MEDO, see *FRUS,* vol. 5 and vol. 9, part 1, 168–377.
28. *New York Times,* Mar. 3, 1953.
29. *Washington Post,* Mar. 2, 1953.
30. *FRUS,* vol. 9, part 2, Secretary of State to Director of Mutual Security Agency (Stassen), Feb. 19, 1953, 1991.
31. Eban, Dulles History; also in Ben-Gurion Diary, Mar. 3, 1953.
32. *New York Times,* Feb. 15, 1953.
33. Soon after the creation of the state of Israel in May 1948, Ben-Gurion and Sharett attempted to steer a middle course of "nonidentification" between East and West. By the end of 1950, however, the country's democratic character, its links with Western Jewry, the need for U.S. economic aid, and the Korean conflict made nonidentification untenable. It was replaced by full identification with the West. For a thorough discussion of the subject, see Bialer, *Between East and West,* 249–75.
34. Bedell Smith, the number-two man in the State Department, was an old friend of Eisenhower, his chief of staff when the president commanded the Allied forces in North Africa and Western Europe during World War II. Bedell Smith was also involved in caring for the Jewish DPs, and like Eisenhower, he met Ben-Gurion in Frankfurt late in 1945. After the war he was named ambassador to the Soviet Union, a post he held for three years, where he befriended the late Golda Meir, Israel's first ambassador to Moscow. In 1950 Smith became director of the CIA.
35. Full details of the memorandum are contained in ISA, 2479/10, Feb. 11, 1953.

36. *FRUS*, vol. 9, part 1, Memo of conversation by Officer in Charge of Palestine-Israel-Jordan Affairs (Waller), Feb. 11, 1953, 1125–28.

37. ISA, 2382/22, Feb. 11, 1953. Of General Smith's sympathetic view of Israel, its importance in the Middle East, and its military capabilities, also see Ben-Gurion Diary, Mar. 23, 1953.

38. In his diary, Ben-Gurion emphasized how important it was to keep reminding the United States of Israel's military strength and its industrial potential, including its roads, airfields, and ports, which must be rebuilt so they could be at the West's disposal in case of war. Ben-Gurion Diary, Mar. 28, 1953.

39. ISA, 2382/22, Feb. 26, 1953. David Goitein, an embassy staff member, was present at the meeting. He summarized the discussion between Dulles and Eban and then added a few unkind observations about the secretary of state. "Unlike his predecessor Acheson, who might be a Palmerston or a Gladstone sitting attentively and calmly throughout the ambassador's presentation, the new secretary of state shows a nervousness and lack of calm frightening in one holding so important a position. At times, his left eye twitches and at times his right. He plays with his hair, now smoothing one side down with one hand and then smoothing the other side down with his second hand. He runs his pencil down the parting of his hair and then sucks his pencil as if to avoid the use of chewing gum." Goitein added that Dulles came to the meeting without having read his brief, which was on the table in front of him. When Eban began speaking, the secretary picked it up and tried to read it "like a schoolboy having a last look."

40. President Truman appointed Byroade assistant secretary of state for Near East, South Asian, and African affairs in April 1952, replacing George McGhee, who became ambassador to Turkey. Before assuming his new post, Byroade distinguished himself in military service during World War II and held important positions in the State Department. His recommendations would play an important role in the decision-making process concerning the Middle East.

41. ISA, 2479/11, Mar. 6, 1953.

42. *FRUS*, vol. 9, part 1, Memorandum of conversation by Officer in Charge of Palestine-Israel-Jordan Affairs (Waller), Apr. 8, 1953, 1164–70.

43. ISA, 2479/11, Apr. 14, 1953. Information pertaining to these issues is also found in memorandum of conversation between Ben-Gurion, Sharett, and the U.S. ambassador to Israel, Mannett Davis, in ISA, 84/20, Feb. 19, 1953.

44. Sharett tried to impress them with Israel's military capabilities, as well as with its being the most reliable pro-Western country in the region. Wilson, who showed little understanding of the regional problems, concentrated on the need for peace. Sharett agreed but argued that military planning with Israel for the defense of Western interests in the area should begin immediately.

45. The information concerning Sharett's talks in Washington was gathered from ISA, 2479/11, Apr. 14 and Apr. 17, 1953.

46. Ibid., Apr. 14 and 17, 1953.

47. Ibid., Apr. 14, 1953.

48. ISA, 389/2/6, Apr. 28, 1953.

49. ISA, 2479/11, May 1, 1953.

50. Ibid., May 1 and 4, 1953.

Chapter 3. Dulles's "Listen and Learn" Tour of the Middle East

1. For a comprehensive study of Dulles's diplomatic career and the events shaping his world outlook, see Ronald W. Pruessen, *John Foster Dulles: The Road to Power*.

2. Sherman Adams, *First Hand Report: The Story of the Eisenhower Administration*, 89. Dulles also wrote two books on the subject of foreign policy, *War, Peace, and Change* and *War and Peace*, and numerous articles.

3. Among the numerous works critical of Dulles, the most comprehensive is Townsend Hoopes, *The Devil and John Foster Dulles*.

4. For this view, see Michael Guhin, *John Foster Dulles: A Statesman and His Times;* John Robinson Beal, *John Foster Dulles: A Biography;* Mildred H. Comfort, *John Foster Dulles, Peacemaker;* Eleanor Lansing Dulles, *John Foster Dulles: The Last Year;* Leonard Mosley, *Dulles: A Biography of Eleanor, Allen, and John Foster Dulles and Their Family Network*.

5. Dwight D. Eisenhower, *The White House Years: Waging Peace, 1956–1961*, 362–64.

6. Ibid., 365; European statesmen thought very little of Dulles. Anthony Eden told Eisenhower of his inability to work with Dulles long before his nomination as the Republican candidate for the presidency. Churchill thought Dulles to be "a stupid man and could hardly stand the sight of him, derogatorily referring to him as 'Dullith.' " See Anthony Eden, *Full Circle: The Memoirs of Anthony Eden*, 64; Ambrose, *Eisenhower*, 2:21.

7. For a new look at Dulles and his relationship with Eisenhower, see Richard Immerman, "Eisenhower and Dulles: Who Made the Decisions?"

8. Whitman File, Name Series, box 18, Oct. 23, 1954; Parmet, *Eisenhower and the American Crusades*, 475–76.

9. State Department replies to written questions submitted by Senator J. William Fulbright; see U.S. Congress, Senate Committee on Foreign Relations and Committee on Armed Services, *Hearings: The President's Proposal on the Middle East*, 171.

10. Whitman File, National Security Council Series, NSC 5428, box 12, Progress Report, May 17, 1956, "U.S. Policy Toward the Middle East."

11. Eban, Dulles History. Ultimately, Truman's own reversal on the question in the final weeks of the presidential campaign, coupled with Dewey's and Dulles's opposition, led to the demise of the Bernadotte proposals. Subsequently, Dulles played a key role in negotiating the Dec. 11, 1948, resolution that established the Conciliation Commission on Palestine charged with bringing about a resolution of the Arab-Israeli conflict. See Eban, *Personal Witness,* 177–78.

12. John Foster Dulles Papers, Seeley G. Mudd Manuscript Library, box 39, Dec. 17, 1948 (hereafter Dulles Papers). Moshe Sharett, *B'Sha'ar Ha-Umot,* 310, 336.

13. Eban, Dulles History.

14. *DSB,* vol. 28, no. 717, Mar. 23, 1953.

15. The negotiations between Egypt and Britain over the future status of the military base were broken off on May 8, 1953. The British agreed to withdraw three combat divisions but insisted that arrangements be made to permit British technicians to continue maintenance duties after the base reverted to Egyptian control. The Egyptians refused to be drawn into technical discussions and demanded complete evacuation.

16. Mohammed Heikal, *The Cairo Documents: The Inside Story of Nasser and His Relationship with World Leaders, Rebels and Statesmen,* 51–52; Erskine Childers, *The Road to Suez: A Study of Western Arab Relations,* 121; Miles Copeland, *The Game of Nations: The Amorality of Power Politics,* 147–49. According to Heikal, a close confidant of Nasser, a gentlemen's agreement was reached between Dulles and Nasser that Egypt under Nasser's leadership would be permitted to take the lead in building up a purely Arab defense alliance free from formal links with an outside power. They also agreed that the Suez base negotiations should resume and reach a final agreement with a view to achieving an Arab regional alliance against communism. In addition, Dulles promised to supply arms for Egyptian security as well as to support Nasser in any possible showdown between him and Naguib within the RCC.

17. Dulles Papers, Conferences, Dossiers, and Special Subjects File, Near East Trip, May 1953, Important points of trip, 1.

18. *FRUS,* vol. 9, part 1, Memorandum of conversation, May 11, 1953, 3–8, 9–18, 19–25.

19. *Ha'aretz,* May 10, 1953.

20. ISA, 2414/29, Apr. 30, 1953; Ben-Gurion Diary, Apr. 30, 1953; the Israeli records regarding Dulles's visit to Israel are included in file 2414/29.

21. Ibid., May 13, 1953. Parallel talks were held between Walter Eytan and junior officials of the U.S. delegation. MacArthur pointed out that Israel would have to make some territorial concessions to Egypt, providing a passage to Jordan. He found Nasser dynamic, shrewd, flexible, and danger-

ous. The new administration, he said, would have a clear-cut policy for the Middle East. Meade asked Eytan whether Israel would be prepared to accept some refugees. Eytan gave the official Israeli reply.

22. When Israel moved the ministry, Dulles's reaction was quite critical of Israel. By that time the United States had already formulated its Mideast policy of "friendly impartiality."

23. In Sharett's study a discussion took place on Israel's economic problems. The participants were Levi Eshkol, Israel's finance minister, and Teddy Kollek representing Israel, and Stassen, Matteson, McDaniel, and Fried for the United States. The main topic was Israel's critical foreign exchange problem. Total indebtedness was said to be approximately $380 million, of which $100 million would mature within the next twelve months. The Israelis asked the U.S. delegation to assist them with a U.S. government loan or another arrangement through the U.S. Export-Import Bank. *FRUS*, vol. 9, part 1, Memorandum of conversation by First Secretary of the Embassy in Israel (Jones), May 14, 1953, 42.

24. ISA, 2424/29, May 14, 1953.

25. Ibid., May 14, 1953; Ben-Gurion Diary, May 14, 1953.

26. DS File, 784A.00(W)5-2353.

27. ISA, 2414/29, May 29, 1953.

28. *FRUS*, vol. 9, part 1, Memorandum of conversations in Jordan, May 15, 1953, 48–54, and in Lebanon, May 16, 1953, 64–67. While Arab leaders looked to the United States to come up with a solution to their conflict with Israel, Dulles, significantly, pointed out that a peace based on the UN resolution of 1947 "was impractical, an impossible achievement." He hoped the Arab states "would agree to a settlement on more moderate terms." *FRUS*, vol. 9, part 1, Memorandum of conversation in Amman, May 15, 1953, 49.

29. *New York Times*, May 15, 1953.

30. *Time*, May 25, 1953.

31. ISA, 2414/29, May 29, 1953.

32. Whitman File, Dulles-Herter Series, box 1, May 17, 1953.

33. *FRUS*, vol. 9, part 1, Memorandum of discussion at 147th meeting of the National Security Council, June 1, 1953, 381.

34. Dulles Papers, box 73, May 29, 1953.

35. For the entire speech see *DSB*, 28, no. 729, June 15, 1953, 831–35; Reich, *Quest for Peace*, 25–26.

36. *Divrei Ha-Knesset*, vol. 14, May 27, 1953, 1412; June 10, 1567–78; June 15 and 16, 1581–87 (hereafter *DK*).

37. *Davar*, June 5, 1953; *Omer, Herut, and Hatsofeh*, June 3, 1953.

38. ISA, 2382/22, June 22, 1953; DS File, 611.84A/6-2353.

39. ISA, 2382/22, June 22, 1953; DS File, 611.84A/6-2353.

Chapter 4. Friendly Impartiality

1. Dulles Papers, box 73, June 20, 1953.
2. They included John D. Jernegan, deputy assistant secretary of state; Parker J. Hart, director of the Division of Near East Affairs; Stephen P. Dorsey, acting deputy director; Fred E. Waller, officer in charge of Palestine, Israel, and Jordan; and Richard Funkhouser, officer in charge of Lebanon, Syria, and Iraq.
3. They often represented the interests of American oil companies; see Divine, *Eisenhower and the Cold War*, 73; Joseph Kraft, "Those Arabists in the State Department," *New York Times Magazine*, Nov. 7, 1971, 88–89, 92–96. See also Steven F. Windmueller, "American Jewish Interest Groups: Their Role in Shaping United States Foreign Policy in the Middle East: A Study of Two Time Periods: 1945–1948; 1955–1958," 93–95.
4. ISA, 2478/1 July 7, 1952; 2420/10, June 19, 1952.
5. ISA, 2475, Sept. 9, 1953.
6. ISA, 2475/2, Nov. 20, 1953.
7. Whitman File, National Security Council Series, NSC 155/1, N.E. (1), box 5, July 30, 1954.
8. Spiegel, *The Other Arab-Israeli Conflict: Making America's Middle East Policy from Truman to Reagan*, 59.
9. Nadav Safran, *Israel: The Embattled Ally*, 348–49.
10. Benjamin Schwadran, *The Middle East, Oil, and the Great Powers*, 451; Herbert Feis, *New York Herald Tribune*, Oct. 28, 1958.
11. "Oil and the State Department Policy on Palestine," *Nation Associates*, June 1948, 1.
12. Blanche Wiesen Cook, *The Declassified Eisenhower: A Divided Legacy*, 220–21; Ewald, *Eisenhower the President*, 171; Peter Lyon, *Eisenhower: Portrait of a Hero*, 546.
13. *FRUS*, vol. 9, part 1, July 11, 1953, 1254.
14. Dulles Papers, box 71, July 13, 1953; *FRUS*, vol. 9, part 1, Secretary of State to Rabbi Hillel Silver, July 13, 1953, 1256.
15. *DSB*, 29, no. 734, July 20, 1953; Reich, *Quest for Peace*, 26.
16. DS File, 611.84A/9-2553, 3. Particularly irksome to Israel was the absence of the U.S. representative at the opening ceremonies on Sept. 22, 1953, of the Conquest of the Desert International Exhibition and Fair in Jerusalem. Personnel of the U.S. embassy in Tel Aviv were instructed not to transact official business in Jerusalem with the Israeli Foreign Ministry or attend official functions there. DS File, 611.84A/10-2153.
17. Eban in a report to the secretary general of the UN, Mar. 16, 1953; see also DS File, 784A.00/6-953. An additional report was submitted to the State Department; *FRUS*, vol. 9, part 1, Apr. 22, 1953. See also Sachar, *A History of Israel*, 443–44.

18. Eisenhower, *Waging Peace*, 24n; *FRUS*, vol. 9, part 1, Acting Secretary of State to Israeli Ambassador, May 25, 1953, 1126–27.

19. *FRUS*, vol. 9, part 1, Secretary of State to U.S. Ambassador in Jordan, Feb. 12, 1953, 1131; Eytan, *The First Ten Years*, 106.

20. Of the four demilitarized zones established by the armistice agreements, the one between Syria and Israel was the most volatile. The zone consisted of two strips of 40 square miles. The first strip ran from the southern half of Lake Hula along the Jordan River to the mouth of Lake Tiberias (Kinneret). The other strip ran "along the southeastern shore of Lake Tiberias with a tail projecting eastward for about three miles." In this area, the DMZ, Israel intended to carry out development projects, such as draining the Hula swamps, to build hydroelectric power stations, and to divert water to the Negev. In 1951, Syria objected to Israel's Hula drainage program outside the DMZ, which aimed at bringing about 45,000 acres under cultivation, under the pretext that the road that would have to be built would affect Arab-owned land in the DMZ. Sachar, *A History of Israel*, 445–47.

21. Ernest Stock, *Israel on the Road to Sinai: 1949–1956*, 63; Reich, *Quest for Peace*, 26; Kenen, *Israel's Defense Line*, 100–101.

22. For more details on the subject, see Nissim Bar-Yaacov, *The Israel-Syrian Armistice: Problems of Implementation*, 117–18.

23. *FRUS*, vol. 9, part 1, Acting Secretary of State to U.S. Embassy in Israel, Sept. 19, 1953, 1317; see also 1320–23.

24. Israel was greatly concerned lest this action might set a precedent of linking U.S. economic aid with political issues between Israel and the Arab states.

25. DS File, 611.84A/9-2553, 3.

26. Ibid., 4.

27. The question of Jewish immigration to Israel was discussed at the highest echelons of the U.S. government. The Operation Control Board (OCB) was in the process of preparing a memorandum on other subjects. Byroade would elaborate on this issue in a major address in April 1954.

28. DS File, 611.84A/9-3053. In the subsequent meeting between Dulles and Eban, the secretary referred only indirectly to Byroade's list of charges and chose instead to discuss the basic problem in U.S.-Israeli relations by explaining the importance of an impartial policy. He advised Eban to take up specific problems with Byroade.

29. Ibid., 10-1235.

30. ISA, 2403/13, Oct. 24, 1953.

31. Stock, *Israel on the Road to Sinai*, 67.

32. For more details on the subject, see *FRUS*, vol. 9, part 1, Chargé in Israel (Russell) to Department of State, Sept. 25, 1953. Paper prepared in the Bureau of Near Eastern, South Asian, and African Affairs (undated), 1406–9; Secretary of State to Department of State, Apr. 13, 1954, 1513–

14; Memorandum of conference with the President, Apr. 19, 1954, 1527–28.

33. ISA, 2403/13, Oct. 25, 1953.

34. Donald Neff, *Warriors at Suez: Eisenhower Takes America into the Middle East*, 48–49.

35. For a full report on the incident, see *FRUS*, vol. 9, part 1, Chargé in Jordan (Seelye) to Department of State, Oct. 15, 1953, 1358–59.

36. *New York Times*, Oct. 19 and 20, 1953.

37. Moshe Sharett, *Yoman Ishi* (Personal Diary) 1:39, 51.

38. ISA, 2382/22, Oct. 23, 1953. On the way to New York, Dayan surveyed the situation with Rafael. He told Rafael that Israel would not stop work on the Jordan canal, that the Kibya raid was carried out with Sharett's knowledge, and that Ben-Gurion was thoroughly satisfied with the successful outcome. Rafael remarked that Sharett opposed the attack, but that he (Rafael) would not enter into an argument with Dayan over the issue.

39. ISA, 2403/13, Nov. 28, 1953.

40. Ben-Gurion's biographers include Michael Bar-Zohar, *Ben-Gurion: A Biography* and *Ben-Gurion: The Armed Prophet;* Robert St. John, *Ben-Gurion: A Biography;* Dan Kurzman, *Ben-Gurion: Prophet of Fire;* Shabtai Teveth, *Ben-Gurion: The Burning Ground, 1886–1948.*

41. Neff, *Warriors at Suez*, 48.

42. Michael Brecher, *The Foreign Policy System of Israel: Setting, Images, Process*, 253.

43. Bar-Zohar, *Ben-Gurion: A Biography*, 218–19.

44. From Brecher's interviews with both statesmen. For more on the philosophical differences between them, see Brecher, *Foreign Policy System of Israel*, 254–90; Avi Shlaim, "Conflicting Approaches to Israel's Relations with the Arabs: Ben-Gurion and Sharett, 1953–1956," 180–83; Eban, *Personal Witness*, 249–50.

45. Bar-Zohar, *Ben-Gurion: A Biography*, 202, 203.

46. Kibya was a watershed as far as retaliation was concerned. It did not mean that during Sharett's short term as prime minister there were no acts of retaliation, but that they were rationalized and their application was restricted. Under Sharett's leadership, said Eytan, the policy was not to harm innocent civilians, but to limit attacks to police forces, military posts, and bases from which raiders operated. Eytan, *The First Ten Years*, 108.

47. Dulles Papers, Telephone Call Series, box 1, Conversation between Byroade and Dulles, Oct. 22, 1953.

48. Coincidentally, while they were calling on Dulles on Israel's behalf, the president at the White House received Abdel Khalad Hassanna, secretary general of the Arab League, who praised the U.S. decision to cut aid to Israel.

49. *FRUS,* vol. 9, part 1, Memorandum of conversation, Oct. 16, 1953, 1384–87; Kenen, *Israel's Defense Line,* 102–3.

50. Dulles Papers, Telephone Call Series, box 1, Conversations between Dulles and Lodge, Oct. 26, 1953, 4:00 P.M.; Oct. 27, 1953, 2:50 P.M., 6:20 P.M.

51. *FRUS,* vol. 9, part 1, Oct. 28, 1953, 1390. Although political considerations in this case had some effect on the secretary and the president to find a face-saving device, such pressures would not change the overall direction of U.S. Middle East policy. A survey of U.S. editorial opinion and press attitudes during Oct. 17–31, 1953, was conducted by the Israeli embassy in Washington. The survey was based on analysis of 396 editorials appearing in 281 daily newspapers throughout the country. The period analyzed was notable for a succession of important political developments in connection with Israel. Over half of the editorials, 53.7%, gave unquestioning support to the State Department's actions; 28% were friendly toward Israel; and 10% were openly hostile. ISA, 2472/1, Nov. 5, 1953.

52. Whitman File, Dulles-Herter Series, box 1, Oct. 28, 1953.

53. Melvin I. Urofsky, *We Are One! American Jewry and Israel,* 237–38.

54. Marshall Sklare and Mark Vosk, *The Riverton Study,* 22; the information on the subject is reprinted from Isaac Alteras, "Eisenhower, American Jewry, and Israel," *American Jewish Archives* 37 (Nov. 1985):261–62.

55. Will Herberg, *Protestant, Catholic, Jew,* 190.

56. In the 1952 elections, about three-quarters of U.S. Jewry supported Adlai Stevenson. In fact, Stevenson did better among Jews than Truman in 1948. See Lawrence Fuchs, *Political Behavior of American Jews,* 83–85.

57. Alteras, "Eisenhower, American Jewry, and Israel," 260.

58. DS File, 884 A.00/10-2653.

59. Dwight D. Eisenhower Papers, White House Central File, Eisenhower Library, File OCB, Records 1953–54 (hereafter WH File). On July 9, 1953, the NSC with Eisenhower present discussed the deteriorating situation at the frontiers between Israel and its neighbors. Dulles focused on the impending financial crisis in Israel, pointing out that the United States was compelled to loan Israel $7 million to prevent default. He expected Israel to come back with a request for $100 million to stave off bankruptcy. And yet, he continued, Israel had been planning to bring in two million new immigrants. The vice-president, Richard Nixon, remarked that he was disturbed by the fact that the United States had been for some time under heavy political pressure to subsidize the Israeli economy, which could never balance itself. "It began to look as though they'd come back again and again for handouts from the U.S. with no prospect of permanent stabilization or improvement." *FRUS,* vol. 9, part 1, Memorandum of discussion at 153d meeting of National Security Council, July 9, 1953, 397.

60. Sachar, *A History of Israel,* 395; Eban, *Personal Witness,* 171–72.

61. *DSB,* May 16, 1954, 22.
62. *DSB,* Apr. 16, 1954, 628; Reich, *Quest for Peace,* 27.
63. Whitman File, Special Assistant for National Security Affairs, NSC Series: Policy Papers Subseries, box 5, NSC155/Progress Report on U.S. Objectives and Policies with Respect to the Near East by the OCB, July 30, 1954.
64. DS File, 611.84A/5-1454.
65. Ibid., 811.84A; 784A.00(W)5-754.
66. *DK,* vol. 16, May 12, 1954, 1596. On May 17, the Knesset (Israel's Parliament) concluded its foreign affairs debate and adopted the following resolution: "The Knesset sees the supply of arms to Iraq or any other Arab state as a threat to the security of Israel and peace and stability in the Middle East. The Knesset looks with concern on the policy expressed by U.S. Assistant Secretary of State Byroade, since it does not conform to the traditional friendship between the Jewish people returning to their homeland and the U.S. The Knesset expresses concern at the attempt to interfere in the internal affairs of the state . . . and proclaims that ingathering of exiles is the supreme ideal of Israel and the State of Israel will continue to strengthen the bonds between the State and Jews everywhere in order to enrich Jewish spiritual and cultural life." *DK,* vol. 16, May 17, 1954, 1712.
67. DS File, 611.84A/5-1354.
68. Ibid., 611.84A/5-1454. On May 12, Dulles met with Jacob Blaustein, the president of the prestigious American Jewish Committee. Although he had been a strong supporter of administration policy in the Middle East, he felt that "impartiality" was going a little far in certain respects, particularly in U.S. intentions to provide military aid to Iraq. Those arms, Blaustein contended, could be used against Israel rather than against the Soviet threat. He did, however, find Israel's reaction to Byroade's speech too harsh. While Dulles defended the U.S. policy of arms to Iraq and spoke of the importance of the "northern tier," Blaustein commented that U.S. policy made Sharett's moderate policy unpopular at home. Sharett, he said, "is a moderate and we need to hold his hand." *FRUS,* vol. 9, part 1, Memorandum from Director of the Office of Near Eastern Affairs (Hart), May 12, 1954, 1555–56.
69. *DSB,* May 17, 1954, 782
70. Whitman File, National Security Council Series, NSC 155/1, box 5, July 30, 1954; for documentation concerning the genesis of the Baghdad Pact, see *FRUS,* vol. 9, 1952–54, part 1, 377–438; Spiegel, *The Other Arab-Israeli Conflict,* 62; Safran, *Israel: The Embattled Ally,* 350.
71. DS File, 611.84A/5-1354.
72. Whitman File, National Security Council Series, NSC 155/1, box 5, July 30, 1954.
73. Stock, *Israel on the Road to Sinai,* 81; Safran, *Israel: The Embattled Ally,* 350–51.

74. DS File, 784.00(W)17-3054.

75. *New York Times,* July 29, 1954.

76. A group of Conservatives in Parliament led by Captain Charles Waterhouse and Julian Amery and known as the Suez Group ardently campaigned against surrendering the base. Amery thought that Britain had already gone too far in surrendering bases in the Middle East.

77. Eytan, *The First Ten Years,* 101.

78. Moshe Dayan, *Diary of the Sinai Campaign,* 10–12.

79. For more on the subject see Amos Perlmutter, *Military and Politics in Israel: Nation Building and the Role of Expansion.*

80. DS File, 784A.00/8-2654.

81. Ibid., 611.84A/5-2454, 611.84A/7-1654.

82. Ibid., 611.84A/8-1654; see also *FRUS,* vol. 9, part 1, Memorandum of conversation by Director of the Office of Near Eastern Affairs (Hart), Oct. 10, 1954, 1673–74, 1723.

83. DS File, 611.84A/8-1954.

84. Ibid., 611.84A/8-3054, 611.84A/10-1254.

85. *FRUS,* vol. 9, part 1, Memorandum of conversation by Acting Assistant Secretary of State for Near Eastern, South Asian, and African Affairs (Jernegan), Dec. 17, 1954, 1720–23.

86. DS File, 611.84A/9-2154.

87. *FRUS,* vol. 9, part 1, Memorandum of conversation by Officer in Charge of Israel-Jordan Affairs (Bergus), Oct. 8, 1954, 1667–69.

88. Whitman File, National Security Council Series, Policy Papers Subseries, NSC 5428, box 12, July 23, 1954.

89. Georgiana G. Stevens, *Jordan River Partition,* 17–18; Sachar, *A History of Israel,* 456–57. U.S. officials were under strong pressure from Congress to find a solution to the refugee problem, as most of the cost for UNRWA came from U.S. contributions. By the summer of 1953 the United States had spent a total of $153 million on refugee aid. Arthur Gardiner, the political and economic adviser for the Office of Near Eastern, South Asian, and African Affairs, testifying before the House Committee on Foreign Affairs on June 4, 1953, asked for an additional $30 million for 1954. Committee members reluctantly approved the request. U.S. Congress, House, Committee on Foreign Affairs, *Hearings: Mutual Security Act Extension,* 83d Cong., 1st sess., (Washington, D.C.: U.S. Government Printing Office, 1953), 1033.

90. The quest for water had been a most important and consistent theme for the Jewish Agency in Palestine decades prior to the establishment of the Jewish state. In the early 1920s the Jewish national movement in Palestine tried but failed to secure control over the headwaters of the Jordan-Yarmuk river system and hydroelectric potential of the Litani. Subsequently, various plans for the use of the Jordan waters were discussed by Zionist leaders: the

Ionides Report (1937), the W. C. Lowdermilk recommendations (1944), the Hayes Plan (1948), the Bunger Plan (1953), and finally the Main Plan. For the Yishuv in Palestine and later Israel the expansion of irrigation and electric power resources were a means for enhancing the state's economic viability and absorptive capacity for new immigrants. Growth, economic independence, and security were all linked. For a full chronological listing and details of these and other plans, see American Friends of the Middle East, *The Jordan Water Problem: An Analysis and Summary of Available Documents*.

91. For details of the Main Plan see Main, (Chas. T.) Inc., *The Unified Development of the Water Resources of the Jordan Valley Region*, 7. See also Georgiana G. Stevens, "The Jordan River Valley."

92. *FRUS*, vol. 9, part 1, Secretary of State to Chairman of the Advisory Board for International Development (Johnston), Oct. 13, 1953, 1348–53. In his speech on June 1, Dulles said, "Throughout the area the cry is for water for irrigation. U.N. contributions and other funds available to help refugees . . . could well be spent in large portion on a coordinated use of rivers run through the Arab countries and Israel." *DSB*, 28, no. 729, June 15, 1953, 832; for the White House statement, see, *DSB*, vol. 29, no. 751, Oct. 26, 1953, 553; Michael Brecher, *Decisions in Israel's Foreign Policy*, 192.

93. Brecher, *Decisions in Israel's Foreign Policy*, 194.

94. Ibid., 195–96.

95. *DSB*, vol. 30, no. 778, May 24, 1954, 788–91.

96. *FRUS*, vol. 14, 1955–57, Feb. 3, 1955, 43–45.

97. *FRUS*, vol. 9, part 1, 1400–1402, 1410–12.

98. Stevens, *Jordan River Partition*, 29; Brecher, *Decisions in Israel's Foreign Policy*, 196.

99. *New York Herald Tribune*, Paris Edition, Nov. 7, 1953; ISA, 2403/13, Nov. 13, 1953. On Nov. 17, Johnston reported to the president and the secretary of state about his efforts thus far. Dulles gave an optimistic assessment. He was "gratified by Johnston's report." The political tensions in the area, said Dulles, "might well have resulted in outright rejection of the ideas set out in the U.N. report," but they were still very much alive. *DSB*, vol. 39, no. 753, Nov. 30, 1953, 749–50.

100. For the complete text of the Arab response, see *Egyptian Economic and Political Review* 2 (Oct. 1955): 42–46; see also *FRUS*, vol. 9, part 1, Memorandum of a proposal from the State Department, Dec. 20, 1954, 1727–30.

101. Brecher, *Decisions in Israel's Foreign Policy*, 197. A summary of Israel's plan was published by the Israeli Office of Information in New York, February 1955.

102. Whitman File, Dulles-Herter Series, box 2, May 7, 1954.

103. Ibid., National Security Council Series, Progress Report prepared by the

OCB for National Security Council, NSC 155/1, box 5, July 30, 1954. See also, *New York Times,* June 27, 1954.

104. *New York Times,* Aug. 27, 1955.
105. *New York Herald Tribune,* Oct. 7, 1955.
106. Whitman File, Dulles-Herter Series, box 2, May 7, 1954.
107. Eisenhower, *Waging Peace,* 23.

Chapter 5. Security and Arms

1. For a detailed discussion of the subject, see *FRUS,* vol. 9, part 2, Byroade to Dulles, July 15, 1954, 2283–84; see also, 2291–95, 2312, 2322–23, and Spiegel, *The Other Arab-Israeli Conflict,* 62.
2. ISA, Feb. 25, 1955, 2460/10/B.
3. ISA, March 5, 1955, 2456/4/16.
4. Ben-Gurion to U.S. Ambassador Lawson, Ben-Gurion Diary, May 12, 1955.
5. ISA, 2456/4/6, Feb. 23, 1955; 2455/2, March 3, 1955.
6. ISA, 2460/10/B, Apr. 16 and 19, 1955.
7. On the origins of ALPHA, see *FRUS,* vol. 9, part 1, 1683–1720.
8. Dulles Papers, box 3, May 5, 1955. For more details about the meeting and agreement on the ALPHA Project, see Evelyn Shuckburgh, *Descent to Suez: Diaries, 1951–1956,* 242–43.
9. In order to maintain utmost secrecy, Harold Beeley of the British embassy in Washington was instructed by the British foreign secretary, Anthony Eden, to discuss with U.S. officials the exact location, timing, and "cover plan" for the proposed Anglo-American discussions slated to begin in early or mid-January 1955. *FRUS,* vol. 9, part 1, Dec. 17, 1954, 1724–25.
10. ISA, 2456/3, Dec. 12, 1955; Shuckburgh, *Descent to Suez,* 246.
11. ISA, 2455/2, Dec. 27, 1954; 2460/10/B, Jan. 27, 1955. The U.S. and British officials discussed the various inducements to be offered to Egypt and Israel in exchange for a peace settlement. In the context of a peace settlement, Egypt would be granted military and economic assistance in building the Aswan Dam and political recognition as the focal point of power in the Middle East. Israel would get a security guarantee, U.S. economic aid, removal of the blockade at the Suez Canal, and the termination of all boycotts of Israel by Arab states. *FRUS,* vol. 14, 24–25.
12. The following is a precise listing of the required funds (see Dulles Papers, box 3, Feb. 14, 1955):
    (A) *Funds probably required under a continuation of the present situation (in millions of dollars):* Funds appropriated and presently being held in the U.S. Treasury for UNRWA Sinai aid and Syrian resettlement project, $44; U.S. commitment as of UNRWA five-year plan for Arab refugee relief, $80; Main Plan (if agreement reached by Ambassador Johnston), $112; Probable

regular economic aid to Israel and Arab states over next five years on basis of present program, $250. Total: $486.

(B) *Additional funds probably needed for Israeli-Arab settlement:* U.S. loan to Israel for fund for payment of compensation to Arab refugees (repayment doubtful), $200; Additional economic aid to Egypt, Jordan, Syria, and Lebanon, $145; Military aid to Israel and neighboring Arab states, conditional upon settlement, $250. Total: $595.

13. Dulles Papers, box 3, Feb. 15, 1955; *FRUS,* vol. 14. Memorandum of conversation between President and Secretary of State, Feb. 16, 1955, 53–54.

14. Dulles Papers, box 3, Feb. 14, May 5, 1955; Shuckburgh, *Descent to Suez,* 252. On February 20, Anthony Eden visited Cairo and sounded out Nasser about a possible settlement with Israel. The Egyptian leader did not react unfavorably but stressed the importance of Egypt's need for territorial contiguity with Arab states. The idea of a corridor in the Negev was unsatisfactory to Nasser. *FRUS,* vol. 14, 70.

15. Dulles Papers, box 3, May 5, 1955; *FRUS,* vol. 14. Memorandum from Russell to Secretary of State, May 18, 1955, 200–204.

16. There was considerable debate between U.S. and British officials as to the timing of making ALPHA public. The British officials and Eric Johnston wanted to wait until 1956, lest the proposals included in ALPHA interfere with Johnston's mission. But Dulles, with the president's concurrence, decided that there was no time to waste; 1956, said Dulles, would be a presidential election year, and the whole plan might get mired in domestic politics.

17. ISA, 2455/4, Sept. 7, 1955.

18. In the foreign aid allocations submitted by the administration to Congress, two proposals dealt with the resettlement of the refugees. They suggested that in the Sinai anywhere from 70,000 to 80,000 refugees could be settled by irrigation of desert land at a cost of $50 million. The project would take two years to complete. In addition, the Johnston plan would make possible the resettlement of 150,000 refugees at a cost of $90 million. ISA, 2460/10/B, May 10, 1955.

19. For more details on Dulles's speech see *DSB,* Sept. 5, 1955, "The Middle East," address by Secretary Dulles, 376–80. On August 24, the U.S. ambassadors in Cairo and Tel Aviv provided Nasser and Sharett a draft of Dulles's upcoming speech. Nasser found it satisfactory. Sharett was apprehensive and noncommittal. *FRUS,* vol. 14, 389, 391. Their views would be less favorable once the speech became public.

20. ISA, 2460/10/B, Aug. 26, 1955.

21. Dulles Papers, box 8, Aug. 26, 1955.

22. *FRUS,* vol. 14, Telegram from Embassy in Israel to Department of State, Aug. 26, 1955, 391.

23. *DK,* 18, Oct. 18, 1955, 88.
24. *FRUS,* vol. 14, Telegram from Embassy in Egypt to the Department of State, Aug. 23, 1955, 402.
25. *FRUS,* vol. 14, Sept. 1, 1955, 439.
26. Eytan, *The First Ten Years,* 108.
27. Ibid.
28. Eedson L. M. Burns, *Between Arab and Israeli,* 47; Stock, *Israel on the Road to Sinai,* 71.
29. Ibid.; *Ha'aretz,* Jan. 25 and 26, 1955.
30. In September 1951 the Security Council called upon Egypt to allow Israeli ships to pass through the Suez Canal, but Egypt rejected the resolution. Moreover, in Apr. 1954, Egypt occupied the two islets of Tiran and Sanapir in the Gulf of Aqaba, which ships had to pass to reach the southern Israeli port of Eilat.
31. *FRUS,* vol. 14, Telegram from Embassy in Egypt to Department of State, Mar. 4, 1955, 82. For additional documentation on the motives behind the launching of the attack on Gaza, see ibid., 81, 88–89; Israel's raid on Gaza had greatly increased the problems in launching ALPHA, 90. Nonetheless, informal, nonofficial secret talks aimed at achieving peace between Israel and Egypt took place in Paris, Cairo, and Jerusalem during autumn 1954 and spring 1955. On those mediation efforts, see Elmore Jackson, *Middle East Mission: The Story of a Major Bid for Peace in the Time of Nasser and Ben-Gurion,* 26–57.
32. Michael Bar-Zohar, *Ben-Gurion: The Armed Prophet,* 184; Bar-Zohar, *Ben-Gurion: A Biography,* 216. In a note to Sharett, Dulles strongly condemned the Israeli attack on Gaza; *FRUS,* vol. 14, Mar. 9, 1955, 92; for Sharett's indignation about the devastation caused by the raid, see Sharett, *Yoman Ishi,* 3:799–801, 805.
33. Neff, *Warriors at Suez,* 83.
34. Ibid., 73.
35. Ibid., 72.
36. ISA, 2456/7, May 11, 1955.
37. *FRUS,* vol. 14, 238, 255, 271. Eisenhower, *Waging Peace,* 24–25.
38. *FRUS,* vol. 14, June 21, 1955, 261.
39. Ibid., Letter from Acting Director of the CIA to Secretary of State, Aug. 25, 1955, 221.
40. Ibid., July 29, 1955, 304–5.
41. Ibid., Sept. 19, 1955, 481.
42. Ibid., Sept. 20, 1955, 490.
43. Ibid., Sept. 26, 1955, 517.
44. Ibid., Memorandum of telephone conversation between President and Secretary of State, Sept. 23, 1955, 509. Nonetheless, the president, while recuperating

from a heart attack in Denver, Colorado, on Oct. 11 sent a message to the Soviet Prime Minister, Nikolai Bulganin, stating: "I am concerned about the new prospective arms shipments to Egypt. I fear they will not promote the goals which I hope we share in common . . . that is a relaxation of tension between us and a peaceful constructive solution to the Arab-Israeli problem." Bulganin's calming reply that those arms were "no grounds" for concern did not satisfy Eisenhower. In a second message on Oct. 24 the president wrote: "On the basis of all my information, this large transaction has created a greatly increased danger of a major outbreak of violence in the area. I am asking Secretary Dulles to discuss this situation further with Foreign Minister Molotov at Geneva." Speaking about the Middle East with the Acting Secretary of State, Herbert Hoover, Jr., the president said, "We should pay more attention to the Middle East, get a little tough about that one"—presumably with the Russians. There is little evidence of any action taken in that regard. Whitman File, Dulles-Herter Series, box 4, Oct. 11, 21, and 24, 1955. See also Dulles Papers, Telephone call to President in Denver, box 5, Sept. 23, 1955.

45. *FRUS,* vol. 14, Sept. 23, 1955, 504.
46. Ibid., Oct. 1, 1955, 537; ISA, 2450/7, Oct. 19, 1955; Neff, *Warriors at Suez,* 96–97.
47. ISA, 2456/7, Oct. 14, 1955; 2456/7, Oct. 6, 1955. According to the CIA the Egyptian-Soviet arms deal would run for five years. The Egyptian initial order included the following items: 200 jet aircraft (MIG 15s), 100 to be delivered by December 1955, 6 jet training planes, 100 tanks, 6 torpedo boats, 2 submarines. *FRUS,* vol. 14, 507.
48. ISA, 2415/2B, Oct. 1, 1955; Stock, *Israel on the Road to Sinai,* 115.
49. On May 25, 1950, the United States, Britain, and France issued a tripartite declaration aimed at preserving the status quo in the Middle East and preventing the Arab-Israeli arms race from eluding Western control. The declaration stated: "The three governments recognize that the Arab states and Israel all need to maintain a certain level of armed forces for the purposes of legitimate self-defense of the area as a whole. All applications for arms or war materials for those countries will be considered in light of these princi-ples." *DSB,* vol. 22, no. 570 (1950), 886.
50. Burns, *Between Arab and Israeli,* 99.
51. Although Sharett continued to head the government until Nov. 1955, Ben-Gurion's influence on defense and foreign policy was overwhelming. General elections were held in July 1955, and Ben-Gurion conducted the political negotiations with the various parties to form a coalition government. In November, Ben-Gurion assumed the premiership as well as the portfolio of defense. Sharett continued as foreign minister but resigned his post in June 1956 with the announcement that he no longer found it possible to continue under Ben-Gurion's direction.

52. *New York Times*, Oct. 5, 1955.

53. On Oct. 27, 1955, the NSC (NSC 5468) adopted measures the United States would take should war break out between Israel and its Arab neighbors. Those measures included discontinuing U.S. government aid to the aggressor, an embargo of U.S. trade, and preventing the direct or indirect transfer of funds or other assets subject to U.S. control. If these actions did not end hostilities, the United States would consider the feasibility of military action, including the imposition of a blockade and UN sanctions. *FRUS*, vol. 14, Oct. 27, 1955, 667.

54. ISA, 2403/9, Oct. 26, 1955; 2474/16B, Oct. 31, 1955.

55. *FRUS*, vol. 14, Telegram from Delegation at the Foreign Minister Meeting to the Department of State, Oct. 27, 1955, 657.

56. Eban, *An Autobiography*, 146. See also *FRUS*, vol. 14, Nov. 1, 1955, 691–92.

57. Whitman File, Dulles-Herter Series, box 5, Nov. 2, 1955. According to Schuckburgh, Macmillan not only rejected Sharett's plea for arms but told the Israeli that "he should consider making concessions for the sake of a settlement." Shuckburgh, *Descent to Suez*, 293.

58. Even so, Sharett came home disillusioned with the meager results of the trip. Sharett, *Yoman Ishi*, 5:1254. Israel's cabinet, at a meeting on Oct. 28, 1955, decided on an expanded arms procurement plan with $50 million for French-made weapons, with special emphasis on the purchase of Mystère IV jets and AMX tanks. *FRUS*, vol. 14, From Embassy in Israel to Department of State, Oct. 28, 1955, 673.

59. Sylvia K. Crosbie, *A Tacit Alliance: France and Israel from Suez to the Six Day War*, 36.

60. Shimon Peres, *David's Sling: The Arming of Israel*, 51.

61. Crosbie, *A Tacit Alliance*, 45.

62. Ibid., 61. For more details on the burgeoning Franco-Israeli alliance, see Michael Bar-Zohar, *Gesher 'al ha-yam ha-tichon. Yahasei Tsarfat-Israel, 1947–1963*; Sachar, *A History of Israel*, 483.

63. The United States also learned that Israel was seeking equipment from Italy. The U.S. air attaché in Rome was informed on October 31 that Israel's request included 40 F-51 fighters, 59 Sherman tanks, 50 M-F self-propelled guns, 120 armored cars, and 500 bazookas and machine guns. In late October, the Israeli cabinet voted to spend $50 million for these arms. The Italian government, according to the State Department, would probably sell the arms in order to play a larger role in Mideast policy. Whitman File, Dulles-Herter Series, box 5, Nov. 3, 1955.

64. Whitman File, Dulles-Herter Series, box 4, Nov. 2, 1955.

65. Sharett was now only foreign minister, as Ben-Gurion became prime minister on November 3. He also held the post of defense minister.

66. *FRUS*, vol. 14, Nov. 8, 1955, 717.

67. Whitman File, Dulles-Herter Series, box 5, Nov. 9, 1955.

68. Francis Russell in a conversation with Walter Eytan, ISA, 2446/4, Nov. 12, 1955.

69. ISA, 2446/4, Nov. 18, 1955.

70. ISA, 2403/9, Nov. 22, 1955.

71. On Nov. 16, Israel submitted a request for U.S. defensive weapons to correct the "local imbalances."

72. *FRUS*, vol. 14, Nov. 9, 1955, 725.

73. Ibid., Nov. 17, 1985, 781; see also 773, 832.

74. ISA, 2456/3, Nov. 21, 1955.

75. ISA, 2455/4, Nov. 21, 1955.

76. ISA, 2456/3, Dec. 6, 1955.

77. *FRUS*, vol. 14, Dec. 6, 1955, 832.

78. ISA, 2456/3, Dec. 12, 1955. But in Shuckburgh's view, the Soviet-Egyptian arms deal made a peaceful settlement based on the ALPHA Project all but impossible. Shuckburgh, *Descent to Suez*, 278–79.

79. *FRUS*, vol. 14, Memorandum of conversation between President and Secretary of State, Dec. 8, 1955, 837.

80. ISA, 2456/3, Dec. 29, 1955.

81. *FRUS*, vol. 14, Memorandum of discussion at 268th meeting of the NSC, Dec. 1, 1955, 812–13.

82. Eli Ginzberg, *My Brother's Keeper*, 78. Professor Ginzberg, an economist with expertise in the study of manpower and human resources, taught at Columbia University in New York. He became acquainted with Eisenhower in 1946–47 through his friendship with Eisenhower's personal physician, Major General Howard Snyder. When Eisenhower served as president of Columbia University, he asked Ginzberg to design a research project on "Conservation of Human Resources"—a study of U.S. military manpower in World War II. In subsequent years they remained in contact in person and through correspondence. Ginzberg, a supporter of Israel, met Ben-Gurion and other Israeli leaders during his frequent visits there and relayed his findings and messages to the White House. During the Sinai crisis he would serve as a go-between for the two governments.

83. Dulles Papers, box 5, Nov. 3, 1955.

84. Selwyn I. Troen, "The Sinai Campaign as a 'War of No Alternative': Ben-Gurion's View of the Israel-Egyptian Conflict," 181–84.

Chapter 6. Prelude to War: Tension and Violence

1. Burns, *Between Arab and Israeli*, 76.

2. Ibid., 86–87.

3. Ibid., 88.
4. Ibid., 90; Neff, *Warriors at Suez,* 103.
5. *Ha'aretz,* July 10, 1955.
6. *DK,* Nov. 2, 1955, 19, 232.
7. Dayan, *Diary,* 12. See also Mordechai Bar-On, "The Influence of Political Considerations on Operational Planning in the Sinai Campaign," 197–98.
8. Burns, *Between Arab and Israeli,* 104; Stock, *Israel on the Road to Sinai,* 164.
9. Neff, *Warriors at Suez,* 114.
10. For Sharett's opposition to war, see Sharett, *Yoman Ishi,* 5:1328, 1517; Dayan, *Diary,* 13.
11. Sharett, *Yoman Ishi,* 5:1307–18; Gideon Rafael, *Destination Peace: Three Decades of Israeli Foreign Policy,* 48.
12. Burns, *Between Arab and Israeli,* 119.
13. Neff, *Warriors at Suez,* 124–25.
14. Adams, *First-Hand Report,* 248.
15. Whitman File, International Series, box 8, Dec. 16, 1955.
16. Transcript of recorded interview with Herman Phleger, State Department legal adviser, Dulles History, July 21, 1964.
17. *FRUS,* vol. 15, Jan. 5, 1956, 9.
18. Whitman File, Name Series, Dec. 8, 1956; also in Diary Series, box 9, Jan. 12, 1956. In 1987 at the age of seventy-six Anderson was convicted of tax evasion and sent to prison in Texas.
19. Parmet, *Eisenhower and the American Crusades,* 479–80; Ewald, *Eisenhower the President,* 194–95.
20. Whitman File, Diary Series, box 19, Jan. 12, 1956.
21. As quoted in Neff, *Warriors at Suez,* 135–36; Ewald, *Eisenhower the President,* 193–94.
22. *FRUS,* vol. 15, Message from Robert Anderson to Department of State, Jan. 21, 1956, 43–47.
23. Ben-Gurion Diary, Jan. 15, 1956.
24. *FRUS,* vol. 15, Message from Robert Anderson to Department of State, Jan. 23, 1956, 51–58; Jan. 24, 1956, 63–66.
25. Rafael, *Destination Peace,* 51.
26. *FRUS,* vol. 15, Message from Robert Anderson to Department of State, Jan. 27, 1956, 80–82.
27. Whitman File, Diary Series, box 13, Feb. 27, 1956; also in Miscellaneous, Feb. 27, 1956.
28. Ibid.
29. King of Jordan, murdered on July 10, 1951, by a Palestinian nationalist.
30. *FRUS,* vol. 15, Message from Robert Anderson to Department of State, Mar. 6, 1956, 302–14.

31. Ewald, *Eisenhower the President*, 194–96.
32. For Ben-Gurion's account of Anderson's meetings in Israel, see David Ben-Gurion, *My Talks with Arab Leaders*, 274–325.
33. Ibid., 323; *FRUS*, vol. 15, Message from Robert Anderson to Secretary of State, Mar. 9, 1956, 333–35.
34. Whitman File, Diary Series, box 9, Mar. 13, 1956.
35. *FRUS*, vol. 15, Message from Prime Minister Eden to President Eisenhower, Mar. 12, 1956, 364–65.
36. Whitman File, Diary Series, box 13, Mar. 12, 1956.
37. Ibid., March 28, 1956.
38. Ibid.
39. ISA, 2467/7, Dec. 8, 1955; Bialer, *Between East and West*, 272.
40. ISA, 2456/3, Jan. 16, 1956.
41. Ibid., Jan. 23, 1956.
42. *DSB*, Feb. 6, 1956; Dulles Papers, box 107.
43. ISA, 2422/8, Feb. 10, 1956.
44. Ibid., Feb. 28, 1965.
45. Whitman File, White House Memoranda Series, box 4, Mar. 2, 1956.
46. *FRUS*, vol. 15, 209.
47. Whitman File, Memoranda Series, box 4, Mar. 16, 1956.
48. ISA, 2474/16, Mar. 30, 1956; Eisenhower, *Waging Peace*, 29.
49. Whitman File, Memoranda Series, box 4, Apr. 26, 1956; Raphael, *Abba Hillel Silver*, 200.

Chapter 7. Setting the Stage for Preemptive War

1. Burns, *Between Arab and Israeli*, 139.
2. *Ha'aretz*, Apr. 5, 1956.
3. *New York Times*, Apr. 5–10, 1956.
4. *Jerusalem Post*, Mar. 7, 1956.
5. To add further importance to the mission, Eisenhower sent identical letters to Ben-Gurion and Nasser pledging his support "of the mission in fullest measure. . . . It is my earnest hope that in view of the awful calamity which general hostilities would surely visit upon the area you will even under extreme provocation avoid retaliatory action which could have the greatest consequences." Whitman File, International Series, box 8, Apr. 9, 1956. *FRUS*, vol. 15, Apr. 9, 1956, 502.
6. *FRUS*, vol. 15, Apr. 10, 1956, 517.
7. Letter from Jon Kimche to Nahum Goldmann, Aug. 2, 1956, Central Zionist Archives, General J.R. 1956, part 1, Z 6/1085.
8. *New York Times*, Apr. 14, 1956.
9. Hammarskjöld to Goldmann, July 26, 1956, Central Zionist Archives,

General 1956, part 1, Z 6/1085. There had long been a basic disagreement between Israel and the United Nations over the functions of the observers. Israel had taken the position that the observers were merely to investigate breaches of the armistice agreements. General Burns has maintained that the observers have a preventive role in maintaining the cease-fire. In order to fulfill that duty, he maintained, they must have free access on all fronts, something Israel had prevented in the past.

10. In fact, the agreed-upon truce was violated by Egypt while Hammarskjöld was still shuttling between Arab capitals. On April 29, a civilian guard at Nahal Oz was shot while attempting to prevent Arab infiltrators from reaping the settlement's wheat. His body, which had been dragged across the demarcation line to prove that he had crossed into Egyptian territory, was later returned mutilated. The same day an Israeli soldier was killed and two were wounded along the Gaza Strip. That incident marked the first serious breach of the Egyptian-Israeli cease-fire negotiated by Hammerskjöld on April 18. On April 24, three Israeli surveyors and the driver of their automobile were ambushed and slain in the Negev by Arab infiltrators from Jordan.

11. Bar-Zohar, *Ben-Gurion: A Biography*, 226.

12. Records of the U.S. Joint Chiefs of Staff, JCS Chairman Radford's Files, National Archives, File 091 Egypt 1954–Aug. 1956, box 8, Oct. 12, 1955 (hereafter, JCS Records).

13. Sharett, *Yoman Ishi*, 2:376–78, 418–19, 5:1334, 8:2397–2400; Troen, "Sinai Campaign," 183; Rafael, *Destination Peace*, 55.

14. Rafael, *Destination Peace*, 56. In Washington, Eban attributed Sharett's resignation to a deterioration in U.S.-Israeli relations, demonstrated by U.S. unwillingness to provide Israel with arms to counter the shipments of Soviet arms to Egypt. *FRUS*, vol. 15, Letter from Arthur M. Dean to Secretary of State, July 11, 1956, 809.

15. Bar-Zohar, *Ben-Gurion: A Biography*, 229.

16. Ibid.

17. For more information on this interesting subject, see Abel Thomas, *Comment Israel fût sauvé*, 105–10; Peres, *David's Sling*, 31–65, 183–214; Dayan, *Story of My Life*, 183.

18. Neff, *Warriors at Suez*, 253–54.

19. Chester L. Cooper, *The Lion's Last Roar: Suez, 1956*, 96; Parmet, *Eisenhower and the American Crusades*, 480–81.

20. As quoted in Philip Briggs, "Congress and the Middle East: The Eisenhower Doctrine, 1957," 253.

21. Whitman File, Diary Series, box 13, Mar. 28, 1956.

22. The Soviet Foreign Minister, Dmitri Shepilov, in a visit to Cairo was reported to have offered Soviet assistance in financing the Aswan Dam. Eisenhower often said that if some country came to him and said, "If you don't give us aid

we will go to the Russians," he was going to reply with great enthusiasm, "Well, go and try. Don't come to me with that line." See George V. Allen, Dulles History. For more on the subject see *FRUS*, vol. 15, 862–73.

23. Whitman File, Dulles-Herter Series, box 5, July 19, 1956. For a most comprehensive analysis of the economic and diplomatic aspects relating to the Aswan High Dam, see the excellent study by Diane B. Kunz, *The Economic Diplomacy of the Suez Crisis*, 36–72.

24. Evidence suggests that Nasser anticipated the U.S. and British rebuff and used the loan cancellation as a pretext for nationalizing the Suez Canal. The move had been under consideration since 1954, although it was not until June 1956 with the evacuation of the last British troops that an opportunity for swift action appeared. By that time, presumed Soviet backing shifted the balance in Nasser's favor. Dulles Papers, Central Correspondence and Memoranda Series, box 1, May 26, 1957. In other words, the refusal of the loan did not cause Nasser's action but influenced its timing. See interview with Herman Phleger, Dulles History.

25. JCS Records, File 091 Egypt 1954–Aug. 1956, box 8, Aug. 7, 1956.

26. Whitman File, Diary Series, box 20, July 28, 1956.

27. Robert Murphy, *Diplomat among Warriors*, 377–78; J. A. Sellers, "Military Lessons: The British Perspective," 17.

28. Whitman File, Diary Series, box 20, July 31, 1956; see also Eisenhower, *Waging Peace*, 39–44.

29. Whitman File, Diary Series, box 20, July 31, 1956.

30. Dwight D. Eisenhower Papers, White House Central File, Eisenhower Library, Legislative Meetings Series, box 2, Aug. 12, 1956.

31. According to Dulles, Egypt refused to attend because of the strong personal attacks on Nasser by Anthony Eden. In a nationally televised speech on August 8, the prime minister attacked Nasser by declaring, "Our quarrel is not with Egypt, still less with the Arab world; it is with Colonel Nasser."

32. Whitman File, National Security Council Series, box 8, Aug. 30, 1956.

33. Neff, *Warriors at Suez*, 291.

34. In a memorandum to the secretary of defense, the chairman of the Joint Chiefs of Staff warned about the serious implications for the United States arising from Nasser's action. In his view the nationalization act might affect continued U.S. control of military bases and facilities in the general area, the future of the Baghdad Pact, and the economic and military strength of NATO. If Nasser's arbitrary action was tolerated, a precedent for similar arbitrary action would be established. Other Arab states would use his successful act of nationalization as justification for themselves expropriating and nationalizing U.S. and Western enterprises with little fear of consequences. The memorandum advised the State Department that "the United States should consider the desirability of taking military action in support of

the United Kingdom, France and others as appropriate." JCS Records, File 092 Egypt, July 28, 1956–Aug. 3, 1956.

35. Whitman File, Dulles-Herter Series, box 6, Sept. 8, 1956.

36. For full documentation concerning the establishment of the Suez Canal Users Association, see *FRUS*, vol. 16, 448 passim.

37. From October 5 to October 13 the matter was before the Security Council. At the same time, private meetings were held between the UN secretary general and the British, French, and Egyptian foreign ministers. These discussions resulted in a council endorsement of six principles to provide the basis for further exploration between the interested parties. Their efforts were interrupted by the Israeli, British, and French military action in late October.

38. Murphy, *Diplomat among Warriors*, 388.

39. While at the outset of the crisis the Labour party in Britain supported the government's insistence on the validity of using military action, by late August that support had all but vanished. Hugh Gaitskell, the leader of the party, told Dulles that Britain could not afford to ignore the United Nations and that he doubted whether Britain "would be in a position to go to war against Egypt, if the Labor Party opposed such a plan." Whitman File, National Security Council Series, box 8, Aug. 30, 1956. See also *FRUS*, vol. 16, Annex to Watch Committee Report, Oct. 3, 1956, 629.

40. Bar-Zohar, *Ben-Gurion: A Biography*, 230.

41. Dayan, *Story of My Life,* 201; Peres, *David's Sling,* 183; Bar-On, "Influence," 202.

42. Ben-Gurion Diary, Sept. 3, 1956; Dayan, *Story of My Life,* 183–84; Troen, "Sinai Campaign," 190.

43. Ben-Gurion Diary, Sept. 7, 1956.

44. Ibid., Sept. 24, 1956.

45. Bar-Zohar, *Ben-Gurion: A Biography*, 132.

46. Ibid., 234.

47. Ben-Gurion Diary, Oct. 1, 1956.

48. Ibid., Oct. 3, 1956.

49. Dayan, *Story of My Life,* 203.

50. Bar-Zohar, *Ben-Gurion: A Biography*, 233.

51. Dayan, *Story of My Life,* 212.

52. Ibid., 212

53. Ben-Gurion Diary, Oct. 22, 1956.

54. Ibid.; Dayan, *Story of My Life,* 215; Bar-Zohar, *Ben-Gurion: A Biography*, 236.

55. Dayan, *Story of My Life,* 218; Selwyn Lloyd in *Suez, 1956: A Personal Account* denies that Britain colluded with Israel. At no time did Britain request that Israel take military action. British representatives at the meeting, according to Lloyd, merely expressed the steps Britain would take should

"certain things happen" (186–88). For a French view of what transpired at Sèvres, see Christian Pineau, *Suez 1956*, 149–52, and Thomas, *Comment Israel fût sauvé*, 105–200. Anthony Eden initially was very reluctant to accept any Israeli participation in a British-French assault on Egypt. His aversion to what transpired at Sèvres was demonstrated by his desperate attempt to have all records of the agreement or protocol destroyed. See Robert Rhodes James, "Eden," 105–8.

56. Ben-Gurion Diary, Oct. 24, 1956.
57. With no relationship to the Sèvres talks but in an obvious boost to Israeli morale and air power, Canada on Sept. 21, 1956, announced that it would make available to Israel 4 F-86s per month up to a total of 24. *FRUS*, vol. 16, 559.
58. Dayan, *Story of My Life*, 233.
59. Ben-Gurion Diary, Oct. 26, 1956.
60. Ibid., Oct. 2, 1956.
61. Bar-On, "Influence," 214–15.
62. *FRUS*, vol. 16, Oct. 26, 1956, 790; Parmet, *Eisenhower and the American Crusades*, 471.

Chapter 8. Operation Kadesh: The Sinai Campaign

1. Chaim Herzog, *The War of Atonement, October 1973*, 2–3.
2. Dayan, *Diary*, 25–28.
3. Burns, *Between Arab and Israeli*, 172. The *Jerusalem Post*, which frequently reflected the views of the Israeli government, editorialized on Oct. 7, 1956, "Jordan is the sick man of the Middle East and Israel has the major misfortune to find herself next door to this disintegrating body." The article contended that Jordanian attacks against Israeli citizens were carried out under Egyptian orders, enabling Egypt to strike at Israel without incurring retaliation. The editorial suggested that the Jordanian government had lost control of the situation, in which case, the editorial concluded: "If Jordan crumbles, Israel will not sit with folded hands, and Egypt will not inherit."
4. Dayan, *Diary*, 43–57.
5. Whitman File, Diary Series, box 9, Oct. 15, 1956.
6. Ambrose, *Eisenhower*, 2:352. See also *FRUS*, vol. 16, 799–800. The CIA, however, had a more accurate assessment of the situation. See Peter L. Hahn, *The United States, Great Britain, and Egypt, 1945–1956: Strategy and Diplomacy in the Early Cold War*, 226–28.
7. Ben-Gurion Diary, Oct. 1, 1956.
8. *FRUS*, vol. 16, Oct. 1, 1956, 622.
9. ISA, 2453/10, Oct. 12 and 19, 1956; see also *FRUS*, vol. 16, Oct. 15, 1956, 728.

10. Dayan, *Diary*, 59.

11. The plan was no longer practical anyway. The Jordanian parliamentary elections on Oct. 15 resulted in a victory for Nasser's supporters, whereupon the Jordanian government hastened to cancel its military agreement with Iraq, Nasser's enemy. The Egyptian leader promised military aid to Jordan in case of an Israeli attack, and Jordan in turn agreed to join the Egyptian-Syrian joint military command.

12. As part of a deception plan Israeli troops were moved openly to the northern and eastern borders against Syria and Jordan. Those units designated for war against Egypt were dispatched secretly southward.

13. Dayan, *Diary*, 67. Throughout October 25 and 26, U.S. Intelligence in Israel sent reports to the State Department about large-scale mobilization. On October 28 Lawson cabled reports to that effect as well. Herman Finer, *Dulles over Suez: The Theory and Practice of His Diplomacy*, 348–49.

14. Eban, *An Autobiography*, 211.

15. Whitman File, Diary Series, Oct. 27, 1956; ISA, 2448/6, Oct. 27, 1956. Nonetheless, the Watch Committee set up by the CIA to monitor developments in the Middle East, in analyzing the motives behind Israel's full-scale mobilization, did consider the possibility of an Israeli attack against Egypt under the pretext of retaliation for the most recent border incidents. The U.S. military attaché in Tel Aviv speculated that the French might be working with the Israelis and that an Israeli move against the Straits of Tiran was a "good bet." *FRUS*, vol. 16, 787–800.

16. Eban, *An Autobiography*, 211.

17. Whitman File, Diary Series, box 9, Oct. 27, 1956; *FRUS*, vol. 16, 801–2.

18. ISA, 2448/6, Oct. 29, 1956.

19. Dayan, *Diary*, 74. Dayan was overly optimistic. In fact, Eisenhower and Dulles strongly suspected British and French knowledge of and even acquiescence in the Israeli action. *FRUS*, vol. 16, 803–5, 815.

20. Dayan, *Diary*, 71.

21. ISA, 2448/6, Oct. 28, 1956.

22. Escorting the transport planes were ten Meteor fighters, while twelve Mystères patrolled the length of the Suez Canal ready to engage any Egyptian aircraft that attacked the Israeli transport planes.

23. Soon after, an announcement from Israel's Foreign Ministry declared that Israel was engaged in "security measures to eliminate the Egyptian *fedayeen* bases in the Sinai Peninsula." The announcement continued, "It is not Israel which has sought to encircle Egypt with a ring of steel with the purpose of annihilating" the state of Israel.

24. *FRUS*, vol. 16, Memorandum of conversation of the Department of State, Oct. 29, 1956, 821.

25. Haggai Eshed, *Mossad shel Ish Ehad: Reuven Shiloah—Avi Ha-Modyin Ha-Israeli*, 218.

26. Eban, *An Autobiography*, 221–23; Finer, *Dulles over Suez*, 353–54.

27. Whitman File, Diary Series, box 18, Phone calls, Oct. 29, 1956. See also *FRUS*, vol. 16, Memorandum of conversation, Department of State, Oct. 29, 1956, 829.

28. Ambrose, *Eisenhower*, 2:354.

29. Throughout the summer and fall of 1956, Ben-Gurion kept reassuring General Burns that Israel would not start a preemptive war. On August 30, he assured the Mapai Congress that "the first principle of our policy is to maintain the peace to the extent that this depends on us." On September 21, Ben-Gurion told a reporter, "As long as it is for me to decide, we shall make no war . . . I will never make war. Never." On October 15, two weeks prior to the Sinai campaign, he defended in Parliament his policy against preemptive war. Quoted in Sachar, *A History of Israel*, 493.

30. Emmet J. Hughes, *The Ordeal of Power: A Political Memoir of the Eisenhower Years*, 212.

31. Eisenhower, *Waging Peace*, 73; Neff, *Warriors at Suez*, 365.

32. *FRUS*, vol. 16, Oct. 26, 1956, 790. Finer, *Dulles over Suez*, 335–36.

33. Whitman File, Diary Series, box 19, Oct. 29, 1956; Neff, *Warriors at Suez*, 366–67.

34. Ambrose, *Eisenhower*, 2:353.

35. Whitman File, Diary Series, box 20, Nov. 2, 1956. Eisenhower was often critical of Truman for exploiting foreign policy in order to gain domestic political advantage, implying that Truman's decision to recognize the state of Israel was not based on national security considerations but was rather a means to gain Jewish votes. On a number of occasions, Eisenhower instructed Dulles to keep domestic politics out of U.S. policy in the Middle East.

36. Ironically, Anthony Eden insisted on October 29 as the date for the opening of Israel's attack against Egypt. One of the reasons for Eden's agreement to collaborate with Israel against an Arab state had been his assumption that Eisenhower, out of concern for the Jewish vote, would refrain from applying pressure on Israel and that by extension no pressures would be brought to bear on Britain and France. David Carlton, *Anthony Eden: A Biography*, 438.

37. Brecher, *Decisions in Israel's Foreign Policy*, 274.

38. *FRUS*, vol. 16, Memorandum of conference with President, Oct. 30, 1956, 855.

39. Whitman File, Diary Series, box 19, Memorandum of conference with President, Oct. 30, 1956.

40. Finer, *Dulles over Suez*, 362.

41. Ibid., 357; Neff, *Warriors at Suez*, 376.

42. *New York Times*, Nov. 4, 1956.

43. Whitman File, Diary Series, Telephone call, Dulles to Eisenhower, 2:17 P.M., Oct. 30, 1956.

44. Dayan, *Diary*, 97.

45. Brecher, *Decisions in Israel's Foreign Policy*, 242.

46. Dayan, *Diary*, 96.

47. Carlton, *Anthony Eden*, 443.

48. According to Eban, the assumption in Jerusalem had been that an Anglo-French veto in the Security Council would remove the United Nations from the arena of the conflict. Little attention was paid to the constitutional change in the United Nations under the United Nations for Peace resolution of 1951, which made it possible for the UN General Assembly to act if the Security Council was deadlocked by a veto. See also Rafael, *Destination Peace*, 59.

49. Eshed, *Reuven Shiloah*, 219. Shiloah was instrumental in cultivating friendships with those individuals. He also tried to gain the support of prominent non-Jews such as General Lucius Clay and John McCloy. See Ginzberg, *My Brother's Keeper*, 80; Eban, *Personal Witness*, 224.

50. As quoted in Eban, *An Autobiography*, 117. From Thomas Dewey, Eban learned that Eisenhower's main apprehension "lay in the suspicion that Israel intended a permanent occupation" of the Sinai. In the Pentagon, Dewey told Eban, there was concern that unless hostilities came to a quick end, the Soviet Union might intervene, resulting in a "world conflagration." Eban relayed those messages to Ben-Gurion, urging him to signal the administration in Washington that Israel intended to end the hostilities and did not aim at annexing the Sinai.

51. Eban, *An Autobiography*, 218.

52. *New York Times*, Nov. 1, 1956.

53. Eden, *Full Circle*, 604. Eden was shocked at that unexpected move by the United States. He and Harold Macmillan, the chancellor of the exchequer, were convinced that on the eve of a presidential election Eisenhower and Dulles would tacitly support their allies against Nasser, especially since the U.S. leaders had come to detest the Egyptian ruler. Carlton, *Anthony Eden*, 445. The worst the British expected from the United States was a public statement of disapproval. Robert Rhodes James, *Anthony Eden*, 544.

54. Ambrose, *Eisenhower*, 2:364. Hours after the news of the Israeli attack reached Washington, the Commerce Department issued a temporary stop order to export licenses that were not yet issued on selected items destined for Israel. See also, Kunz, *The Economic Diplomacy of the Suez Crisis*, 163, 166–67.

55. *FRUS*, vol. 16, Nov. 1, 1956, 925–27. Eban, *An Autobiography*, 219–20. Eban, *Personal Witness*, 269–70. Finer, *Dulles over Suez*, 392.

56. *DSB*, Nov. 12, 1956, 754. Finer, *Dulles over Suez*, 394–97.

57. Eban's remarks to Dulles earlier in the day had an effect on the secretary. Dulles added a paragraph to the U.S. resolution presented to the General Assembly urging that once a cease-fire was established, steps must be taken to reopen the canal and restore freedom of navigation. Most important, he added to his speech a statement calling for the nonreturn of the status quo ante bellum.

58. *New York Times*, Nov. 2, 1956.

59. Spiegel, *The Other Arab-Israeli Conflict*, 76. By Nov. 10 Dulles would receive State Department cables at his hospital bed.

60. Dayan, *Story of My Life*, 249.

61. Ibid., 234.

62. Ibid., 239–50; for a detailed discussion of Israel's military campaign, see Dayan, *Diary*; S. L. A. Marshall, *Sinai Victory*; Edgar O'Ballance, *The Sinai Campaign, 1956*; Robert Henriques, *A Hundred Hours to Suez: An Account of Israel's Campaign in the Sinai Peninsula*; Kenneth Love, *Suez: The Twice-Fought War: A History*; Aviezer Golan, *Ma'arechet Sinai*; Bar-On, "Influence," 209–14; Bar-On, "The Sinai Campaign, 1956—Objectives and Expectations," 94–104.

63. The United States watched helplessly as Soviet troops invaded Hungary. All it could do was offer assistance to Hungarians fleeing across the Austrian border. The United States, challenged by both friend and foe, found itself in the unenviable position of being tough with its allies but helpless to punish its enemy, the Soviet Union, indeed a most embarrassing double standard. Spiegel, *The Other Arab-Israeli Conflict*, 77. No doubt the crisis in the Middle East helped divert world attention from Soviet actions in Hungary.

64. Eban, *An Autobiography*, 219.

65. Dayan, *Story of My Life*, 251. In fact, Eisenhower too was dismayed by both British tactics and strategy. In a letter to Alfred Gruenther, NATO commander, he lamented the poor planning of the allied operation. "If one has to fight then that is that," he wrote. Ambrose, *Eisenhower*, 2:365.

66. As for Israel's benefits from its collaboration with the British and the French, the facts speak for themselves. The allied bombardment of Egyptian airfields destroyed most of the Egyptian air force on the ground, thereby alleviating Ben-Gurion's fears of Egyptian bombardment of Israeli cities. In addition, French fighter planes protected Israeli cities just in case the Egyptian air force attempted to strike against Israeli population centers. A French destroyer, *Kersaint*, attacked and immobilized an Egyptian destroyer that had attempted to attack the port of Haifa. The warship and crew surrendered to Israeli naval forces.

67. Eban, *An Autobiography,* 226.

68. On Nov. 4, the Soviet Prime Minister, Nikolai Bulganin, in a letter to Eisenhower proposed that the two powers jointly use their air and sea power to help Egypt defeat the "aggressors." Eisenhower considered such joint action "unthinkable and warned that any entry of new troops" (i.e., Soviet troops) would be met by countermeasures from all UN members, including the United States. Although the president did not take seriously the Soviet threat of intervention, he nonetheless used that possibility to pressure the allies and Israel to cease hostilities. Love, *Suez,* 614; Adams, *First-Hand Report,* 258.

69. Eden, *Full Circle,* 620.

70. *FRUS,* vol. 16, Nov. 6, 1956, 1025–27. Finer, *Dulles over Suez,* 432–33.

71. Shuckburgh, *Descent to Suez,* 365; Carlton, *Anthony Eden,* 452; James, *Anthony Eden,* 556. On November 6, Humphrey informed Macmillan that Britain's urgent loan application for $1 billion from the International Monetary Fund would not be approved unless Britain ceased fire at once. The loan was urgently needed to help arrest the decline of the British pound sterling. Compounding Britain's problems, the Suez Canal was blocked with shipwrecks, resulting in a cutoff of oil shipments. The United States refused to make up the loss. For more information on the tremendous economic pressures applied by the United States, see also Kunz, *The Economic Diplomacy of the Suez Crisis,* 143–52.

72. Finer, *Dulles over Suez,* 429.

73. Pineau, *Suez 1956,* 186–88.

74. But according to Eden it would have taken more than just two days to complete the entire operation. Eden in his memoirs observed that General Keightly estimated that he could occupy Ismailia by November 8, and the remaining length of the canal by November 12 (*Full Circle,* 620.) Eden's assertion was correct, but only theoretically. Practically, the conquest of Ismailia would have all but assured allied control of the canal. For a French perspective, see, Jean-Paul Cointet, "Guy Mollet, the French Government, and the SFIO," 136–38.

75. Shuckburgh, *Descent to Suez,* 365.

76. Carlton, *Anthony Eden,* 454. See also Gilbert, *Churchill: A Life,* 950.

77. As quoted in James, *Anthony Eden,* 577; Finer, *Dulles over Suez,* 446–47; Parmet, *Eisenhower and the American Crusades,* 487.

78. Eden, *Full Circle,* 625.

79. Ambrose, *Eisenhower,* 2:372.

80. Eshed, *Reuven Shiloah,* 220–21.

81. Finer, *Dulles over Suez,* 419; for the full texts of the letters between Ben-Gurion and Bulganin, see Moshe Zak, *Arbayim Shnot Du-Siach im Moskva,* 181–83.

82. Brecher, *Foreign Policy System of Israel,* 43, 266.
83. Zak, *Arbayim Schnot Du-Siach,* 180.
84. *FRUS,* vol. 16, Nov. 6, 1956, 1014.
85. Ben Gurion Diary, Nov. 7, 1956.
86. Zak, *Arbayim Schnot Du-Siach,* 190.
87. Ben-Gurion Diary, Nov. 10, 1956; Sachar, *A History of Israel,* 501; Brecher, *Decisions In Israel's Foreign Policy,* 275.
88. Ben-Gurion Diary, Nov. 7, 1956.

Chapter 9. Israel's Withdrawal from the Sinai and Gaza: The Diplomatic Struggle

1. *DK,* 20 (Nov. 1956), part 2, 736–40.
2. Eban, *An Autobiography,* 229; According to Shimon Peres, Ben-Gurion's statement was solely for negotiating purposes. He never considered holding on to the Sinai. See Shimon Peres, "The Road to Sèvres: Franco-Israeli Strategic Cooperation," 145; but ten years later Ben-Gurion, in a moment of candor, confessed his error in making that speech. In an interview with Michael Brecher he said, "You see . . . the victory was too quick. I was too drunk with victory." Brecher, *Decisions in Israel's Foreign Policy,* 263.
3. Finer, *Dulles over Suez,* 446.
4. ISA, 2448/13, Nov. 8, 1956. Furthermore, during a visit to the recuperating secretary of state on Nov. 7 at Walter Reed Hospital, the president and Dulles agreed on the need to pressure Israel to return to the armistice lines in compliance with UN resolutions. Dulles suggested that Eban should be informed immediately that unless the Israelis complied, the United States would place an embargo on all funds going to Israel. With the elections over, Dulles observed, "this was the time to take this step with the Israelis." They agreed that the Treasury Department could make all remittances to Israel taxable, which would have a "profound effect" on the Israeli government. *FRUS,* vol. 16, 1049–52, 1057.
5. Dulles Papers, Telephone Call Series, box 6, conversation between Hoover and Eisenhower, Nov. 8, 1956.
6. Eban, *An Autobiography,* 231.
7. During November and early December 1956, the main UN efforts were concentrated on evicting British and French troops from the Suez Canal area and opening the canal to the flow of Arab oil to Europe and the rest of the world. By November 20, only 700 UN troops from "neutral" countries had arrived in the Canal Zone. Another 3,000 were on their way. On November 22, the British and French withdrawal began. Eban's advice, therefore, would satisfy U.S. demands for withdrawal and also buy time for negotiations with the United States about the conditions under which Israeli withdrawal would take place.

8. As quoted in Bar-Zohar, *Ben-Gurion: A Biography*, 252.

9. ISA, 2456/4/B, Nov. 8, 1956. By contrast, his letter to Bulganin sent the same day was one of defiance and contained no promise of withdrawal.

10. Since early evening the citizens of Israel had been told that Ben-Gurion was about to broadcast an address to the nation.

11. Whitman File, International Series, Israel (3) box 29, Nov. 9, 1956.

12. Ben-Gurion Diary, Nov. 10, 1956.

13. On November 15, 1956, Bulganin in a letter to Ben-Gurion rejected Israel's linkage of withdrawal to the conclusion of "satisfactory arrangements with the UN" and demanded an immediate withdrawal of Israeli troops without preconditions. ISA, 2474/8, Nov. 15, 1956.

14. Eban, *An Autobiography*, 233.

15. Ben-Gurion Diary, Dec. 23, 1956. Dayan favored withdrawal eastward only as far as El-Arish, "and there we will stay." It is clear that until late December, Israel was not considering withdrawing from Gaza. Ben-Gurion in his diary (Nov. 14, 1956) wrote about a meeting with Ziama Divon, a foreign ministry Arab affairs expert. Divon told Ben-Gurion that Golda Meir had ordered him and Ezra Donin to persuade the inhabitants of Gaza to express their views by demonstrating in favor of Israeli rule there.

16. Ben-Gurion Diary, Dec. 29, 1956.

17. ISA, 2448/6, 2459/4, Dec. 30, 1956; see also *FRUS*, vol. 17, Jan. 12, 1957, 31; Jan. 14, 1957, 35–36.

18. Ben-Gurion Diary, Dec. 28, 1956.

19. Author's interview with Eban, New York City, Apr. 8, 1990.

20. After the meeting, Dean called Rountree and informed him of the Israeli position. Rountree briefed Dulles in advance of the secretary's meeting with Meir and Eban. Dulles Papers, Telephone Call Series, box 6, Dec. 28, 1956.

21. ISA, 2459/14, Dec. 30, 1956.

22. Both Meir and Eban were taken aback by Dulles's admonition. The Israeli foreign minister could not conceal her disappointment about the secretary's remarks. The secretary, she said, had forgotten that since 1948 Israel had stretched out its hand for peace with its Arab neighbors and been constantly rebuffed. Dulles was not convinced and pointed to the death and destruction among Arabs caused by Israel's retaliatory policy. Hammarskjöld told him that in most cases Israel was responsible for the border incidents. Ben-Gurion was angered by Dulles's remarks and protested to the U.S. ambassador in Tel Aviv. In a letter to Bedell Smith he complained about Dulles's insensitivity to Israel's problems and achievements in a short period of eight years despite Arab hatred and belligerency.

23. ISA, 2459/14, Jan. 21 and 22, 1957.

24. Ben-Gurion Diary, Jan. 7, 1957.

25. Ibid.

26. Whitman File, International Series, box 21, June 12, 1956.

27. The verbatim record of the January 25 debate is in *DK*, 21, part 2, 830–51. Only Begin's right-wing Herut party termed any withdrawal "a political defeat after a military victory." Ben-Gurion's position had already been conveyed privately on January 8, 1957, to the U.S. ambassador in Tel Aviv. *FRUS*, vol. 17, Jan. 8, 1957, 13.

28. *FRUS*, vol. 17, 45–47.

29. ISA, 2448/6, Feb. 3, 1957.

30. Ambrose, *Eisenhower*, 2:385.

31. ISA, 2448/6, Feb. 8, 1957.

32. Whitman File, International Series, Telephone call from Dulles to President, Feb. 6, 1957.

33. On January 5, 1957, the president asked Congress to support his Middle East policy by passing a resolution that would endorse the giving of aid to any Middle East country that "asked for help against an overt attack by a government dominated by international communism." The resolution also called for the supply by the United States of arms to Middle East countries to be used against internal threats. Dulles maintained that a "power vacuum" existed in the area and that the Soviet Union might fill it, to the detriment of Western interests. The Senate Foreign Relations Committee was debating the president's proposal when his policy toward Israel came under severe criticism.

34. Dulles Papers, Telephone Call Series, box 6, Feb. 9, 1957. The aide-mémoire stated that on January 28, 1950, when Egypt occupied the two islands of Tiran and Sanapir at the entrance of the Gulf of Aqaba, Egypt informed the United States that its action would not obstruct the innocent passage through the waters separating the two islands in conformity with international practice and recognized principles of the law of nations. Egypt, of course, violated that promise.

35. ISA, 2448/6, Feb. 11, 1957. *FRUS*, vol. 17, Feb. 11, 1957, 132–34.

36. Dulles Papers, Telephone Call Series, box 6, Nov. 9, 1957.

37. Eban, *An Autobiography*, 241.

38. Ben-Gurion Diary, Feb. 12, 1957; Eban, *An Autobiography*, 241.

39. ISA, 2459/18, Feb. 15, 1957; Eban, *An Autobiography*, 242; see also Dulles Papers, Telephone Call Series, box 6, Feb. 15, 1957.

40. Dulles Papers, Telephone Call Series, box 6, Feb. 15, 1957.

41. Ambrose, *Eisenhower*, 2:386–87.

42. Dulles Papers, Telephone Call Series, box 6, Feb. 12, 1957.

43. Ibid., Feb. 16, 1957.

44. ISA, 2459/15, Feb. 17, 1957.

45. Ibid., Feb. 16, 1957.

46. As quoted in Eban, *An Autobiography*, 244.

47. Dulles Papers, Telephone Call Series, box 6, Feb. 18, 1957.

48. Ibid., Feb. 19, 1957.
49. *FRUS*, vol. 17, Feb. 19, 1957, 208–11.
50. ISA, 2448/16, Feb. 19, 1957.
51. *New York Times*, Feb. 18, 1957.
52. WHCF-DDE, Legislative Meetings Series, box 21, Feb. 20, 1957.
53. Ibid.
54. Dulles Papers, Telephone Call Series, box 6, 11:45 A.M. call to Dr. Roswell Barnes, Feb. 22, 1957.
55. Neff, *Warriors at Suez*, 433–34.
56. Finer, *Dulles over Suez*, 485.
57. Eban, *An Autobiography*, 245; Brecher, *Decisions in Israel's Foreign Policy*, 298.
58. On February 21, in response to the president's speech, Ben-Gurion told the Knesset that the people of Israel would not submit to discrimination in international relations. In what seemed like a direct appeal to the people of the United States over the head of the administration, he drew a distinction between the injurious policy of the administration and the friendship of the people toward Israel.
59. ISA, 2448/6, Feb. 22, 1957; Eban, *An Autobiography*, 244–45. Lodge succeeded in convincing Hammarskjöld to postpone a UN vote until February 26. *FRUS*, vol. 17, Feb. 18, 1957, 203; Feb. 20, 1957, 225.
60. Rafael, *Destination Peace*, 64.
61. ISA, 2448/6, Feb. 24, 1957.
62. Burns, *Between Arab and Israeli*, 269.
63. Dulles Papers, Telephone Call Series, box 6, 7:02 P.M. call to Lodge, Feb. 24, 1957.
64. Ibid., Conversation between Arthur Dean and Dulles, Feb. 24, 1957.
65. Finer, *Dulles over Suez*, 486.
66. *FRUS*, vol. 17, Memorandum of conversation, Department of State, Feb. 26, 1957, 285–98.
67. ISA, 2459/15, 2456/4/B, Feb. 27, 1957.
68. Ben-Gurion Diary, Feb. 27 and 28, 1957.
69. ISA, Mar. 1, 1967.
70. ISA, 2459/15, Mar. 1, 1957. For complete text of Golda Meir's speech, see UN General Assembly, Official Records, 11th sess., 666th meeting, 1275–76; also in *New York Times*, Mar. 2, 1957.
71. Lodge's speech apparently went through a last-minute revision as a result of the intervention and input of the Indian representative, Krishna Menon, who spearheaded the Egyptian campaign in the United Nations. Menon and Lodge had worked very closely since the inception of the crisis. Golda Meir considered Menon malicious, anti-Israel, and even anti-Semitic. Brecher,

Decisions in Israel's Foreign Policy, 300. For full details of Lodge's speech and his deviation from the Dulles-Eban agreement, see UN General Assembly, *Official Records,* 11th sess., 666th and 667th plenary meetings, 1277–1304; also in *New York Times,* Mar. 2, 1957.

72. ISA, 2459/15, Mar. 3, 1957.
73. Finer, *Dulles over Suez,* 488.
74. ISA, 2448/6, Mar. 2, 1957.
75. Rafael, *Destination Peace,* 64. Eban contacted Bedell Smith to tell him about the anxieties caused in Israel by Lodge's speech. Smith called the president, who assured him that despite Lodge's speech there had not been any last-minute change in U.S. policy. ISA, 1459/15, Mar. 2, 1957. Also on March 2, Meir and Eban talked with the French leaders, now in Ottawa, Canada. They agreed to support Israel's efforts to undo the damage caused by Lodge and urged the Israelis to proceed with the withdrawal, Lodge's comments notwithstanding.
76. ISA, 2459/15, Mar. 3, 1957.
77. *DK,* 22, Mar. 5, 1957, 1240–43.
78. Gideon Rafael drafted the contents of the cable to Ben-Gurion and subsequently convinced Meir not to dispatch it. In all likelihood, he told the foreign minister, Ben-Gurion had already received the same information about the Egyptian return to Gaza. Should he decide to halt the withdrawal, he would do it without her message. But should he decide to proceed with the withdrawal, her message would make things more difficult for him than they were already. Golda Meir was persuaded not to put additional burdens on Ben-Gurion. Rafael, *Destination Peace,* 65–66.
79. Author's interview with Eban, New York City, Apr. 8, 1990.
80. ISA, 2456/4/B, Mar. 6, 1957.
81. Burns, *Between Arab and Israeli,* 257.
82. ISA, 2456/4, Mar. 14, 1957.
83. ISA, 2459/15, Mar. 19, 1957.
84. Rafael, *Destination Peace,* 65; Bar-Zohar, *Ben Gurion: A Biography,* 256.
85. Ben-Gurion Diary, Mar. 10, 1957.
86. Ibid., Feb. 19, Mar. 3, 1957.
87. As quoted in Bar-Zohar, *Ben Gurion: A Biography,* 256.
88. Itamar Rabinovich, "The Suez-Sinai Campaign: The Regional Dimension," 169–70. Although Israel's ongoing security situation had improved, the more fundamental threats to its existence still persisted, and that called for adjustments in Israel's military strategy. For changes in Israel's military strategy vis-à-vis the Arab states in the aftermath of the Sinai campaign, see Elhannan Orren, "Changes in Israel's Concept of Security after Kadesh," 218–28.

Chapter 10. U.S. Jewry and the Sinai Campaign

1. Isaac Alteras, "Eisenhower, American Jewry, and Israel," 262.
2. Dulles Papers, Telephone Call Series, box 6, Feb. 22, 1957; Neff, *Warriors at Suez,* 432–33.
3. *New York Times,* Sept. 15, 1985.
4. James Lee Ray, *The Future of American-Israeli Relations: A Parting of the Ways?* 29. The Presidents' Conference functioned in the 1955–58 period as an "assembly" type of communication organization, hosting briefings and sharing basic information with its member units. Windmueller, "American Jewish Interest Groups," 325–26.
5. Kenen, *Israel's Defense Line,* 111. Author's interview with Yehuda Hellman, executive director of the Conference of Presidents of Major American Jewish Organizations, New York City, Apr. 16, 1985; see also Urofsky, *We Are One,* 300–302.
6. Stephen Birmingham, *Our Crowd,* 89.
7. Michael Brecher, "American Jewry's Influence on Israeli-U.S. Relations, Reality, and Images," 3. For a detailed examination of some of their activities as pressure groups throughout the first decade of Israel's existence, see Windmueller, "American Jewish Interest Groups," 294–300.
8. U.S. Agency for International Development, Bureau for Program Policy Coordination; also in Report of the Comptroller General of the United States, U.S. Assistance to Israel, General Accounting Office, June 24, 1983.
9. Nadav Safran, *The United States and Israel,* 278–80.
10. In November 1956, the American Jewish Committee published a document entitled "Some Press Views on the Middle East Conflict." Seventy-five editorials in fifty-seven newspapers from thirty-six cities were examined. Ten papers were critical of U.S. policy, and thirty-seven endorsed the government's negative reaction to the British-French-Israeli attack on Egypt. In addition, although public opinion polls indicated that Americans in general demonstrated more sympathy toward Israel than Egypt, only a small proportion felt that Israel's invasion was justified.
11. ISA, 2474/8, Nov. 2, 1956; Nahum Goldmann, *The Autobiography of Nahum Goldmann: Sixty Years of Jewish Life,* 299; Eban, *An Autobiography,* 213.
12. Author's interview with Abba Eban, New York City, Apr. 8, 1990.
13. *Jewish Telegraphic Agency,* Nov. 18 and 26, 1956, Jan. 4. 1957 (hereafter, *JTA*); American Jewish Congress, *Congress Record,* vol. 9, no. 3; Jewish Labor Committee, "American Labor on the Middle East," Jan. 1957.
14. ISA, 2463/20, Nov. 3, 1956; see also the American Jewish Committee, *Vigilant Brotherhood,* 27–30.

15. Naomi Cohen, *Not Free to Desist: The American Jewish Committee, 1906–1966*, 323–24.

16. *American Zionist* 47, no. 2 (Oct.–Nov. 1956): 17.

17. Ibid., 1–3.

18. *Jewish Frontier*, Nov. 1956, 6.

19. *American Zionist* 47, no. 2 (Oct.–Nov. 1956): 1–3.

20. Alteras, "Eisenhower," 267.

21. Nahum Goldmann warned Ben-Gurion that U.S. Jews would not stand behind Israel if it persisted in its occupation of the Sinai. Abba Hillel Silver conveyed to Ben-Gurion two messages from Eisenhower containing threats and promises to Israel. Bar-Zohar, *Ben Gurion: The Armed Prophet*, 226–28, 235.

22. Philip Klutznick, Oral History, B'nai B'rith, Anti-Defamation League, New York.

23. Michael Reiner, "The Reaction of U.S. Jewish Organizations to the Sinai Campaign and Its Aftermath," 34.

24. ISA, 2448/6, Mar. 1957.

25. Eisenhower, *Waging Peace*, 178.

26. For the background to the Eisenhower Doctrine, see Eisenhower, *Waging Peace*, 180–83; for congressional views and action on the president's proposal, see "The Administration's New Middle East Doctrine," *Congressional Digest* 36 (Mar. 1957): 67–69; U.S. Congress, Senate, *Hearings: The President's Proposal*, 7, 9, 21, 247, 326; Michael Yizhar, "The Formulation of the United States Middle East Resolution," 2–7, and "The Eisenhower Doctrine: A Case Study of American Foreign Policy Formulation and Implementation."

27. Kenen, *Israel's Defense Line*, 139.

28. *JTA*, Jan. 17, 1957.

29. American Jewish Congress, "Statements of the American Jewish Congress on the Eisenhower Doctrine," Feb. 4, 1957, 1–4.

30. U.S. Congress, House, Committee on Foreign Affairs, *Hearings: Economic and Military Cooperation with Nations in the General Area of the Middle East*, 145.

31. *Near East Report* 1, no. 12 (Nov. 15, 1957); Michael Yizhar, "Israel and the Eisenhower Doctrine," 58–64.

32. *JTA*, Jan. 23, 1957.

33. ISA, 2448/6, Mar. 1957.

34. Finer, *Dulles over Suez*, 475.

35. *JTA*, Feb. 7, 1957.

36. Kenen, *Israel's Defense Line*, 130.

37. The stand taken by the majority leader enlisted the support of the whole

Democratic Policy Committee of the Senate—the likes of Mansfield, Demo-
cratic whip and one of the party's chief voices on foreign policy; Thomas
Hennings of Missouri, the secretary of the Democratic Conference and
chairman of the powerful Rules Committee; Theodore Green of Rhode
Island, chairman of the Foreign Relations Committee; Richard Russell of
Georgia, chairman of the Armed Services Committee, and Carl Hayden of
Arizona, chairman of the Appropriations Committee.

38. As quoted in Peter Golden, *Quiet Diplomat: A Biography of Max M. Fisher,*
xviii.

Chapter 11. From Confrontation to Cooperation

1. Eshed, *Reuven Shiloah,* 250.
2. Eytan, *The First Ten Years,* 156.
3. Abba Eban, interview with the author, New York City, April 8, 1992.
4. For more details on the debate regarding the Eisenhower Doctrine, see *Jewish
Agency Digest of Press and Events,* Jan. 10, 1957, 578–79; Jan. 24, 1957,
650–51; May 16, 1957, 1154–55; May 30, 1957, 1186; June 6, 1957,
1202–3, 1217–20; June 13, 1957, 1221–22.
5. Bar-Zohar, *Ben-Gurion: A Biography,* 260; Eshed, *Reuven Shiloah,* 255.
6. ISA, Sept. 11, 1957, 4374/26, Sept. 17, 1957, 4374/26.
7. Bar-Zohar, *Ben-Gurion: A Biography,* 263.
8. Eisenhower, *Waging Peace,* 272–75; Bar-Zohar, *Ben Gurion: A Biography,*
263. For a critical evaluation of the Eisenhower Doctrine and its failure to
achieve its objectives, see Robert D. Schulzinger, "The Impact of Suez on
United States Middle East Policy, 1957–1958," 251–64.
9. WH File, Official File Series, box 29 (Israel) (2), July 1958 (1), July 20, 1958.
10. Eshed, *Reuven Shiloah,* 270.
11. Ben-Gurion Diary, July 20, 1958.
12. Ben-Gurion Diary, July 22, 1958; also in Eshed, *Reuven Shiloah,* 268–69.
13. WH File, Official File Series, box 29 (Israel) (2), July 25, 1958.
14. ISA, 4374/26, Aug. 2, 1958.
15. As quoted in Eshed, *Reuven Shiloah,* 272.
16. Dan Raviv and Yossi Melman, *Every Spy a Prince: The Complete History of
Israel's Intelligence Community,* 83.
17. Dulles Papers, Telephone call to Rountree, Oct. 12, 1958.
18. Christian Herter Papers, Dwight D. Eisenhower Library, 1957–61, Chronological File, box 8, Aug. 4, 1960. The latest U.S. offer, however, fell short
of Israel's request of arms supplies worth a quarter of a billion dollars as a
grant. The Israeli shopping list included tanks, squadrons of 104s, and Hawk
antiaircraft missiles. Eisenhower turned down the request out of fear that a

new arms race would develop in the Middle East. Herter Papers, 1957–61, Chronological File, Feb. 17, 1960.

19. *New York Times,* Mar. 11, 1960.

20. Herter Papers, 1957–61, Chronological File, box 8, Mar. 25, 1960. Ill health forced Dulles to resign from the cabinet on Apr. 21, 1959; he died on May 24, 1959.

Bibliography

Manuscript Sources

United States

Dwight D. Eisenhower Library, Abilene, Kansas
  Dwight D. Eisenhower Papers, Ann Whitman File
    Administrative Series
    Cabinet Series
    Diary Series
    Dulles-Herter Series
    International Series
    Memoranda Series
    Name Series
    National Security Council Series
  Dwight D. Eisenhower Papers, White House Central File
    Legislative Meetings Series
    Official File Series
    Operations Coordinating Board Central File Series
  Christian Herter Papers, 1957–61
National Archives, Washington, D.C.
  Record Group 59: General Records of Department of State
    Central Decimal File
Records of the United States Joint Chiefs of Staff, 1954–56:
    JCS Chairman Radford's Files
Seeley G. Mudd Manuscript Library, Princeton University, Princeton, New Jersey

John Foster Dulles Oral History Collection
John Foster Dulles Papers
Women's Zionist Organization of America, New York, New York
  Hadassah Archives
YIVO Institute for Jewish Research, New York, New York
  American Jewish Committee Archives

Israel

Ben-Gurion Research Institute and Archives, S'deh Boker
  David Ben-Gurion Diary
  David Ben-Gurion Correspondence
Prime Minister's Office, Hakirya, Jerusalem
  Israel State Archives
Central Zionist Archives, Jerusalem

Published Sources

Official State Documents

Israel. *Divrei Ha-Knesset* (Israeli parlimentary proceedings), 1954–58.
————. *Government Year Book,* 1953–54, 1959–60.
UN General Assembly. *Official Records,* 1953–57.
UN Security Council. *Official Records,* 1953–57.
U.S. Congress. House. Committee on Foreign Affairs. *Hearings: Economic and Military Cooperation with Nations in the General Area of the Middle East.* 85th Cong., 1st sess. Washington, D.C.: U.S. Government Printing Office, 1957.
————. Senate. Committees on Foreign Relations and Armed Services. *Hearings: The President's Proposal on the Middle East.* 85th Cong., 1st sess. Washington, D.C.: U.S. Government Printing Office, 1957.
U.S. Department of State. *The Department of State Bulletin.* Washington, D.C., U.S. Government Printing Office, 1949, 1953–61.
————. *Foreign Relations of the United States, Diplomatic Papers, 1948–1957.* Washington, D.C.: U.S. Government Printing Office.
————. *The Suez Canal Problem, July 16-September 22, 1956.* Publication no. 6392. Washington, D.C.: U.S. Government Printing Office, 1956.
————. *United States Policy in the Middle East, September 1956-June 1957.* Washington, D.C.: U.S. Government Printing Office, 1958.

Books and Articles

Adams, Sherman. *First-Hand Report: The Story of the Eisenhower Administration.* New York: Harper, 1961.
Allon, Yigal. "Israel at Bay." *Midstream* 2 (Spring 1956): 5–11.

Alteras, Isaac. "Eisenhower, American Jewry, and Israel." *American Jewish Archives* 37 (November 1985): 257–74.

———. "Eisenhower and the State of Israel: Supporter or Distant Sympathizer?" In *Dwight D. Eisenhower: Soldier, President, Statesman,* edited by Joann P. Krieg, 237–47. Westport, Conn.: Greenwood, 1987.

Ambrose, Stephen E. *Eisenhower.* 2 vols. New York: Simon & Schuster, 1983–84.

———. *Eisenhower: Soldier and President.* New York: Simon & Schuster, 1990.

American Friends of the Middle East. *The Jordan Water Problem: An Analysis and Summary of Available Documents.* Washington, D.C., 1964.

Badeau, John. "The Middle East: Conflicts in Priority." *Foreign Affairs* 36 (January 1958): 232–40.

Ball, George W., and Douglas B. Ball. *The Passionate Attachment: America's Involvement with Israel, 1947 to the Present.* New York: Norton, 1992.

Bar-On, Mordechai. "The Influence of Political Considerations on Operational Planning in the Sinai Campaign." In *The Suez-Sinai Crisis, 1956: Retrospective and Reappraisal,* edited by Selwyn I. Troen and Moshe Shemesh, 196–215. New York: Columbia University Press, 1990.

———. "The Sinai Campaign, 1956—Objectives and Expectations." *Zemanim,* no. 23 (Autumn 1986): 94–104.

Bar-Yaacov, Nissim. *The Israel-Syrian Armistice: Problems of Implementation.* Jerusalem: Magnes Press/Hebrew University of Jerusalem, 1967.

Bar-Zohar, Michael. *Ben-Gurion: A Biography.* New York: Delacorte, 1977.

———. *Ben-Gurion: The Armed Prophet.* Englewood Cliffs, N.J.: Prentice-Hall, 1968.

———. *Gesher al Ha-Yam Ha-Tichon: Yahasei Tsarfat-Israel, 1947–1963* (Bridge over the Mediterranean: French-Israeli relations, 1947–1963). Tel Aviv: Am Ha-Sefer, 1964.

Beal, John R. *John Foster Dulles: A Biography.* New York: Harper, 1957.

Bein, Keith. *March to Zion: U.S. Policy and the Founding of Israel.* College Station: Texas A & M University Press, 1980.

Ben-Gurion, David. "Israel's Security and Her International Position before and after the Sinai Campaign." *Israel Government Year Book, 1959–1960.*

———. *My Talks with Arab Leaders.* Jerusalem: Keter, 1972.

Bialer, Uri. *Between East and West: Israel's Foreign Policy Orientation, 1948–1956.* Cambridge: Cambridge University Press, 1990.

Birmingham, Stephen. *Our Crowd.* New York: Harper & Row, 1967.

Blitzer, Wolf. *Between Washington and Jerusalem.* New York: Oxford University Press, 1985.

Brands, H. W. *Cold Warriors: Eisenhower's Generation and American Foreign Policy.* New York: Columbia University Press, 1972.

Brecher, Michael. "American Jewry's Influence on Israeli-U.S. Relations: Reality and Images." *Weiner Library Bulletin* 25 (1971): 2–7.

———. *Decisions in Israel's Foreign Policy.* New Haven, Conn.: Yale University Press, 1967.

———. *The Foreign Policy System of Israel: Setting, Images, Process.* New Haven, Conn.: Yale University Press, 1972.

Briggs, Philip. "Congress and the Middle East: The Eisenhower Doctrine, 1957." In *Dwight D. Eisenhower: Soldier, President, Statesman,* edited by Joann P. Krieg, 249–69. Westport, Conn.: Greenwood, 1987.

Brilliant, Moshe. "Israel's Policy of Reprisal." *Harper's* (March 1955): 68–72.

Burns, A. A. "A New Balance of Power." *Journal of International Affairs* 24 (January 1960): 61–69.

Burns, Eedson M. *Between Arab and Israeli.* Toronto: Clarke, Irwin, 1963.

Butcher, Harry. *My Three Years with Eisenhower.* New York: Simon & Schuster, 1946.

Carlton, David. *Anthony Eden: A Biography.* London: Penguin, 1981.

Childers, Erskine B. *The Road to Suez: A Study of Western-Arab Relations.* London: MacGibbon, 1962.

Clifford, Clark M., with Richard Holbrooke. *Memoir: Counsel to the President.* New York: Random House, 1991.

Cohen, Michael J. *Palestine and the Great Powers, 1945–1948.* Princeton, N.J.: Princeton University Press, 1982.

———. *Truman and Israel.* Berkeley & Los Angeles: University of California Press, 1990.

Cohen, Naomi. *Not Free to Desist: The American Jewish Committee, 1906–1966.* Philadelphia: Jewish Publication Society, 1972.

Cointet, Jean-Paul. "Guy Mollet, the French Government, and the SFIO." In *The Suez-Sinai Crisis, 1956: Retrospective and Reappraisal,* edited by Selwyn I. Troen and Moshe Shemesh, 127–39. New York: Columbia University Press, 1990.

Comfort, Mildred H. *John Foster Dulles: Peacemaker.* Minneapolis: Edison, 1960.

Cook, Blanche W. *The Declassified Eisenhower.* Garden City, N.Y.: Doubleday, 1981.

Cooper, Chester L. *The Lion's Last Roar: Suez, 1956.* New York: Harper & Row, 1978.

Coplend, Miles. *The Game of Nations: The Amorality of Power Politics.* London: Weidenfeld & Nicolson, 1969.

Crosbie, Sylvia K. *A Tacit Alliance: France and Israel from Suez to the Six Day War.* Princeton, N.J.: Princeton University Press, 1974.

Cutler, Robert. *No Time for Rest.* Boston: Little, Brown, 1965.

Dayan, Moshe. *Diary of the Sinai Campaign.* London: Weidenfeld & Nicolson, 1966.

————. "Israel's Border and Security Problem." *Foreign Affairs* 33 (January 1955): 250–67.

————. *Story of My Life*. New York: Morrow, 1967.

Divine, Robert A. *Eisenhower and the Cold War*. New York: Oxford University Press, 1981.

Donovan, Robert J. *Eisenhower: The Inside Story*. New York: Harper, 1956.

————. *Tumultuous Years: The Presidency of Harry S. Truman, 1949–1953*. New York: Norton, 1982.

Dulles, Eleanor Lansing. *John Foster Dulles: The Last Year*. New York: Harcourt, Brace & World, 1963.

Dulles, John F. *War and Peace*. New York: Macmillan, 1950.

————. *War, Peace, and Change*. New York: Harper, 1939.

Eban, Abba S. *An Autobiography*. New York: Random House, 1977.

————. *Personal Witness: Israel through My Eyes*. New York: Putnam's, 1992.

Eden, Anthony. *Full Circle: The Memoirs of Anthony Eden*. Boston: Houghton Mifflin, 1960.

Eisenhower, Dwight D. *At Ease: Stories I Tell to Friends*. Garden City, N.Y.: Doubleday, 1967.

————. *Crusade in Europe*. Garden City, N.Y.: Doubleday, 1948.

————. *Dwight D. Eisenhower: Letters to Mamie*. Edited by John S. D. Eisenhower. Garden City, N.Y.: Doubleday, 1978.

————. *The Eisenhower Diaries*. Edited by Robert H. Ferrell. New York: Norton, 1981.

————. *The Papers of Dwight D. Eisenhower: The War Years*. Edited by Alfred D. Chandler, Jr. Vols. 4, 7, 8, 9. Baltimore: Johns Hopkins University Press, 1970.

————. *The White House Years: Mandate for Change, 1953–1956*. Garden City, N.Y.: Doubleday, 1963.

————. *The White House Years: Waging Peace, 1956–1961*. Garden City, N.Y.: Doubleday, 1965.

Eshed, Haggai. *Mossad shel Ish Ehad: Reuven Shiloah—Avi Ha-Modyin Ha-Israeli* (One man's Mossad: Reuvan Shiloah, father of the Israeli Intelligence Service). Tel Aviv: Edonim, 1988.

Ewald, William Bragg, Jr. *Eisenhower the President: Crucial Days, 1951–1960*. Englewood Cliffs, N.J.: Prentice-Hall, 1981.

Eytan, Walter. *The First Ten Years: A Diplomatic History of Israel*. New York: Simon & Schuster, 1958.

————. "Israel's Foreign Policy and International Relations." *Middle Eastern Affairs* 2 (May 1951): 155–60.

Finer, Herman. *Dulles over Suez: The Theory and Practice of His Diplomacy*. Chicago: Quadrangle, 1964.

Flapan, Simha. *The Birth of Israel: Myths and Realities*. New York: Pantheon, 1987.

Fuchs, Lawrence. *Political Behavior of American Jews*. Glencoe, Ill.: Free Press, 1956.

Ganin, Zvi. *Truman, American Jewry, and Israel, 1945–1948*. New York: Holmes & Meier, 1979.

Garcia-Granados, Jorge. *The Birth of Israel*. New York: Knopf, 1948.

Ginzberg, Eli. *My Brother's Keeper*. New Brunswick, N.J.: Transaction, 1989.

Gilbert, Martin. *Churchill: A Life*. New York: Holt, 1991.

———. *The Holocaust: A History of the Jews of Europe during the Second World War*. New York: Holt, 1985.

Gilboa, Eytan. *American Public Opinion Toward Israel and the Arab-Israeli Conflict*. Lexington, Mass.: Lexington Books, 1987.

Golan, Aviezer. *Ma'arechet Sinai* (The Sinai campaign). Tel Aviv: Am Oved, 1966.

Golden, Peter. *Quiet Diplomat: A Biography of Max M. Fisher*. New York: Herzl, 1992.

Goldmann, Nahum. *The Autobiography of Nahum Goldmann: Sixty Years of Jewish Life*. New York: Holt, Rinehart & Winston, 1969.

Green, Stephen. *Taking Sides: America's Relations with a Militant Israel*. New York: Morrow, 1984.

Greenstein, Fred I. *The Hidden-Hand Presidency: Eisenhower as Leader*. New York: Basic, 1982.

Guhin, Michael. *John Foster Dulles: A Statesman and His Times*. New York: Columbia University Press, 1979.

Hahn, Peter L. *The United States, Great Britain, and Egypt, 1945–1956: Strategy and Diplomacy in the Early Cold War*. Chapel Hill: University of North Carolina Press, 1991.

Heikal, Mohammed. *The Cairo Documents: The Inside Story of Nasser and His Relationship with World Leaders, Rebels, and Statesmen*. Garden City, N.Y.: Doubleday, 1973.

Henriques, Robert. *A Hundred Hours to Suez: An Account of Israel's Campaign in the Sinai Peninsula*. New York: Viking, 1957.

Herberg, Will. *Protestant, Catholic, Jew*. Garden City, N.Y., Doubleday, 1960.

Herzog, Chaim. *The War of Atonement, October 1973*. Boston: Little, Brown, 1974.

Hoopes, Townsend. *The Devil and John Foster Dulles*. Boston: Atlantic-Little, Brown, 1973.

Hughes, Emmet J. *The Ordeal of Power: A Political Memoir of the Eisenhower Years*. New York: Atheneum, 1963.

Immerman, Richard H. "Eisenhower and Dulles: Who Made the Decisions?" *Political Psychology* 1 (1979): 21–39.

———, ed. *John Foster Dulles and the Diplomacy of the Cold War: A Centennial Reappraisal*. Princeton, N.J.: Princeton University Press, 1990.

Jackson, Elmore. *Middle East Mission: The Story of a Major Bid for Peace in the Time of Nasser and Ben-Gurion*. New York: Norton, 1983.

James, Robert Rhodes. *Anthony Eden*. New York: McGraw-Hill, 1987.

———. "Eden." In *The Suez Canal Crisis, 1956: Retrospective and Reappraisal*, edited by Selwyn I. Troen and Moshe Shemesh, 100–109. New York: Columbia University Press, 1990.

Kenen, Isaiah L. *Israel's Defense Line: Her Friends and Foes in Washington*. New York: Prometheus, 1981.

Kraft, Joseph. "Those Arabists in the State Department." *New York Times Magazine*, November 7, 1971, 38–39ff.

Kunz, Diane B. *The Economic Diplomacy of the Suez Crisis*. Chapel Hill: University of North Carolina Press, 1991.

Kurzman, Dan. *Ben-Gurion: Prophet of Fire*. New York: Simon & Schuster, 1983.

Kyle, Keith. *Suez*. New York: St. Martin's, 1991.

Laqueur, Walter Z. "Israel and the Arab Blocs." *Commentary* 24 (September 1957): 185–91.

Lloyd, Selwyn. *Suez, 1956: A Personal Account*. New York: Mayflower, 1978.

Love, Kenneth. *Suez: The Twice-Fought War*. New York: McGraw-Hill, 1969.

Lyon, Peter. *Eisenhower: Portrait of a Hero*. Boston: Little, Brown, 1974.

MacDonald, James G. *My Mission to Israel, 1948–1951*. New York: Simon & Schuster, 1951.

Main, (Chas. T.) Inc. *The Unified Development of the Water Resources of the Jordan Valley Region*. Boston, 1953.

Marshall, S. L. A. *Sinai Victory*. New York: Morrow, 1965.

McCullough, David. *Truman*. New York: Simon & Schuster, 1992.

Morris, Benny. *The Birth of the Palestinian Refugee Problem*. New York: Cambridge University Press, 1987.

Mosley, Leonard. *Dulles: A Biography of Eleanor, Allen, and John Foster Dulles and Their Family Network*. New York: Dell, 1978.

Murphy, Robert. *Diplomat among Warriors*. Garden City, N.Y.: Doubleday, 1964.

Nadich, Judah. *Eisenhower and the Jews*. New York: Twayne, 1953.

Nasser, Gamal A. "The Egyptian Revolution." *Foreign Affairs* 33 (January 1955): 199–211.

Neff, Donald. *Warriors at Suez: Eisenhower Takes America into the Middle East*. New York: Simon & Schuster, 1981.

Novik, Nimrod. *The United States and Israel: Domestic Determinants of a Changing U.S. Commitment*. Boulder, Colo.: Westview Press, 1986.

O'Ballance, Edgar. *The Sinai Campaign, 1956*. New York: McGraw-Hill, 1960.

Orren, Elhannan. "Changes in Israel's Concept of Security after Kadesh." In *The Suez-Sinai Crisis, 1956: Retrospective and Reappraisal,* edited by Selwyn I. Troen and Moshe Shemesh, 218–29. New York: Columbia University Press, 1990.

Parmet, Herbert S. *Eisenhower and the American Crusades.* New York: Macmillan, 1972.

Pearlman, Moshe. *Ben-Gurion Looks Back in Talks with Moshe Pearlman.* New York: Simon & Schuster, 1965.

Peres, Shimon. *David's Sling: The Arming of Israel.* London: Weidenfeld & Nicolson, 1970.

———. "The Road to Sèvres: Franco-Israeli Strategic Cooperation." In *The Suez-Sinai Crisis, 1956: Retrospective and Reappraisal,* edited by Selwyn I. Troen and Moshe Shemesh, 140–49. New York: Columbia University Press, 1990.

Peretz, Dan. "Development of the Jordan Valley Waters." *Middle East Journal* 9 (Autumn 1955): 397–410.

Perlmutter, Amos. *Military and Politics in Israel: National Building and Role of Expansion.* New York: Praeger, 1969.

Pineau, Christian. *Suez 1956.* Paris: Lamont, 1976.

Pruessen, Ronald W. *John Foster Dulles: The Road to Power.* New York: Free Press, 1982.

Rabinovich, Itamar. *The Road Not Taken: Early Arab-Israeli Negotiations.* New York: Oxford University Press, 1991.

———. "The Suez-Sinai Campaign: The Regional Dimension." In *The Suez-Sinai Crisis, 1956: Retrospective and Reappraisal,* edited by Selwyn I. Troen and Moshe Shemesh, 162–71. New York: Columbia University Press, 1990.

Rafael, Gideon. *Destination Peace: Three Decades of Israeli Foreign Policy.* New York: Stein & Day, 1981.

Raphael, Marc L. *Abba Hillel Silver: Profile in American Judaism.* New York: Holmes & Meier, 1989.

Raviv, Dan, and Yossi Melman. *Every Spy a Prince: The Complete History of Israel's Intelligence Community.* Boston: Houghton Mifflin, 1990.

Ray, James L. *The Future of American-Israeli Relations: A Parting of the Ways?* Lexington: University Press of Kentucky, 1989.

Reich, Bernard. *Quest for Peace: United States-Israeli Relations in the Arab-Israeli Conflict.* New Brunswick, N.J.: Transaction, 1977.

———. *The United States and Israel: Influence in the Special Relationship.* New York: Praeger, 1984.

Reiner, Michael. "The Reaction of U.S. Jewish Organizations to the Sinai Campaign and Its Aftermath." *Forum on the Jewish People, Zionism, and Israel,* no. 40 (Winter 1980–81).

Robertson, Terence. *Crisis: The Inside Story of the Suez Conspiracy.* New York: Atheneum, 1965.

Robinson, John B. *John Foster Dulles: A Biography*. New York: Harper, 1957.

Sachar, Abram L. *The Redemption of the Unwanted: From the Liberation of the Death Camps to the Founding of Israel*. New York: St. Martin's, 1983.

Sachar, Howard M. *Egypt and Israel*. New York: Marek, 1981.

———. *A History of Israel from the Rise of Zionism to Our Time*. New York: Knopf, 1979.

———. *A History of the Jews in America*. New York: Knopf, 1992.

Safran, Nadav. *Israel: The Embattled Ally*. Cambridge, Mass.: Harvard University Press, 1981.

———. *The United States and Israel*. Cambridge, Mass.: Harvard University Press, 1963.

St. John, Robert. *Ben-Gurion: A Biography*. Garden City, N.Y.: Doubleday, 1977.

Schechtman, Joseph B. *The United States and the Jewish State Movement: The Crucial Decade, 1939–1949*. New York: Herzl, 1966.

Schoenbaum, David. *The United States and the State of Israel*. New York: Oxford University Press, 1993.

Schulzinger, Robert D. "The Impact of Suez on United States Middle East Policy, 1957–1958." In *The Suez-Sinai Crisis, 1956: Retrospective and Reappraisal*, edited by Selwyn I. Troen and Moshe Shemesh, 251–73. New York: Columbia University Press, 1990.

Schwadran, Benjamin. *The Middle East Oil and the Great Powers*. New York: Council for Middle East Affairs Press, 1959.

Segev, Tom. *1949: The First Israelis*. New York: Free Press, 1986.

Sellers, J. A. "Military Lessons: The British Perspective." In *The Suez-Sinai Crisis, 1956: Retrospective and Reappraisal*, edited by Selwyn I. Troen and Moshe Shemesh, 17–53. New York: Columbia University Press, 1990.

Sharett, Moshe. *B'Sha'ar Ha-Umot* (At the gate of nations). Tel Aviv: Am Oved, 1958.

———. *Yoman Ishi* (Personal diary). 8 vols. Tel Aviv: Sifriyat Ma'ariv, 1978.

Shlaim, Avi. "Conflicting Approaches to Israel's Relations with the Arabs: Ben-Gurion and Sharett, 1953–1956." *Middle East Journal* 37 (Spring 1983): 180–201.

Shuckburgh, Evelyn. *Descent to Suez: Diaries, 1951–1956*. New York: Norton, 1987.

Sklare, Marshall, and Mark Vosk. *The Riverton Study*. New York: American Jewish Committee, 1957.

Snetsinger, John. *Truman, the Jewish Vote, and the Creation of Israel*. Stanford, Calif.: Hoover Institute, 1974.

Spiegel, Steven L. *The Other Arab-Israeli Conflict: Making America's Middle East Policy from Truman to Reagan*. Chicago: University of Chicago Press, 1985.

Stevens, Georgiana G. *Jordan River Partition*. Stanford, Calif.: Hoover Institute, 1965.

———. "The Jordan River Valley." *International Conciliation*, no. 506 (January 1956): 27–39.

Stock, Ernest. *Israel on the Road to Sinai: 1949–1956*. Ithaca, N.Y.: Cornell University Press, 1967.

Teveth, Shabtai. *Ben-Gurion: The Burning Ground, 1886–1948*. Boston: Houghton Mifflin, 1987.

Thomas, Abel. *Comment Israel fût sauvé?* Paris: Albin Michel, 1974.

Troen, Selwyn I. "The Sinai Campaign As a 'War of No Alternative': Ben-Gurion's View of the Israel-Egyptian Conflict." In *The Suez-Sinai Crisis, 1956: Retrospective and Reappraisal*, edited by Selwyn I. Troen and Moshe Shemesh, 180–95. New York: Columbia University Press, 1990.

Truman, Harry S. *Memoirs*. 2 vols. Garden City, N.Y.: Doubleday, 1955–56.

Urofsky, Melvin I. *We Are One! American Jewry and Israel*. Garden City, N.Y.: Doubleday, 1982.

———. "The Formulation of the United States Middle East Resolution." *Wiener Library Bulletin* 26 (1972–73): 2–7.

———. "Israel and the Eisenhower Doctrine." *Wiener Library Bulletin* 28 (1975): 58–64.

Zak, Moshe. *Arbayim Shnot Du-Siach im Moskva* (Forty years of dialogue with Moscow). Tel Aviv: Ma'ariv Guild, 1989.

Dissertations

Muftah, Saleh Mustafa. "The Influences of American-Israeli Relations upon American-Egyptian Relations, 1948 through the Suez War of 1956." University of Denver, 1984.

Windmueller, Steven F. "American Jewish Interest Groups: Their Role in Shaping United States Foreign Policy in the Middle East. A Study of Two Time Periods: 1945–1948; 1955–1958." University of Pennsylvania, 1973.

Yizhar, Michael. "The Eisenhower Doctrine: A Case Study of American Foreign Policy Formulation and Implementation." New School of Social Research, 1969.

Yungher, Israel. "United States-Israeli Relations: 1953–1956." University of Pennsylvania, 1985.

Index